Manual of
Christian Reformed Church
Government

Manual of Christian Reformed Church Government

1980 Edition

William P. Brink
Richard R. De Ridder

Board of Publications of the Christian Reformed Church
Grand Rapids, Michigan

© 1980 by the Board of Publications of the Christian Reformed Church
2850 Kalamazoo Ave. SE
Grand Rapids, Michigan 49560
Printed in the United States of America
Library of Congress Cataloging in Publication Data

Brink, William P   1916-
  Manual of Christian Reformed Church government.

  Includes indexes.
  1. Christian Reformed Church--Government--Handbooks,
manuals, etc.   I. De Ridder, Richard, joint author.
II. Title.
BX6826.B74   1980   262'.05731   80-24129
ISBN O-933140-19-3

*All things should be done
decently and in order.*

I CORINTHIANS 14:40

Contents

Preface xi
Introduction: Polity of the Christian Reformed Church 1
Church Order of the Christian Reformed Church in North America 7
Manual of Christian Reformed Church Government 27
   Introduction
        1. Purpose and Basis of the Church Order 28
   I. The Offices of the Church
      A. General Provisions
        2. Special Offices of the Church 32
        3. Eligibility for Ecclesiastical Offices 39
        4. Calling to Special Offices 42
        5. Signing the Form of Subscription 44
      B. Ministers of the Word
        6. Eligibility for Admission to the Ministry of the Word 48
        7. Admittance to the Ministry without Prescribed Training 53
        8. Ministers Eligible for Call 58
        9. Function of a Counselor 66
       10. Ordination and Installation 68
       11. The Function of the Minister of the Word 74
       12. Specific Tasks and Calling of Ministers of the Word 76
       13. Supervision of Ministers 82
       14. Release from Ministerial Office 85
       15. The Support of Ministers 88
       16. Temporary Release from Service (Leave of Absence) 93
       17. Release from Ministry in a Congregation 95
       18. Retirement of Ministers 98
       19. Theological Seminary 101
       20. Tasks of Professors of Theology 102
       21. Student Fund 105
       22. Licensure of Students 106
      C. Elders, Deacons, and Evangelists
       23. Appointment, Ordination, and Tenure 109

    24. Ministry of the Elders and Evangelists........................113
    25. Ministry of the Deacons.................................117

II. The Assemblies of the Church
  A. General Provisions
    26. Assemblies..120
    27. Authority of Ecclesiastical Assemblies........................121
    28. Matters Legally before Assemblies...........................123
    29. The Character of Assembly Decisions.........................129
    30. Appeals 132
    31. Request for Revision of a Decision...........................140
    32. Procedure and Order in Assemblies..........................143
    33. Assembly Committees..................................153
    34. Delegation to Assemblies.................................163
  B. The Consistory
    35. Composition of a Consistory...............................165
    36. Frequency of Meetings and Mutual Censure....................167
    37. Congregational Meetings.................................170
    38. Unorganized Churches..................................173
  C. The Classis
    39. Constituency of a Classis.................................176
    40. The Sessions of Classis..................................177
    41. Questions to Each Consistory at Classis.......................181
    42. Church Visitors.......................................184
    43. Classical Licensure to Exhort..............................190
    44. Joint Action of Neighboring Classes.........................192
  D. The Synod
    45. The Constituency of Synod...............................194
    46. Meetings of Synod....................................197
    47. The Task of Synod.....................................201
    48. Synodical Deputies....................................204
    49. Interchurch Relations..................................207
    50. Reformed Ecumenical Synods.............................212

III. The Task and Activities of the Church
  A. Worship Services
    51. The Elements and Occasions for Worship Services..............214
    52. Consistorial Regulation of Worship Services...................218
    53. The Conducting of Worship Services.........................224
    54. Preaching...226
    55. The Administration of the Sacraments........................228
    56. Administration of Infant Baptism...........................230
    57. Administration of Adult Baptism...........................233
    58. Valid Baptism..235
    59. Admission to Communicant Membership.....................238
    60. Administration of the Lord's Supper.........................241
    61. Prayer in Public Worship Services...........................244
    62. Offerings 246

  B. Catechetical Instruction
     63. The Purpose of Catechetical Instruction......................250
     64. The Implementation of Catechetical Instruction...............254
  C. Pastoral Care
     65. The Exercise of Pastoral Care..............................257
     66. Membership Transfers......................................260
     67. Absentee Members...263
     68. Membership Records.......................................266
     69. Solemnization of Marriage................................267
     70. Funerals...275
     71. Christian Schools..276
     72. Congregational Societies..................................279
  D. Missions
     73. The Church's Mandate to Missions.........................281
     74. Congregational Evangelism................................284
     75. Classis Mission Work.....................................287
     76. Denominational Home Missions............................289
     77. Denominational World Missions...........................294
IV. The Admonition and Discipline of the Church
  A. General Provisions
     78. The Nature of and Responsibility for Discipline...............298
     79. The Purpose of Admonition and Discipline...................301
     80. The Subjects of Admonition and Discipline...................302
     81. Occasions for Discipline..................................304
     82. Preliminary Requirements.................................308
  B. The Admonition and Discipline of Members
     83. Discipline of Baptized Members............................309
     84. Reconciliation of Disciplined Members......................311
     85. Discipline of Confessing Members..........................312
     86. Excommunication 313
     87. Restoration of Excommunicated Persons.....................317
  C. The Admonition and Discipline of Office-bearers
     88. The Relationship of General and Special Discipline.............319
     89. Grounds and Procedures for Special Discipline................320
     90. Suspension and Deposition of Ministers.....................323
     91. Suspension and Deposition of Elders and Deacons.............326
     92. Discipline of a Minister Whose Membership Resides with a
         Congregation Other than His Calling Church.................327
     93. Lifting of Suspension......................................329
     94. Reinstatement of Deposed Office-bearers.....................330
 Conclusion
     95. Equality of Churches and Office-bearers......................332
     96. Revision of the Church Order..............................334
Appendix..337
General Index..345
Index of Scripture References......................................367

Preface

This edition of the *Manual of Christian Reformed Church Government* was revised to incorporate decisions made by the Synods of 1979 and 1980. Materials not included in the first edition were added as well. Wherever necessary, we have made corrections as they were brought to our attention. Some changes have also been made in the original works, but they are insubstantial consisting mostly of modernizing spellings and punctuation and improving grammar.

We are grateful for the splendid reception which the first edition has received and trust that this revision will serve the church even better.

Preface to the First Edition

For many years a succession of authors has served the Christian Reformed Church well by their collation of decisions of its synods and by means of commentaries on its Church Order. The names of Hemkes, Heyns, Bos, Beets, Schaver, Monsma, Van Dellen, and Spaan are well known among us, and their contributions in this area of the church's life have been substantial.

In recent years, however, no up-to-date volume has been available to which church members and office-bearers could turn for direction and information concerning the practices of the church and its synodical regulations. With this need in mind the Synodical Interim Committee of the Christian Reformed Church approved a project already conceived and initiated by William P. Brink, Stated Clerk of the denomination, and Richard R. De Ridder, Associate Professor of Church Polity at Calvin Theological Seminary, to prepare a volume that would meet these urgent needs. This volume represents nearly three years of work on their part.

The splendid cooperation of the Education Department of the Board of Publications and the inestimable editorial services of Edwin Walhout are deeply appreciated. We also give special recognition to Mary Braat and Adrianna De Ridder for their secretarial services and skills in preparing the final manuscript. And we also thank the students of Calvin Seminary in whose classes in Church Order these materials were first "tried out." Their helpful suggestions and encouragement enabled these materials to be tested before publication.

Present projections call for revisions of the volume to appear every few years in order to keep the contents up to date. An annual, cumulative index incorporating decisions of intervening synods will be made available between editions.

The book is sent forth with the hope, not merely that it will serve as an adequate replacement of volumes which the passing of time alone has made inadequate, but also with the hope that it will be widely used as a guide in the development of the denomination's polity and lead to a deeper appreciation and understanding of the principles which regulate the church's ecclesiastical life.

Introduction

POLITY OF THE CHRISTIAN REFORMED CHURCH

A. REFORMED CHURCH POLITY

The Christian Reformed Church in North America, in harmony with the Word of God and the Reformed creeds as an interpretation of that Word, acknowledges Jesus Christ as the only head and ruler of the church. To carry out his rule the church has adopted a Church Order so that all things in the church may be done decently and in order (I Cor. 14:40). The general pattern of the organization provided by the Church Order is presbyterian: that is, a system of leadership by elders (presbyters) who represent Christ in his church. Reformed church polity is not strictly presbyterian in all respects, however, and differs in approach from traditional presbyterian polity in that the polity of Reformed churches, while regulative, is not confessional in nature; that is, the Reformed Church Order does not have the status of a creed.

Reformed churches have never claimed that every detail of their system is determined by the Scriptures. Only certain basic principles are found there, providing general directions to the church. Details may and do vary from one Reformed family of churches to another because expediency and specific circumstances often require varying approaches.

Church polity is not—and should not be made into—a fixed, rigid system of rules. Whenever the profit of the churches requires, the specific application of the general principles derived from Scripture must be changed. In a previous version of its Church Order the Christian Reformed Church expressed this in the following way: "The Articles...have been so drafted and adopted by common consent, that they (if the profit of the Church demand otherwise) *may and ought to be* altered, augmented, or diminished." There is, as a result, an amazing amount of flexibility in procedures and practices possible within the polity of the Christian Reformed Church.

B. THE ORIGIN OF THE CHURCH ORDER

The Church Order of the Christian Reformed Church has its origin in the Calvinist Reformation in the Netherlands where a uniform form of government for the emerging Reformed churches of the Lowlands gradually developed in the late 1500s. Eventually, the final structure was refined and adopted by the National Synod of Dort in 1618-19. Although the Church Order of 1618-19 was widely used, it never received the official approval of the state government which controlled the national church.

Later, in the aftermath of the Napoleonic era a new Church Order was officially imposed on the Dutch church by King William II (1816). This new Church Order was viewed by some church leaders as part of a general drift toward liberalism and political control of the churches. Their concern included not only the polity but also the liturgy and doctrine of the church and led to the *Afscheiding* (secession movement) which split the national church in 1834. The secession churches repudiated King William's Church Order and restored the original Church Order adopted by the Synod of Dort. At their Synod of Amsterdam (1840) a revision of the Church Order of Dort became the official polity of the secession churches.

The 1840 revision was adopted by the immigrants who constituted the early colonies of Western Michigan and who organized their congregations into Classis Holland and early united with the Reformed Church in America. Complaints with respect to departures from the Dort Church Order were among the grounds cited by those who seceded in 1857 from the Reformed Church in America to form what became the Christian Reformed Church. The newly founded denomination adopted the 1840 Church Order as its own in one of its earliest sessions.

Comparatively few revisions were made of this Church Order in succeeding years. The Synod of 1912 adopted a revision which incorporated the stance of Dr. Abraham Kuyper, whose American followers tended toward a kind of congregationalism. This trend toward congregationalism was not at all congenial to opponents who maintained that broader assemblies of the church (classis and synod) were legitimately acting in the capacity of the church of Jesus Christ when in assembly. These tensions have never been resolved completely within the polity of the Christian Reformed Church. Each position serves, however, to keep the other in balance and serves to prevent either one from assuming the dominant role in the practice of the church.

C. THE REVISION OF 1965

A long revision process was begun by the Synod of 1950 in response to an official request from the Gereformeerde Kerken in the Netherlands that the Reformed Churches of the Netherlands, South Africa, and the Christian Reformed Church cooperate in producing an international, uniform Church Order. Although this international attempt ultimately proved unrealistic, it did focus the attention of the church on matters of church polity and created a new impetus for change. Contemporary society was undergoing rapid change. This, together with the exposure of the church members to the world at large and the exhilarating adjustments demanded by the vast number of Dutch immigrants to Canada and the United States, required a new investigation of the polity of the church. In order to respond to the changes in society and the place of the church's witness to the world, the church began to reflect seriously on the nature of its Church Order. A vital part of the Reformed heritage is found in the principle that the polity of the church must always respond to the times in which the church serves its generation.

In 1965 a revised Church Order was adopted, retaining by specific direction of preceding synods the basic format of the Church Order of Dort. The revised Church Order of 1965 demonstrates that the church is awake to its responsibilites in the contemporary world and is desirous of responding to that world in obedience to her Lord.

D. Recent Trends Reflected in the Church Order

Observant students of the Church Order's development will note that there are a number of trends within the church in recent years which are increasingly reflected in the manner in which the Christian Reformed Church deals with its Church Order.

1. Revisions

A surprising number of revisions of the Church Order have been made since its adoption in 1965. Between the years 1912 and 1965 only two significant changes were made in the Church Order. From 1965 to 1978 twenty-three articles have been revised! Almost an equal number of requests for revision of other articles has been rejected by the synods in that period. Still other articles have been clarified as to their intent and/or application.

2. The Office of Every Believer

Increased concern has been expressed during the last two decades for a clearer understanding of (and putting into practice) the fundamental scriptural teaching of "the office of every believer." Although the structure of the Church Order has historically been oriented toward official functions performed by ordained office-holders and ecclesiastical assemblies, some recent modifications have been in the direction of the responsibilities of the believers (see for example, Article 73b and Article 78b).

3. The Nature of Office in the Church

Significant concerns have also been expressed for clear definition of the nature of office in the church. The report on "Ecclesiastical Office and Ordination" (Report 44, *Acts of Synod 1973*) established and defined basic biblical principles. The impact of that report is already felt in the church. The report will continue to influence the church for a long time to come.

While the functions of elders, deacons, and pastors continues to be studied, the place of the diaconate in church structures and assemblies is receiving particular attention in certain areas. This is a wholesome concern arising from concerted efforts to give the diaconal office its proper place in the affairs of the church and the church's ministry in the community and the world. The opening of the office of deacon to all confessing members of the church by the Synod of 1978 is another significant change with respect to the diaconal office.

The Synod of 1978 also established the office of evangelist, recognizing that there were circumstances in which specific authorization needed to be given to selected and qualified persons to perform functions which previously had been reserved for ordained ministers.

4. Synodical Study Committees

Synodical study committees continue to serve the church with significant biblical and theological research. It is a joyful experience to note that biblical data and norms continue to govern these studies and the conclusions of the committees.

3

The impact of these reports cannot be measured simply by synodical approval or action, and it sometimes requires a number of years before the conclusions of these studies are translated into action.

In this volume reference will be made under specific Church Order articles to appropriate studies on related subjects. We cannot afford to ignore the work which has been done before us and upon the basis of which we are challenged to build today.

5. Healthy Tensions

Within Reformed church polity we continue to see healthy tensions between the rights and autonomy of the local congregation and the delegated authority of the broader assemblies. Some plead for greater uniformity and look back to the time when all the churches did most things the same way, no matter where they were located. Others rejoice at discovering that the church's polity is flexible enough to allow greater liberty to the local church while holding to a common, basic, confessional commitment. To maintain balance between these two is not easy. But the welfare of the church (and churches) must always govern the direction we take.

6. North American Environment

Any comparative review of Christian Reformed Church government with its European antecedents demonstrates how clearly the church has become a part of its North American environment. As a denomination the Christian Reformed Church in North America still maintains close ties with the Netherlands churches and is affected by theological movements and developments among them. But many of the concerns shared by the Netherlands and American churches are based less on our common roots then on the tenor of our age. There are other concerns which arise from our peculiar situation in Canada and the United States. The very failure of the 1950 attempt to produce an internationally uniform Church Order for Reformed churches evidenced wholesome changes within each denomination as each responded to its specific environment. It is to be hoped that in the future we shall likewise profit from our associations with churches from within our own traditions with which we maintain close ties of ecclesiastical fellowship as well as from national and emerging churches with which we cooperate in mission and benevolent ministries.

E. How to Use the Church Order

This Manual of Christian Reformed Church Government must not be used merely as a resource book to be consulted when one wants to know whether synod said something or what it has decided on a particular subject or issue. Nor is its primary purpose to settle arguments over fine points raised in consistory rooms. To use it in this way would defeat the purpose both of this volume and of the Church Order itself. Our desire is that a search be made for the basic principles which govern decisions of the past and which are regulative for the future.

In one sense the things contained in this manual are *prescriptive* since the Christian Reformed Church, by means of its Church Order "regulates its ecclesiastical organization and activities" (Church Order Art. 1). In another sense this material is *descriptive* of where the Christian Reformed Church finds herself at this particular moment of her existence.

This volume collates and interprets synodical decisions, reports and advice. It has been written and compiled with the conscious realization that a book such as this is out of date as soon as it is printed. Therefore, insertions or substitutions will be provided periodically to keep the volume up-to-date. The compilers welcome suggestions of material from synodical sources which they may have overlooked but which would contribute to the completeness of this volume.

The task of compilation is not always easy. Judgments as to what to include and what to exclude had to be made. The criteria employed was the welfare of the church today and what will serve to guide the church into the future. When reviewing the multitude of regulations, decisions, and advice which synods have adopted through the years, we have tried to follow as faithfully as possible synod's own judgment that "the retention of rules that are obsolete and are no longer complied with does more harm than good" (*Acts of Synod 1936*, p. 93).

It is hoped that this volume will challenge the church by encouraging office-bearers and members to undertake a serious and ongoing appraisal of how our church can best serve its Lord in "such a time as this." We must all seek to be more like the men of Issachar who "had understanding of their times to know what Israel ought to do" (I Chron. 12:23).

5

Church Order of
The Christian Reformed Church
in North America

INTRODUCTION

ARTICLE 1

a. The Christian Reformed Church, confessing its complete subjection to the Word of God and the Reformed creeds as a true interpretation of this Word, acknowledging Christ as the only head of his church, and desiring to honor the apostolic injunction that in the churches all things are to be done decently and in order (I Cor. 14:40), regulates its ecclesiastical organization and activities in the following articles.

b. The main subjects treated in this Church Order are: The Offices of the Church, The Assemblies of the Church, The Task and Activities of the Church, and The Admonition and Discipline of the Church.

I. THE OFFICES OF THE CHURCH
A. GENERAL PROVISIONS

ARTICLE 2

The church recognizes the offices of minister of the Word, elder, deacon, and evangelist. These offices differ from each other only in mandate and task, not in dignity and honor.

ARTICLE 3

Confessing male members of the church who meet the biblical requirements for office-bearers are eligible for office. Only those who have been officially called and ordained or installed shall hold and exercise office in the church.

CHURCH ORDER

ARTICLE 4

a. In calling to an office, the consistory shall present to the congregation a nomination of at least twice the number to be elected. In special circumstances the consistory may submit a nomination which totals less than twice the number to be elected, giving reasons for this departure from the rule.

b. Prior to making nominations the consistory may give the congregation an opportunity to direct attention to suitable persons.

c. The election by the congregation shall take place under the supervision of the consistory after prayer and in accordance with the regulations established by the consistory. The right to vote shall be limited to confessing members in good standing.

d. After having called the elected persons to their respective offices and having announced their names, the consistory shall proceed to ordain or install them if no valid impediment has arisen. The ordination or installation shall take place in the public worship services with the use of the prescribed ecclesiastical forms.

ARTICLE 5

All office-bearers, on occasions stipulated by consistorial, classical, and synodical regulations, shall signify their agreement with the doctrine of the church by signing the Form of Subscription.   [Supplement contained in this manual, Art. 5, section 4.]

B. THE MINISTERS OF THE WORD

ARTICLE 6

a. The completion of a satisfactory theological training shall be required for admission to the ministry of the Word.

b. Graduates of the theological seminary of the Christian Reformed Church who have been declared candidates for the ministry of the Word by the churches shall be eligible for call.

c. Those who have been trained elsewhere shall not be eligible for call unless they have met the requirements stipulated in the synodical regulations and have been declared by the churches to be candidates for the ministry of the Word.

[Supplement contained in this manual, Art. 6, section 2b, 2.]

ARTICLE 7

a. Those who have not received the prescribed theological training but who give evidence that they are singularly gifted as to godliness, humility, spiritual discretion, wisdom, and the native ability to preach the Word, may, by way of exception, be admitted to the ministry of the Word, especially when the need is urgent.

b. The classis, in the presence of the synodical deputies, shall examine these men concerning the required exceptional gifts. With the concurring advice of the synodical deputies, classis shall proceed as circumstances may warrant and in accordance with synodical regulations.   [Supplement contained in this manual, Art. 7.]

8

ARTICLE 8

a. Ministers of the Christian Reformed Church are eligible for call, with due observance of the relevant rules.

b. Ministers of other denominations desiring to become ministers in the Christian Reformed Church shall be declared eligible for a call by a classis only after a thorough examination of their theological training, ministerial record, knowledge of and soundness in the Reformed faith and their exemplarincss of life. The presence and concurring advice of the synodical deputies are required.

c. Ministers of other denominations who have not been declared eligible for a call shall not be called unless all synodical requirements have been met.

[Contents of Supplement contained in this manual, Art. 8.]

ARTICLE 9

In nominating and calling a minister the consistory shall seek the approval of the counselor who acts in behalf of classis to see that the ecclesiastical regulations have been observed. The consistory and counselor shall sign the letter of call and the counselor shall render an account of his labors to classis.

ARTICLE 10

a. The ordination of a candidate for the ministry of the Word requires the approval of the classis of the calling church and of the synodical deputies. The classis, in the presence of the deputies, shall examine him concerning his doctrine and life in accordance with synodical regulations. The ordination shall be accompanied by the laying on of hands by the officiating minister.

b. The installation of a minister shall require the approval of the classis of the calling church or its interim committee, to which the minister shall have previously presented good ecclesiastical testimonials of doctrine and life which have been given him by his former consistory and classis.

[Contents of Supplement contained in this manual, Art. 10.]

ARTICLE 11

The calling of a minister of the Word is to proclaim, explain and apply Holy Scripture in order to gather in and build up the members of the church of Jesus Christ.

ARTICLE 12

a. A minister of the Word serving as pastor of a congregation shall preach the Word, administer the sacraments, conduct public worship services, catechize the youth, and train members for Christian service. He, with the elders, shall supervise the congregation and his fellow office-bearers, exercise admonition and discipline, and see to it that everything is done decently and in order. He, with the elders, shall exercise pastoral care over the congregation, and engage in and promote the work of evangelism.

b. A minister of the Word who enters into the work of missions or is appointed directly by synod shall be called in the regular manner by a local church, which acts in cooperation with the appropriate committee of classis or synod.

c. A minister of the Word may also serve the church in other work which relates directly to his calling, but only after the calling church has demonstrated to the satisfaction of classis, with the concurring advice of the synodical deputies, that said work is consistent with the calling of a minister of the Word.

[Supplement contained in this manual, Art. 12c, section 4b.]

ARTICLE 13

a. A minister of the Word is directly accountable to the calling church, and therefore shall be supervised in doctrine, life and duties by that church. When his work is with other than the calling church, he shall be supervised in cooperation with other congregations, institutions or agencies involved.

b. A minister of the Word may be loaned temporarily by his calling church to serve as pastor of a congregation outside of the Christian Reformed Church, but only with the approval of classis, the concurring advice of the synodical deputies, and in accordance with the synodical regulations. Although his duties may be regulated in cooperation with the other congregation, the supervision of his doctrine and life rests with the calling church.   [Supplement contained in this manual, Art. 13b, section 4.]

ARTICLE 14

a. A minister of the Word shall not leave the congregation with which he is connected for another church without the consent of the consistory.

b. A minister of the Word, once lawfully called, may not forsake his office. He may, however, be released from office to enter upon a nonministerial vocation for such weighty reasons as shall receive the approval of the classis with the concurring advice of the synodical deputies.

c. A former minister of the Word who was released from his office may be declared eligible for call upon approval of the classis from which he obtained his release, with the concurring advice of the synodical deputies. Upon acceptance of a call, he shall be reordained.

ARTICLE 15

Each church shall through its consistory provide for the proper support of its minister(s).

ARTICLE 16

A minister who for weighty reasons desires a temporary release from service to the congregation must have the approval of his consistory, which shall continue to have supervision over him.

ARTICLE 17

a. A minister who is neither eligible for retirement nor worthy of discipline may, because of an intolerable situation existing between him and his church, be released from active ministerial service in his congregation. The consistory shall give such a release only with the approval of the classis, with the concurring advice of the synodical deputies and in accordance with synodical regulations.

b. The consistory shall provide for the support of a released minister in such a way and for such a time as shall receive the approval of classis.

c. Eventually, if no call is forthcoming, he may at the discretion of classis and the synod be completely released from his ministerial office.

[Supplement contained in this manual, Art. 17, section 5.]

ARTICLE 18

a. A minister who has reached retirement age, or who because of physical or mental disability is incapable of performing the duties of his office, is eligible for retirement. Retirement shall take place with the approval of the consistory and classis and in accordance with synodical regulations.

b. A retired minister shall retain the honor and title of a minister of the Word and his official connection with the church which he served last, and this church shall be responsible for providing honorably for his support and that of his dependents according to synodical regulations.

c. Should the reasons for his retirement no longer exist, the minister emeritus shall request the consistory and classis which recommended him for retirement to declare him eligible for call.   [Contents of Supplement 18 are contained in this manual, Art. 18.]

ARTICLE 19

The churches shall maintain a theological seminary at which men are trained for the ministry of the Word. The seminary shall be governed by synod through a board of trustees appointed by synod and responsible to it.

ARTICLE 20

The task of the ministers of the Word who are appointed as professors of theology is to train the seminary students for the ministry of the Word, expound the Word of God, and vindicate sound doctrine against heresies and errors.

ARTICLE 21

The churches shall encourage young men to seek to become ministers of the Word and shall grant financial aid to those who are in need of it. Every classis shall maintain a student fund.

ARTICLE 22

Students who have received licensure according to synodical regulations shall be permitted to exhort in the public worship services.

(Supplement contained in this manual, Art. 22, section 2.]

C. THE ELDERS, DEACONS, AND EVANGELISTS

ARTICLE 23

a. The elders and deacons shall serve for a limited time as designated by the consistory. As a rule a specified number of them shall retire from office each year. The retiring office-bearers shall be succeeded by others unless the circumstances and the profit of the church make immediate eligibility for re-election advisable. Elders and deacons who are thus re-elected shall be reinstalled.

b. The evangelist shall be acknowledged as an elder of his calling church with corresponding privileges and responsibilites. His work as elder shall normally be limited to that which pertains to his function as evangelist. His office will terminate when the group of believers is formed into an organized church.

[Supplement contained in this manual, Art. 23, section 5.]

ARTICLE 24

a. The elders, with the minister(s), shall have supervision over the congregation and their fellow office-bearers, exercising admonition and discipline and seeing to it that everything is done decently and in order. They shall, with the minister(s), exercise pastoral care over the congregation, and engage in and promote the work of evangelism.

b. The evangelist shall minister only to that emerging congregation in which he is appointed to labor.

1) The task of the evangelist is to witness for Christ and to call for a comprehensive discipleship through the means of the preaching of the Word and the administration of the sacraments, evangelism, church education for youths and adults, and pastoral care, in order that the church may be built and unbelievers won for Christ. Any service or assignment beyond his specific field of labor requires the authorization of his consistory and the approval of classis.

2) The evangelist shall function under the direct supervision of the consistory, give regular reports to the consistory, and be present at the meetings of the consistory whenever possible, particularly when his work is under consideration.

3) The evangelist shall have authority to administer the Word and the sacraments in the work of evangelism in the emerging church to which he is called.

ARTICLE 25

a. The task of the deacons is to administer Christian mercy toward those who are in need, first of all toward those of the household of faith, but also toward the needy in general. In executing this task they shall diligently collect, administer, and distribute monies and other gifts, and shall serve the distressed with counsel and assistance.

b. They shall enable the needy under their care to make use of Christian institutions of mercy.

c. They shall confer and cooperate with diaconates of neighboring churches when this is desirable for the proper performance of their task.

d. They may also seek mutual understandings with other agencies in their community which are caring for the needy, so that the gifts may be distributed properly.

II. THE ASSEMBLIES OF THE CHURCH
A. GENERAL PROVISIONS

ARTICLE 26

The assemblies of the church are: the consistory, the classis and the synod.

ARTICLE 27

a. Each assembly exercises, in keeping with its own character and domain, the ecclesiastical authority entrusted to the church by Christ; the authority of consistories being original, that of major assemblies being delegated.

b. The classis has the same authority over the consistory as the synod has over the classis.

ARTICLE 28

a. These assemblies shall transact ecclesiastical matters only, and shall deal with them in an ecclesiastical manner.

b. A major assembly shall deal only with those matters which concern its churches in common or which could not be finished in the minor assemblies.

c. Matters referred by minor assemblies to major assemblies shall be presented in harmony with the rules for classical and synodical procedure.

[Supplement contained in this manual, Art. 28, section 5.]

ARTICLE 29

Decisions of ecclesiastical assemblies shall be reached only upon due consideration. The decisions of the assemblies shall be considered settled and binding, unless it is proved that they conflict with the Word of God or the Church Order.

ARTICLE 30

a. Assemblies and church members may appeal to the assembly next in order if they believe that injustice has been done or that a decision conflicts with the Word of God or the Church Order. Appellants shall observe all ecclesiastical regulations regarding the manner and time of appeal.

b. When written charges requiring formal adjudication by an ecclesiastical assembly are made, the relevant provisions of the Judicial Code shall be observed.

[Supplement contained in this manual, Art. 30, section 2c.]

ARTICLE 31

A request for revision of a decision shall be submitted to the assembly which made the decision. Such a request shall be honored only if sufficient and new grounds for reconsideration are presented.

ARTICLE 32

a. The sessions of all assemblies shall begin and end with prayer.

b. In every assembly there shall be a president whose duty it shall be to state and explain the business to be transacted, and to see to it that the stipulations of the Church Order are followed and that everyone observes due order and decorum in speaking. There shall also be a clerk whose task it shall be to keep an accurate record of the proceedings. In major assemblies the above named offices shall cease when the assembly adjourns.

c. Each assembly shall make proper provision for receiving communications, preparing agenda and acts, keeping files and archives, and conducting the financial transactions of the assembly.

d. Each assembly shall provide for the safeguarding of its property through proper incorporation.

ARTICLE 33

a. The assemblies may delegate to committees the execution of their decisions or the preparation of reports for future consideration. They shall give every committee a well-defined mandate, and shall require of them regular and complete reports of their work.

b. Each classis shall appoint a classical interim committee, and synod shall appoint a synodical interim committee, to act for them in matters which cannot wait action by the assemblies themselves. Such committees shall be given well-defined mandates and shall submit all their actions to the next meeting of the assembly for approval.

ARTICLE 34

The major assemblies are composed of office-bearers who are delegated by their constituent minor assemblies. The minor assemblies shall provide their delegates with proper credentials which authorize them to deliberate and vote on matters brought before the major assemblies. A delegate shall not vote on any matter in which he himself or his church is particularly involved.

B. THE CONSISTORY

ARTICLE 35

a. In every church there shall be a consistory composed of the office-bearers. The consistory is responsible for the general government of the church.

b. Where the number of elders is at least four, a distinction may be made between the general consistory, to which all office-bearers belong, and the restricted consistory, in which the deacons do not participate.

c. When such a distinction is made, the supervision and discipline of the congregation shall be vested in the restricted consistory. The work of Christian mercy shall be the task of the deacons, who shall render account of their work to the general consistory. All other matters belong to the general consistory.

ARTICLE 36

a. The consistory shall meet at least once a month, at a time and place announced to the congregation. Ordinarily the meeting shall be presided over by the minister, or in the absence of the minister by one of the elders.

b. The consistory, at least four times per year, shall exercise mutual censure, which concerns the performance of the official duties of the office-bearers.

ARTICLE 37

The consistory, besides seeking the cooperation of the congregation in the election of office-bearers, shall also invite its judgment about other major matters, except those which pertain to the supervision and discipline of the congregation. For this purpose the consistory shall call a meeting at least annually of all members entitled to vote. Such a meeting shall be conducted by the consistory, and only those matters which it presents shall be considered. Although full consideration shall be given to the judgment expressed by the congregation, the authority for making and carrying out final decisions remains with the consistory as the governing body of the church.

ARTICLE 38

a. Groups of believers among whom no consistory can as yet be constituted shall be under the care of a neighboring consistory, designated by classis.

b. When a consistory is being constituted for the first time the approval of classis is required.

C. THE CLASSIS

ARTICLE 39

A classis shall consist of a group of neighboring churches. The organizing of a new classis and the redistricting of classes require the approval of synod.

ARTICLE 40

a. The consistory of each church shall delegate a minister and an elder to the classis. If a church is without a minister, or the minister is prevented from attending, two elders shall be delegated. Office-bearers who are not delegated may also attend classis and may be given an advisory voice.

b. The classis shall meet at least every four months, unless great distances render this impractical, at such time and place as was determined by the previous classical meeting.

c. The ministers shall either preside in rotation, or one shall be chosen to preside; however, the same minister shall not be chosen twice in succession.

ARTICLE 41

In order properly to assist the churches, the president, on behalf of classis, shall among other things present the following questions to the delegates of each church:

1. Are the consistory meetings regularly held in your church; and are they held according to the needs of the congregation?

2. Is church discipline faithfully exercised?

3. Are the needy adequately cared for?

4. Does the consistory diligently promote the cause of Christian education from elementary school through institutions of higher learning?

5. a. Have you submitted to the secretary of our Home Mission Board the names and addresses of all baptized and communicant members who have, since the last meeting of classis, moved to a place where no Christian Reformed churches are found?

b. Have you informed other consistories or pastors about members who reside, even temporarily, in the vicinity of their church?

c. Have you, having been informed yourself of such members in your own area, done all in your power to serve them with the ministry of your church?

6. Does the consistory diligently engage in and promote the work of evangelism in its community?

ARTICLE 42

a. The classis shall appoint at least one committee composed of two of the more experienced and competent office-bearers, two ministers, or one minister and one elder, to visit all its churches once a year.

b. The church visitors shall ascertain whether the office-bearers faithfully perform their duties, adhere to sound doctrine, observe the provisions of the Church Order, and properly promote the edification of the congregation and the extension of God's kingdom. They shall fraternally admonish those who have been negligent, and help all with advice and assistance.

c. The churches are free to call on the church visitors whenever serious problems arise.

d. The church visitors shall render to classis a written report of their work.

ARTICLE 43

The classis may grant the right to exhort within its bounds to men who are gifted, well-informed, consecrated, and able to edify the churches. When the urgent need for their services has been established, the classis shall examine such men and license them as exhorters for a limited period of time.

ARTICLE 44

A classis may take counsel or joint action with its neighboring classis or classes in matters of mutual concern.

D. THE SYNOD

ARTICLE 45

The synod is the assembly representing the churches of all the classes. Each classis shall delegate two ministers and two elders to the synod.

ARTICLE 46

a. Synod shall meet annually, at a time and place determined by the previous synod. Each synod shall designate a church to convene the following synod.

b. The convening church, with the approval of the synodical interim committee, may call a special session of synod, but only in very extraordinary circumstances and with the observance of synodical regulations.

c. The officers of synod shall be elected and shall function in accordance with the Rules for Synodical Procedure.

ARTICLE 47

The task of synod includes the adoption of the creeds, of the Church Order, of the liturgical forms, of the Psalter Hymnal, and of the principles and elements of the order of worship, as well as the designation of the Bible versions to be used in the worship services.

No substantial alterations shall be effected by synod in these matters unless the churches have had prior opportunity to consider the advisability of the proposed changes.

ARTICLE 48

a. Upon the nomination of the classes, synod shall appoint ministers, one from each classis, to serve as synodical deputies for a term designated by synod.

b. When the cooperation of the synodical deputies is required as stipulated in the Church Order, the presence of at least three deputies from the nearest classes shall be prescribed.

c. Besides the duties elsewhere stipulated, the deputies shall, upon request, extend help to the classes in the event of difficulties in order that proper unity, order, and sound doctrine may be maintained.

d. The synodical deputies shall submit a complete report of their actions to the next synod.

ARTICLE 49

a. Synod shall appoint a committee to correspond with other Reformed churches so that the Christian Reformed Church may exercise Christian fellowship with other denominations and may promote the unity of the church of Jesus Christ.

b. Synod shall decide which denominations are to be received into ecclesiastical fellowship, and shall establish the rules which govern these relationships.

ARTICLE 50

a. Synod shall send delegates to Reformed ecumenical synods in which the Christian Reformed Church cooperates with other denominations which confess and maintain the Reformed faith.

b. Synod may present to such gatherings matters on which it seeks the judgment of the Reformed churches throughout the world.

c. Decisions of Reformed ecumenical synods shall be binding upon the Christian Reformed Church only when they have been ratified by its synod.

III. THE TASK AND ACTIVITIES OF THE CHURCH
A. WORSHIP SERVICES

ARTICLE 51

a. The congregation shall assemble for worship at least twice on the Lord's day to hear God's Word, to receive the sacraments, to engage in praise and prayer, and to present gifts of gratitude.

b. Worship services shall be held in observance of Christmas, Good Friday, Easter, Ascension Day, and Pentecost, and ordinarily on Old and New Year's Day, and annual days of prayer and thanksgiving.

c. Special worship services may be proclaimed in times of great stress or blessing for church, nation, or world.

ARTICLE 52

a. The consistory shall regulate the worship services.

b. The consistory shall see to it that the synodically approved Bible versions, liturgical forms, and songs are used, and that the principles and elements of the order of worship approved by synod are observed.

c. The consistory shall see to it that if choirs or others sing in the worship services, they observe the synodical regulations governing the content of the hymns and anthems sung. These regulations shall also apply when supplementary hymns are sung by the congregation.

ARTICLE 53

a. The ministers of the Word shall conduct the worship services.

b. Persons licensed to exhort and anyone appointed by the consistory to read a sermon may conduct worship services. They shall, however, refrain from all official acts of the ministry.

c. Only sermons approved by the consistory shall be read in the worship services.

ARTICLE 54

a. In the worship services the minister of the Word shall officially explain and apply Holy Scripture.

b. At one of the services each Lord's day, the minister shall ordinarily preach the Word as summarized in the Heidelberg Catechism, following its sequence.

ARTICLE 55

The sacraments shall be administered upon the authority of the consistory in the public worship service, by the minister of the Word, with the use of the prescribed forms.

ARTICLE 56

The covenant of God shall be sealed to children of believers by holy baptism. The consistory shall see to it that baptism is requested and administered as soon as feasible.

ARTICLE 57

Adults who have not been baptized shall receive holy baptism upon public profession of faith. The Form for the Baptism of Adults shall be used for such public professions.

ARTICLE 58

The baptism of one who comes from another Christian denomination shall be held valid if it has been administered in the name of the triune God, by someone authorized by that denomination.

ARTICLE 59

a. Members by baptism shall be admitted to the Lord's Supper upon a public profession of Christ according to the Reformed creeds, with the use of the prescribed form. Before the profession of faith the consistory shall examine them concerning their motives, doctrine, and conduct. The names of those who are to be admitted to the Lord's Supper shall be announced to the congregation for approval at least one Sunday before the public profession of faith.

b. Confessing members coming from other Christian Reformed congregations shall be admitted to communicant membership upon the presentation of certificates of membership attesting their soundness in doctrine and life.

c. Confessing members coming from churches in ecclesiastical fellowship shall be admitted to communicant membership upon presentation of certificates or statements of membership after the consistory has satisfied itself concerning the doctrine and conduct of the members. Persons coming from other denominations shall be admitted to communicant membership only after the consistory has examined them concerning doctrine and conduct. The consistory shall determine in each case whether to admit them directly or by public reaffirmation or profession of faith. Their names shall be announced to the congregation for approval.

ARTICLE 60

a. The Lord's Supper shall be administered at least once every three months.

b. The consistory shall provide for such administrations as it shall judge most conducive to edification. However, the ceremonies as prescribed in God's Word shall not be changed.

c. The Lord's Supper shall ordinarily be preceded by a preparatory sermon and followed by an applicatory sermon.

ARTICLE 61

a. The public prayers in the worship service shall include adoration, confession, thanksgiving, supplication, and intercession for all Christendom and all men.

b. In the ministry of prayer the approved liturgical prayers may be used.

ARTICLE 62

In the worship services Christian alms shall be received regularly.

B. CATECHETICAL INSTRUCTION

ARTICLE 63

Each church shall instruct its youth—and others who are interested—in the teaching of the Scriptures as formulated in the creeds of the church, in order to prepare them to profess their faith publicly and to assume their Christian responsibilities in the church and in the world.

ARTICLE 64

a. Catechetical instruction shall be supervised by the consistory.

b. The instruction shall be given by the minister of the Word with the help, if necessary, of the elders and others appointed by the consistory.

c. The Heidelberg Catechism and its Compendium shall be the basis of instruction. Selection of additional instructional helps shall be made by the minister in consultation with the consistory.

C. PASTORAL CARE

ARTICLE 65

Pastoral care shall be exercised over all the members of the congregation. The minister of the Word and the elders shall conduct annual home visitation, and faithfully visit the sick, the distressed, the shut-ins, and the erring.

They shall encourage the members to live by faith, comfort them in adversity, and warn them against errors in doctrine and life.

ARTICLE 66

a. Confessing members who remove to another Christian Reformed church are entitled to a certificate, issued by the consistory, concerning their doctrine and life. When such certificates of membership are requested, they shall ordinarily be mailed to the church of their new residence.

b. Members by baptism who remove to another Christian Reformed church shall upon proper request be granted a certificate of baptism, to which such notations as are necessary shall be attached. Such certificates shall as a rule be mailed to the church of their new residence.

c. Ecclesiastical certificates shall be signed by the president and clerk of the consistory.

ARTICLE 67

Members who move to localities where there is no Christian Reformed church may, upon their request, either retain their membership in the church of their former residence, or have their certificates sent to the nearest Christian Reformed church.

[Supplement contained in this manual, Art. 67, section 2.]

ARTICLE 68

Each church shall keep a complete record of all births, deaths, baptisms, professions of faith, receptions and dismissals of members, and excommunications and other terminations of membership.

ARTICLE 69

a. Consistories shall instruct and admonish those under their spiritual care to marry only in the Lord.

b. Christian marriages should be solemnized with appropriate admonitions, promises, and prayers, as provided for in the official form. Marriages may be solemnized either in a worship service, or in private gatherings of relatives and friends.

c. Ministers shall not solemnize marriages which would be in conflict with the Word of God.

ARTICLE 70

Funerals are not ecclesiastical but family affairs, and should be conducted accordingly.

ARTICLE 71

The consistory shall diligently encourage the members of the congregation to establish and maintain good Christian schools, and shall urge parents to have their children instructed in these schools according to the demands of the covenant.

ARTICLE 72

The consistory shall promote societies within the congregation for the study of God's Word and shall serve especially the youth organizations with counsel and assistance. All such societies are under the supervision of the consistory.

D. MISSIONS

ARTICLE 73

a. In obedience to Christ's great commission, the churches must bring the gospel to all men at home and abroad, in order to lead them into fellowship with Christ and his church.

b. In fulfilling this mandate, each consistory shall stimulate the members of the congregation to be witnesses for Christ in word and deed, and to support the work of home and foreign missions by their interest, prayers, and gifts.

ARTICLE 74

a. Each church shall bring the gospel to unbelievers in its own community. This task shall be sponsored and governed by the consistory.

b. This task may be executed, when conditions warrant, in cooperation with one or more neighboring churches.

ARTICLE 75

The classes shall, whenever necessary, assist the churches in their local evangelistic programs. The classes themselves may perform this work of evangelism when it is beyond the scope and resources of the local churches. To administer these tasks each classis shall have a classical home missions committee.

ARTICLE 76

a. Synod shall encourage and assist congregations and classes in their work of evangelism, and shall also carry on such home missions activities as are beyond the scope and resources of minor assemblies.

b. To administer these activities synod shall appoint a denominational home missions committee, whose work shall be controlled by synodical regulations.

[Contents of Supplement are contained in this manual, Art. 76.]

ARTICLE 77

a. Synod shall determine the field in which the joint foreign mission work of the churches is to be carried on, regulate the manner in which this task is to be performed, provide for its cooperative support, and encourage the congregations to call and support missionaries.

b. To administer these activities synod shall appoint a denominational foreign missions committee, whose work shall be controlled by synodical regulations.

[Contents of Supplement are contained in this manual, Art. 77.]

IV. THE ADMONITION AND DISCIPLINE OF THE CHURCH
A. GENERAL PROVISIONS

ARTICLE 78

a. The admonition and discipline of the church are spiritual in character and therefore require the use of spiritual means.

b. The exercise of admonition and discipline by the consistory does not preclude the responsibility of the believers to watch over and to admonish one another in love.

ARTICLE 79

The purpose of the admonition and discipline of the church is to maintain the honor of God, to restore the sinner, and to remove offense from the church of Christ.

ARTICLE 80

All members of the congregation are subject in both doctrine and life to the admonition and discipline of the church.

ARTICLE 81

Commission of sins which give public offense or which are brought to the attention of the consistory according to the rule of Matthew 18:15-17 shall make one liable to the discipline of the church.

ARTICLE 82

Disciplinary measures shall be applied only after an adequate investigation has been made and the member involved has had ample opportunity to present his case.

B. THE ADMONITION AND DISCIPLINE OF MEMBERS

ARTICLE 83

a. Members by baptism who willfully neglect to make public profession of faith, or are delinquent in doctrine or life, and do not heed the admonitions of the consistory shall be dealt with in accordance with the regulations of synod and, if they persist in their sin, shall be excluded from the church of Christ.

b. Members by baptism who have been excluded from the church and who later repent of their sin shall be received again into the church only upon public profession of faith.   [Supplement contained in this manual, Art. 83, section 1b.]

ARTICLE 84

Confessing members who have offended in doctrine or in life and who have responded favorably to the admonitions of the consistory shall be reconciled to the church upon sufficient evidence of repentance. The method of reconciliation is to be determined by the consistory.

ARTICLE 85

Confessing members who have offended in doctrine or in life and who obstinately reject the admonitions of the consistory shall be barred from partaking of the Lord's Supper, responding to the baptismal questions, and exercising any other rights of membership.

ARTICLE 86

a. Confessing members who have been barred from the Lord's Supper and who after repeated admonitions show no signs of repentance shall be excommunicated from the church of Christ. The Form for Excommunication shall be used for this purpose.

b. The consistory, before excommunicating anyone, shall make three announcements in which the nature of the offense and the obstinacy of the sinner are explained and the congregation is urged to pray for him and to admonish him. In the first announcement the name of the sinner shall ordinarily be withheld but may be mentioned at the discretion of the consistory. In the second, after the classis has given its approval to proceed with further discipline, his name shall be mentioned. In the third, the congregation shall be informed that unless the sinner repents he will be excommunicated on a specified date.

ARTICLE 87

When anyone who has been excommunicated desires to become reconciled to the church, the consistory, having satisfied itself as to the sincerity of his repentance, shall announce these developments to the congregation. If no valid objections are presented, he shall be restored to the fellowship of the church of Christ. The Form for Readmission shall be used for this purpose.

C. THE ADMONITION AND DISCIPLINE OF OFFICE-BEARERS

ARTICLE 88

a. Ministers, elders, deacons, and evangelists, besides being subject to general discipline, are also subject to special discipline, which consists of suspension and deposition from office.

b. General discipline shall not be applied to an office-bearer unless he has first been suspended from office.

ARTICLE 89

a. Special discipline shall be applied to office-bearers if they violate the Form of Subscription, are guilty of neglect or abuse of office, or in any way seriously deviate from sound doctrine and godly conduct.

b. The appropriate assembly shall determine whether, in a given instance, deposition from office shall take place immediately, without previous suspension.

ARTICLE 90

a. The suspension of a minister of the Gospel shall be imposed by the consistory of his church with the concurring judgment of the consistory of the nearest church in the same classis.

b. If the neighboring consistory fails to concur in the position of the consistory of the minister involved, the latter consistory shall either alter its original judgment or present the case to classis.

c. The deposition of a minister shall not be effected without the approval of classis together with the concurring advice of the synodical deputies.

ARTICLE 91

a. The suspension or deposition of an elder, deacon, or evangelist shall be imposed by the consistory with the concurring judgment of the consistory of the nearest church in the same classis.

b. If the neighboring consistory fails to concur in the position of the consistory of the elder, deacon, or evangelist involved, the latter consistory shall either alter its original judgment or present the case to classis.

ARTICLE 92

a. A minister of the Word whose membership resides with a congregation other than his calling church is subject to the admonition and discipline of the consistories of both churches. Either consistory may initiate disciplinary action, but neither shall act without conferring with the other.

b. If the consistories disagree, the case shall be submitted to the classis of the calling church for disposition.

ARTICLE 93

a. The suspension of an office-bearer shall be lifted only upon sufficient evidence of repentance.

b. The lifting of suspension is the prerogative of the assembly which imposed suspension.

ARTICLE 94

a. A deposed office-bearer shall not be restored unless he gives sufficient evidence of genuine repentance. It must further be evident that, should he be restored to office, he could then serve without being hindered in his work by the handicap of his past sin and that his restoration would be to the glory of God and for the true welfare of the church.

b. The judgment as to whether a deposed minister shall subsequently be declared eligible for call shall be made by the classis in which he was deposed, together with the concurring advice of the synodical deputies. Upon acceptance of a call, he shall be re-ordained.

CONCLUSION

ARTICLE 95

No church shall in any way lord it over another church, and no office-bearer shall lord it over another office-bearer.

ARTICLE 96

This Church Order, having been adopted by common consent, shall be faithfully observed, and any revision thereof shall be made only by synod.

INTRODUCTION

ARTICLE 1

PURPOSE AND BASIS OF THE CHURCH ORDER

a. The Christian Reformed Church, confessing its complete subjection to the Word of God and the Reformed creeds as a true interpretation of this Word, acknowledging Christ as the only head of his church, and desiring to honor the apostolic injunction that in the churches all things are to be done decently and in order (I Cor. 14:40), regulates its ecclesiastical organization and activities in the following articles.
b. The main subjects treated in this Church Order are: The Offices of the Church, The Assemblies of the Church, The Task and Activities of the Church, and The Admonition and Discipline of the Church.

Article 1 of the Church Order presents "the justification for, and [the] purpose of the Church Order," as the Committee for Revision expressed it in 1960 (*Acts of Synod 1960,* p. 134).

1. Principles of Reformed Church Polity
   Article 1a expresses three principles of Reformed church polity:

   a. Complete Subjection to the Word of God and to the Reformed Creeds
   The Bible is the final court of appeal in matters of church government and practice. For example, Article 29 states that "the decisions of the assemblies shall be considered settled and binding, unless it is proved that they conflict with the Word of God or the Church Order."
   Even a casual reading of the Church Order will impress one as to the frequent reference to "the Word." Pastors are called "minister[s] of the Word" (Art. 2); the preaching of the Word is an essential element in public worship services (Arts. 51, 54); synod approves the Bible versions used in worship (Art. 47); church societies have as their purpose "the study of God's Word" (Art. 72).
   Only three direct references are made to specific Scripture passages, however. (1) Article 1 refers to I Corinthians 14:40 and states the principle that "in the churches all things are to be done decently and in order." (2) Article 73 refers to the great commission (Matt. 28:19-20 and parallels are implied) to which the churches must be obedient. (3) Article 81 establishes procedures in discipline matters on the basis of Matthew 18:15-17.

28

As its confessional expression of God's Word the Christian Reformed Church subscribes to the Belgic Confession, the Heidelberg Catechism, and the Canons of Dort. In addition the church receives three ecumenical creeds: the Apostles' Creed, the Nicene Creed, and the Athanasian Creed.

b. Christ Is the Only Head of His Church

The Bible speaks of the church as the body of Christ and of Christ as its head. He is in the closest and most vital relationship to the church. He is, in fact, a part of that church. As the church's true and only head he has complete authority over its life. The church renders him joyful obedience. His headship is exercised in love and grace (Eph. 5:23-27).

"The ministry of the church is Christ's ministry, and as Christ's ministry it functions with the power and authority of Christ the Lord."

(Acts of Synod 1973, p. 63)

"Christian authority involves service in the name of the authoritative Christ, and Christian service involves authority in the name of the serving Christ. Both before and after his ascension as our victorious Lord, Jesus is the authoritative Son of God who serves the Father and those whom the Father has given him.

"Christ only is Lord of the church, and no one may presume to rule in his place. Service and authority exercised in the church are in his Name and according to his Word." *(Acts of Synod 1973,* p. 62)

c. All Things Must Be Done Decently and in Order

The third principle of Reformed church polity as expressed in Article 1a is "the apostolic injunction that in the churches all things are to be done decently and in order (I Cor. 14:40)."

The Synod of 1973 stated that "although in the New Testament the organization of the church is not clear as has sometimes been assumed, nevertheless there is the insistence that the church shall have organizational structure" *(Acts of Synod 1973,* p. 62).

The Belgic Confession, Article 30, expresses this principle when it says that "everything will be carried on in the Church with good order and decency, when faithful men are chosen, according to the rule prescribed by St. Paul in his Epistle to Timothy."

2. Relationship of Scripture, the Reformed Creeds, and the Church Order

a. Scripture

The Bible is the final authority in Reformed church polity. The Belgic Confession defines one of the marks of the true church as being that "all things are managed according to the pure Word of God, all things contrary thereto rejected, and Jesus Christ acknowledged as the only head of the church" (Belgic Confession, Art. 29).

b. The Reformed Creeds

Article 1a describes the Reformed creeds as "a true interpretation of this Word."

The creeds are themselves subject to the Word and subordinate to it. The Belgic Confession states:

"Neither may we consider any writings of men, however holy these men may have been, of equal value with those divine Scriptures, nor ought we to consider custom, or the great multitude, or antiquity, or succession of times, persons, councils, decrees or statutes, as of equal value with the truth of God, since the truth is above all." (Belgic Confession, Art. 7)

Article 5 of the Church Order requires all office-bearers in the church to subscribe to the creeds as a condition for holding office.

c. The Church Order

The Church Order is subordinate to both Scripture and the Reformed creeds. It contains statements of principles derived from both sources as well as many provisions which reflect the contemporary situation of the church in a particular age and place. Reformed church polity has always maintained that the Church Order must be changed whenever the profit of the church requires.

This aspect of Reformed church polity was more explicitly stated in the 1914 Church Order (Art. 86) than in the 1965 Revised Church Order (Art. 96). The 1914 Church Order provided:

"These articles, relating to the lawful order of the church, have been so drafted and adopted by common consent, that they (if the profit of the church demands otherwise) may and ought to be altered, augmented or diminished."

The Scripture is the infallibly inspired Word of God, and is not subject to alteration.

The creeds also ought to be altered only with great caution and in the light of new understanding of the Word of God.

The Church Order, however, while it must be in harmony with the Word of God and the creeds of the church, is adaptable to such changes as will promote good order in the church; and therefore, if and when the profit of the church demands it, the Church Order "may and ought to be altered, augmented or diminished" (Pre-1965 Church Order, Art. 86). Only by such usage can it fulfill its stated purpose of causing all things to be done decently and in good order.

The Church Order does, however, constitute a court of appeal inasmuch as it is in harmony with both Scripture and the Reformed creeds (cf. Art. 29).

3. Divisions of the Church Order

Article 1b states "the main subjects treated in this Church Order." They are:

a. The Offices of the Church (Arts. 2-25)
b. The Assemblies of the Church (Arts. 26-50)
c. The Task and Activities of the Church (Arts. 51-77)
d. The Admonition and Discipline of the Church (Arts. 78-94)

Each of these deals with some aspect of the organizational structure and function of the church. The Church Order is concerned with the question of how the principles of the Word and the contemporary life of the church affect the way things are done.

30

The scope of the Church Order's frame of reference is therefore limited. It touches on the life of the individual member only occasionally and marginally. Even then it does this in terms of one's relationship to the structured church. Many details of procedure and practice are omitted, giving each local church great liberty to structure its life and service in harmony with the broad statements of polity. We can illustrate this as follows: The Church Order specifies (Art. 51) that the congregation must assemble for worship at least twice each Lord's day and lists the main components of the worship service. It does not say what times the services must be held, nor how many services may be held, how many hymns must be sung, nor what the order of worship must be. It does not give details concerning the way the sacraments are to be celebrated although the churches have consented together to do this in harmony with certain basic provisions. The very brevity of the Church Order as compared to the very lengthy Rules and Discipline of some denominations confirms this feature.

I. THE OFFICES OF THE CHURCH
A. GENERAL PROVISIONS

ARTICLE 2

SPECIAL OFFICES OF THE CHURCH

The church recognizes the offices of minister of the Word, elder, deacon, and evangelist. These offices differ from each other only in mandate and task, not in dignity and honor.

(Amended—*Acts of Synod 1979,* p. 66)

1. General Observations
   It should be noted that Article 2 deals with the special offices of the church. This calls for a few observations about the concept of offices in the Scripture and our confessions.

   a. The word *office* as we understand it in the church is not an accurate translation of any Old Testament Hebrew word nor of any New Testament Greek word.

   As a general term for what we call *office* (namely, a certain type of service within the church) the word *diakonia* (which means ministry or service) is generally used in the New Testament. We therefore follow the biblical pattern more closely when we designate the functions performed in and by the church and its members as *ministries* (services) rather than *offices.*

   b. We have titled Church Order Article 2 "Special Offices of the Church" because the ministries (offices) described in this article are distinguished from and must be understood in the light of the broader background of the ministry of *all* believers.

   In the New Testament we are taught that Christ dwells in his church. The church is the temple of the Holy Spirit, and God lives in it (I Cor. 3:16). Thus every believer and all believers are called to Christ's ministry, and we speak of the office or ministry of all believers.

   John writes about the anointing (ordination or calling) of all believers to office or ministry when he writes, "You have been anointed by the Holy One, and you all know" (I John 2:20); and again, "The anointing which you received from him abides in you, and you have no need that any one should teach you; as his anointing teaches you about everything, and is true" (I John 2:27).

   The Heidelberg Catechism describes the ministry or office of all believers in Lord's Day 12, Question and Answer 32:

32

"32 Q.   BUT WHY ARE YOU CALLED A CHRISTIAN?
   A.   Because by faith I am a member of Christ
           and so I share in his anointing.
             I am anointed
               to confess his name,
               to present myself to him as a living sacrifice
                 of thanks,
               to strive with a good conscience against sin
                 and the devil in this life,
               and afterward to reign with Christ
                 over all creation
                 for all eternity."

c. Those who wish to make a more complete study of the offices of the church should consult Study Report 44, "Ecclesiastical Office and Ordination," which appears in the *Acts of Synod 1973* (pp. 635-716). This comprehensive report presents both an in-depth biblical study on office and ordination and an account of the historical development of the concepts of office and ordination.

d. While our present Church Order speaks of three special offices of the church, the Church Order of Dort and our own early Church Order listed four special offices in the church; in addition to the three we now list they included the office of professor of theology.

   The Church Order clearly specifies that these offices do not differ "in dignity and honor" but only "in mandate and task."

   It may be noted also that the Synod of 1973 mandated a committee "to study the implications of the Guidelines for Understanding the Nature of Ecclesiastical Office and Ordination, especially as they relate to ordaining 'layworkers in evangelism' " (*Acts of Synod 1973,* p. 64; also see section 3 below).

2. Decisions of Synod re Ecclesiastical Office and Ordination
   a. The Synod of 1973 adopted the following statements as "Guidelines for Understanding the Nature of Ecclesiastical Office and Ordination":

   "(Comprehensive Ministry: 'Office of all believers')
   "1)   The general term for 'office' in the Greek New Testament is DIAKONIA, meaning 'service' or 'ministry.' In this basic sense ecclesiastical office is one and indivisible, for it embraces the total ministry of the church, a ministry that is rooted in Christ.
   "2)   This comprehensive ministry (office) is universal, committed to all members of the church, and the task of ministry is shared by all. The ministry of the church is Christ's ministry, and as Christ's ministry it functions with the power and authority of Christ the Lord. This minstry of the church is shared by all who are in Christ.

   "(Particular Ministries)
   "3)   It is not inconsistent with this universal office-sharing and is in keeping

with apostolic practice that some individuals, in whom the church has discerned the required gifts, be appointed to special tasks. The Scriptures report a setting apart to particular ministries or services. Both in the Old and New Testaments God calls certain people for particular tasks.

''4) From the beginning these particular ministries were functional in character, arising under the guidance of the Spirit in the interests of good order and efficiency in the church, to enable the church to carry out Christ's work in the world most effectively.

''5) The particular ministries are characterized by service, rather than by status, dominance or privilege. These ministries function with Christ's power and authority, a power and authority rooted in obedience to his Word and expressed in loving service. In turn, those who are served are to respond with obedience and respect.

''6) The particular ministries are to be distinguished in function, not in essence, from the comprehensive ministry shared by all believers, and distinctions among the particular ministries themselves are functional. Since all members are commissioned to serve, there is only a difference in the kinds of service of deacons, elders, ministers, and all other members.

''(The Word and The Sacraments)

''7) The tasks of the preaching of the Word and of the administration of the sacraments have been given by Christ to the church. Although in the Scriptures these tasks are not explicitly limited to special office-holders, historically they have been assigned to and carried out by those whom the church has appointed on Christ's authority.

''8) There is no valid biblical or doctrinal reason why a person whom the church has appointed to bring the Word may not also be appointed to administer the sacraments.

''(Appointment to Particular Ministries)

''9) 'Ordination' should be understood as the appointment or setting apart of certain members of the church for particular ministries that are strategic for the accomplishment of the church's total ministry. In this sense of appointment or setting apart, ordination has biblical precedent, and is valuable for the good order and well-being of the church.

''10) The ceremony of the laying on of hands is not a sacrament but a symbolic act by which the church may publicly confirm its call and appointment to particular ministries. As such it is useful but not essential.

''11) To invite only ministers, and not elders also, to participate in the laying on of hands is a departure from biblical example. Furthermore, there is no biblical warrant for limiting the laying on of hands to the occasion of setting apart for the particular ministry of the Word and the sacraments.

''12) Because the Scriptures do not present a definitive, exhaustive description of the particular ministries of the church, and because these particular ministries as described in Scripture are functional in character, the Bible

34

leaves room for the church to adapt or modify its particular ministries in order to carry out effectively its service to Christ and for Christ in all circumstances." *(Acts of Synod 1973*, pp. 62-64)

b. The Synod of 1973 also adopted the following observations as the framework within which the "Guidelines for Understanding the Nature of Ecclesiastical Office and Ordination" are to be understood:

"1) Although in the New Testament the organization of the church is not as clear as has sometimes been assumed, nevertheless there is insistence that the church shall have organizational structure, and that this organizational structure shall include designated leaders to whom respect and submission is due.

"2) Nowhere in the New Testament is there a conflict between authority and service, or between ruling and love. Christian authority involves service in the name of the authoritative Christ, and Christian service involves authority in the name of the serving Christ. Both before and after his ascension as our victorious Lord, Jesus is the authoritative Son of God who serves the Father and those whom the Father has given him.

"3) Christ only is Lord of the church, and no one may presume to rule in his place. Service and authority exercised in the church are in his Name and according to his Word.

"4) Because God is a God of order, and because the people of God are subject to many weaknesses and errors and in need of spiritual leadership in the face of a hostile world, Christ grants, by his Holy Spirit, gifts of ruling service and serving authority (service and authority) to particular people whom the church must recognize, in order that their gifts may be officially exercised for the benefit of all.

"5) The office-bearers, i.e., certain people appointed to particular tasks, are not appointed without the call and approbation of the church. When so appointed, however, they are recognized by the church to be representatives of Christ in the special functions for which they have been appointed. As such they serve both Christ and the church, and are worthy of honor, especially if they serve and rule well.

"6) These guidelines are intended to offer helpful directions to the churches as they continue to seek practical solutions to the questions pertaining to the status and functions of 'layworkers in evangelism' and related questions. These guidelines do not re-define the basic types of service currently assigned to deacons, elders, and ministers; nor do these guidelines now authorize anyone other than ministers to administer the sacraments along with the preaching of the Word. *In keeping with our church polity, such changes may be introduced only by way of revision of the Church Order as decided by synod."* *(Acts of Synod 1973,* p. 62)

3. The Office of Evangelist
The Synod of 1978 established a fourth office, that of evangelist, and appointed a

committee to advise a future synod concerning the revisions of the Church Order necessitated by this decision. Synod also instructed the Liturgical Committee to prepare a form for the ordination of evangelists.

The decisions of the Synod of 1978 are:

a. Synod declared that "the office of minister of the Word with the prescribed requirements for admission to that office is the ordinary and usual way in which the church fulfills Guideline 8 [of the Synod of 1973].

   "Grounds:

   "1) The ministry of the Word and sacraments has been reserved for the office of the minister of the Word in universal Christian practice.

   "2) The theology of Guideline 8 is such as to require a complete ministry of Word and sacraments for those who are admitted to the office of minister of the Word, but does not compel the church to grant the same privilege to those who may be permitted to exhort."   (*Acts of Synod 1973,* p. 63)

b. Synod declared that "while evangelism is mandated to the church and is, therefore, an essential aspect of the task committed to her ordained ministers, nevertheless the church should make use of other members who have the necessary gifts for the task.

   "Grounds:

   "a) Article 73 of the Church Order:

      "1) In obedience to Christ's great commission, the churches must bring the gospel to all men at home and abroad in order to lead them into fellowship with Christ and his church.

      "2) In fulfilling this mandate, each consistory shall stimulate the members of the congregation to be witnesses for Christ in word and deed, and to support the work of home and foreign missions by their interest, prayers and gifts.

   "b) Article 74 of the Church Order:

      "1) Each church shall bring the gospel to unbelievers in its own community. This task shall be sponsored and governed by the consistory.

      "2) This task may be executed, when conditions warrant, in cooperation with one or more neighboring churches.

   "c) Guidelines 1, 2, and 7 (*Acts of Synod 1973,* p. 63):

      "1: The general term for 'office' in the Greek New Testament is DIAKONIA, meaning 'service' or 'ministry.' In this basic sense, ecclesiastical office is one and indivisible, for it embraces the total ministry of the church, a ministry that is rooted in Christ.

      "2: This comprehensive ministry (office) is universal, committed to all members of the church, and the task of ministry is shared by all. The ministry of the church is Christ's ministry and as Christ's ministry it functions with the power and authority of Christ the Lord. This ministry of the church is shared by all who are in Christ.

      "7: The tasks of the preaching of the Word and of the administration of the sacraments have been given by Christ to the church. Although in the

Scriptures these tasks are not explicitly limited to special officeholders, historically they have been assigned to and carried out by those whom the church has appointed on Christ's authority.''

c. Synod established ''the office of evangelist with authority to administer the Word and sacraments in the work of evangelism of his calling church.

''Grounds:

''a) In the discharge of this basic evangelistic task of the church, one who has been chosen by the church to perform this specialized ministry on behalf of the local congregation should be ordained to an office which enables him to fulfil the special function to which he has been called by the church. (cf. Guideline 7)

''b) Because the Scriptures do not present a definitive, exhaustive description of the particular ministries of the church, and because these particular ministries as described in Scripture are functional in character, the Bible leaves room for the church to adapt or modify its particular ministries in order to carry out effectively its service to Christ and for Christ in all circumstances. (Guideline 12)''

d. Synod declared that ''the evangelist be acknowledged as an elder of his calling church with corresponding privileges and responsibilities.

''Ground:

''This acknowledgement is also accorded the minister of the Word in his relationship to the consistory with whom he labors.''

e. Synod declared that one who is ordained to the office of evangelist ''shall function under the following regulations:

''a) His ordination to the office of evangelist shall not take place until he has proven his ability to function adequately in the work of evangelism, and he has sustained the classical examination for evangelists.

''b) His term of ordination shall correspond to his term of appointment by the local church.

''c) His work as elder shall normally be limited to that which pertains to his function as evangelist.

''d) He shall function under the direct supervision of the consistory. He shall give regular reports to the consistory, and be present at the meetings of the consistory whenever possible, and particularly when his work is under consideration.

''e) His work as evangelist shall be limited to that emerging congregation in which he is appointed to labor only until the congregation is organized.

''f) The membership of the emerging congregation shall be held by his calling church.

''g) When he accepts an appointment to another field, he shall submit to such examination as is considered appropriate by the classis to which his calling church belongs, and he shall be ordained in his new field of labor.''

f. Synod declared that "the classical examination for evangelist shall include at least the following elements:

"a) Presentation of the following documents:

"1) A consistorial recommendation from the church in which the appointee holds membership.

"2) Any evidence (diplomas, transcripts) of formal general education and of specialized training in Bible and evangelism.

"3) A copy of his appointment from the church which is requesting his ordination as evangelist.

"b) Presentation of a message to classis based upon an assigned text of Scripture, a written copy of which shall be examined by a committee of the classis and an oral presentation made before classis. The length of the oral presentation shall be left to the discretion of classis.

"c) Examination before classis in the following areas:

a) Knowledge of Scripture

b) Knowledge of Reformed Doctrine

c) Knowledge of the Standards of our Church

d) Practical matters regarding Christian testimony, walk of life, relation to others, love for the church, interest in evangelism and promotion of Christ's kingdom." *(Acts of Synod 1978, pp. 76-78)*

I. THE OFFICES OF THE CHURCH
A. GENERAL PROVISIONS (continued)

ARTICLE 3

ELIGIBILITY FOR ECCLESIASTICAL OFFICES

Confessing male members of the church who meet the biblical requirements are eligible for office. Only those who have been officially called and ordained or installed shall hold and exercise office in the church.

1. Eligibility for Office.
   Article 3 limits eligibility to "confessing male members who meet biblical requirements." Eligibility includes the following according to this article:

   a. Confession of Faith
   Persons considered for these offices must be confessing members of the church.

   b. Male
   Article 3 limits eligibility to male members only.

   c. Biblical Requirements
   Article 3 specifies that office-bearers must meet biblical requirements. They must:
   1) Possess the Necessary Gifts Required for a Particular Function
      a) In Romans 12 Paul writes that the church is like the body—its members have different gifts. Believers have "gifts that differ according to the grace given to us" (vs. 6) and we should be conscious that "all members do not have the same function" (vs. 4).
      b) In I Corinthians 12 Paul writes, "Now there are varieties of gifts, but the same Spirit; and there are varieties of services, but the same Lord; and there are varieties of working, but it is the same God who inspires them all in every one" (vss. 4-6).
   2) Possess the Gift of Leadership
      Hebrews 13:7 lays a great emphasis on an exemplary life and leadership: "Remember your leaders, those who spoke to you the word of God; consider the outcome of their life, and imitate their faith."
   3) Live an Exemplary Life
      Biblical requirements for office-bearers are indicated in many passages in the Book of Acts and the New Testament Epistles. Several desirable qualifications

for office-bearers are listed in I Timothy 3:1-7 and Titus 1:5-9, indicating that office-bearers should be above reproach, temperate, self-controlled, hospitable, able to teach, good managers of their families, respected both inside and outside of the church, and holding firm to the Word of God. These passages also tell us that there are characteristics—such as bigamy, drunkenness, a violent temper, quarrelsomeness, greed or love of money—which disqualify persons for special offices.

The Forms for Ordination of office-bearers also call attention to the importance of the life of the office-bearer in the discharge of his responsibility, and provide: "To fill worthily so sacred an office, [they] should set an example of godliness in their personal life, in their home life, and in their relations with their fellow-men."

d. Gifts of Believers
All believers have gifts which must be used for the Lord. Peter writes, "As each has received a gift, employ it for one another, as good stewards of God's varied grace" (I Pet. 4:10).

Though gifts of believers differ, the church ought not to think of one type of gift as superior to all others.

1) Not all believers have the peculiar gifts needed in the specific offices of the church.

2) Many of the most gifted persons in the church never serve in the special offices but function wonderfully in the ministry of the gifts entrusted to them by the Lord.

3) It is the responsibility of the consistory and congregation of believers to select prayerfully persons with the necessary qualifications for all functions in the church.

2. Eligibility for the Office of Deacon
The Synod of 1975 decided "that the practice of excluding women from ecclesiastical offices recognized in the Church Order be maintained unless compelling biblical grounds are advanced for changing that practice," and "that sufficient biblical grounds have not been adduced to warrant a departure from our present practice of excluding women from the ecclesiastical offices recognized in the Church Order" (*Acts of Synod 1975*, p. 78).

But in 1978 synod decided "that consistories be allowed to ordain qualified women to the office of deacon, provided that their work is distinguished from that of elders" and proposed to revise Article 3 of the Church Order accordingly (*Acts of Synod 1978*, p. 104). The proposed revision broadens eligibility for the office of deacon to "all confessing members."

The ratification of the proposed revision of Article 3 was deferred by the Synod of 1979 until a study committee on this matter reports to a later synod.

3. Eligibility for the Office of Evangelist
The office of evangelist was established by the Synod of 1978. Necessary revisions of the Church Order with respect to this office were made by the Synod of 1979 (*Acts of*

Synod 1979, pp. 64-68) and are contained in this manual (cf. Arts. 2, 23, 24, 88, 91).

4. Other Considerations Regarding Eligibility
From time to time synods have responded to certain questions about eligibility for ecclesiastical office. Two of these follow:

a. Christian Education
1) "Synod urges all ministers and consistories with their strengths and gifts to support heartily the establishment and growth of the Christian schools."
                                                    (*Acts of Synod 1892*, p. 12)
2) "Although such as heartily support Christian instruction do not thereby automatically qualify for the nomination of office-bearers, yet Synod wishes to emphasize that this element should be given very weighty consideration, and advises consistories to do so, since our principles logically call for it and our Christian schools are constantly in need of whole-hearted support from consistories."   (*Acts of Synod 1934*, p. 167-68)
     The above declaration was made in dealing with a protest to a specific nomination. Synod did not sustain the protest, and noted in the grounds that "local conditions in a congregation may make it difficult to find suitable material for office-bearers" and that "the nominees in question do not in principle object to Christian instruction."

b. Labor Union Membership
Synod declared that membership in a labor union does not necessarily disqualify an office-bearer (*Acts of Synod 1955*, p. 91-93).

5. Ordination and Installation
Article 3 specifies that "only those who have been officially called and ordained or installed shall hold and exercise office in the church."
     For regulations concerning the ordination and installation of office-bearers, see Article 4; of ministers, see Article 10; of elders and deacons, see Article 23; of evangelists, see Article 2.

I. OFFICES OF THE CHURCH
A. GENERAL PROVISIONS (continued)

ARTICLE 4
CALLING TO SPECIAL OFFICES

a. In calling to an office, the consistory shall present to the congregation a nomination of at least twice the number to be elected. In special circumstances the consistory may submit a nomination which totals less than twice the number to be elected, giving reasons for this departure from the rule.
b. Prior to making nominations the consistory may give the congregation an opportunity to direct attention to suitable persons.
c. The election by the congregation shall take place under the supervision of the consistory after prayer and in accordance with the regulations established by the consistory. The right to vote shall be limited to confessing members in good standing.
d. After having called the elected persons to their respective offices and having announced their names, the consistory shall proceed to ordain or install them if no valid impediment has arisen. The ordination or installation shall take place in the public worship services with the use of the prescribed ecclesiastical forms.

1. Nomination
   a. Number of Nominations
      Article 4a states that nominations of ministers, elders, and deacons shall ordinarily consist of twice the number to be elected. If circumstances lead a consistory to nominate less than twice the number, the consistory should give reason for departing from the rule. The procedure of having less than twice the number should be very exceptional.

   b. Notifying the Congregation
      The Church Order requires that the consistory submit nominations for special offices. The first announcement should be made early enough for members to present possible objections at a regular meeting of the consistory. If no lawful objections are received, the names shall be presented at a congregational meeting for election.

2. Congregational Suggestions for Nominations
   Article 4b states that before making nominations the congregation may be given op-

42

portunity to direct attention to suitable persons. This is not required, but permitted. Its inclusion in the Church Order would indicate that this is generally a desirable procedure.

3. Election
   a. Election by the congregation shall take place at a regular congregational meeting under supervision of the consistory.
   b. The right to vote shall be limited to confessing members in good standing, that is, not under formal church discipline. Synod affirmed in 1957 and reaffirmed in 1972 "that it is the right... of women members, as full members of Christ and his church and sharers in the office of believers, to participate in and vote at congregational meetings on a level of equality with men" (*Acts of Synod 1972*, p. 103).
   c. The regulations for congregational meetings are dealt with in Article 37.

4. Ordination
   a. The names of those elected to special offices are ordinarily announced to the congregation on two Sundays prior to ordination.
   b. The ordination (or installation) shall take place in a public worship service with the use of synodically approved ecclesiastical forms. Further guidelines are found in Articles 3, 10, and 23.
   c. For the understanding of ordination and the meaning of the ceremony of ordination the "Guidelines for Understanding the Nature of Ecclesiastical Office and Ordination" (Guidelines 9-12) will be helpful. These guidelines are listed in this manual under Church Order Article 2. Report 44 of the Synod of 1973 contains a helpful section on "The Meaning of Ordination." (See *Acts of Synod 1973*, pp. 638-649.)

I. THE OFFICES OF THE CHURCH
A. GENERAL PROVISIONS (continued)

ARTICLE 5

SIGNING THE FORM OF SUBSCRIPTION

All office-bearers, on occasions stipulated by consistorial, classical, and synodical regulations, shall signify their agreement with the doctrine of the church by signing the Form of Subscription.

1. Occasions Requiring Signature
   The Form of Subscription is signed by each office-bearer at the time of induction into office in a specified consistory or classis, or at the first meeting the office-bearer attends in the consistory or classis in which he is to serve.

   When an office-bearer assumes his office in another consistory or classis, he must sign the Form of Subscription of that assembly at the time of induction, or at the first meeting he attends.

   At synodical gatherings delegates affirm their public declaration of agreement with the Forms of Unity by rising, or by verbal consent, after the "Public Declaration of Agreement with the Forms of Unity" has been read.

2. Use of the Official Copy
   Each consistory and each classis should preserve and maintain its official copy of the Form of Subscription (with the accumulated signatures) along with its official minutes, and it should be on hand when new office-bearers are inducted.

3. The Form of Subscription
   "We, the undersigned, Professors of the Christian Reformed Church, Ministers of the Gospel, Elders and Deacons of the Christian Reformed congregation of_____, of the Classis of _____, do hereby sincerely and in good conscience before the Lord, declare by this our subscription that we heartily believe and are persuaded that all the articles and points of doctrine contained in the Confession and Catechism of the Reformed church, together with the explanation of some points of the aforesaid doctrine made by the National Synod of Dordrecht, 1618-'19, do fully agree with the Word of God.

   "We promise therefore diligently to teach and faithfully to defend the aforesaid doctrine, without either directly or indirectly contradicting the same by our public preaching or writing.

"We declare, moreover, that we do not only reject all errors that militate against this doctrine and particularly those which were condemned by the above mentioned synod, but that we will neither publicly nor privately propose, teach, or defend the same, either by preaching or writing, until we have first revealed such sentiments to the consistory, classis, or synod, that the same may there be examined, being ready always cheerfully to submit to the judgment of the consistory, classis, or synod, under the penalty, in case of refusal, of being by that very fact suspended from our office.

"And further, if at any time the consistory, classis, or synod upon sufficient grounds of suspicion and to preserve the uniformity and purity of doctrine, may deem it proper to require of us a further explanation of our sentiments respecting any particular article of the Confession of Faith, the Catechism, or the explanation of the National Synod, we do hereby promise to be always willing and ready to comply with such a requisition, under the penalty above mentioned, reserving for ourselves, however, the right of appeal in case we should believe ourselves aggrieved by the sentence of the consistory or the classis; and until a decision is made upon such an appeal, we will acquiesce in the determination and judgment already passed."

4. Gravamina

Differing sentiments, dissent, or difficulties pertaining to the confessional standards must be dealt with in accord with the stipulations of the Form of Subscription. When a person presents a difficulty with or an objection to some aspect of the creedal standards, it is called a *gravamen*. The Synod of 1976 made the following decisions with respect to any gravamen which might be presented to the assemblies and included them as Supplement 5 to the Church Order:

a. "Synod declares that gravamina fall into at least two basic types:

   "1) A *confessional-difficulty gravamen:* a gravamen in which a subscriber expresses his personal difficulty with the confession but does not call for a revision of the confessions, and

   "2) A *confessional-revision gravamen:* a gravamen in which a subscriber makes a specific recommendation for revision of the confessions.

b. *"Guidelines* as to the meaning of subscription to the confessions by means of the Form of Subscription:

   "1) The person signing the Form of Subscription subscribes without reservation to all the doctrines contained in the standards of the church, as being doctrines which are taught in the Word of God.

   "2) The subscriber *does not* by his subscription declare that these doctrines are all stated in the best possible manner, or that the standards of our church cover all that the Scriptures teach on the matters confessed. Nor does he declare that every teaching of the Scriptures is set forth in our confessions, or that every heresy is rejected and refuted by them.

   "3) A subscriber is only bound by his subscription to those doctrines which are confessed, and is not bound to the references, allusions and remarks that are

45

incidental to the formulation of these doctrines nor to the theological deductions which some may draw from the doctrines set forth in the confessions. However, no one is free to decide for himself or for the church what is and what is not a doctrine confessed in the standards. In the event that such a question should arise, the decision of the assemblies of the church should be sought and acquiesced in.

c. "*Regulations* concerning the procedure to be followed in the submission of a *confessional-difficulty gravamen:*

"1) Ministers (whether missionaries, professors, or others not serving congregations as pastors), elders or deacons shall submit their 'difficulties and different sentiments' to their consistories for examination and judgment. Should a consistory decide that it is not able to judge the gravamen submitted to it, it shall submit the matter to classis for examination and judgment. If the classis, after examination, judges that it is unable to decide the matter, it may submit it to synod, in accordance with the principles of the Church Order, Article 28b.

"2) In all instances of confessional-difficulty gravamina, the matter shall not be open for discussion by the whole church since this type of gravamen is a personal request for information and/or clarification of the confession. Hence this type of gravamen should be dealt with pastorally and personally by the assembly addressed.

d. "*Regulations* concerning the procedure to be followed in the submission of a *confessional-revision gravamen:*

"1) The basic assumption of the church in requiring subscription to the Form of Subscription is that 'all the articles and points of doctrine' contained in the confessions of the church 'do fully agree with the Word of God.' The burden of proof, therefore, rests upon the subscriber who calls upon the church to justify or revise her confessions.

"2) Ministers (including missionaries, professors or all others not serving congregations as pastors), elders or deacons shall submit their gravamina calling for revision of the confessions to their consistories for examination and judgment. Should the consistory decide that it is not able to judge the gravamen submitted to it, it shall submit the matter to classis for examination and judgment. If the classis, after examination, judges that it is unable to decide the matter, classis may submit to the synod, in accordance with the princples of the Church Order, Article 28b.

"3) If the gravamen is *adopted* by the consistory and the classis as its own, it becomes an overture to the broader assemblies and therefore it is open for discussion in the whole church.

"4) If the gravamen is *rejected* by the classis it may be appealed to synod; and when the constituted synod declares the matter to be legally before it for action, all the signers of the Form of Subscription shall be free to discuss it together with the whole church until adjudicated by synod.

"5) Since the subscriber has the right of appeal from the judgment of a consistory to classis and from classis to synod, the mere fact that the matter is being appealed shall not be a reason for suspending or otherwise disciplining an office-bearer, provided other provisions of the Form of Subscription and the Church Order are observed.

"6) A revision of the confessions shall not be adopted by synod until the whole church membership has had adequate opportunity to consider it.
"Grounds:
"a. The history of the functioning of the Form of Subscription shows that if such guidelines and regulations had been available and followed, considerable delay and confusion might have been avoided.
"b. These guidelines and regulations will make the signing of the Form of Subscription more meaningful and will remove some common misunderstandings that now exist on the part of many office-bearers.
"c. These guidelines and regulations will prove helpful to consistory, classis and synod in dealing with matters submitted to them for examination in accordance with the Form of Subscription.

e. "That synod print the above guidelines and regulations in future official editions of the Church Order as a supplement to Article 5."

(Acts of Synod 1976, pp. 68-70)

I. THE OFFICES OF THE CHURCH
B. MINISTERS OF THE WORD (Articles 6-22)

ARTICLE 6
ELIGIBILITY FOR ADMISSION TO THE MINISTRY OF THE WORD

a. The completion of a satisfactory theological training shall be required for admission to the ministry of the Word.

b. Graduates of the theological seminary of the Christian Reformed Church who have been declared candidates for the ministry of the Word by the churches shall be eligible for call.

c. Those who have been trained elsewhere shall not be eligible for call unless they have met the requirements stipulated in the synodical regulations and have been declared by the churches to be candidates for the ministry of the Word.

1. Theological Training

Article 6a requires a candidate for the ministry of the Word to have completed a "satisfactory theological training."

a. Calvin Theological Seminary

Training for the ministry of the Word in the Christian Reformed Church is provided by Calvin Theological Seminary. The curriculum adopted by the faculty, the Board of Trustees, and approved by synod is designed to provide a satisfactory theological training for future ministers in the Christian Reformed Church.

b. Degree Requirements

Synod has stipulated the following degree requirements for candidacy:

1) Synod recognizes the M.Div. degree as the degree qualifying for the Christian Reformed ministry.

2) After the Synod of 1978 no one is to be "admitted to ministerial candidacy in the regular way who does not possess the Calvin Seminary M.Div. degree or its equivalent, with the exception of anyone who, previous to the Synod of 1978, met the established requirements for candidacy by means of the B.D. degree plus the program of field education required for candidacy at the time he received that degree" (*Acts of Synod 1975*, p. 25).

2. Candidacy

Article 6b stipulates that seminary graduates who "have been declared candidates

48

for the ministry of the Word by the churches shall be eligible for call." Both the synod and the Board of Trustees of Calvin College and Seminary (as a committee of synod) cooperate in the process leading to candidacy.

a. The Board of Trustees of Calvin College and Seminary

"First, an aspirant to the ministry is admitted to the seminary only after the board has received from the seminary faculty information as to his academic record, recommendation by his home consistory and college advisers, and an interview with members of the seminary faculty.

"Second, the aspirant submits to an interview by the Board of Trustees, in consultation with the seminary faculty, before obtaining preaching license.

"Third, the aspirant submits to periodic examinations by the faculty, and is regularly visited by the members of the faculty during his years as a student.

"Fourth, pursuant to the decision of the Synod of 1961, the board makes provision for one-to-one visits with senior seminarians about to enter the ministry.

"Fifth, the aspirant submits to a thorough examination by the seminary faculty prior to the obtaining of a...M.Div. degree, and the seminary faculty presents a complete statement to the Board of Trustees of the student's qualifications and a recommendation regarding doctrinal soundness, spiritual fitness, and personality.

"Sixth, the aspirant submits to an interview before the Board of Trustees for candidacy, and two sermon manuscripts are submitted for evaluation. The Board of Trustees presents its recommendations and report of interviews to synod, with synod's right to additional interview prior to declaration of candidacy.

"Seventh, the aspirant has been under the scrutiny of the church during his two years of preaching, his summer field work assignment, and, in some instances, his year of service as seminary intern." *(Acts of Synod 1976, p. 12)*

b. Synod

1) Examination for Candidacy

Synod conducts the examination for candidacy by way of its committee, the Board of Trustees, prior to the convening of synod (see "Sixth" above).
"Grounds:
"a) The Board of Trustees is a duly constituted committee of synod which is broadly representative of the Christian Reformed Church.
"b) The reasons for which synod referred this task to the Board of Trustees in the past are still valid." *(Acts of Synod 1977, p. 128)*
Synod instructed the Board of Trustees "to continue to seek ways to make synod's involvement in candidacy decisions more meaningful" *(Acts of Synod 1977, p. 128).*
Synod decided to publish the names and pictures of candidates for the ministry in the Christian Reformed Church in *The Banner* and *De Wachter* only when they are actually eligible for call *(Acts of Synod 1976, p. 13).*
The Synod of 1978 adopted the following regulations for processing applications for candidacy:

a) The Board of Trustees must submit to synod the following materials regarding each prospective candidate:
   1) Consistorial recommendation
   2) Candidate's one-page statement of faith
   3) Candidate's one-paragraph statement of reasons for seeking candidacy
   4) Picture and personal data
   5) Report of visit by board member
   6) Board's evaluation

b) The Board of Trustees must also provide the appropriate advisory committee with the following materials regarding each prospective candidate:
   1) Faculty evaluation
   2) Transcript

c) Synod adopted the following procedure:
   1) The advisory committee shall give early attention to this matter.
   2) The advisory committee shall advise synod which candidates, if any, should be reexamined and how the reexamination is to be continued.
   3) The advisory committee shall submit its recommendations to synod by Thursday of the first week.
   4) The advisory committee shall be available to any delegate wishing to contact it regarding any candidate.
   5) Synod shall declare the applicants to be candidates in a formal meeting at which all candidates are to be present (insofar as possible).
   6) Synod shall designate its officers as the persons responsible for making the appropriate arrangements for the declaration of candidacy meeting.
   (Acts of Synod 1978, p. 22-23)

Note: A complete report of the history of synodical procedures re candidates is contained in the *Acts of Synod 1977,* pp. 126-131.

2) Declaration of Candidacy between Synods (Church Order Supplement, Art. 6)
   The Synod of 1975 decided that candidacy may be declared both at the time of synod and between annual synods. The following regulations govern declaration of candidacy between synods:
   "a) Applications for candidacy examination may be made by students who:
      1) Have completed all core courses and field education practicums, and
      2) Are within twelve hours of completing course work, and
      3) Are within ten units of completing field education requirements.
   "b) Synod may declare such students to be candidates contingent upon completion of all remaining requirements.
   "c) When a student completes all remaining requirements, the executive committee of the Board of Trustees shall so inform the Stated Clerk, who will then announce the candidate's eligibility for call.
   "d) Any student who does not complete the remaining requirements by March 1 must re-apply for candidacy to the secretary of the Board of Trustees.
   "e) Any such candidate who has not received and accepted a call to one of

our churches and desires to have his candidacy continued must make application to the secretary of the Board of Trustees by May 15.

"Grounds:

"1) This procedure will avoid lengthy delay for students who complete these studies between the annual synods.

"2) Under this arrangement the exceptional cases are made to conform as nearly as possible to the ordinary procedures governing candidacy.

"3) This procedure appropriately implements the decision of synod 'that candidacy shall be for a period of one year' *(Acts of Synod 1961,* p. 55)." *(Acts of Synod 1975,* p. 111)

3) Eligibility for Call

Regulations governing eligibility for call and the term of candidacy are as follows:

a) Candidates are eligible to receive calls two weeks after they have been declared eligible by synod or after announcement by the Stated Clerk of synod. (See *Acts of Synod 1970,* p. 11; *1975,* p. 111.)

b) The candidate shall be given a period of three weeks to consider a call *(Acts of Synod 1928,* p. 75).

c) Candidacy for the ministry of the Word is for a period of one year, after which a candidate must be interviewed by the Calvin College and Seminary Board of Trustees if he wishes an extension of candidacy *(Acts of Synod 1961,* p. 55).

3. Students Trained in Other Seminaries (Church Order Supplement, Art. 6)

Article 6c requires that students trained elsewhere than at Calvin Seminary must meet "the requirements stipulated in the synodical regulations" and must be "declared by the churches to be candidates" before they shall be eligible for call. Synod and its Calvin College and Seminary Board of Trustees have made the following rules and provisions pertaining to students trained in other seminaries:

a. Students having studied theology at other seminaries shall at least take the senior year at our seminary before they shall be declared eligible for call in our churches *(Acts of Synod 1924,* p. 38).

b. Students who have been trained in other seminaries are not eligible for candidacy unless they have met the requirements stipulated by synod and have been declared candidates through the same procedure stipulated for graduates of Calvin Theological Seminary. *(Acts of Synod 1961,* p. 55)

c. Special Program for Ministerial Candidacy in the CRC

Calvin Theological Seminary provides a special program according to synodical regulations which, under exceptional circumstances, qualifies graduates of other seminaries for ministerial candidacy in the Christian Reformed Church. This program does not diminish the overall academic standards for candidacy which have been officially established for those who follow the regular course of study at the Seminary. At least three quarters in residence are required. These, in combination with all previous study, must form an acceptable equivalency to the total pre-seminary and seminary program required of Calvin Seminary graduates as preparation for the Christian Reformed ministry.

In order that the faculty may fulfill its obligation to prepare an informed recommendation for candidacy for a student enrolled in the Special Program for Ministerial Candidacy in the Christian Reformed Church, it holds an interview with each student during his year of residence at Calvin Seminary. This interview is more than a casual conversation with the student and focuses primarily on the following areas:

1) The prospective candidate's personal background and sense of vocation.
2) An investigation of the student's knowledge of Systematic Theology and of the History of Doctrine.
3) An examination of the student's doctrinal soundness and creedal awareness.
4) An assurance of the student's willingness to sign the Formula of Subscription in good conscience.

Note: See Article 10 for further information about ordination and installation of candidates.

I. THE OFFICES OF THE CHURCH
B. MINISTERS OF THE WORD (continued)

ARTICLE 7

ADMITTANCE TO THE MINISTRY WITHOUT PRESCRIBED TRAINING

a. Those who have not received the prescribed theological training but who give evidence that they are singularly gifted as to godliness, humility, spiritual discretion, wisdom, and the native ability to preach the Word, may, by way of exception, be admitted to the ministry of the Word, especially when the need is urgent.
b. The classis, in the presence of the synodical deputies, shall examine these men concerning the required exceptional gifts. With the concurring advice of the synodical deputies, classis shall proceed as circumstances may warrant and in accordance with synodical regulations.

1. Conditions for Admittance without Theological Training
   Article 7a prescribes the conditions under which persons without prescribed theological training may be admitted to the ministry:
   a. An applicant must be blessed with the unique gifts described in the article.
      1) The gifts mentioned in Article 7 "should be possessed by a candidate in a very exceptional measure. No one should be considered unless he has extraordinary qualities."
      2) Besides the qualifications mentioned in Article 7, "such a candidate should also possess exceptional knowledge of the Word, knowledge of spiritual needs, and native ability to apply the Word." *(Acts of Synod 1947,* p. 94).
   b. There should be evidence of an urgent need of the church for such an applicant. The Synod of 1947 adopted the following declarations regarding the admittance to the ministry by way of Article 7:
      1) "Synod reminds the churches that Article 8 [now Article 7] of the Church Order was adopted in a time when there was a dire need for ministers of the Word. This article should function only in case of great need.
      2) "This article should never be used as a means to ordain all layworkers who may desire such, and whose prestige would be increased by such action. The churches are reminded that the regular door to the ministry is a thorough academic training. This must be maintained in theory and practice."
      (Acts of Synod 1947, p. 94)

c. The Synod of 1979 considered a proposal from one of the classes to change the wording of Article 7 so that the words "when the need is urgent" to read "when these gifts meet a ministry need within the church." The synod did not accede to this overture on the following grounds:

"1. The regular door to the ministry is through a thorough academic training.

(Acts of Synod 1947, p. 94)*

"2. The presence of exceptional gifts does not require the church to ordain the person who possesses them.

"3. The synodical and church order regulations have always kept a balance in the application of Article 7 between gifts and needs."

(Acts of Synod 1974, pp. 76-77)*

2. Seminary Training for Persons of More Mature Years

The Synod of 1971 adopted the following declarations:

a. "If a classis, in fulfilling the requirements of Article 7b...wishes to enlist the cooperation of the seminary, the seminary shall lend its assistance according to the following provisions:

1) "When the classis, with the concurring advice of the synodical deputies, has satisfied itself as to the presence of exceptional gifts in the prospective candidate, the classis may enlist the cooperation of the seminary in his further preparation. This shall take place when the classis is ready to commit itself to a candidate to a certain extent, but prior to the final decision as to his eligibility for a call.

2) "The seminary shall accept such a person for class work under the following conditions:

a) "He shall be classified as an auditor and pay tuition accordingly.

b) "His program of education and testing will be worked out between the seminary and classis in agreements covering such matters as the areas of instruction and the duration of his course of studies.

c) "Although classified as an auditor because he has not met seminary entrance requirements, he will receive work assignments approximately equal to those of regular students in the course followed.

3) "At the conclusion of the agreed period of instruction, the seminary shall provide the classis with a thorough evaluation of his work. This will provide the classis with information leading to a decision with respect to candidacy but it is to be in no way a substitute for the decision itself. The classis shall then proceed to the consideration of his ordination according to the provisions of Article 7, C. O.

b. "To keep Article 7 in the 'extraordinary' category, only men who are at least forty years of age at the beginning of the program shall be admitted.

c. "It is to be clearly understood that in outlining a way in which the seminary can be serviceable to classes which are contemplating the ordination of candidates under the provisions of Article 7, synod is not promoting a third way of preparing men for the ministry. The educational cooperation hereby made available is not an adequate substitute for a regular theological education. Nor is it intended to weaken in any way the restrictions laid down in Article 7, *viz.* 'exceptional gifts,' 'by way of exception,' 'especially when the need is urgent.' These elements shall be scrupulously observed by each classis, and synod through its synodical deputies shall underscore them."

(Acts of Synod 1971, pp. 124-125)

3. Examination Procedures for Article 7 Applicants (Church Order Supplement, Art. 7)

   a. Examination for Licensure to Exhort
   If anyone wishes to be admitted to the ministry of the Word in accordance with Article 7, he should apply to his consistory. If the consistory is convinced that the applicant has the required exceptional gifts, the consistory shall endorse the request and present its recommendation along with the applicant's request to the classis.

   Together with the synodical deputies from the neighboring classes, the classis shall first of all examine the written credentials of the consistory concerning the required qualifications as stated in Article 7 and thereupon the classis itself shall proceed to examine him to ascertain whether these qualifications be present.

   If the preliminary judgment is favorable, the petitioner is to be given the right, for some time, to exhort in vacant churches within the classis. He shall also exhort a few times in churches that are not vacant in the presence of the respective ministers of these churches. The length of this period of probation is to be determined by classis.

   b. Examination for Candidacy
   At the close of the period of probation, the classis, together with the synodical deputies, shall take a final decision regarding the petitioner's "exceptional gifts." If the decision is in the affirmative, the classis shall subject the petitioner to a preparatory examination in the following subjects: a. Exegesis of the Old and New Testament, b. Bible History, c. Dogmatics, d. General and American Church History.

   If the examination is favorable, the petitioner shall be declared eligible for a call.

   c. Examination for ordination
   The final examination of classis takes place after the candidate receives and accepts a call, and is conducted according to the regular schedule for examination with the exception of ancient languages. (*Agenda for Synod 1920,* pp. 36-37; *Acts of Synod 1922,* pp. 72-73; see also Article 6 of the Church Order.)

4. Special Procedures for the Indian Mission Field
   To meet the special needs for native workers on the Indian Mission field, the Synod of 1958 adopted the following advice of the Christian Reformed Board of Foreign Missions:
   a. That the following be the method by which the ordination of native workers is to be effected:

1) That capable men, who feel the call to the gospel ministry, be encouraged to pursue the regular course of study for ordination.

2) That those who are not able to pursue that course, and who possess exceptional gifts, be advised to seek ordination under the pattern prescribed by Article 7 of the Church Order, and make known their desire to their consistory, or Council of Indian Churches, where no consistory exists.

b. For those seeking ordination by way of Article 7, Church Order, the following procedure is recommended:

1) The written credentials of the consistory or Council of Indian Churches concerning the required qualifications stated in Article 7 are to be forwarded to Classis Rocky Mountain.

2) Upon receipt of application, together with the recommendation of the consistory or the favorable advice of the Council of Indian churches, the classis, in conjunction with synodical deputies, shall determine whether it considers the aspirant eligible for further examination under Article 7.

3) If the preliminary judgment is favorable, the applicant will be instructed to speak a word of edification at several of the preaching centers on the Indian Field in the presence of the missionary and in at least two of the churches of the classis in the presence of the ministers of these churches. Classis shall regulate these appointments and determine the length of this period of probation.

4) At the termination of this period of probation the classis, in conjunction with the synodical deputies, shall take a final decision regarding the qualifications of the candidate. If the decision is in the affirmative, then the classis shall give the applicant a preliminary examination in the following branches: (a) Bible History; (b) Exegesis of the English Old and New Testaments; (c) Dogmatics; (d) Church History; (e) Practica.

5) The missionary of the applicant as representative of Council of Indian Churches shall be present in an advisory capacity at those sessions of classis in which the case of the applicant is being considered.

6) If the applicant is successful in the examination he is declared eligible to a call.

7) The examination for ordination follows later according to existing rules, except in the classical languages.

Note: The regulations above are an updated statement of the Synod of 1958 (*Acts of Synod 1958,* pp. 87-88).

5. Synodical Deputies' Role in Article 7
   a. The synodical deputies are required to be present at all examinations for candidacy and for ordination *(Acts of Synod 1962,* pp. 77-78).
   b. "The synodical deputies are to be involved from the very beginning. The synodical deputies are to give advice regarding both the need and the requisite 'gifts.' They are not mere witnesses at the preliminary interview which the classis" has with the applicant... (*Acts of Synod 1970,* p. 151).
   c. It has been observed by synod that "the issue of 'need' or 'urgent' need has given rise to differences of opinion...the need must be judged in the context of the

whole denomination. The very fact that the synodical deputies are to be present at the examinations reveals the denominational character of the need" *(Acts of Synod 1970,* p. 53).

d. The synodical deputies are required to determine whether a classis may proceed with the examination of an applicant. Without a prior approval of synodical deputies, a classis may not proceed with an examination. (Cf. *Acts of Synod 1968,* Art. 86, XI, p. 60). The initial hearing of an applicant and the approval of the synodical deputies should precede the scheduling of the examinations for candidacy and for ordination.

I. THE OFFICES OF THE CHURCH

B. MINISTERS OF THE WORD (continued)

ARTICLE 8

MINISTERS ELIGIBLE FOR CALL

a. Ministers of the Christian Reformed Church are eligible for call, with due observance of the relevant rules.

b. Ministers of other denominations desiring to become ministers in the Christian Reformed Church shall be declared eligible for a call by a classis only after a thorough examination of their theological training, ministerial record, knowledge of and soundness in the Reformed faith and their exemplariness of life. The presence and concurring advice of the synodical deputies are required.

c. Ministers of other denominations who have not been declared eligible for a call shall not be called unless all synodical requirements have been met.

(Amended—*Acts of Synod 1974*, p. 57)

1. Eligibility for Call
   All ordained ministers of the Christian Reformed Church are eligible for a call by any congregation without further examination, even when the calling church is in a different classis.

2. Relevant Rules re Calling a Minister

   a. Permission to Call
      "Every church has an inherent right and duty to call a minister" *(Acts of Synod 1957,* p. 38).

      The only restriction to the above right and duty applies to an organized church which is too small for self-support or is dependent upon the Fund for Needy Churches.

      Synod has ruled that "an organized church which cannot support itself, should not ordinarily become a calling church until it has reached at least a level of thirty families. . . . Exceptions to this rule shall be made only after a thorough investigation by the classis involved in cooperation with the FNC [Fund for Needy Churches] Committee and approval of both bodies" *(Acts of Synod 1971,* p. 23).

b. Length of Pastorate (Supplement, Article 8, Section A)
The Synod of 1916 adopted the following statement regarding the nominating of ministers who have served their present churches less than two years:
"Synod judges that consistories of vacant congregations in drawing up a nomination shall not place on it the name of a minister who has served less than two years in the congregation he presently is serving, unless there are particular, overriding reasons, and that a counselor, where such a name appears, which he must approve in the name of the classis, shall give an account to classis of the reasons for approving the same." (*Acts of Synod 1916*, p. 29)
The Synod of 1947 rejected an overture to lengthen the minimum stay to four years (*Acts of Synod 1947*, p. 46).

c. Repetition of a Call (Supplement, Article 8, Section B)
Calling of the same minister twice during the same vacancy shall not take place within a year without the advice of classis *(Acts of Synod 1906,* p. 16).

d. Period of Consideration
Ministers shall be given a period of three weeks for consideration of a call *(Acts of Synod 1916,* p. 26).

e. Moving Expenses of Ministers
1) The calling church shall be responsible for all moving and transportation expenses of a minister.
2) Reimbursement of expenses—"If a minister leaves a church within a year, the calling church shall refund the church he leaves expenses in full; if he leaves within two years, three-fourths; if within three years, one-half; if within four years, one-fourth of his moving expenses. . . . This rule applies to all agencies which are responsible for the payment of moving expenses of ministers" *(Acts of Synod 1966,* p. 88).

f. Salary Responsibility for Ministers
Salary responsibility terminates and begins with the farewell sermon (*Acts of Synod 1926,* p. 71).

3. Letter of Call
The calling of a minister must be certified by the sending of an official letter of call. The letter of call should be in accord with the stipulations of the Church Order and the decisions of synod pertaining to the work and proper support of the minister of the Word.

The letter of call must be signed by the consistory as representatives of the congregation and by the counselor as a representative of the classis in which the calling church is located.

A letter of call which meets the requirements of the Church Order and synodical decisions is available from the Board of Publications of the Christian Reformed Church. A sample copy of the letter of call appears in the Appendix (p. 337).

4. Ministerial Information Service

The Synod of 1972 established the Ministerial Information Service as a standing synodical committee with the following regulations:

"a. *Mandate:*

"1) to introduce ministers who are seeking a call to churches which are vacant,

"2) to introduce ministers who are seeking specialized ministries to appropriate boards and committees,

"3) to compose and distribute questionnaires to churches and ministers to obtain the necessary information,

"4) and to serve the churches and ministers with other needed advice in matters pertaining to calling.

"b. *Guidelines:*

"1) The committee shall serve in an informational capacity.

"2) The committee shall offer no unsolicited advice.

"3) Ministers and churches shall make use of the Ministerial Information Service at their own discretion.

"4) Information about ministers and churches shall be obtained by the committee only from the parties involved, and their files shall be open to them at any time.

"5) Ministers and churches shall have the right to withdraw or amend the information in their files at any time.

"6) The committee shall be composed of six members, three of whom shall be ministers.

"7) The mandate and guidelines may be amended only by synod.

"c. *Implementation:*

"1) The committee shall serve according to the rules for standing synodical committees.

"2) The committee shall develop the Ministerial Information Service in keeping with the mandate and guidelines which have been adopted and shall present a complete report to the Synod of 1973.

"Grounds:

"a. A large majority of the consistories have indicated their desire for such a service to be provided.

"b. This method is being used effectively in other denominations similar to ours in church polity.

"c. Such a service can be very helpful in assisting both churches and ministers in making meaningful contacts with each other when vacancies occur and ministers desire a change of pastorate.

"d. Through this service, boards and committees can be alerted to men who desire specialized ministries." *(Acts of Synod 1972,* pp. 72-73.)

Synod declared it "a proper practice for ministers to indicate their desire for a call in general or for a call to a specific church.

"Grounds:
"a. This practice is consistent with the work of the Holy Spirit in the process of calling in that it recognizes both the divine and human factors involved.
"b. This method is followed with profit in several related churches which follow Reformed church polity.
"c. The flexibility which is desirable within our system would be increased."

(Acts of Synod 1972, p. 73)

Synod declared that "it is acceptable procedure for vacant churches to advertise for available ministers.

"Grounds:
"a. While not traditional in our churches, this practice is already being followed by certain consistories.
"b. Adoption of the MINISTERIAL INFORMATION SERVICE concept suggests the appropriateness of this procedure as a method whereby greater openness and flexibility can be provided within our system." *(Acts of Synod 1972,* p. 73)

The Synod of 1976 authorized the Ministerial Information Service "to function as an assisting agency for pastoral exchanges and to apprise the churches and ministers of this service. This assistance is to be given in accordance with the following *guidelines....*

"a. Ministers and churches who are interested in an exchange of pastorates will make the initial contact with the committee indicating their desires and preferences. They will subsequently provide other pertinent information which will be of value to the committee in performing its task. The local church council and pastor must mutually agree on a request for a pastoral exchange before the committee will be able to take the next step. Prior confidential inquiries to the committee, however, may be made by either the council or the minister before reaching mutual agreement on the local level.
"b. When two or more churches and ministers have made requests, the committee will approach the executive committee of the councils, with strict confidence, to reveal the names of the ministers involved and to determine the feasibility of proceeding further.
"c. Simultaneous with step b, the committee will approach the ministers, with strict confidence, to reveal the names of the churches involved and to determine the feasibility of proceeding further.
"d. When steps b and c have been completed satisfactorily, the names of the ministers will be revealed to the councils to determine the feasibility of proceeding further. This also must remain in confidence.
"e. When all the above steps have been satisfactorily completed the councils will reveal the information to the congregations and announce the name of the minister to be placed on mono for congregational vote on a specified date and place. If one congregation does not gain a majority vote to call the given minister, the call of the other church will be nullified. Dates of the congregational meetings should coincide very closely for the benefit of all concerned.

"Grounds:
"1) The original questionnaire indicated that this type of service should be considered by the committee.
"2) Several churches and ministers have requested this type of service.
"3) Churches and ministers who would currently appreciate such an exchange would profit by an objective party to assist them."

(Acts of Synod 1976, pp. 24-25)

The Synod of 1978 adopted the following: (1) Synod urged "vacant churches who desire the services of this committee to provide them with their church profile"; (2) Synod authorized "the extension of the pastoral exchange concept approved by the Synod of 1976, until 1980, since the committee has not had opportunity to test this concept" *(Acts of Synod 1978, p. 25).*

5. Ministers from Other Denominations (Supplement, Article 8, Section C)
Synod has adopted the following set of regulations regarding the calling and admitting of ministers from other denominations:
"a. When Initiated by Action of the Consistory
    "1) Ministers from other denominations may be called by Christian Reformed churches in exceptional cases.
    "2) Before a consistory nominates a minister from another denomination it must:
        "a) Establish that there is a pressing local need.
        "b) Establish that the needs of the local church can best be met by the proposed nominee.
        "c) Obtain the approval of classis or of the counselor in the name of classis.
        "d) Obtain the approval of three synodical deputies who shall have conferred with each other before rendering their advice (by mail if necessary).
    "3) Classes and synodical deputies shall give objective consideration to such proposed nominations, seeking to be entirely faithful to established regulations and furnishing reasons in the event of disapproval.
    "4) Synodical deputies shall use the following criteria for approving or disapproving of proposed nominee:
        "a) Soundness of doctrine.
        "b) Sanctity of life.
        "c) Knowledge and appreciation of Christian Reformed practice and usage.
        "d) Sufficient formal education. The nominee shall submit a diploma, or statement of credits, from an accredited college and recognized seminary to indicate his scholastic attainment. A measure of discretionary power is granted the classis in connection with the matter of scholastic attainment of the nominee, but when such power is exercised by classis, it shall be in consultation with the synodical deputies.

62

Only when classis and the synodical deputies are agreed may the nominee be approved.

"e) Need of calling other than Christian Reformed ministers.

"5) When ministers from foreign countries are being proposed for nominations, the synodical deputies shall use the following additional standards:
"a) Ability to speak or to learn the English language.
"b) Ability to adjust to the American-Canadian situation.
"c) Age limit of 40 as a general rule.

"6) Before a pastor-elect from another denomination may be installed, the consistory must arrange with the classis for a 'colloquium doctum' to be conducted. When the classis and the synodical deputies are satisfied with the results of this colloquium, the pastor-elect is admitted to our denomination and may be installed.

"b. When Initiated by Action of the Individual Minister
"1) A minister of another denomination desiring to be declared eligible for a call in the Christian Reformed Church shall make application to the Christian Reformed classis in which, or nearest which, his field of labor is located.

"2) The approval of three synodical deputies shall be obtained before the classis shall proceed to honor the request of the applicant.

"3) A classis and synodical deputies, considering such a request, must be convinced that there is in the Christian Reformed Church a need which the applicant is qualified to fulfill.

"4) Classis and the synodical deputies shall give objective consideration to such requests, seeking to be entirely faithful to established regulations and furnishing reasons in the event of disapproval.

"5) The minister making application to be declared eligible for a call, shall present the following documents to the classis or classical committee in ample time so that the documents may be examined and considered in consultation with the synodical deputies prior to the classical examination:

"a) A testimonial from his consistory or classis, session or presbytery, concerning his purity of doctrine and sanctity of life. It is conceivable that just because the applicant is loyal to the Word and creeds that he is adjuged persona non grata by his own ecclesiastical assemblies and that he would not be granted such a testimonial. Should such be the case a careful preliminary investigation must be made by the classis in consultation with the synodical deputies. The report of this investigation, if satisfactory to the classis and synodical deputies, will serve under such circumstances in lieu of the testimonial.

"b) A diploma, or statement of credits, from an accredited college and recognized seminary to indicate the scholastic attainment of the applicant. A measure of discretionary power is granted the classis in connection with the matter of scholastic attainment of the applicant, but when such power is exercised by classis, it shall be in consultation with the synodical deputies. Only when both classis and synodical deputies are agreed, may the applicant be examined.

"c) A statement of health from a recognized physician.

"6) The various documents and reports having been presented and adjudged satisfactory by classis and the synodical deputies, the applicant must submit to a careful examination regarding his soundness in the Reformed faith and the exemplariness of his life. Classis in conjunction with the synodical deputies shall determine whether the applicant shall submit to a 'colloquium doctum' or a full classical examination.

"7) The following criteria shall be applied for approving or disapproving the applicant:

"a) Soundness of doctrine.

"b) Sanctity of life.

"c) Knowledge and appreciation of Christian Reformed practice and usage.

"8) The applicant, having sustained the examination, and having received the approbation of the synodical deputies, may now be declared eligible for call. No further examination or 'colloquium doctum' will be required of the minister thus declared eligible."

(Church Order Supplements, pp. 31-34)

Note: Cf. *Acts of Synod 1963,* pp. 20-24; *1968,* pp. 21-22; *1974,* pp. 21, 390-392.

c. Determination of Need

"a) Synod directs its synodical deputies to take specific and special note of the 'need' factor when requested to give their advice to the consistories and/or classes in the calling of ministers from other denominations and in declaring ministers from other denominations available for call in the Christian Reformed Church at their own request.

"b) Synod requires of the consistories and/or classes such written specification of the 'need' for approving such ministers and their calling as will satisfy the synodical deputies in their concurrence, which written specification shall then become part of the report of the synodical deputies to be submitted for synodical approval.

Grounds:

"1) The requirement that there be a clear need for admitting ministers from other denominations is adequately set forth in synodical regulations.

"2) Without a specific report on the matter of need there is no way for synod to know whether this aspect of its concern is being taken seriously, since present regulations do not require a report on the grounds of concurrence.

"3) It is the judgment of many that the Christian Reformed Church is at present not in need of admitting any more ministers from other denominations. However, such ministers are still being admitted each year. If there is such a need it ought to be demonstrable.

"4) There are clear indications that many candidates will be available for service in the Christian Reformed Church, having been trained specifically for the Christian Reformed Church ministry, who may not be able to find a place for service to the church because of a limited number of churches in need of ministers. Therefore, the matter of demonstrated need becomes crucially important."

(*Acts of Synod 1979*, p. 73-74)

Consistories may call a minister of another denomination only after the above synodical requirements have been met.

6. Proper Procedure for Eligibility for Call

In 1954 synod declared the following with regard to three ministers examined by synod and declared eligible for call:

"Synod decides to record in its Acts that it proceeded to examine these brethren and decided to declare them eligible, by way of concession, in the face of certain prior developments, but that the present procedure is not meant to be a precedent for possible future requests, inasmuch as the course of procedure to be followed is indicated in Art. 9 [now Art. 8] of the Church Order. . . . The ministers declared eligible for a call, by this Synod, must submit to a colloquium doctum by Classis before installation." *(Acts of Synod 1954*, pp. 123-124)

I. THE OFFICES OF THE CHURCH
B. MINISTERS OF THE WORD (continued)

ARTICLE 9

FUNCTION OF A COUNSELOR

In nominating and calling a minister the consistory shall seek the approval of the counselor who acts in behalf of classis to see that the ecclesiastical regulations have been observed. The consistory and counselor shall sign the letter of call and the counselor shall render an account of his labors to classis.

1. Appointment of a Counselor
When a church is without a pastor and takes steps to call a minister, the consistory is required to ask the classis to appoint a counselor, or advisor, and may request the services of a specific pastor for this purpose. The counselor of a vacant church must be appointed by classis and acts in behalf of classis. The classis, or the interim committee, then appoints a minister to counsel the vacant church in all matters pertaining to the calling of a new minister.

Upon request the counselor should attend consistory meetings to advise the calling church with respect to proper procedure and ecclesiastical regulations involved in calling a minister. The advice of the counselor should be requested early in the calling (or nomination) process. He also ordinarily presides at congregational meetings during a vacancy.

The appointment of a minister as a counselor involves no obligation to perform pastoral services for the calling church. If a consistory desires pastoral help for worship services, teaching, pastoral counseling or calling, funerals, weddings, or other services, the consistory must make such arrangements with the minister of its choice regardless of whether or not he is the classically appointed counselor.

The term of a counselor ends when the vacancy is filled and his report is presented to classis, or when classis replaces him for other reasons.

2. Counselor's Reports
Since the counselor represents the classis, he must present an account of his labors to classis.

3. Responsibilities of a Counselor
A counselor in order to fulfill his responsibilities should be fully aware of the ecclesiastical regulations for calling adopted by synod. These are contained in this volume in the explanation of Article 8.

A consistory may not proceed with the calling of a minister without the approval of the counselor. If a difference of judgment between the consistory and the counselor cannot be resolved, the consistory may appeal to classis or its interim committee.

"If it appears to the counselor that improper influence has been exerted in the calling of a minister, either by himself (the minister) or by others, the name of that minister shall be removed from the trio" *(Acts of Synod 1872,* p. 141).

The letter of call must be signed by the counselor as the representative of the classis in which the calling church is located.

I. THE OFFICES OF THE CHURCH
B. MINISTERS OF THE WORD (continued)

ARTICLE 10
ORDINATION AND INSTALLATION

a. The ordination of a candidate for the ministry of the Word requires the approval of the classis of the calling church and of the synodical deputies. The classis, in the presence of the deputies, shall examine him concerning his doctrine and life in accordance with synodical regulations. The ordination shall be accompanied by the laying on of hands by the officiating minister.

b. The installation of a minister shall require the approval of the classis of the calling church or its interim committee, to which the minister shall have previously presented good ecclesiastical testimonials of doctrine and life which have been given him by his former consistory and classis.

1. Article 10a—Ordination of Candidates

   a. Prerequisites for Classical Examination
   Before a candidate may be ordained to the ministry of the Word, he must be examined by the classis of the calling church.

   The rules for theological training, declaration of candidacy, and processing of candidacy prior to the classical examination are dealt with in Article 6. Certain supplementary decisions of synod follow:

   1) Provisional Nature of the Call
   "The letter of call to a candidate must indicate the provisional nature of this call until the classical examination has been sustained.
   "Grounds:
   "a) The calling church cannot issue an unconditional call to a candidate before the classical examination has been sustained.
   "b) This conditional character of the letter of call underscores the decisive nature of the classical examination." *(Acts of Synod 1972,* pp. 44-45)

   2) Moving into the Parsonage
   The Synod of 1972 declared that "no candidate [shall] move into the parsonage of the calling church before he has sustained the classical examination" *(Acts of Synod 1972,* p. 45; *1975,* p. 89).

The Synod of 1978 nullified "its decisions of 1972/1975 re moving of candidates and allow[s] a candidate to move into the parsonage of the calling church before he has sustained the classical examination" *(Acts of Synod 1978,* p. 65).

3) Setting the Date of Ordination
"The date of ordination [shall] be officially announced only after the candidate has passed the examination [by the classis].
"Ground: Announcing the date of ordination before the classical examination is completed tends to prejudge the outcome of the examination."
(Acts of Synod 1972, p. 45)

b. The Importance of the Classical Examination
Synod emphasized "the importance of the examination for ordination by the classis in which the calling church is located after a candidate has accepted a call.
"Grounds:
1) "This examination is an integral part of the lawful calling as outlined in Art. 4 of the Church Order.
2) "There has been a danger of considering this examination superfluous when synod conducted a previous examination." *(Acts of Synod 1961,* p. 55)

c. Credentials Required by Classis
Synod advises "the classes, with reference to the credentials required by classes, that synod's declaration of candidacy may be taken to certify that the candidates have met the academic requirements for candidacy, have been found in good health, and have been recommended by a consistory. No further inquiry into these matters need ordinarily be made by a classis at the examination for ordination" *(Acts of Synod 1978,* p. 24).

d. The Sermon
The following are the synodical regulations concerning the candidate's classical sermon:
1) "The candidate is to prepare a sermon on a text assigned by classis. A copy of this sermon is to be submitted to the sermon critics two weeks before the examination. . . . The sermon critics shall discuss the sermon with the candidate prior to the examination in the other branches." *(Acts of Synod 1961,* p. 56)
2) "The candidate should preach a sermon on a text assigned by classis, in an official worship service in the presence of classical representatives, preferably on the Sunday preceding the meeting of classis, and in the church to which he has been called.
"Grounds:
"a) The sermon is such an important part of the examination that it warrants delivery in a regular worship service.
"b) It is extremely difficult for a candidate to preach and to proclaim the Word of God in a deliberative meeting such as a classis."
(Acts of Synod 1972, p. 45)

69

3) "Classis itself, or those assigned to this task by classis, shall assign the text for the candidate's sermon" (*Acts of Synod 1975*, p. 89). Synod noted that the regulations demand that classis assign the text rather than agree to the text.

4) "A copy of the candidate's sermon [must] be provided by classis to the synodical deputies and to the delegates to classis.
"Ground: This will be conducive to a thorough examination of the contents of the sermon by all who are called upon to pass judgment at classis."
(Acts of Synod 1972, p. 45)

5) "In addition to the required sermon on an assigned text, the candidate shall submit to each of the sermon critics of classis copies of two other sermons which he has preached as a student, one based on a Scripture text and the other on a Lord's Day of the Heidelberg Catechism. The combination of Scripture texts should include both the Old Testament and the New Testament. These sermons shall not include those which have been used in practice preaching, or for academic evaluation, in the seminary.
"Grounds:
"a) The submission of additional sermons provides a better basis for sermon evaluation at this examination which is decisive for the candidate's ordination.
"b) The inclusion of a sermon on the Heidelberg Catechism is consistent with the requirement of the Church Order regarding catechism preaching (Article 54b)." *(Acts of Synod 1975,* p. 90)

6) "The sermon critics shall report to classis prior to the examination in the other branches." *(Acts of Synod 1970,* p. 69)

7) "Four classical delegates should be appointed as the official examiners, two to function as sermon critics and to be present at the worship service in which the total sermon is being preached, and two to conduct the actual examination at the time classis meets.
"Grounds:
"a) A better rapport with the candidate will be established with a smaller number of examiners.
"b) The small number of examiners needed enables the classis to make a more appropriate selection of men for this task." *(Acts of Synod 1972,* p. 45)

e. Schedule for the Classical Examination:
"1) Introduction: a classical examiner shall introduce the candidate to the classis.
"2) The examination proper shall consist of inquiry into three main areas, as follows:
"PRACTICA (no time limit)
"1. The classical examiner shall inquire into the candidate's relationship to God and his commitment to the ministry, his understanding of the meaning and relevance of the ministry for our times, his loyalty to the church, and related matters.
"2. The synodical deputies and delegates shall have opportunity to ask additional questions.

"3. Before proceeding to the next area of inquiry, a motion to proceed shall carry.

"SERMON EVALUATION

"1. In the presence of the candidate, the written sermon shall be evaluated, and attention shall be given to his manner of conducting a worship service.

"2. Additional questions with reference to the sermon and its delivery shall be allowed.

"3. Before proceeding to the next area, a motion to proceed shall carry with the concurrence of the synodical deputies.

"BIBLICAL AND THEOLOGICAL POSITION (minimum, 30 minutes per candidate)

"1. The examiner shall inquire into the candidate's biblical and theological judgment, competence, and soundness.

"2. Opportunity shall be provided for additional questions. (No specific time limit).

"3) Procedure for admitting to the ministry:

"1. A motion to admit shall be received and given preliminary consideration in executive session.

"2. Prayer for the guidance of the Holy Spirit shall be offered.

"3. The synodical deputies shall leave the floor to prepare their recommendation.

"4. The classis shall vote by ballot.

"5. The synodical deputies shall offer their written statement, from which it will become evident whether or not they can concur with the decision of classis.

"6. In the event they do not concur, the classis and the synodical deputies may try to reach a unified decision.

"7. In the event that agreement cannot be reached between them, the matter is automatically referred to the synod for final adjudication.

"*Grounds:*

"a. This procedure will allow both the classis and the synodical deputies to arrive at their decisions independently.

"b. The procedure previously adopted can influence the classis unduly.

"c. The Church Order consistently speaks about 'concurring advice of the synodical deputies.' There can be no concurring advice if the classis does not reach its decision at the same time as the synodical deputies." *(Acts of Synod 1972,* pp. 45-46)

Note: The Synod of 1912 decided that in the case of disagreement between a classis and the synodical deputies no other call may be extended nor may another classis examine the candidate until synod has adjudicated the matter. (See *Acts of Synod 1912,* p. 54.)

f. Reexamination of a Candidate

If a candidate does not pass the examination, he may be given another opportunity at the following classical meeting to be examined in the areas in which he failed (*Acts of Synod 1894,* p. 30).

The classis and synodical deputies may recommend a reexamination and specify its nature. Since an examination is conducted at the request of the calling consistory, a reexamination should also take place at the request of this consistory. Since the call of a candidate is tentative and provisional upon the passing of the examination, the consistory must officially request a reexamination or the candidate is left without a call. In this sense, failure of the consistory officially to request a reexamination implies withdrawal of the call.

If a candidate fails to pass his classical examination and/or reexamination, his candidacy terminates.

g. Classical Diploma and Certificate of Ordination
Generally when a candidate has successfully sustained the examination by classis, he is awarded a diploma by the classis certifying the fact. A copy of the form in common usage is in the Appendix (p. 338). The classis authorizes the consistory of the congregation whose call the candidate has accepted to proceed to his ordination.

The Stated Clerk of synod provides a Certificate of Ordination following the candidate's induction into the ministry of the Word.

h. Laying on of Hands
Church Order Article 10a states that "the ordination shall be accompanied by the laying on of hands by the officiating minister." A few observations should be made on this matter.

The form neither states nor implies that "the laying on of hands" effects or accomplishes an ordination. As the synodically adopted guidelines indicate, *ordination should be understood as "the appointment* or setting apart of certain members of the church for *particular ministries* that are strategic for the accomplishment of the church's total ministry" (Guideline 9 for Office and Ordination, *Acts of Synod 1973,* p. 63).

The laying on of hands is the church's way of symbolizing its ordination of a minister of the Word.

"The ceremony of the laying on of hands is not a sacrament but a symbolic act by which the church may publicly confirm its call and appointment to particular ministries. As such it is useful but not essential" (Guideline 10 for Office and Ordination, *Acts of Synod 1973,* p. 64).

Article 10a, while speaking of "the laying on of hands by the officiating minister," does not indicate that he alone is to lay on the hands. Others may also be asked to participate. As a matter of custom, other ministers present are generally asked to participate, as parenthetically noted in the Form for the Ordination of Ministers. In some congregations other office-bearers have also participated in this symbolic act of appointment.

"To invite only ministers, and not elders also, to participate in the laying on of hands is a departure from biblical example. Furthermore, there is no biblical warrant for limiting the laying on of hands to the occasion of setting apart for the particular ministry of the Word and the sacraments" (Guideline 11 for Office and Ordination, *Acts of Synod 1973,* p. 64; cf. also biblical studies on "Special ceremonies accompanying appointments," *Acts of Synod 1973,* pp. 640-649).

2. Article 10b—Installation of Ministers of the Word

   a. The Necessity of Installation
   While Article 10a deals with the first commission to the ministry of the Word, Article 10b deals with inductions into successive pastorates.
   Article 10b deals with the process by which a minister assumes a new pastorate or appointment. The Church Order specifies that he shall be publicly installed in his office with the use of the prescribed form for ordination.

   b. Prerequisites of Installation
   The following procedures are required prior to installation:
   1) A Testimonial of His Former Consistory
   The minister's former consistory must hold a formal meeting to approve "good ecclesiastical testimonials of doctrine and life." Although synod has never adopted a specific statement of the minister's credential, the copy in the Appendix (p. 339) represents the testimonial that has come into common use.
   2) Approval of the Former Classis
   The classis to which the minister belonged, or its interim committee, must approve the testimony of the consistory and forward the credentials to the classis of the church to which he has been called.
   3) Approval of the New Classis
   The classis to which the minister has been called must approve the above credentials and forward the testimony with its endorsement to the consistory and notify the classically appointed counselor. Only after the testimonial has been received by the new consistory may the installation take place.

   It should be noted that the installation of every minister involves not only the local consistory but also the broader classical assembly to which the congregation belongs.

3. The Effectiveness of the Ministerial Testimonial
   The credential gives an enthusiastic endorsement of the minister being transferred. It is to be hoped that such a credential can be given to all of our ministers. However, churches must also be zealous for truthfulness and the well-being of the church.
   The authors believe that endorsements and testimonials ought to be worded in accord with the sincere observations and convictions of the consistories and classes involved. Recommendations adopted merely as a matter of form can be deceptive and harmful to the church of Christ. The testimonial in common usage (see copy in the Appendix, p. 339) ought to be amended as necessary.
   It is regrettable, when a minister has difficulties in his charge, to learn that the same difficulties had been a problem in his previous charges, but no word of advice had been offered in the testimonial. When difficulties have been experienced in a charge, it is to the best interest of the church of Christ for the consistory to present a brief description in its testimonial.

I. THE OFFICES OF THE CHURCH
B. MINISTERS OF THE WORD (continued)

ARTICLE 11

THE FUNCTION OF THE MINISTER OF THE WORD

The calling of a minister of the Word is to proclaim, explain
and apply Holy Scripture in order to gather in and build up
the members of the church of Jesus Christ.

(Amended—*Acts of Synod 1978*, p. 46)

1. The Basic Task of the Minister
   Article 11 defines the function of the minister as that of proclaiming, explaining, and
   applying Holy Scripture. While all members of the church are "members of
   Christ...and share in his anointing," and are called "to confess his name"
   (Heidelberg Catechism, Q. and A. 32), Article 11 describes the professional vocation
   and regular duties of those whom the church appoints (or ordains) to the ministry of
   the Word as an ecclesiastical function.
   The Church Order emphasizes that the special and particular function of *every
   minister* of the Word is "to proclaim, explain and apply Holy Scripture."
   It should be observed that the church, which is called to carry out the ministry of
   Christ, is commissioned by Christ to proclaim the good news of salvation and to
   teach men to observe all that Christ commanded. For the church to carry out this
   commission, it recognizes and appoints persons who have special gifts as well as
   theological and professional training to provide biblically informed and profes-
   sionally competent leadership both within the church and on behalf of the church.
   Article 54a states that the special function of the minister of the Word is to "officially explain and apply Holy Scripture." Article 11 speaks of the ministry of the
   Word as an *ecclesiastical* office. The person appointed to this service is directly accountable for his work to the church as an organization (consistory, classis, or
   synod). This includes those ministers of the Word who are employed by church-
   related or private Christian organizations and also those who serve in chaplaincies
   for governmental or private agencies. Ministers of the Word retain official account-
   ability to the church which appoints them to their office.

2. The Purpose of Ministry
   Article 11 mentions two purposes or goals which belong to the ministry of the Word:
   a. "To gather in...the members of the church." The minister of the Word, along
      with the entire congregation, must reach out into all the world with the gospel of

74

Jesus Christ, so that unbelievers may be won for Christ. The preaching of the gospel, which is the power of God unto salvation to everyone who believes, is the means by which this may be done.

b. "To build up the members of the church." The minister's task is to build up the church, equipping each member with the gifts of the Spirit, so that the church may carry out the mission of the Lord in the world. Paul describes the goal of ministry when he writes,

> "His gifts were that some should be apostles, some prophets, some evangelists, some pastors and teachers, for *the equipment of the saints,* for the work of ministry, for the building up of the body of Christ, until we all attain to the unity of the faith and of the knowledge of the Son of God, to mature manhood, to the measure of the stature of the fulness of Christ."
>
> (Eph. 4:11-13)

I. THE OFFICES OF THE CHURCH
B. MINISTERS OF THE WORD (continued)

ARTICLE 12

SPECIFIC TASKS AND CALLING OF MINISTERS OF THE WORD

a. A minister of the Word serving as pastor of a congregation shall preach the Word, administer the sacraments, conduct public worship services, catechize the youth, and train members for Christian service. He, with the elders, shall supervise the congregation and his fellow office-bearers, exercise admonition and discipline, and see to it that everything is done decently and in order. He, with the elders, shall exercise pastoral care over the congregation, and engage in and promote the work of evangelism.

b. A minister of the Word who enters into the work of missions or is appointed directly by synod shall be called in the regular manner by a local church, which acts in cooperation with the appropriate committee of classis or synod.

c. A minister of the Word may also serve the church in other work which relates directly to his calling, but only after the calling church has demonstrated to the satisfaction of classis, with the concurring advice of the synodical deputies, that said work is consistent with the calling of a minister of the Word.

(Amended—*Acts of Synod 1978,* pp. 46-47)

1. Distinctions with Respect to Ministers of the Word
   Article 12 makes distinctions with respect to the work of ministers of the Word who serve as congregational pastors (Art. 12a), ministers who serve in the work of missions (Art. 12b), and ministers who serve the church in specialized ministerial tasks (Art. 12c).

   a. Differences of Setting for Ministry
      The pastor of a congregation labors primarily within the context of the congregation. Other ministers of the Word, such as missionaries, Bible teachers, chaplains, administrators, or theological professors, labor primarily outside the context of the local congregation.

   b. Differences in Specific Tasks
      While the pastor of a congregation conducts a "general" ministry of the Word with responsibility in the various aspects of the life of the congregation (cf. Art.

12a), other ministers of the Word, such as missionaries, teachers, chaplains, and counselors, serve as specialists in some aspect of the church's ministry to its members and the world (cf. Art. 12b and 12c).

c. Recognition of Distinctions
Synod has recognized distinctions applicable to ministers of the Word by the adoption of a Form for Ordination (or Installation, or Commissioning) of Ministers of the Word to be used in the following ways:
1) For the Pastor in an Established Congregation
2) For a Foreign Missionary
3) For a Home Missionary
4) For a Teacher of Theology
5) For Commissioning of Ministers to Extraordinary (Specialized) Tasks

(Acts of Synod 1971, pp. 528-538)

2. Duties of Pastors of Congregations (Art. 12a)

a. Preaching the Word and Administering the Sacraments
The Bible couples the preaching of the Word and the administration of the sacraments (Matt. 28:19-20 and the history in Acts). The oral proclamation of the Word should be accompanied by the visible signs and seals of God's grace contained in the sacraments.

In 1973 synod decided "there is no valid biblical or doctrinal reason why a person whom the church has appointed to bring the Word may not also be appointed to administer the sacraments" ("Guidelines for Understanding the Nature of Ecclesiastical Office and Ordination," *Acts of Synod 1973,* pp. 62-64).

b. Conducting Public Worship
Article 12a also mentions the conduct of public worship as a fundamental task of the minister of the Word. In the conduct of public worship the preaching of the Word and administration of the sacraments become effective in the life of the entire congregation. The essential elements of worship services and the proper regulation of worship are dealt with in Church Order Articles 51-54. Article 54a stipulates that in every worship service "the minister of the Word shall officially explain and apply Holy Scripture" (*Acts of Synod 1973,* p. 55).

c. Catechizing the Youth
Article 12a also states that it is the responsibility of the minister to "catechize the youth." Articles 63 and 64 provide further regulations for catechetical instruction, among which is the provision that elders or others appointed by the consistory may help the minister if necessary.

d. Training Members for Service
The pastor of a congregation has a mandate to teach not only the youth, but all members of the church for the service of Christ. The members of the congregation must be instructed in their responsibility as those who are called by Christ to

77

be his body in the world. Coupled with discipling and baptizing, Jesus spoke of "teaching them to observe all that I have commanded you" (Matt. 28:20).

Synod recognized the special need of training in education for ministers of the Word to train members for service. In 1974 a seminary professor was appointed to the position in the Church and Ministry Division, with special assignment in Church Education. It was noted as a ground that "the pressing needs in the area of church education" require of the professor of Church Education "substantial amounts of training in pedagogy, and experience in student teacher supervision" *(Acts of Synod 1974,* pp. 28, 150, 160).

Through the Education Committee of the Board of Publications of the Christian Reformed Church, synod has received, studied, and approved curricula and study courses for children, youth, and adults. Catalogs and complete information are available from the Board of Publications.

The Christian Reformed Board of Home Missions also serves the churches with seminars, training, and education materials for development of the evangelistic ministry of the members of the congregations.

e. Exercising Pastoral Care
Article 12a defines the pastoral task of the minister of the Word. He is called to give pastoral care and supervision, along with the elders, to the congregation and his fellow office-bearers. This care includes the total ministry to the spiritual needs of the congregation including the exercise of admonition and discipline and seeing to it that everything in the congregation is done decently and in order.

f. Engaging in and Promoting Evangelism
Both the pastor and the elders are called to "engage in and promote the work of evangelism," giving leadership as well as setting a zealous example for the congregation in the promotion of this work. The church of Jesus Christ is called to bear the good news, to let the light of Christ shine through all the world, and the pastor is called to show such love and leadership in reaching out to bring the gospel to the community that the entire congregation may be deeply motivated in bringing the gospel to all men.

3. Missionaries and Other Synodical Appointees (Art. 12b)

a. The Calling of Missionaries
In the interest of good order, Article 12b specifies that missionaries are to be called by a local church in the same manner as regular ministers. Article 75 of the Church Order requires each classis to "have a classical home missions committee"; Article 77 requires synod to "appoint a denominational foreign missions committee." Local congregations must act in cooperation with these committees when calling a minister to be a missionary.

b. Appointees of Synod or Its Agencies
"In the case of all appointments made or approved by Synod, 'Synod or the synodical committee shall designate the calling church in consultation with the

person and consistory involved.' ... In all other instances the calling church shall be decided upon by the agency desiring the services of a minister in consultation with the person and the consistory involved.''   *(Acts of Synod 1964,* p. 58)

c. Geographical Locations
"He shall be called by a local church lying within the geographical district of the classis where the service is to be performed. A measure of flexibility shall be allowed where two or more classes border each other and the minister's place of residence differs from that of the place where the service is to be performed. The geographical provision may also be impossible to carry out in the case of foreign and home missionaries and chaplains in the armed forces. However, wherever it is possible and feasible the geographical provision must be observed.''
(Acts of Synod 1964, p. 58)

d. Ordination, Credentials, and Membership
"He shall be properly ordained (installed) in his office with the use of the form(s) (and adaptations) approved by synod. His ministerial credentials shall be held by the calling church, and the consistory of the calling church shall exercise supervision over his doctrine and life. His membership shall also reside with the calling church. The latter may be impossible in the case of foreign and home missionaries, and chaplains in the armed forces. However, in all cases where possible, it must be observed.''   *(Acts of Synod 1964,* p. 58)

4. Ministers of the Word in Specialized Services (Art. 12c)

a. Prerequisites for Calling Ministers for Specialized Services

1) Approval of the Position by Assemblies
Before a minister of the Word may serve the church in other work which relates to his calling, the assemblies of the church must determine that the task is "consistent with the calling of a minister of the Word." All of the assemblies must assume their responsibility in the above determination: the calling church is required to demonstrate this consistency; the classis must express satisfaction; and the synod through its synodical deputies must concur.

2) Pension Arrangements
"Synod instructs the Synodical Deputies, in granting permission to ministers to engage in specialized service, to determine that suitable arrangements have been made for defraying the cost of his pension.'' *(Acts of Synod 1969,* p. 48)

b. Regulations for the Application of Article 12c (Supplement, Art. 12c)
1) "The calling church shall secure the prior approval of classis, with concurring advice of the synodical deputies, for each new ministerial position, by providing classis with the following information:
    a) "The description of the official position (purposes, duties, qualifications, etc.) as determined by the calling church in consultation with cooperating agencies as applicable.

b) "The evidence that the minister will be directly accountable to the calling church, including an outline of requirements for reporting to the calling church and supervision by the calling church, in consultation with cooperating agencies as applicable.

c) "The demonstration that the position will be consistent with his calling as a minister of the Word.

d) "When any position having been declared by a classis to be 'spiritual in character and directly related to the ministerial calling' prior to June, 1978, becomes vacant, this position shall be reviewed in the light of Articles 11-14 of the Church Order before another call is issued. . . .

2) "When a new ministry opportunity can be met only by immediate action, the calling church (and the appropriate denominational agency) may obtain provisional approval from the classical committee, subject to subsequent approval by classis with the concurring advice of the synodical deputies. In the event that the provisional approval is not sustained and he desires to maintain his position, the minister may be honorably released from office and may be readmitted according to the regulations of the Church Order. (Cf. Art. 14c.)

3) "Prior to calling a minister of the Word to a military or institutional chaplaincy, the calling church also is urged to obtain the endorsement of the Chaplain Committee of the Christian Reformed Church" (*Acts of Synod 1973,* p. 56).

4) "The church visitors of classis shall inquire annually into the supervision of the calling church toward said minister(s), as well as the reporting of said minister(s) to the calling church. The church visitors shall inform classis of departure from the approved provisions for supervision and reporting."

(Acts of Synod 1978, pp. 47-48)

c. Additional Synodical Rules re Calling of Chaplains

1) Recommendation or Endorsement of a Field

Synod has authorized the "Chaplain Committee to enlarge the scope of its responsibility so as to include institutional chaplaincies, to the extent of investigating openings and opportunities wherever chaplains are appointed or needed and of recruiting qualified men among our ministers and seminarians" *(Acts of Synod 1957,* p. 19).

Consistories, when contemplating the beginning of a chaplaincy, should seek the endorsement of the committee appointed by synod for this purpose.

Synod has reminded the churches that all new positions for extraordinary ministerial tasks do require the approval of the classis, with the concurring advice of the synodical deputies (*Acts of Synod 1976,* p. 48).

2) Endorsement of Candidates for Chaplaincies Authorized and Required

Synod has given the Chaplain Committee authority "to grant ecclesiastical endorsement to qualified ministerial candidates for chaplaincies in mental and general hospitals—both public and private—and in federal, state, and local prisons, when this is required, and in a way similar to that now in practice for the military chaplaincy" *(Acts of Synod 1959,* p. 14).

"Synod strongly urges that classis require that any ordained person working full time in pastoral care or counseling, not serving a local church or a denominational agency, be endorsed by the Chaplain Committee in order to receive approval by his classis for work in a special ministry. Endorsement shall consist of the following:

a) "The approval of the man as a qualifed candidate in terms of ministerial skills and training for his specialized position. Such qualifications are to be judged on the basis of personal interviews, recommendations, and other standards of the Chaplain Committee. (Classis shall retain the task of judging the spiritual nature of the position and granting permission for a man to be called to that position.)

b) "The approval of the field as a 'worthy field' with a potential great enough to justify the full-time employment of an ordained minister.

Grounds:
(1) "Article 95 of the Church Order stipulates the proper equality among churches and office-bearers.
(2) "This arrangement is consistent with the general policy adopted by synod in 1961, 'that a Christian Reformed minister entering the institutional chaplaincy, in addition to consistorial and classical endorsement, be urged to secure ecclesiastical endorsement from the Synodical Chaplain Committee' " (*Acts of Synod 1961,* Art. 44, p. 13; *1973,* p. 56).

d. Prior Synodical Precedents
Prior to the decisions of the Synod of 1978 (contained in section 4b above) some of the specialized positions approved by synod included presidents of Calvin, Dordt, and Trinity colleges; editors of our periodicals and educational committees; officers of denominational boards and committees; chaplains; Bible translators; Bible teachers in our high schools and colleges; and various other positions relating to the ministry of the Word.

I. THE OFFICES OF THE CHURCH
B. MINISTERS OF THE WORD (continued)

ARTICLE 13

SUPERVISION OF MINISTERS

a. A minister of the Word is directly accountable to the calling church, and therefore shall be supervised in doctrine, life
and duties by that church. When his work is with other than
the calling church, he shall be supervised in cooperation
with other congregations, institutions or agencies involved.
b. A minister of the Word may be loaned temporarily by his
calling church to serve as pastor of a congregation outside
of the Christian Reformed Church, but only with the approval
of classis, the concurring advice of the synodical deputies,
and in accordance with the synodical regulations. Although
his duties may be regulated in cooperation with the other
congregation, the supervision of his doctrine and life rests
with the calling church.

(Amended—*Acts of Synod 1976*, p. 33; *Acts of Synod 1978*, p. 47)

1. Supervision of All Ministers
   Article 13a stipulates the basic rule for every minister of the Word. Each minister of
   the Word is directly accountable to his calling church, and therefore shall be supervised in doctrine, life, and duties by that church.
   The minister of the Word must recognize himself as a servant of Christ and accountable to him. However, he is called by Christ through a specific congregation
   and its consistory and serves the church for Christ's sake.
   Each consistory must recognize its responsibility for the supervision of its
   ministers of the Word. Supervision does not imply mere watchfulness but love,
   counsel, encouragement, and assistance in the work of the Lord. The service of the
   minister of the Word and the total ministry of the church are intricately and vitally
   interrelated as Paul indicates in Ephesians 4:11-13.

2. The Supervision of Missionaries
   Article 13b distinguishes between *regulation of duties* of a missionary and the *supervision of doctrine and life*. Classical and synodical mission boards have "mission
   orders" which regulate the duties of a missionary, but the calling church retains
   responsibility for supervising the doctrine and life of such ministers. Mission boards

and committees are not substitute consistories, since they neither call ministers nor supervise their doctrine and life. Likewise consistories are not substitute mission boards or committees regulating the work of ministers in mission service.

The respective responsibilites of mission agencies and consistories noted above demand close cooperation and consultation when necessary. Neither the agency nor the consistory may overstep the boundaries of its mandates.

3. Supervision of Other Ministers

Church Order Article 13 recognizes that some ministers are called to work in areas other than the calling church. In all such cases the supervision of his doctrine, life, and duties remains with the calling church. It is recognized, however, that the calling churches must exercise this supervision in cooperation with any other congregations, institutions, or agencies involved. (See this manual under Art. 92).

In such cases, as in the supervision of missionaries (noted in section 2 above), the respective responsibilities of the calling church and the agency involved demand close cooperation and consultation.

4. Supervision and Regulations re Ministers in Other Denominations (Supplement, Art. 13b)

Synod has approved the following regulations pertaining to Article 13b of the Church Order: "A minister whose service is requested by a congregation outside the CRC may be loaned temporarily to serve such a church while still retaining his ministerial status in the CRC in keeping with the following regulations:

"a. The congregation seeking the services of the CR minister is desirous of the Reformed faith and seriously contemplates affiliation with the CRC or some other Reformed denomination, or is already in a Reformed denomination and seeks to be strengthened in the Reformed faith.

"b. The minister contemplating service in an undenominational church acknowledges it as his duty to bring such a church into the CRC, or at least into a Reformed denomination similar to the CRC.

"c. The duties of the minister are spiritual in character and directly related to the ministerial calling, and such duties do not conflict with his commitment to the faith and practice of the CRC as required by his signature to the Form of Subscription.

"d. If the congregation to be served is in close proximity to a CR congregation of another classis, the approval of that classis shall be required, in addition to the approval of the classis of the minister's calling church, and the synodical deputies.

"e. The loaning of such ministerial services may be for a period of time not to exceed two years. Extensions of not more than two years each may be granted if circumstances warrant, with the approval of classis and the synodical deputies.

"f. Should the minister become subject to discipline, the non-CR congregation which he is serving shall have the right to suspend him from his service to that church, but his suspension from office and deposition may be applied only by the CRC.

"g. Continuation under the CRC Pension Plan shall require that the minister, or the non-CR church which he serves, shall contribute to the Ministers' Pension Fund an amount which is determined annually by the Ministers' Pension Fund Committee for ministers serving in extraordinary positions outside of our denomination." *(Acts of Synod 1976,* pp. 33-34)

I. THE OFFICES OF THE CHURCH
B. MINISTERS OF THE WORD (continued)

ARTICLE 14

RELEASE FROM MINISTERIAL OFFICE

a. A minister of the Word shall not leave the congregation with which he is connected for another church without the consent of the consistory.

b. A minister of the Word, once lawfully called, may not forsake his office. He may, however, be released from office to enter upon a nonministerial vocation for such weighty reasons as shall receive the approval of the classis with the concurring advice of the synodical deputies.

c. A former minister of the Word who was released from his office may be declared eligible for call upon approval of the classis from which he obtained his release, with the concurring advice of the synodical deputies. Upon acceptance of a call, he shall be reordained.

(Amended—*Acts of Synod 1978,* p. 47)

1. Transfer from One Congregation to Another
   Church Order Article 14a is designed to protect the binding character of the tie between a minister and his congregation. It prescribes that no minister shall be permitted to leave the congregation he serves for another congregation "without the consent of the consistory." This clearly implies that before a minister decides to accept a call from another congregation, he should discuss the matter with his consistory and seek its consent. There should be a free and open discussion between the pastor and a consistory before a call is accepted and a minister leaves the responsibility for his congregation. (See this manual under Art. 10b.)

2. Release from the Ministry of the Word
   Article 14b declares that a minister is bound to his calling as a minister of the Word. He may not forsake it lightly. If, however, a minister of the Word feels that he should enter upon a nonministerial vocation, he may "be released from office to enter upon a nonministerial vocation for such weighty reasons as shall receive the approval of the classis with the concurring advice of the synodical deputies."

   Synod has defined a nonministerial vocation as one "that lies entirely outside of the sphere of the Ministry of the Gospel and does not have its purpose in that Ministry" (*Acts of Synod 1932,* p. 165).

A minister of the Word who feels that he must temporarily or permanently enter upon a nonministerial vocation should consult with his consistory and give good reason for his decision. If the reason is judged sufficient by the consistory, the classis and the synodical deputies are called upon to take the official action in declaring that the given minister is released from his ministerial office.

Historically, ministers have requested and been granted release from the ministry of the Word to enter into other occupations.

3. Legitimacy of an Honorable Release from the Ministry of the Word
The synodical study committee which proposed to the Synod of 1978 revisions of Church Order Articles 11 to 14 (*Acts of Synod 1978,* pp. 474-483) addressed the question of whether provisions should be made for those who for legitimate reasons wish to leave the ministry of the Word temporarily for other occupations. The committee wrote:

"We know of no biblical warrant for requiring that the ministry of the Word be 'for life,' whereas the offices of elder and deacon are not. A second reason is that there are *numerous* Christian occupations that can be well served by a person with theological training and ministerial experience, but that are not ecclesiastical in nature and are not directly related to the purpose and primary task of the ministry of the Word. Let us be clear about this matter! Just because a (former) minister of the Word is able to do a job does not automatically make that job either ecclesiastical or directly related to the purpose and primary task of the ministerial office.

"As a matter of fact, in frequent instances we think it would be appropriate and even helpful if a minister of the Word could honorably and without prejudice set aside his ordination for a specific time (such as two years minimum, five years maximum) while he engage[s] in an occupation that [does] not satisfy the requirements of Articles 11-13 as proposed. Essentially such action is no different than in the case of elders and deacons who conclude a term of service on the consistory, only to be reelected and installed at a later date. When the other assignment is completed, the (former) minister could then follow the appropriate steps for returning to a ministerial vocation." *(Acts of Synod 1978,* pp. 479-480)

4. Faulty Terminology and Procedure in Releases
In some cases, ministers have "resigned" from office. A word of caution should be used about the concept of resignation. Resignation implies a deliberate forsaking of office. In the case of the resignation of members, synod "warns against such expressions as 'accepting the resignation' since the responsibility for his sinful act must remain with the person who withdraws himself from the church" (*Acts of Synod 1951,* p. 17).

When a minister of the Word resigns from his office, the assemblies should deal with this person in the way of discipline, and as a last resort may have to acquiesce in the resignation but ought not to use the terminology of "accepting the resignation."

The misuse of terminology described above is apparent in two decisions of the Synod of 1977. This synod dealt with two cases of "resignation from the ministry."

One of these cases was in actuality a request for release from the ministry and dismission to another denomination. The second case was a request for release to enter another occupation. Synod informed both classes involved that release from the office of the ministry of the Word requires action by the classis and concurring advice of synodical deputies. (See *Acts of Synod 1977*, p. 71.)

The Synod of 1949 in a specific case of a minister of the Word who was guilty of a sin which made it impossible for him to serve in the ministry, who had confessed this sin and subsequently resigned his office, thereby evading further disciplinary action, declared that "his status will be considered that of one deposed from office" (*Acts of Synod 1949*, p. 48).

Synod has instructed "all our churches and classes that in all cases of resignation a proper resolution of dismissal must be adopted with the concurring advice of synodical deputies" *(Acts of Synod 1978*, p. 73).

5. Effective Date of Release or "Resignation"
The effective date of the termination of ministerial office is determined by the consistory and/or classis which approved the release of the minister of the Word (*Acts of Synod 1977*, pp. 65ff., 452-454).

6. Return to Office of a Minister of the Word Honorably Released
Article 14c makes provisions for the minister who has been honorably released to return to the office of the minister of the Word.

A former minister of the Word desiring to return to ministerial office must request the classis by which he was released to declare him eligible to receive a call. The classis, with the concurring advice of the synodical deputies, may grant his request and declare the applicant eligible for a call.

Upon acceptance of a call a former minister of the Word shall be reordained to this office. In accord with the scriptural teaching that " 'ordination' should be understood as the appointment or setting apart of certain members of the church for particular ministries" (Guideline 9 re Office and Ordination, *Acts of Synod 1973*, p. 63), Article 14c provides that ministers of the Word, as elders and deacons and evangelists, may be reordained after periods of release from office.

7. Return to Office of a Minister of the Word Who Was Released (or Who Resigned) While Subject to Disciplinary Action
In the case of a minister of the Word who resigns his office or who requests release from office because he has committed some sin which makes it impossible to continue in office, the conditions and procedures of Church Order Article 94 would have to be followed.

I. THE OFFICES OF THE CHURCH
B. MINISTERS OF THE WORD (continued)

ARTICLE 15

SUPPORT OF MINISTERS

Each church shall through its consistory provide for the proper support of its minister(s).

Church Order Article 15 requires that each church through its consistory provide for the proper support of its minister or ministers. It has always been the position of the Church Order of the Christian Reformed Church to insist that those who are called to the ministry of the Word ought to be properly cared for as servants of Jesus Christ. A number of regulations have been adopted to insure that ministers of the Word shall be properly cared for in all of our churches and by all of our agencies.

1. Salary Responsibility of the Calling Church
   Salary responsibility terminates and begins with the farewell sermon (*Acts of Synod 1926*, p. 71).

2. Guidelines for Ministers' Salaries and Additional Benefits

   a. Salary
      Each year synod adopts a suggested base salary for ministers. This does not mean that the minimum should in any way be construed as the maximum, but that it becomes the base from which to proceed responsibly to a realistic salary on the basis of an annual reevaluation of need, the increase or decrease in the cost of living, and prevailing salary standards.
         Synod adopted the following grounds for the fixing of an annual, suggested base salary:
      1) "The minister's salary should be compared with average incomes of other professionals and the Bureau of Labor Statistics of living costs (which are updated and made available regularly for various areas in the United States) rather than the average income of his congregation.
      2) "All consistories should take into consideration the increased cost of living as a basic ingredient in determining the salary increment for the minister.
      3) "In considering its ability to grant an increase, the consistory should set its minister's salary increase as a primary obligation, ahead of capital expenditures, etc. Meeting its financial responsibilities to its minister should take priority over responsibilities to classis and synod.

4) "A realistic salary should be in terms of actual costs to feed, clothe, educate, to absorb personal expenses of the minister's salary, and to accumulate enough savings to retire debt occasioned by his education, and to assure him of a roof over his head upon retirement. To set a minimum salary figure below these needs is unrealistic." *(Acts of Synod 1970,* p. 45)

b. Additional Benefits

In addition to salary provision synod urged consistories and other employing agencies to adopt the other recommendations made by the study committee concerning additional benefits as follows:

1) *"Housing.* In addition to the base salary the local consistory should provide adequate housing, including major appliances, utilities, and telephone, except for personal calls, for the minister and his family.

2) *"Travel Expense.* A car allowance should be granted each minister to the extent of ___¢ per mile driven for the church, plus prompt payment of other travel and lodging expenses incurred when out of town on business for the local church. [The mileage allowance in 1980 is 20¢ per mile.]

3) *"Tools for Continuing Education.* A reasonable allowance should be authorized to purchase new books and periodicals and the cost of attending conferences other than church business which are means to strengthen the ministry and its service to the church.

4) *"Hospital and Medical Insurance.* The congregation should provide adequate hospital and medical insurance for the minister and his family. The Christian Reformed survey shows that two-thirds of our ministers are paying their own, whereas the trend in industry today is that the employer pays all hospital and medical insurance expense.

5) *"Social Security.* Social Security is now mandatory for the minister as a self-employed person. . . . Consistories in the U.S.A should take this into account when setting the minister's salary.

6) *"Memberships.* The minister should be given the privilege of an expense account or a reasonable allowance be included in his salary to join service clubs and professional organizations and attend meetings of a civic nature in the interest of the commitment of the church to the community. The church should pay annual dues and other expenses incurred.

7) *"Hospitality.* The church often expects its minister to do extensive entertaining on behalf of the church and therefore should reimburse him when such expenses are incurred." *(Acts of Synod 1970,* pp. 45-46)

c. Ordained Men's Compensation Survey

In 1974, in answer to a mandate of synod, the Synodical Interim Committee presented a supplement to the Guidelines for Ministers' Salaries adopted by the Synod of 1970 as a report entitled "Ordained Men's Salary Survey and Findings." Synod adopted this report in form and substance and requested the Synodical Interim Committee to continue to acquire and retain data for the updating of ministers' compensation reviews on a year-to-year basis.

The appropriate portions of this report are published in "Your Church in Action," the handbook of the Christian Reformed Church. Current information gathered by the Synodical Interim Committee is also published in the handbook as an annual Ministers' Compensation Survey.

Synod also instructed the Fund for Needy Churches (FNC) Committee to make every attempt to comply with the Guidelines for Ministers' Salaries and to take into consideration current information available from the Synodical Interim Finance Committee as published in the annual Ministers' Compensation Survey.

In 1975, synod adopted several additional guidelines pertaining to the Ministers' Compensation Survey:

1) Synod urged "all of our church consistories to adopt the Ordained Men's Compensation Study report as a guide for their pastor's annual compensation and particularly, where compensation as shown in the study falls considerably below the Cost of Living Index, [to take] corrective measures...immediately to adjust such inequities."

2) Synod urged "our consistories to make use of the data published under 'Ministers' Salary Guide' in our Handbook of the Christian Reformed Church—'Your Church in Action' to be mailed to them in the fall of [each] year."

3) Synod urged "our ministers and/or consistories to cooperate with the Synodical Interim Committee in furnishing the information required annually to up-date compensation studies for the benefit of all concerned."

4) Synod instructed "the FNC and our boards and agencies employing ordained men to make every attempt to comply with the 'Guidelines for Ministers' Salaries' published in 1970 and to take into consideration current information available in the Ministers' Compensation Study Report from the Synodical Interim Finance Committee, as published in the annual handbook, 'Your Church In Action.' "   *(Acts of Synod 1975, p. 117)*

3. The Fund for Needy Churches

For over forty years synods have appointed a committee to administer the Fund for Needy Churches. In 1958 the following synodical rules were adopted for the administration of the Fund for Needy Churches:

"a. The purpose of the Fund for Needy Churches is the granting of salary assistance and other financial allowances (such as children's allowance and mileage) to churches which have done their utmost to meet the minimum salary as set by synod and have found themselves unable to do so.

"b. The administration of this fund is entrusted to the Fund for Needy Churches Committee, appointed by synod and comprised of two ministers and three laymen. Synod stipulated that this committee shall be incorporated under the laws of the state or province from which its members are appointed.

"c. Qualification for assistance from this fund shall be based on conditions of need as related to congregational income, congregational giving toward its own financial requirements, and congregational giving toward synodically set denominational quotas; with special consideration being given to exceptional causes (e.g., heavy debt on church property, poverty of the congregation, or special conditions in pastor's home, etc.).

"d. At each Synod the FNC Committee shall recommend a minimum salary for the year following, a mileage allowance, and a children's allowance applicable through the high school age. The final decision shall be left to Synod.

"e. At each synod the FNC Committee shall recommend a minimum contribution that each family, belonging to a subsidized church, shall make toward the minister's salary for the following year. The final decision shall be left to Synod.

"f. The individual congregations desiring assistance from this fund shall make application annually by filing a questionnaire provided by the synodically appointed committee. This questionnaire, together with the congregation's annual financial report, shall be forwarded with the action of classis as to the amount requested. In cases of special need classis shall furnish information necessary to establish need. This information shall be sent to the FNC Committee not later than the first day of November of the year preceding the one for which the request is made.

"g. The FNC Committee, in consultation with the classes concerned, shall urge the following:
   "1) That recipient congregations shall become self-supporting as soon as possible.
   "2) That congregations which have no promise of future growth merge with neighboring congregations wherever possible and feasible.
   "3) That churches assist in the financial needs of daughter churches until they become self-supporting.

"h. When a minister leaves a church which is receiving aid from the FNC, that church, through its classis, shall take up the matter of continued support with the FNC Committee before calling another minister.

"i. The amount of aid given to each church shall be published in the *Acts of Synod* annually." *(Acts of Synod 1958, pp. 75-76)*

4. Combining Fields
The Synod of 1928 decided that in order to assist in the proper support of our ministers every classis should "strive to induce two or more small, weak and subsidized churches to combine into one field of labor having one minister" *(Acts of Synod 1928, p. 110)*.

5. Responsibilities of Consistories, Classes, and Church Visitors
All churches are obliged to provide for the proper support of their ministers. Synod has been aware of the fact that at times churches which are not receiving assistance from the Fund for Needy Churches are paying substandard salaries to their ministers. In their churches ministers are receiving less salary than ministers who are serving in the neediest of our churches, those supported by the FNC. Such an arrangement is unfair to the ministers.

With the above in mind, synod urges "all consistories, classes and church visitors to exert themselves to the end that all of our ministers receive salaries at least commensurate with the minimum set annually for 'needy churches,' and where the consistory is unable to meet that minimum, that it unhesitatingly appeal to the Fund [FNC]'' for assistance *(Acts of Synod 1948,* p. 18).

All consistories, classes, and church visitors should be aware of their full responsibility with respect to meeting the minimum annual salary.

I. THE OFFICES OF THE CHURCH

B. MINISTERS OF THE WORD (continued)

ARTICLE 16

TEMPORARY RELEASE FROM SERVICE (LEAVE OF ABSENCE)

A minister who for weighty reasons desires a temporary release from service to the congregation must have the approval of his consistory, which shall continue to have supervision over him.

1. Temporary Release

Article 16 provides for what is commonly called a "leave of absence." It should be noted that this article deals only with *temporary* release from service to the congregation. In 1928 synod decided that an *indefinite* leave of absence is not permissible *(Acts of Synod 1928,* p. 141).

A leave of absence must always be requested (and given) for a specific period of time, which should be clearly recorded in the minutes of the consistory. This should include both a beginning date and a termination date.

2. Valid Reasons for Leave of Absence

A leave of absence may be requested (and granted) only for weighty reasons. The reason should be clearly stated in the consistory minutes.

One such reason, recognized by synod as valid, is advanced study. This is the only way a minister doing advanced study can retain his official ministerial status as he prepares himself for continued work in the church. (See *Acts of Synod 1932,* p. 165.)

Another reason for requesting a leave of absence is illness or temporary incapacity. Again, the reason should be clearly recorded, and the time limit should be set. If it appears that the incapacity will be indefinite in length or that it is of a serious nature, consideration should be given to emeritation according to Article 18.

3. Invalid Reasons for Leave of Absence

There are many invalid reasons for requesting a leave of absence:
a. When a minister desires to serve a congregation outside the Christian Reformed Church, the provisions of Article 13b should be followed.
b. When a minister wishes to temporarily pursue a nonministerial vocation, the provisions of Article 14b should be followed.
c. When an intolerable situation exists between the minister and his congregation, the provisions of Article 17 should be followed.

93

4. Terms of the Leave of Absence

When a leave of absence is granted according to Article 16, the terms of that leave of absence with respect to the obligations of the minister and the congregation should be spelled out. If the minister is to return to his church after a given period of time, such a stipulation should be clearly agreed upon. Likewise, if the minister and the congregation believe that the congregation will be better served by calling another minister, definite arrangements should be made with respect to the termination of salary, the use of the parsonage, and other material arrangements. Furthermore, the consistory not only remains the custodian of the credentials and the supervisor of the life and doctrine of the minister involved, but at the termination of the leave of absence, it shall be the responsibility of this consistory to announce that the minister is available for a call from another church.

5. Responsibilities of the Consistory

Article 16 specifies that the minister who desires a temporary release from service to the congregation must have the approval of his consistory. This means that the tie which unites the minister and his congregation may not be broken without serious consideration of both the minister and his consistory. The minister, moreover, has an obligation to respect the decision of his consistory in such a matter.

When a temporary release from the service of the congregation is given in accord with Article 16 of the Church Order, the consistory continues to have supervision over the minister who is on leave of absence.

6. Pension Arrangements

When a minister is given a leave of absence arrangements should be made with respect to his pension rights. A minister on leave of absence will become a nonactive participant in the Christian Reformed Ministers' Pension Fund unless payments are made to the Ministers' Pension Fund either by his consistory or by the minister himself in accordance with the provisions of the Ministers' Pension Plan.

(Acts of Synod 1978, p. 376)

I. THE OFFICES OF THE CHURCH

B. MINISTERS OF THE WORD (continued)

ARTICLE 17

RELEASE FROM MINISTRY IN A CONGREGATION

a. A minister who is neither eligible for retirement nor worthy of discipline may, because of an intolerable situation existing between him and his church, be released from active ministerial service in his congregation. The consistory shall give such a release only with the approval of the classis, with the concurring advice of the synodical deputies and in accordance with synodical regulations.

b. The consistory shall provide for the support of a released minister in such a way and for such a time as shall receive the approval of classis.

c. Eventually, if no call is forthcoming, he may at the discretion of classis and the synod be completely released from his ministerial office.

1. Release from the Congregation

Article 17a provides for the release of a minister who is neither eligible for retirement nor worthy of discipline. The intent of this article is to provide for proper severance of a minister from a congregation when relationships have become so strained that effective ministry has become impossible.

This article must not be used for ministers who either for illness or age are eligible for retirement. (Article 18 is applicable for such ministers.) Nor may this article be employed for ministers whose doctrine or conduct make them subject to formal discipline (Article 88-94 provide regulations governing such cases), since Article 17a is no substitute for proper discipline in the church.

2. Approval of Release from a Congregation

Because a minister serves not only the local congregation but also the classis and the denomination, he may be released from active ministerial service in a congregation only after classis gives its approval and synod, through its synodical deputies, concurs. No consistory may release its pastor without such approval.

3. Support of a Released Minister

Article 17b provides that when a minister is released from a congregation, the consistory must provide for the support of this minister in such a way and for such a time as shall receive the approval of classis. Since the minister involved is not worthy of discipline, the church maintains a responsibility with respect to his support. This responsibility must be met by mutual consultation of the minister and the consistory involved and must have the approval of classis.

4. The Status of a Released Minister

When a minister has been released, it becomes the responsibility of the congregation from which he has been released to declare him available for a call to another church.

A minister who has been released from service in his congregation does not immediately lose his ministerial status. He continues to be a minister in good standing and is available for a call to another congregation. Since there is no disciplinary matter involved when Article 17 is employed, the consistory should be able in good conscience to recommend the released pastor for a call to another church. (See *Acts of Synod 1960,* p. 46.)

Announcement of the release of a minister should be made periodically in our church papers indicating that he is available for a call.

5. Transfer of Credentials (Supplement, Art. 17)

The Synod of 1973 declared that "a minister who has been released from active ministerial service in his congregation according to Article 17 of the Church Order, and who has transferred his membership to another congregation, may, with the approval of classis and after a time agreed upon by classis, have his official connection transferred to the consistory of the congregation of which he is a member.

"*Grounds:*

"a. The 'intolerable situation' which first precipitated the release of a minister from his consistory is likely to influence adversely their continuing relationship.

"b. A neutral consistory may be in a better situation to deal fairly and objectively with a released minister and to receive that minister's cooperation than would be the consistory from which the minister is estranged.

"c. The consistory of the congregation of which he is a member is in a better position to exercise the appropriate supervision of the brother's doctrine and life."

(Acts of Synod 1973, p. 35)

6. If No Call Is Received

Article 17c provides that eventually, if no call is forthcoming, a minister released from his congregation may at the discretion of classis and the synod be released from the ministerial office as well. This section of the Church Order demands an adequate period of time for a minister to receive a call.

Before a minister is finally released from the ministerial office, a definite time limit should be determined by the classis and the consistory holding his ministerial credentials. *Final release shall take place only when classis, with the approval of the synodical deputies, has made an official declaration of such release.* (See Acts of Synod 1977, p. 71.)

Release from the ministerial office, it should be noted, is not given because of the intolerable situation which led to the minister's release from active service in his congregation. The release of which Article 17c speaks takes place because, after a sufficiently long period of time, if no call is received there is no outward confirmation to the internal call to the ministry of the Word. The procedure in such an instance is similar to that which applies when a candidate does not receive a call.

I. THE OFFICES OF THE CHURCH
B. MINISTERS OF THE WORD (continued)

ARTICLE 18

RETIREMENT OF MINISTERS

a. A minister who has reached retirement age, or who because of physical or mental disability is incapable of performing the duties of his office, is eligible for retirement. Retirement shall take place with the approval of the consistory and classis and in accordance with synodical regulations.
b. A retired minister shall retain the honor and title of a minister of the Word and his official connection with the church which he served last, and this church shall be responsible for providing honorably for his support and that of his dependents according to synodical regulations.
c. Should the reasons for his retirement no longer exist, the minister emeritus shall request the consistory and classis which recommended him for retirement to declare him eligible for call.

1. Eligibility for Retirement
   Article 18a specifies two valid reasons for retirement of a minister:
   a. Retirement Age
      The Synod of 1956 decided that "ministers shall have the privilege of retiring at the age of 65 years" (*Acts of Synod 1956,* p. 19).
      The age stipulation of synod does not *require* retirement at sixty-five but grants to each minister the privilege of retirement if he so desires.
      The Synod of 1980 decides that "ministers of the Word shall be granted the privilege of retiring at the age of sixty-two, with the approval of the classes involved, under the reduced pension scale adopted by the Synod of 1978" (*Acts of Synod 1980,* p. 22).
   b. Physical or Mental Disability
      A minister is eligible for retirement if his physical or mental disability is of such a nature that he is incapable of performing the duties of his office. Before a minister is declared eligible for such retirement, his physical or mental disability must be certified by a physician.

2. Approval of Retirement
   Requests for retirement must be approved by the consistory and the classis and the

date of emeritation must be specified by the classis. The stated clerk of classis shall notify the stated clerk of synod and the Ministers' Pension Fund Committee of the date and reason for each emeritation.

3. The Status of Retired Ministers
   a. A retired minister retains the honor and title of a minister of the Word and is authorized to perform all services pertaining to the office of the ministry.
   b. The official connection of a minister (his credentials and supervision) remains in the church he served last if he remains a member or if his emeritation is expected to be of a temporary nature.

      Synod has ruled that "the supervision of an emeritus minister...may be transferred, at his request, to the church of which he becomes a member after emeritation" *(Acts of Synod 1968,* p. 69). It should be evident that the consistory holding the minister's membership is best able to supervise his doctrine and life.

      The transfer of the credentials of retired ministers does not require processing through the classes. The consistory of the church which the emeritus minister last served formally requests the consistory of the church he wishes to join to exercise supervision over him. (See *Acts of Synod 1968,* p. 69.)

4. The Support of Retired Ministers
   Article 18b requires that a retired minister and his dependents be supported honorably by the church which he served last. Recognizing that this requirement may impose undue hardship on some churches, synod has established a Ministers' Pension Fund to provide for retired ministers, and their widows and families. Through quotas and contributions all congregations in the Christian Reformed Church share in supporting the servants of the Lord who have given their lives for the ministry of the Word.

   The regulations for the support of retired ministers and their dependents are outlined in the Rules for the Ministers' Pension Fund. Copies are available from the Ministers' Pension Fund office in the Christian Reformed Denominational Building, 2850 Kalamazoo Avenue, SE, Grand Rapids, Michigan 49560.

   Notice of the death of a minister should be sent to the Ministers' Pension Fund Committee by his classis or consistory.

   Through the Ministers' Pension Fund Committee synod provides moving expenses of retired ministers, and widows of ministers who died in service, from their last charge to the place of retirement residence. The regulations pertaining to these expenses are available from the Ministers' Pension Fund office.

   The Synod of 1979 reaffirmed the decision of 1969 that the Ministers' Pension Plan is by synodical decision formulated in terms of an advanced funding concept *(Acts of Synod 1969,* p. 47, paragraph 3).

   One of the grounds cited is as follows:

   "A sound pension plan to provide for our ministers upon retirement from the ministry is based on the principle that the cost of providing retirement benefits, which we believe to be mandated by Scripture and our Church Order, for a minister is incurred while he is in active service. Therefore, an amount must be set aside, as deferred compensation, each year during his career so that at retirement, based on age or otherwise, there will be sufficient moneys to pay retirement benefits as needed to sustain him and his family for the remaining years of his life.''

(Acts of Synod 1979, p. 105)

5. Readmission of Retired Ministers

If a minister has retired for mental or physical disability, and the reasons for his retirement no longer exist, such a minister shall not be called until the consistory and classis which approved his retirement declare him eligible for a call and judge that the reasons for his retirement no longer exist. (See *Acts of Synod 1928,* p. 138.)

6. Other Ecclesiastical Employees

The same provisions made for ministers are applicable to other full-time employees of the church or churches, such as evangelists, missions employees, unordained personnel of denominational and classical agencies, and local church employees.

Synod has established an Unordained Employees Pension Fund to enable our agencies, classes, and consistories to provide honorably for retired employees who have served Christian Reformed churches.

Information and application are obtainable from the Unordained Employees Pension Fund Committee, 2850 Kalamazoo Avenue, SE, Grand Rapids, Michigan 49560.

I. THE OFFICES OF THE CHURCH
B. MINISTERS OF THE WORD (continued)

ARTICLE 19

THEOLOGICAL SEMINARY

The churches shall maintain a theological seminary at which men are trained for the ministry of the Word. The seminary shall be governed by synod through a board of trustees appointed by synod and responsible to it.

1. The Relationship of the Church and Seminary
Article 19 affirms that the churches have a responsibility to provide a seminary for training ministers of the Word. Since 1876 the Christian Reformed Church has provided theological training for its ministers at Calvin Theological Seminary. In 1910 synod stated that the theological school should be acknowledged as the property of the church and that theological training should be supported by and be under the jurisdiction of the church *(Acts of Synod 1910,* p. 38).

2. The Function of the Seminary
Article 19 indicates that the primary function of the theological seminary as an agency of the Christian Reformed Church is to provide training for the ministry of the Word.

In various decisions synod has also provided that there may be students other than those who aspire to the ministry of the Word in the Christian Reformed Church who may be trained in Calvin Theological Seminary. The study of theology is not limited to those who wish to enter into the official ministry of the Word.

3. The Government of the Seminary
Article 19 specifies that the seminary shall be governed by a board of trustees appointed by synod and responsible to it. Each classis nominates a prospective board member and alternate who are appointed by synod in accord with the rules for synodical procedure. In addition to the board members representing classes, synod appoints nine members at large to the board of trustees.

Since Calvin College is an outgrowth of Calvin Seminary, both institutions are governed by the same board. The Board of Trustees of Calvin College and Seminary is accountable to synod and reports annually to it.

I. THE OFFICES OF THE CHURCH
B. MINISTERS OF THE WORD (continued)

ARTICLE 20

TASKS OF PROFESSORS OF THEOLOGY

The task of the ministers of the Word who are appointed as professors of theology is to train the seminary students for the ministry of the Word, expound the Word of God, and vindicate sound doctrine against heresies and errors.

1. The Specific Tasks of Professors of Theology

   a. Training of Seminary Students for the Ministry of the Word
   The primary task of seminary professors is to prepare seminary students to be ministers of the Word, "men who as ministers of the Word shall preach the Gospel of salvation to the people of God in the church of Christ and to men outside of the church of Christ" (Form for the Commissioning of Teachers of Theology, *Psalter Hymnal)*. This task is in accord with Paul's words to Timothy, "What you have heard from me before many witnesses entrust to faithful men who will be able to teach others also" (II Tim. 2:2).

   b. Giving Theological Leadership
   In addition to the training of future ministers of the Word, seminary professors are called upon to expound the Word of God and vindicate sound doctrine against heresies and errors. The seminary professors must be deeply committed to the Lord and his Word and have expertise in the knowledge of God's Word. They must also be cognizant of the spiritual, theological, and moral climate in which the church is called to serve Christ. The Church Order properly calls upon our seminary professors to use their gifts not only in the classroom but by leadership in the ministries of the church of Christ.

2. Professors of Theology: Requirements for Appointment
   In 1958 synod adopted the following requirements for instructional staff in the seminary:
   a. "*Personal*
      1) "He must be sound in doctrine and zealous for the system of truth known as the Reformed faith.
      2) "He must be diligent in the vindication of the Reformed faith against all heresy and error.

102

3) "He must be of sound judgment, and must be well balanced, free from fanaticism.

4) "He must be truly godly and must excel in the basic Christian virtues of honesty and humility.

5) "He must possess pedagogical competence on the seminary level.

b. *"Academic*

1) "He must be truly learned in the sense that he has received a broad liberal arts education as well as a thorough Reformed theological training.

2) "He must have special training in the field for which he is nominated.

3) "He must have given evidence of being a scholar, having the ability to express himself with accuracy and to engage in original research.

4) "He must have a thorough acquaintance with contemporaneous theological thought, both Reformed and otherwise.

c. *"Ministerial*

"He should ordinarily be an ordained man who has had pastoral experience."

(Acts of Synod 1958, p. 16)

3. The following rules for nomination and appointment of seminary professors were adopted by the Synod of 1979:

a. "The need for additional teaching help or eventual replacements shall be reviewed annually by the seminary president and the Board of Trustees at its May meeting in order that the board may make the necessary appointment(s) at its February meeting.

b. "When the need for appointments has been established, this need shall be referred to the seminary faculty, whose duty shall be to convass the field of possible candidates; to gather the required personal, academic, ministerial, and other relevant information concerning them; to evaluate them; and to submit a nomination to the board.

c. "At the May meeting the board may submit to the faculty the names of persons whom it wishes the faculty to consider as possible nominees. The faculty shall solicit further recommendations of names for consideration from consistories and classes, establishing a suitable deadline for the submission of such names. All names so submitted shall be reported by the faculty to the board when its nomination is submitted to the board.

d. "The faculty's nomination shall be presented to the board by the seminary president at the February meeting of the board, and shall be accompanied by a file on the nominee(s) and by a written statement prepared by the faculty [in justification of its nomination]. Members of the faculty who cannot subscribe to this statement shall be expected to present to the board their own written evaluation of the faculty's nominee(s). At this February meeting, the faculty having rendered its report, the Board of Trustees shall decide on the advisability of making an appointment to a professorship, an associate professorship, an assistant professorship, or a lectureship.

e. "When presenting the faculty's nomination, the seminary president shall make specific recommendations concerning rank and tenure to be held by the appointee.

f. "In case the board should wish to add to the list of nominees submitted by the faculty, the proposed addition(s) shall first be presented to the faculty for evaluation.

g. "Having given due consideration to the nominee(s) of the faculty, to the accompanying materials, and to the faculty's evalution of other nominees, and having interviewed the nominees, the board shall make the appointment(s).

h. "The board's appointment to be submitted to synod shall be published twice in the church papers immediately after the February meeting of the board so as to give the church ample time for consideration and expression of possible objections.

i. "The board shall submit the appointment to synod for approval. Synod shall interview the appointee before voting on the appointment. If synod does not approve the appointment, the board shall be asked to submit a new appointment in accordance with the aforesaid procedure. The appointment shall be accompanied by supporting materials.

"The teaching needs occasioned by this interim situation shall be filled by the executive committee of the board in consultation with the seminary faculty until the board can make provision for the vacancy.

j. "When the board is not ready to make a regular appointment, it shall make an interim appointment. These are to be submitted to synod for approval.

k. "A regular appointment shall, as a rule, be for the rank of Assistant Professor.

l. "The seminary faculty shall maintain a complete file of information on possible candidates for seminary teaching positions with a view to providing for long-range as well as immediate needs." (*Acts of Synod 1979,* pp. 69-70)

I. THE OFFICES OF THE CHURCH
B. MINISTERS OF THE WORD (continued)

ARTICLE 21

STUDENT FUND

The churches shall encourage young men to seek to become ministers of the Word and shall grant financial aid to those who are in need of it. Every classis shall maintain a student fund.

Article 21 directs the churches to encourage young men to become ministers of the Word. Such encouragement may be given by word, by teaching and example, and by prayer for the ministry.

The Church Order specificaliy states, however, that encouragement for the ministry of the Word shall be given by financial assistance to those students who are in need of it. Such assistance may be provided by the congregation or the classis.

To assist students for the ministry every classis must have a student fund. These funds are regulated in each classis by a Student Fund Committee.

In 1928 and again in 1942 synod has suggested to the various classes that students who enter the ministry should be exempt from repayment. Student aid should be a gift rather than a student loan if we are serious about encouraging students for the ministry of the Word. (See *Acts of Synod 1942,* pp. 122-24.)

I. THE OFFICES OF THE CHURCH
B. MINISTERS OF THE WORD (continued)

ARTICLE 22

LICENSURE OF STUDENTS

Students who have received licensure according to synodical regulations shall be permitted to exhort in the public worship service.

It should be noted that Article 22 deals only with the licensure of seminary students. The licensure of others is dealt with in Article 43.

1. The Purpose of Student Licensure
   The purpose of licensure is to provide the students with the opportunity to conduct worship services in the Christian Reformed Church as part of their field education program and as part of their required preparation for admission to candidacy for the ministry in the Christian Reformed Church.
   No unauthorized person is allowed to preach and conduct an official worship service in the Christian Reformed Church. Students are authorized by means of a license to exhort. Such licensure is an ecclesiastical matter—the church through the Board of Trustees extends this privilege upon recommendation of the Calvin Seminary faculty. Licensure is designed to aid students in their preparation for the ministry of the Word, and only those aiming at such a ministry should seek licensure.
   All student preaching is under the supervision of the Coordinator of Field Education of Calvin Seminary. Many churches offer the opportunity for students to preach. These requests are handled by the Office of Field Education. These assignments are carefully monitored and evaluated by the seminary faculty, and evaluations of the student's performance are solicited from the congregation in which the service was conducted.
   Students are not permitted to conduct services outside the Christian Reformed Church, unless in each case prior approval of the President of Calvin Seminary has been obtained through the Coordinator of Field Education.

2. Synodical Rules for Licensure of Students (Church Order Supplement, Art. 22)
   a. "The Board of Trustees of Calvin College and Seminary may grant licensure to conduct religious services in our churches only to such as:
      1) "Are enrolled as regular students in our seminary.
      2) "Have successfully passed the final examinations of the junior year in the seminary.

106

b. "The board shall not grant licensure to such students till it has made sure of the following with respect to each applicant:
   1) "That he is a member in good standing in our churches.
   2) "That he has spiritual qualifications necessary for the ministry, and that he considers himself called of God to prepare himself for the office of ministering the Gospel of Jesus Christ.
   3) "That he intends to enter the ministry of the Christian Reformed Church.
   4) "That he has sufficient knowledge of the Bible, and especially of our Reformed principles to act as a guide to others.
   5) "That he speaks acceptably and to the edification of the churches. It is left to the discretion of the board, however, whether it will obtain this information by consulting the seminary faculty or by examining the applicants.
c. "The board has the right to extend the licensure of those who want to take post-graduate work, but with the understanding:
   1) "That this privilege is to be granted only to such who are taking post-graduate work in theology, and declare that it is their definite intention to enter the ministry in the Christian Reformed Church.
   2) "That this extension is valid for no more than one year.
   3) "That further extension may be given at the end of the first year in case the applicant makes his request in writing, and at the end of the second year if he appears in person and is willing to submit to another examination (the latter part of rule 3c does not apply to those who are taking post-graduate work in theology outside of the United States or Canada).
d. "The board is obliged to revoke the licensure:
   1) "Of those who have completed their theological studies but have failed to take steps to enter the sacred ministry of the Word.
   2) "Of those undergraduate students who either discontinue their studies or fail to enroll again at the seminary." *(Acts of Synod 1936,* pp. 46-48)

3. Rules for the Licensure by the Board of Trustees of Foreign Students at Calvin Seminary
   a. The student "must be a communicant member of a sound Reformed Church and must be a regular or special student at our seminary."
   b. The student "must have sufficient training at our school so that the faculty can recommend him both as to his academic competence and ability to speak fluent English."
   c. The student "must have completed the course in homiletics required of our students, or passed an equivalent course in some other school, and must demonstrate his ability to exhort to the satisfaction of our professor in Homiletics.
   d. "The request for licensure must be sent to the secretary of the board.
   e. "The board or its executive committee must interview the applicant.
   f. "The exhorting of the student must be under the auspices of the school; he must not make his own arrangements.
   g. "Licensure will be in force while he is a student at school. Extension of licensure must be made by special application." *(Acts of Synod 1961,* p. 36)

4. Procedure for Obtaining Licensure

When a seminary student is nearing completion of the academic requirements for licensure (usually during the third quarter of the first year of full-time study), the steps to apply for and receive licensure are as follows:

   a. An "Application for Licensure," available from the Office of Field Education, must be filled out and returned to the Coordinator of Field Education.
   b. The Coordinator, in close consultation with the Registrar, presents these requests to the Admissions and Standards Committee with a view to recommending them to the Board of Trustees for licensure.
   c. The Admissions and Standards Committee then presents to the Board of Trustees a list of the students, with their applications, whom the Committee recommends for licensure by the Board.
   d. The Board of Trustees interviews each student who is recommended for licensure, reviews his application, and confers licensure on the basis of a satisfactory application and a favorable Admissions and Standards Committee recommendation and student interview.

5. Policy Governing Students of Other Seminaries Who Wish to Qualify for Candidacy for the Christian Reformed Ministry

The Board of Trustees regulates the fulfillment of the requirements relating to licensure according to the following policy:

   A student who desires to begin fulfilling his field education requirements by being assigned and/or supervised through the Field Education Office of Calvin Seminary while he is still in attendance at another seminary must be pre-enrolled in the Special Program for Ministerial Candidacy in the Christian Reformed Church and must be licensed by the Board of Trustees of Calvin College and Seminary to conduct worship services in the Christian Reformed Church. The admission requirements for pre-enrollment in this Special Program for Ministerial Candidacy are the same as those for admission to candidacy for the M.Div. degree, and the academic requirements for licensure to conduct services are the same as those that apply to students in residence at Calvin Seminary.

6. Licensure by a Classis in Relation to Licensure by the Board of Trustees

With respect to students preparing for the ministry of the Christian Reformed Church synod has declared that although the classes have the right to license persons to speak within their respective domains, it is not in the interest of good order to license students other than those who have studied in our own seminary *(Acts of Synod 1924,* p. 38).

Note: See also under Church Order Article 43.

I. THE OFFICES OF THE CHURCH
C. ELDERS, DEACONS, AND EVANGELISTS

ARTICLE 23

APPOINTMENT, ORDINATION, AND TENURE

a. The elders and deacons shall serve for a limited time as designated by the consistory. As a rule a specified number of them shall retire from office each year. The retiring office-bearers shall be succeeded by others unless the circumstances and the profit of the church make immediate eligibility for reelection advisable. Elders and deacons who are thus reelected shall be reinstalled.

b. The evangelist shall be acknowledged as an elder of his calling church with corresponding privileges and responsibilites. His work as elder shall normally be limited to that which pertains to his function as evangelist. His office will terminate when the group of believers is formed into an organized church.

(Amended—*Acts of Synod 1979*, p. 66)

Elders and Deacons

With Church Order Article 23 we begin the third section of the Church Order dealing with the offices of the church. Section A (Arts. 2-5) dealt with general provisions and Section B (Arts. 6-22) dealt with the ministers of the Word. It is noteworthy that while seventeen articles of the Church Order deal with the office of the ministry of the Word, only three articles (23-25) specifically relate to the offices of elders and deacons.

1. Length of Tenure

Article 23 deals specifically with the tenure of elders and deacons. The Christian Reformed Church has designated in its Church Order that they shall serve "for a limited time as designated by the consistory."

Some Reformed and Presbyterian churches ordain elders and deacons for a lifetime of service. In other churches terms of service are limited, but these office-bearers are not divested of their office and retain some advisory function in the congregation.

The Scriptures do not specifically indicate whether ordination to the offices of the church shall be lifelong or limited in character. No doubt, the fact that those who are ordained into the offices of elder and deacon enter into these callings as an avocation rather than as a vocation, as a part-time assignment rather than as a full-time assignment, has led the church for practical reasons to appoint elders and deacons for a limited time.

Article 23 specifies that the length of tenure in any given congregation shall be designated by the consistory. As a general rule Christian Reformed churches have ordained elders and deacons for a three-year term, although in some churches a two-year term has been established. Each consistory has been left to judge what is best for its own constituency in determining the length of terms for elders and deacons.

One of the factors that ought to enter into the consideration of the consistory is the matter of continuity. A new office-bearer requires several months, as a general rule, for orientation. His term should be lengthy enough so that he is able to build on what he has learned about his responsibility and the congregation in which he serves. In every congregation there are a number of matters which must be followed up and too rapid a changeover of office-bearers makes such follow-up difficult and sometimes impossible.

2. Retirement from Office

In order to maintain a measure of continuity, Article 23 declares that as a rule a specified number of elders and deacons shall retire from office each year. This prevents too large a turnover at any given time, and should provide that a majority of the office-bearers will be retained after each election of new office-bearers.

Synodical regulations require that the term of office of retiring elders and deacons shall not be concluded until the installation of new office-bearers takes place (*Acts of Synod 1912,* p. 61).

3. Eligibility for Reelection

Article 23 indicates that ordinarily when the terms of elders and deacons expire they shall be succeeded by others in their office. This means that they are not immediately eligible for reelection to the office which they relinquish.

The Church Order does, however, recognize that there may be times when for the profit of the church it would be wise to consider a person eligible for reelection without a period of retirement. In such cases an adequate explanation for renomination should be made to the congregation.

The term during which an elder or deacon is not eligible for renomination is not specified in the Church Order. In determining the period of ineligibility, consistories should be careful not to exclude competent office-bearers for lengthy periods of time. Consistories should always seek for men with spiritual gifts and effective leadership qualities for the offices in the church.

4. Reordination

"In order to promote uniformity among our churches, synod declares that the reordination of reelected office-bearers is not only advisable but proper.

"Grounds:

"a) The character of office. Office does not reside in the person, but continues only so long as specified in the regulations.

"b) The call to office. Although this [the call] is of foremost importance, it must be followed by ordination, which implies nothing more nor less than the express

110

regulations between the calling church and the person called in relation to the office to which he is appointed.

"c) The similarity of the various offices in Christ's church. Ministers of the Word when they move from one congregation to another must be reinstalled because the former commission is valid only so long as he serves in that specific congregation."
(*Acts of Synod 1928,* p. 83)

5. Evangelists (Supplement, Art. 23b)

Ordination to the office of evangelist shall not take place until a person has proven his ability to function adequately in the work of evangelism, and has sustained the classical examination for evangelist.

The classical examination required for the ordination of an evangelist shall include the following elements:

a. Presentation of the following documents:
1) A consistorial recommendation from the church in which the appointee holds membership.
2) Evidence (diplomas, transcripts, etc.) of formal general education and of specialized training in biblical theology and evangelism.
3) A copy of his letter of appointment from the church which is requesting his ordination as evangelist.
4) A copy of his letter of acceptance.

b. An oral presentation of a message based upon an assigned text of Scripture, a written copy of which shall be examined by a committee of classis. Special attention shall be given to biblical exegesis. The length of the oral presentation shall be left to the discretion of classis.

c. Examination in the following areas:
1) Knowledge of Scripture
2) Knowledge of Reformed doctrine
3) Knowledge of the Standards of the Church and the Church Order
4) Practical matters regarding Christian testimony, walk of life, relation to others, love for the church, interest in evangelism and the promotion of Christ's kingdom.

When he accepts an appointment to another field, he shall submit to such examination as is considered appropriate by the classis to which his calling church belongs, and he shall be ordained in his new field of labor.

(Supplement, Art. 23b, *Acts of Synod 1979,* p. 67ff.)

The Synod of 1979 adopted a provisional form for the Ordination of Evangelists.

(See *Acts of Synod 1979,* pp. 126, 379-80.)

6. Office of Evangelist for World Missions

The Synod of 1979 adopted the following policy governing the procedures for the ordination of evangelists of Christian Reformed personnel serving in World Missions:

a. "Ordination shall be sought only if the national church related to the CRWM outreach itself recognizes the office of evangelist as described in the Acts of Synod 1978."

b. "The applicant's term of service as evangelist shall agree with the term of service overseas to which he is appointed by CRWM, and may be renewed by mutual consent during each home service. The commissioning church shall also agree to such renewal."

c. "His work as evangelist is regulated by Article VII of the synodically approved mission order and is under the supervision of CRWM. He shall report semi-annually concerning his work to CRWM and his commissioning church."

d. "His work shall be conducted according to the regulations of the field council and national church in the country in which the evangelist labors. If he accepts an appointment to another field, is assigned to work with another national church, or becomes a member of another CRC church, he shall not hold the office of ordained evangelist until he submits to such examination as is considered appropriate by the classis to which his calling church belongs, and he shall be ordained again as stipulated by the Acts of Synod 1978, page 78."

(Acts of Synod 1979, pp. 77-78)

I. THE OFFICES OF THE CHURCH
C. THE ELDERS, DEACONS, AND EVANGELISTS (continued)

ARTICLE 24

MINISTRY OF THE ELDERS AND EVANGELISTS

a. The elders, with the minister(s), shall have supervision over the congregation and their fellow office-bearers, exercising admonition and discipline and seeing to it that everything is done decently and in order. They shall, with the minister(s), exercise pastoral care over the congregation, and engage in and promote the work of evangelism.

b. The evangelist shall minister only to that emerging congregation in which he is appointed to labor.

1) The task of the evangelist is to witness for Christ and to call for a comprehensive discipleship through the means of the preaching of the Word and the administration of the sacraments, evangelism, church education for youth and adults, and pastoral care, in order that the church may be built and unbelievers won for Christ. Any service or assignment beyond his specific field of labor requires the authorization of his consistory and the approval of classis.

2) The evangelist shall function under the direct supervision of the consistory, give regular reports to the consistory, and be present at the meetings of the consistory whenever possible, particularly when his work is under consideration.

3) The evangelist shall have authority to administer the Word and the sacraments in the work of evangelism in the emerging church to which he is called.

(Amended—*Acts of Synod 1979*, p. 66)

ELDERS

It should be noted that Article 24 is closely related to other articles in the Church Order. This article relates to Article 12 which states that the minister, "with the elders, shall supervise the congregation and his fellow office-bearers." It is evident from Article 24 that supervision over the congregation and fellow office-bearers is a task devolving upon all who are called to the office of elder or minister of the Word.

Article 24 is also very closely related to the articles of the Church Order that deal with discipline. Here in Article 24 it is mentioned that the elders with the ministers are responsible for "exercising admonition and discipline."

1. Supervision over the Congregation
   The word *supervision* comes from two Latin words which mean "to look over, or to oversee." It is very much like the New Testament Greek word *episkopos* which generally means "overseer." The function of the elder is to promote the welfare of the church, exercising "pastoral care over the congregation."

2. Maintaining Good Order
   One of the tasks ascribed to elders in Article 24 is "seeing to it that everything is done decently and in order." Accordingly, elders should be familiar with the Church Order, as well as with the rules of classis and consistory.
   Included in this task of maintaining good order are items such as the following:
   — providing an edifying liturgy for public worship
   — maintaining good order in the worship service
   — following sound rules of procedure in consistory meetings
   — keeping and preserving accurate files: minute books, treasurers' records, membership records
   — including all essential elements of the work of the congregation in consistory agendas
   — formulating and following clear rules for committees and functionaries in the congregation
   — dealing with problems in an orderly and Christian manner.

3. Pastoral Care over the Congregation
   Article 24 specifies that the elders "shall, with the minister(s), exercise pastoral care over the congregation." Elders discharge this duty by faithful supervision, loving discipline, and good order.
   The very qualifications by which elders are selected for office indicate how they should perform their pastoral task. They are to be
   "full of the Spirit and of wisdom" (Acts 6:3); "above reproach, the husband of one wife, temperate, sensible, dignified, hospitable, an apt teacher,...manage his own household well,...well thought of by outsiders" (I Tim. 3:2-7); "an example in speech and conduct, in love, in faith, in purity" (I Tim. 4:12); "a model of good deeds" (Titus 2:7). Believers are urged, "Remember your leaders...consider the outcome of their life, and imitate their faith" (Heb. 13:7).
   The work of the elders is not a domineering rule over the flock, but conforms to the charge given by Peter, "So I exhort the elders among you....Tend the flock of God that is your charge, not by constraint but willingly, not for shameful gain but eagerly, not as domineering over those in your charge but being examples to the flock" (I Pet. 5:1-3). Spiritual leadership is the primary responsibility of the elders.

   Note: A more detailed description of the content of the pastoral care by elders is found in Church Order Article 65.

4. Admonition and Discipline
   Elders are called to keep the church of Christ in good order by exercising admonition and discipline in a loving spirit, thereby promoting spiritual health and restoration

when necessary. The entire fourth section of the Church Order (Arts. 78-94) deals with this function in detail.

5. The Work of Evangelism

Evangelism is the work of spreading the gospel. Article 24 calls upon the elders not only to promote evangelism but to engage in it. Within the congregation elders should be active in counseling and in Bible study; and among neighbors they should have a ready witness for their Lord, speaking willingly and eagerly of the blessing of God in Christ Jesus.

6. The Exercise of Authority in the Church

The Synod of the Christian Reformed Church in its study committee Report 44, "Ecclesiastical Office and Ordination" (*Acts of Synod 1973,* pp. 635-716), discusses the nature of authority in the church (see Section III, A, pp. 691-709). Some of the pertinent observations of that report are summarized below:

a. The Image and Likeness of God and Authority

"...the biblical phrase, 'God created man in his own image...' means, among other things, that God made man to represent him. One of the most basic things, therefore, which the creation account teaches us about man is that man is God's representative and, therefore, an authority-bearing creature. This holds true for both 'male and female' (Gen. 1:27)" (p. 692).

"...Man who was made in God's image was also created after God's likeness. ...The way in which man exercises his authority should be a reflection of the way in which God exercises his authority. The Creator-Father is so concerned about the welfare of his creatures that he constantly serves them by providing them with food, water, clothing, and many other gifts (Ps. 147; Matt. 6:25-30; 10:29-31). Divine authority, therefore, is a serving authority. Jesus Christ...[also] fed the hungry, healed the sick, and washed the feet of his disciples. He could therefore say..., 'I am among you as one who serves' (Luke 22:27)" (p. 692).

In our redemption, man is restored to the image of God (see Col. 3:10; Eph. 4:24). "Christ, in other words, came to restore to all believers the office which was once theirs by virtue of creation; namely, the office to serve others and to serve the whole creation" (p. 693).

b. Authority of the Special Offices or Ministries

"The special ministries [of the church] have a double function. On the one hand, they serve to keep the people of God in fellowship with their Lord, and, on the other hand, they help the people of God to fulfill their office to serve each other and the world" (p. 693).

"The special ministries [offices], therefore, have as their goal the equipment and preparation of the entire congregation for service....The special ministries are not an end in themselves and have no importance in and of themselves. They function correctly only when they assist the office of all believers to come to its fullest expression. The authority of the special ministries...is correctly exercised only when it is used for the benefit of those over whom it is exercised" (p. 693).

c. The Only Essential Ruler in the Church
There is only one Ruler in the Church—Jesus Christ. The Greek word *archoon* (meaning "ruler" or "chief") is used to describe Roman and Jewish officials. "But the New Testament knows of no 'ruler of the church'—except Christ to whom all authority has been given (Matt. 28:18) and who is the ruler (*archoon*) of the kings of the earth (Rev. 1:5). The church has no 'authoritarian rulers' in the sense that secular governments and synagogues do. Even Christ is not called the ruler *(archoon)* of the church in the New Testament—though it is acknowledged that he is the head of the church and that all authority in heaven and earth has been given to him" (p. 703).

d. The Special Ministries and the Congregation
"The special ministries . . . may not lord it over the congregation, for they are the servants of the congregation. But neither may the congregation dictate to the special ministries. . . . The special ministries remain subject to the congregation in the sense that the special ministries must fulfill the task of representing Christ under the mandate of the congregation and for its benefit.

"The church, therefore, is neither a hierarchy nor an aristocracy, oligarchy, or democracy. It is rather a 'Christ-ruled brotherhood.' The rule of Christ is represented in the special ministries in order to guarantee the growth of the brotherhood. It is also represented in the office of all believers, as they engage in mutual service and service to the world. At the same time, both the special ministries and the universal ministry remain subject to the rule of Christ, the only Lord of the church" (p. 693).

e. Office-bearers will do well to study the several texts that are spoken of in the study committee Report 44 of 1973, "Ecclesiastical Office and Ordination." It will appear that the primary role of office-bearers is that which is described in the Revised Standard Version of Hebrews 13:7, "Remember your leaders, those who spoke to you the word of God; consider the outcome of their life, and imitate their faith."
The nature and authority of the special offices or ministries is best described by the term *service.* Office-bearers are to be leaders and examples. They do this best when they follow the spirit and example of Christ and are able to say with him, "I am among you as one who serves" (Luke 22:27).

I. THE OFFICES OF THE CHURCH
C. ELDERS AND DEACONS (continued)

ARTICLE 25
MINISTRY OF THE DEACONS

a. The task of the deacons is to administer Christian mercy toward those who are in need, first of all toward those of the household of faith, but also toward the needy in general. In executing this task they shall diligently collect, administer, and distribute monies and other gifts, and shall serve the distressed with counsel and assistance.
b. They shall enable the needy under their care to make use of Christian institutions of mercy.
c. They shall confer and cooperate with diaconates of neighboring churches when this is desirable for the proper performance of their task.
d. They may also seek mutual understandings with other agencies in their community which are caring for the needy, so that the gifts may be distributed properly.

1. The Ministry of Mercy
Article 25 defines the fundamental task of the deacons as administering "Christian mercy toward those who are in need." Their primary task is not to serve as financial directors and bookkeepers for the congregation, but to represent the congregation in the work of Christian mercy.

The church represents Jesus Christ and is the embodiment of his Spirit. Jesus healed the sick, gave sight to the blind, made the lame to walk, and showed compassion on the distressed. The deacons are called upon to lead the church in a similar Christlike ministry of mercy.

It ought to be observed that the focus of the work of the deacons is collecting and distributing money or gifts for the needy. The entire work of the deacons is to be Christlike in reaching the distressed. Along with loving deeds and with gifts of money and assistance, the deacons are called upon to serve the needy with counsel and with assistance, to lead them to see the grace of our loving Savior and to recognize the Lord from whom all blessings flow.

2. The Objects of Mercy
a. The Household of Faith
Article 25a requires deacons to administer Christian mercy "first of all toward those of the household of faith." The deacons, the representatives of Jesus Christ

117

in the church, are to minister to the sick, the needy, the hospitalized, the disadvantaged, the widows and widowers, and all who are in special need in the congregation.

b. The Needy in General
Deacons are also required to administer Christian mercy "toward the needy in general." Just as Jesus' ministry reached to Samaritans and Greeks as well as to Jews, so the church's ministry of mercy must also reach out to those who are not Christians.

3. Institutional Care
Article 25b states that deacons "shall enable the needy under their care to make use of Christian institutions of mercy." When institutional care is necessary, deacons should not wait to be asked for assistance, but should themselves inquire as to what help can be given and the best means of providing assistance.

Several Christian institutions of mercy are listed in the denominational *Yearbook* under the heading "Organizations Accredited by Synod." These provide such services as professional counseling for personal or family problems, psychiatric treatment, treatment of alcoholism, education for retarded or handicapped children, rehabilitation for emotional problems, geriatric services, and the like. Deacons should enlist the resources of the Christian community to help the needy avail themselves of such services.

4. Diaconal Conferences
Article 25c recognizes that the work of the deacons does not end with the local church in which they serve. Since the church is called by the Lord to represent him in a broader community, the Church Order properly directs that our deacons "shall confer and cooperate with diaconates of neighboring churches when this is desirable for the proper performance of their task." Every classis and every region in which our churches are located should be reached with the demonstration of the love of Christ in diaconal service.

In 1962 synod established the Christian Reformed World Relief Committee (CRWRC). Its purpose is to reach out in the name of Christ to a needy world stricken with disaster, hunger, or poverty. CRWRC also carries on a number of long-range programs to assist needy people economically, physically, and spiritually. In every area of our church there ought to be strong diaconal conferences working closely with the CRWRC. (See *Acts of Synod 1962,* pp. 106-107, 333-336, for a copy of the Constitution of the CRWRC; also *Acts of Synod 1977,* pp. 55-56, 311-312; *Acts of Synod 1978,* pp. 71-72 for revisions.)

5. Community Involvement
In most areas there are other community benevolence agencies which are sponsored by other denominations, governmental agencies, or volunteer groups. Article 25d encourages deacons to work cooperatively with such agencies "so that the gifts may be distributed properly." Deacons should be aware of what such agencies are doing, and assist them when possible as part of the church's ministry "toward the needy in general."

Accordingly, at every meeting of the deacons there should be at least three items on the agenda:

a. Congregational benevolence—The deacons are the representatives of Jesus Christ and of the church in ministering to the sick, the needy, the hospitalized, the disadvantaged, the widows and widowers, and all who are in special need. They minister not only with funds but also with counsel, with compassion, with prayer, and with encouragement.

b. Community benevolence—The church is called to be the light of the world, demonstrating the love of Christ. It must always be aware of the needy in our community and the opportunity that Christ gives us to minister to these needy. The ministry of Jesus always blended the aspects of loving deeds and words of grace.

c. World relief projects—Our denominational ministries reach places of disaster and difficulty where no local diaconate can reach alone. Discussion of the projects of world relief and ways of assisting in denominational benevolence are the business of the deacons of every congregation.

In connection with the problem of world hunger, the Synod of 1978 made several decisions relative to the responsibility of deacons in world relief projects:

Synod affirmed "that in today's shrinking world the nature of the deacons' responsibilities is international in scope, and that offerings for world benevolence are as necessary as offerings for local benevolence."

Synod instructed the CRWRC "with the assistance of other denominational agencies, along with local deacons and diaconal conferences, to sponsor conferences and workshops on world hunger throughout the denomination."

In the grounds for the above decisions on world hunger, synod noted that "as the world has become one small, international community, and as the benevolent needs of our local churches have been taken over more and more by our government, our deacons' responsibilities have broadened to the national and international needs evident today. The diaconate is an effective means the church may use to alleviate hunger abroad." *(Acts of Synod 1978,* pp. 82-83)

II. THE ASSEMBLIES OF THE CHURCH
A. GENERAL PROVISIONS

ARTICLE 26

ASSEMBLIES

The assemblies of the church are: the consistory, the classis and the synod.

Article 26 begins the second of the four major divisions of the Church Order, *The Assemblies of the Church.* The word *assembly* as used in Article 26 denotes a meeting of the special office-bearers of the church or churches to conduct the business delegated to them.

1. Three Assemblies
   Article 26 specifies three assemblies of the church:
   a. Consistory
      The consistory is the official assembly of the congregation, and is composed of the minister(s), elders, and deacons of a local church. The consistory must meet at least once a month. (See Church Order Art. 36.)
   b. Classis
      The classis is the official assembly of a group of neighboring congregations. It is constituted by two official delegates (a minister and an elder) from each congregation, and ordinarily meets every four months. (See Church Order Art. 39.)
   c. Synod
      The Synod of the Christian Reformed Church is the official assembly representing the churches of all the classes, made up of four delegates (two ministers and two elders) from each of our thirty-eight classes. Synod meets once each year. (See Church Order Art. 45.)

2. Responsibility of the Assemblies
   The assemblies of the church represent Christ in leading local, regional, and denominational efforts to serve Jesus Christ in the world. Their responsibility is to undertake deliberations and enact such legislation or adjudication as may be necessary for the unity of the church, the furtherance of the work of Christ, and the building up of the membership of Christ's body.
   It is worth noting that the congregational meeting is not listed as an official assembly of the church.

120

II. THE ASSEMBLIES OF THE CHURCH
A. GENERAL PROVISIONS (continued)

ARTICLE 27

AUTHORITY OF ECCLESIASTICAL ASSEMBLIES

a. Each assembly exercises, in keeping with its own character and domain, the ecclesiastical authority entrusted to the church by Christ; the authority of consistories being original, that of major assemblies being delegated.
b. The classis has the same authority over the consistory as the synod has over the classis.

1. The Nature of Authority in the Church
   Article 27a indicates that the assemblies of the church exercise "the ecclesiastical authority entrusted to the church by Christ."

   a. Ecclesiastical
      All authority in the church is "ecclesiastical"—it is limited by the nature of the church as the body of Christ. The Bible speaks of various other types of authority, such as the authority of parents over their children and the authority of rulers and judges over a nation. Each type of authority must be exercised within its own sphere and in accord with its own structural purposes.

   b. Entrusted by Christ
      The first principle of all ecclesiastical authority is the headship of Christ. The mandates he gives to his church are based upon Christ's own authority, as the Lord himself indicates in Matthew 28:18-20: "All authority in heaven and on earth has been given to me. Go therefore and make disciples of all nations, baptizing them..., teaching them to observe all that I have commanded you; and lo, I am with you always...."
      The church has no authority other than that of Christ. He is the Lord of every member of the church and the director of the use of every gift and ministry. The assemblies and ministries (offices) are to carry out his will and purpose in the church. He has made some "apostles, some prophets, some evangelists, some pastors and teachers, for the equipment of the saints, for the work of the ministry, for building up the body of Christ, until we all attain to the unity of the faith and of the knowledge of the Son of God, to mature manhood, to the measure of the stature of the fulness of Christ" (Eph. 4:11-13). The essential authority of the church is to make the church what Christ calls it to be.

121

Christ rules his church by his Word and Spirit. Each member, each special office, and each assembly is called upon to build up the body of Christ to fully represent him and do his work, so that in all things his purposes may be accomplished in and through his church.

2. The Authority of Each Assembly
Every member, office-bearer, and assembly exercises only the authority committed to the church by Christ. In accord with Church Order Article 27a each assembly exercises its own peculiar authority "in keeping with its own character and domain": the consistory in relation to the congregation, the classis in matters relating to its several congregations, and the synod for the denomination as a whole.

3. Original and Delegated Authority
Article 27a states that the authority of consistories is original and that of the major assemblies is delegated. Each congregation as a unit is a complete expression of the body of Christ. Congregations are the basic units of the church, comprising all of its members in a given community of faith.

In the local congregations the consistories are called upon under the authority of Christ to build up his body for his honor and service.

To express and maintain the broader unity of the church and to reach out beyond the local boundaries, our consistories (minor assemblies) unite in broader (major) assemblies which we call classes. The churches of the classes (as minor assemblies) unite in a still broader (or major) assembly which we call the synod of the church.

4. The Relative Authority of Assemblies
Each consistory is called by Christ to build his body for his work. Ministering to and with the members of the church constitutes the basic or original mandate of Christ to the church. The major assemblies have only such authority as is delegated to them by the minor assemblies. The limitations of the work of major assemblies are prescribed in Article 28a.

5. Authority of Major and Minor Assemblies
In matters that are properly the province of a major (broader) assembly, the Church Order declares that the major assemblies have authority over the minor assemblies—the classis has authority over the consistory, and the synod has authority over the classis.

In an early decision relating to a disturbance in a local congregation, synod declared that the classis had a right to act in the matter since the classis is above the consistory and it not only may but must concern itself when there are difficulties in a congregation and the problem is legally brought before the classis (*Acts of Synod 1877*, p. 177).

6. Disciplinary Authority of Assemblies
In a case involving deposition of a consistory by a classis the Synod of 1926 judged that the authority which assemblies exercise in the name of Christ is *also* of a disciplinary nature *(Acts of Synod 1926*, pp. 141-142).

II. THE ASSEMBLIES OF THE CHURCH

A. GENERAL PROVISIONS (continued)

ARTICLE 28

MATTERS LEGALLY BEFORE ASSEMBLIES

a. These assemblies shall transact ecclesiastical matters only, and shall deal with them in an ecclesiastical manner.
b. A major assembly shall deal only with those matters which concern its churches in common or which could not be finished in the minor assemblies.
c. Matters referred by minor assemblies to major assemblies shall be presented in harmony with the rules for classical and synodical procedure.

1. Ecclesiastical Matters

Article 28a specifies that the work of the assemblies is limited to ecclesiastical matters. The New Testament indicates many tasks which Christ has assigned his church, such as the ministry of the Word and sacraments, worship, education, works of benevolence, the exercise of discipline, the furtherance of the communion of the saints, and other activities which pertain to the church.

Although Christian people have a responsibility to serve the Lord in all spheres of life—physical sciences, education, political life, art, business, etc.—these are not to be regarded as ecclesiastical matters. Synod has declared that "political, social, and economical questions are ecclesiastical matters only when doctrinal and ethical issues of sufficient moment and magnitude are involved according to the Word of God and our standards." When it follows this fundamental principle, the church will not "invade the rights of the state, nor erase the boundary between our duty as a church institute and the duty as Christian citizens" (*Acts of Synod 1937,* p. 11).

When Article 28a demands that matters be dealt with "in an ecclesiastical manner," it generally means according to ecclesiastical procedures (cf. Art. 28c).

A significant commentary on the meaning of the phrase "ecclesiastical matters" was made by Dr. H. Bouwman in his book *Gereformeerd Kerkrecht,* Vol. II, pp. 41-47, as follows:

"Only ecclesiastical matters are to be transacted at the ecclesiastical meetings. Worldly, economical, and political, society matters must not be dealt with anymore than scientific questions at these assemblies. Under Roman hierarchy all kinds of non-ecclesiastical matters were decided at the synod. The Roman Councils could do this by reason of their principle that the church had authority over

123

all spheres of life and that the entire life, art, science, state and commonwealth were subservient to the church.

"The Reformer, however, pointed out that the state, the home and politics each had their own sphere of life, given it by God. Therefore, according to Calvin, the church must cease to be patron of the natural life, and be nothing else but a gathering of believers. And from that principle must follow for the practical life of the church that at the ecclesiastical assemblies only ecclesiastical matters should be dealt with.

"The meaning of the Reformer has always been, that those cases which do not belong to the task of the church, should not be treated at the ecclesiastical meetings. The church has no right to that. She misses the capability as church to pronounce a judgment in cases pertaining to state, society, science, art, etc.

"The task of the church pertains to things sacred. She has the calling to let the Word of God shine upon the natural life and to inspire her members, that they, each in their own office and calling, conduct themselves according to God's Word, in order that the ordinances of God in every sphere of life are followed, but the church must not endeavor to *rule* in the sphere of the natural life."

(Quoted in the *Acts of Synod 1972,* p. 660)

2. Matters to Be Dealt With by the Major Assemblies

Article 28b says that "a major assembly shall deal only with those matters which concern its churches in common or which could not be finished in the minor assemblies."

a. Matters of Common Concern

Projects and programs which can be carried on by the minor assemblies should be done by these assemblies and not by the major assemblies. A consistory should not ask classis to do work which the consistory is capable of doing, and a classis should not ask synod to do work which could be done by the classis.

However, there are many matters which our consistories delegate to classis because they concern all the churches of classis in common. Likewise classes delegate many matters to synod because they concern all the churches of the denomination.

For example, the churches have delegated to synod such matters as domestic and world missions, radio ministry, church education, publications, world relief, and many other denominational programs. Most of these tasks are carried on by synodically approved boards or standing committees which report to and are responsible to synod.

b. Matters Which Could Not Be Finished in Minor Assemblies

All matters should be carried as far as possible in minor assemblies in accord with the Rules for Synodical Procedure. Matters such as appeals from the decision of a minor assembly (a consistory or classis) necessarily call for adjudication by a major assembly. Matters which the churches and/or classes have in common must also by their very nature be referred to the major assembly.

Minor assemblies must make a complete study before referring matters to a major assembly. In a concrete case synod refused to consider a request of a classis and noted that a classis should not be relieved of its responsibility to study a matter before requesting a study by synod. (Cf. *Acts of Synod 1975,* pp. 103-104; *1976,* pp. 52-53.)

3. Classification of Materials for Synod

APPEALS—An appeal is an official procedure by which a case, or decision, is brought from a lower to a higher assembly for rehearing. (Cf. Church Order Art. 30.)

COMMUNICATIONS—A communication is a document presenting information, ideas, thoughts, or opinions for consideration of the assemblies.

GRAVAMEN—A gravamen is a formal complaint, grievance, or question pertaining to the doctrinal standards of the church.

The Synod of 1976 declared that gravamina fall into two basic types:

"1) A *confessional-difficulty gravamen:* a gravamen in which a subscriber expresses his personal difficulty with the confession but does not call for a revision of the confessions, and

"2) A *confessional-revision gravamen:* a gravamen in which a subscriber makes a specific recommendation for revision of the confessions."

(Acts of Synod 1976, p. 68)

OVERTURES—An overture is a formal proposal sent by a minor assembly requesting the legislation or judgment of the major assembly.

PROTESTS—A protest is a declaration of disapproval made to an assembly expressing a complaint or objection to a decision or course of action followed by that assembly. In distinction from an appeal a protest requires no further action by the assembly.

REPORTS—A report is a document of a board, committee, or agency of synod indicating the work performed in response to assembly mandates and presenting recommendations to the assembly for future mandates or projects.

REQUEST FOR REVISION—A request for revision is a document addressed to the assembly making the decision on the basis of grounds which are new and sufficient for reconsideration. (Cf. Church Order Art. 31.)

4. Rules of Procedure

According to Article 28c, in order to be legally before assemblies each item of business must meet the stipulations of the rules of procedure.

a. Consistorial Rules

Each consistory should adopt its own rules of procedure. These rules should be in accord with the Word of God, the articles of the Church Order, and the decisions of the Synod of the Christian Reformed Church.

Suggestions for Consistorial Rules of Order are presented in the handbook for Christian Reformed Churches—"Your Church in Action," which is supplied to all of our consistories.

Copies of suggested Rules for Consistories are also available from the office of the Stated Clerk of Synod.

b. Classical Rules

Each classis should also adopt its own rules of order. Most of our classes have adopted and published rules of order and procedure in accord with the Church Order and synodical decisions. These rules generally use the Rules for Synodical Procedure as a model.

c. Synodical Rules

Synod has adopted rules pertaining to matters legally before it. The Rules for Synodical Procedure were adopted by the Synod of 1952 and amended by subsequent synods. References to these rules are included in this manual under pertinent articles of the Church Order.

5. Matters Legally Before Synod (adopted by the Synod of 1952 and amended by subsequent synods) (Supplement, Art. 28)

a. Reports

Reports of committees, including boards, appointed by previous synods.

b. Overtures and Communications

"Overtures or communications of individuals or Consistories or Classes, on matters which have been carried *as far as possible* in the minor assemblies."

(Acts of Synod 1959, p. 23)

c. Appeals or Protests

Appeals or protests of consistories or individual members who cannot yield to classical decisions and who have given notice of such appeals or protests to the classes concerned.

The following rules shall pertain in all matters of appeal and protest *which concern persons,* and not their views on issues and programs:

1) "The appellant or protestant shall submit notice and copies of all appeals and protests to the ecclesiastical bodies and/or persons concerned, in time for them to submit their response for consideration by synod.

2) "Appeals and protests to synod must be in the hands of the Stated Clerk by March 15. Allowance shall be made, however, for protests and appeals with reference to actions occurring too late to meet this deadline.

3) "The appellant and the defendant shall have the right to appear before the advisory committee of synod to be heard, and shall be expected to indicate whether and when they will so appear.

4) "The appellant and the defendant shall have the right of hearing the case on the floor of synod and they shall have the privilege of explaining and defending their position on the floor of synod, if synod so decides, upon the recommendation of the advisory committee.

5) "The appellant and the defendant shall have the right to be represented by a spokesman.

6) "The advisory committee shall present a clear and adequate statement of the content of each appeal to the entire synod.

126

7) "Copies of the protests and appeals not appearing in the Agenda, and, if possible, the principal related documents, shall be sent to the pre-appointed synodical advisory committee as soon as possible."

(Acts of Synod 1971, pp. 30-31)

Note: These rules do not pertain when the Judicial Code has been invoked. In the latter procedure the cases of both the complainant and the respondent must be processed according to the rules for the Judicial Code (see Supplement, Art. 30).

d. Appeals of Rejected Overtures
Overtures or communications which have failed to gain the endorsement of classis but which the consistory or individual sponsoring the same desire to submit for synod's consideration.

e. Belated Overtures
Overtures or communications of individuals when they have been unable first to present them to consistory and classis. Such matters shall be received as information, provided that the Stated Clerk of Synod receives evidence that it was impossible for the communicant to present his matter to consistory and classis. Synod shall decide whether it shall act upon such matters received as information.

f. Informative Communications
"Synod urges our assemblies and members to refrain from overtures, appeals, or communications which are repetitious, or mere expressions of agreement or disagreement with matters already on the agenda of synod.

"Synod authorizes the Stated Clerk to omit such items from the printed agenda at his discretion. In such cases they shall merely be listed and accepted as informative communications. The senders shall be notified and their materials shall be given to one of the advisory committees of synod to be received as information. Matters received as information will not ordinarily be mentioned in advisory committee reports or the Acts of Synod." *(Acts of Synod 1971,* p. 46-47)

g. Late Reports and Overtures
No study reports received by the Stated Clerk after February 15 nor overtures received after March 15 shall be considered for decision by synod, with the exception of overtures which deal with matters relevant to reports found in the printed Agenda. Any other overture or study report shall be considered only by special decision of synod on the basis of the most weighty grounds. (See *Acts of Synod 1957,* p. 28; *1974,* p. 41.)

h. The Printed Agenda
The Agenda shall be published not later than April 10. It shall include reports of standing or special committees, overtures of classes or consistories, appeals of classes or consistories, notices of appeals of individuals, the names of delegates, and pertinent announcements. All such material shall be in the hands of the Stated Clerk not later than the deadlines: February 15 for the reports of the stand-

ing committees, study committees, and authorized representatives; ten days after conclusion of board meetings for board reports; and March 15 for overtures and appeals (*Acts of Synod 1974,* p. 41).

i. Supplementary Reports
The Back to God Hour Committee, the Board of Trustees of Calvin College and Seminary, the Board for Christian Reformed World Missions, the Christian Reformed Board of Home Missions, the Board of Publications of the Christian Reformed Church, the Christian Reformed World Relief Committee, and the Synodical Interim Committee are permitted to file a supplementary report after March 15. These boards are urged to incorporate as much of their materials as possible in the printed agenda, and matters for the supplementary reports must be held to the lowest possible minimum.

j. Other Matters
All other matters may be considered which synod by a majority vote declares acceptable.

k. Speakers Representing Agencies
"Agencies receiving denominational support shall not ordinarily send speakers to synod in view of the fact that these agencies have opportunity to make their needs known through our denominational representatives, may prepare exhibits for synod, may consult advisory committees, and may serve their causes better through appeals directly to our congregations." *(Acts of Synod 1972,* p. 14)

II. THE ASSEMBLIES OF THE CHURCH
A. GENERAL PROVISIONS (continued)

ARTICLE 29

THE CHARACTER OF ASSEMBLY DECISIONS

Decisions of ecclesiastical assemblies shall be reached only upon due consideration. The decisions of the assemblies shall be considered settled and binding, unless it is proved that they conflict with the Word of God or the Church Order.

1. "Reached Only upon Due Consideration"
   Decisions of ecclesiastical assemblies pertain to the well-being of the church of Christ. They should, therefore, not be made lightly nor hastily but should be given careful consideration. Our ecclesiastical assemblies must be deliberative assemblies. They should take time for discussion of important issues. Delegates should give careful thought and seek to obey the Word of God with the leading of the Holy Spirit.

2. Decisions Are "Settled and Binding"
   This double statement should be of great value for the church. When decisions have been reached after careful and prayerful consideration, they should be considered settled and binding. It is unsettling and divisive for the same issues to be raised in the church without weighty grounds.
   Article 29 indicates, however, that there are two exceptions to the rule above: "unless it is proved that they conflict with the Word of God or the Church Order." The Word of God is the basic authority given by Christ for the faith and life of the church.
   If "due consideration" is given, the decisions of the assemblies should be in accord with the Word of God and the Church Order. The assemblies, however, are not infallible. If it appears that a decision is not in accord with the Word of God or the Church Order, the members of the church and the minor assemblies should present overtures or appeals for the rectification of the decision reached by an assembly.
   It should be noted, moreover, that when Article 29 speaks of decisions being in accord with the Word of God or the Church Order, God's Word and the Church Order are in no sense placed on a par. The Scripture is God's infallible Word, but the Church Order is a vehicle of organization for decency and good order in the church and should be amended whenever the profit of the church so indicates.
   Article 29 should not be construed as an argument against change in the Church

129

Order. Article 86 of the historic version of the Church Order (prior to synodical revision of 1965) stated:

"These articles, relating to the lawful order of the church, have been so drafted and adopted by common consent, that they (if the profit of the church demand otherwise) may and ought to be altered, augmented or diminished."

The fact that the Church Order may and ought to be altered when the profit of the church so demands in no way diminishes the binding character of the Church Order. Former Article 86 stated further that "no particular congregation" or "classis... shall be at liberty to" make alterations in the articles, but they shall show "all diligence in observing them, until it be otherwise ordained by the general synod."

The intent of Article 29 is clearly to protect the unity of the church and denominational integrity as over against independentism and congregationalism.

3. Declarations of Synod

In 1975 synod clarified the use and function of synodical pronouncements on doctrinal and ethical matters and their relations to the confessions:

"a. The Reformed Confessions are subordinate to the Scripture and accepted "as a true interpretation of this Word" (Church Order, Art. 1). These confessions are binding upon all of the office-bearers as is indicated by their subscription to these confessions in the Form of Subscription. These confessions are binding upon all confessing members of the church as is indicated by their public profession of faith.

"b. Synodical pronouncements on doctrinal and ethical matters are subordinate to the confessions, and they 'shall be considered settled and binding, unless it is proved that they conflict with the Word of God or the Church Order' (Church Order, Art. 29). All office-bearers and members are expected to abide by these synodical deliverances.

"c. The confessions and synodical pronouncements have nuances of differences. They differ in the extent of their jurisdiction, in the nature of their authority, in the distinction of purposes, in the measure of agreement expected, and in their use and function.

"d. The use and function of synodical decisions are explicitly or implicitly indicated by the wording of the particular decision itself:

"1) When a synodical pronouncement is set forth as an interpretation of the confession, this is its use and function.

"2) When a synodical decision involves pronouncements that are related to the confessions or go beyond the confessions, the use and function of such decisions is to further express the faith of the church without such statements thereby becoming additions to the confessions.

"3) When a synodical decision involves adjudication of a certain issue, this is its particular use and function although the decision may have doctrinal and ethical implications for the future.

"4) When a synodical decision is expressed in the form of a testimony or letter, this is its use and function.

"5) When a synodical decision is expressed as a guideline for further study or action, this is its use and function.

"6) When a synodical decision is set forth as pastoral advice to churches or individuals, this is its use and function." *(Acts of Synod 1975,* p. 44)

II. THE ASSEMBLIES OF THE CHURCH
A. GENERAL PROVISIONS (continued)

ARTICLE 30

APPEALS

a. Assemblies and church members may appeal to the assembly next in order if they believe that injustice has been done or that a decision conflicts with the Word of God or the Church Order. Appellants shall observe all ecclesiastical regulations regarding the manner and time of appeal.
b. When written charges requiring formal adjudication by an ecclesiastical assembly are made, the relevant provisions of the Judicial Code shall be observed.

(Amended—*Acts of Synod 1977*, p. 55)

1. Appeals—Article 30a

   a. The Right of Appeal
      Article 30a provides that "assemblies and church members may appeal to the assembly next in order" for one of three reasons: if it is believed that "injustice has been done," or that "a decision conflicts with the Word of God or the Church Order." This rule provides members and assemblies the right of appeal from the decision of a minor assembly (a consistory or a classis).

      Church members who have legitimate reason for appealing the decision of the consistory should address their appeal to the classis. Individuals as well as consistories who for good reason wish to appeal the decision of classis should address their appeal to the synod.

      It should be noted that Article 30 deals only with appeals of decisions made by minor assemblies. Since synod is the broadest judicatory, requests for a change or reversal of a synodical decision are not technically appeals but requests for the revision of a decision. Such requests must be dealt with according to the provisions of Article 31.

   b. The Elements of an Appeal
      Appeals should contain at least the following elements:
      1) The name of the appellant.
      2) The name of the body against which the appeal is being made.
      3) The decision which is being appealed (in exact wording if possible).

132

4) The reason why the appealed decision is believed to be wrong.

5) Background information which will enable the assembly to make a proper decision.

6) A statement defining clearly what action the appellant desires the assembly to take.

c. Proper Procedure

   1) Article 30a declares that "all ecclesiastical regulations regarding the manner and time of appeal" must be observed (as stipulated in remarks on Article 28).

   2) Synod has ruled that classes must consider all appeals legally before them *(Acts of Synod 1916,* p. 44).

   3) Synod has ruled that a copy of an appeal or protest must be sent to the assembly or body from whose decision the appeal is made (*Acts of Synod 1936,* p. 92). The assembly must also furnish a copy of its decisions to the appellant upon request. (Cf. Judicial Code of Rights and Procedures, Art. 6 and 14.)

d. Time Limit for Appeal

   No time limit has been officially set by synod for appeals to be made. Long standing practice (following the practice and rule of the Gereformeerde Kerken) has been that an appeal must be made to the first following meeting of the assembly appealed to. The phrase of Article 30a ("to the assembly next in order") has this meaning. It is used consistently by the Church Order Revision Committee (1950-1965), and in one of its proposed readings the phrase was used in the following context: "...he shall have the right to protest to the assembly next in order, or, *regarding decisions by the general synod, to the next general synod" (Acts of Synod 1958,* p. 396).

c. The Status of Matters under Appeal

   There is no rule in our church requiring that matters remain in *status quo* upon appeal; each concrete case must be decided on its own merits. The well-being of the church may demand that action proceed in spite of the appeal. *(Cf. Acts of Synod 1930,* p. 191.)

2. Judicial Code of Rights and Procedures

   Article 30b provides for proper processing of appeals "when written charges requiring formal adjudication by an ecclesiastical assembly are made." The rules for the application of Article 30b are set forth in the Judicial Code of Rights and Procedures.

   a. Characteristics of Judicial Code Procedure—Article 30b

      The Judicial Code provides for:

      1) *Written* charges and responses

      2) *Rights* of representation and hearing

      3) *Specification* of charges

133

  4) Description of proper judicial proceedings
   a) For consistory
   b) For classis
   c) For synod
  5) Synodical Adjudication Procedure
   a) A standing advisory committee between synods (Judicial Code, Art. 24)
   b) Final judgment by synod

 b. Grounds for the Judicial Code
  The 1977 Synod adopted the following grounds for the adoption of Article 30b, and the Judicial Code of Rights and Procedures:
  1) "The Judicial Code will encourage greater uniformity of procedure throughout our denomination when charges must be adjudicated.
  2) "The Judicial Code will help to insure just treatment of those who are involved in the judgments and decisions of the church.
  3) "Scripture requires that provisions be made to provide impartial judgments among God's people. (Cf. Deut. 1:16-17; Deut. 16:18-20; Lev. 19:15; I Tim. 5:19-21.)
  4) "Article 28 of the Church Order requires that the assemblies of the church deal with ecclesiastical matters in an ecclesiastical manner. Without effective procedural guidelines it is often difficult to deal with substantive issues in an appropriate manner.
  5) "The Judicial Code provides a procedural pattern within which the law of love may be fulfilled. (Cf. James 2:1, 8, 9.) 'My brethren, show no partiality as you hold the faith of our Lord Jesus Christ, the Lord of glory.' 'If you really fulfill the royal law according to the scripture, "you shall love your neighbor as yourself," you do well. But if you show partiality, you commit sin, and are convicted by the law as transgressors' (RSV)."

                  (Acts of Synod 1977, pp. 53, 54.)

 c. Text of the Judicial Code
  The complete text of the Judicial Code follows:

JUDICIAL CODE OF RIGHTS AND PROCEDURES
(Supplement, Article 30)

PREAMBLE TO THE JUDICIAL CODE

 The Judicial Code is not a document of broad applicability. It is intended to be operative in a narrow area, and therefore it contains limiting language. It states that its provisions apply *only:*
 a. in a judicial hearing;
 b. when such a judicial hearing is conducted by a consistory, classis, or synod; and
 c. when written charges requiring formal adjudication are filed.
 The key provision is the last one: there must be written charges that require formal adjudication. The first determination that must be made by the consistory or other

assembly before whom written charges are filed is this: Does this matter require formal adjudication?

In making this determination the consistory or other assembly would ordinarily be in a position to know that spiritual means have or have not been fully utilized. If such means have not been exhausted the assembly should seriously consider postponing the judicial hearing while further informal efforts are employed.

The assembly thus decides whether and when it will hear the matter. The Judicial Code gives guidance: it states that matters of admonition and discipline *do not* require a judicial hearing unless there are written charges which the assembly determines require formal adjudication.

The Judicial Code thereby gives expression to the fundamental and primary role of spiritual means in all matters of admonition and discipline; it recognizes that these matters are best handled by informal counseling and entreaty; and if sanctions are required, it leaves their determination to the church under the Church Order.

A. SCOPE
Article 1

a. These provisions apply to judicial hearing before a consistory, classis or synod occasioned by the bringing of written charges requiring formal adjudication. Such admonition and discipline of the church as does not involve the hearing of written charges requiring formal adjudication are not governed by these provisions.

b. Written charges requiring formal adjudication, whether brought by an individual against an individual or an assembly, or by an assembly against an individual or an assembly, may refer only to alleged offenses in profession or practice against the Word of God, the confessions of the church, or the Church Order.

c. The individual or assembly filing a charge against another individual or assembly shall be called a *complainant* and the individual or assembly against whom the charge is filed shall be called a *respondent*.

d. When the assemblies of the church conduct hearings, they act in a judicial capacity.

B. JUDICIAL RIGHTS
Article 2

Both the complainant and the respondent, if they are individuals, shall have the right to be represented or counseled by a member of the Christian Reformed Church in any judicial hearing.

Article 3

Both the complainant and the respondent shall have the right to be present at each original hearing and hearing on appeal provided for herein, except when the assembly withdraws to decide the issues raised by the hearing.

Article 4

The respondent and complainant shall have the right to have witnesses examined in their presence, except when the respondent fails to appear after due notice.

Article 5

A party against whom a judgment is entered shall have the right to appeal that judgment to the assembly next in order.

135

C. CHARGES

Article 6

A charge, in order to receive a judicial hearing, must be presented to the assembly in writing, must set forth the alleged offense and must specify the facts relied upon to sustain the charge. Such specification shall declare, as far as possible, the time, place and circumstances of the alleged offense and shall be accompanied with the names of the witnesses and the titles of the documents to be cited in its support. A copy of the charge shall be transmitted promptly to the respondent by the clerk of the assembly.

Article 7

A charge shall not allege more than one offense. Several charges, whether brought by one or more complainants against the same individual or assembly, with the specifications under each of them, may, however, be presented at the same time and may, at the discretion of the assembly, be heard together. When several charges are heard at the same time, a decision on each charge must be made separately.

Article 8

a. No charge may be filed for an alleged offense which occurred more than five years prior to the date on which the charge was filed.

b. A hearing for an alleged offense shall begin no later than one year from the time the charge is filed.

D. ORIGINAL HEARING PROCEDURES BEFORE A CONSISTORY ACTING IN ITS JUDICIAL CAPACITY

Article 9

All hearings shall be conducted in a consistent Christian manner. A consistory composed of the elders and deacons, while acting in its judicial capacity, shall be so constituted as to avoid conflicts of interest. The administration of oaths shall not be required.

Article 10

The assembly shall in its judicial capacity determine whether or not the written charges are substantial, requiring formal adjudication. The complainant may appear before the assembly concisely stating his* charge and supporting evidence, whereupon the assembly shall determine whether to constitute a formal hearing.

The hearing, if ordered, shall proceed as follows:

a. The complainant shall repeat concisely his charge and his supporting evidence. The presiding officer may permit the form of the charge to be amended, but not its content.

b. The presiding officer shall request the respondent to plead to the charge, and his plea shall be recorded.

c. If the respondent pleads guilty, the hearing need not be continued. If the respondent denies the charge, the hearing shall proceed.

d. The respondent shall state concisely his defense and his supporting evidence.

e. The complainant shall first produce his evidence and witnesses. The respondent shall then produce his evidence and witnesses. All witnesses may be questioned by both the complainant and the respondent.

---

*When the pronoun "his" is used herein, it refers either to an assembly or an individual, irrespective of gender.

f. The complainant and the respondent shall, in turn, summarize their cases either by oral or written argument.

g. If either party objects to the regularity of the proceedings, the objection must be entered in the record. The presiding officer may sustain or disallow the objection. In any case he must be sustained by a majority of the consistory.

Article 11

If in any case the respondent, after due notice has been given him, shall refuse or neglect to appear at the time and place set forth for the hearing, the investigation or hearing may proceed in his absence. In all cases sufficient time shall be allowed for the respondent to appear at the given place and time to prepare for the hearing. The consistory shall decide what constitutes "sufficient time."

Article 12

The final decision on any case shall be by majority vote of the consistory. Members who have not attended all the sessions and have not heard the case in its entirety shall read the record before a vote is taken.

Article 13

During the hearing, the presiding officer shall not comment on the merits of the case. This restriction does not apply when the consistory enters its final deliberations. After a decision has been reached, the presiding officer shall certify and announce the findings.

Article 14

The testimony shall be recorded verbatim if requested by any party to the proceedings. The record, including all exhibits, papers, evidence, and findings in the case shall be certified by the presiding officer and shall be the basis of any appeal which may be taken. The appellant and respondent may have reasonable access to the record.

E. HEARING AND APPEALS PROCEDURES BEFORE
A CLASSIS ACTING IN ITS JUDICIAL CAPACITY

Article 15

If a consistory is the respondent, the original hearing shall be before the classis and in accordance with the hearing procedures set forth in Article 10.

Article 16

In all cases of appeal to the classis from the consistory, the appellant shall within thirty days after the decision of the consistory give notice of appeal to the stated clerk of classis and to the consistory whose decision is appealed. Within the next thirty days, or such extension as the classis may authorize, the appellant shall furnish to the stated clerk of classis a written statement of the grounds of his appeal. The clerk of the consistory shall thereupon forward to the stated clerk the record referred to in Article 14. The hearing in the classis shall be limited to the grounds set forth in the statement and record.

Article 17

An appeal by an involved party shall not be heard in any case when the appellant has without just cause failed or refused to be present at his hearing on appeal.

Article 18

The right to appeal shall not be affected by the death of the person entitled to such right. His heirs or representative may continue to act in his behalf.

Article 19

If the appellant desires to introduce additional evidence, and shows good cause for it, the classis may receive the evidence or remand the case to the consistory for a rehearing.

Article 20

In all cases the classis shall set a time for the hearing on appeal and send a notice as to the time and date of such hearing to all parties. After the statement and record have been considered and oral arguments concluded, the classis shall withdraw and shall thereupon consider and decide the issues of the case. The final decision on any case shall be by majority vote of the classis. Delegates who have not attended all the sessions and have not heard the case in its entirety shall read the record before a vote is taken. The classis may sustain or reverse in whole or in part the decision of the consistory, or it may return the case to the consistory with instructions for a new hearing.

Article 21

Appeal of the decision of classis may be made to synod. Such an appeal must be made within thirty days after the decision of classis. When such an appeal is made a written notice together with a statement of grounds of appeal shall be sent to the Stated Clerk of Synod and a copy thereof to the stated clerk of classis. The stated clerk of such classis shall thereupon transmit the decision of classis together with the record and papers of the case to the Stated Clerk of Synod, who will place the appeal on the agenda of synod.

F. HEARING AND APPEAL PROCEDURES BEFORE THE SYNOD ACTING IN ITS JUDICIAL CAPACITY

Article 22

Appeal of decisions of assemblies of the church acting in their judicial capacity, and such other matters requiring formal adjudication as synod shall undertake, shall be referred to the Synodical Advisory Committee on Protests and Appeals for consideration and advice.

Article 23

a. The Protests and Appeals Committee advising a given synod shall be appointed by the preceding synod. Approximately half the members shall be lay persons.

b. Any member of the Protests and Appeals Committee advising a given synod may be, but need not be, a delegate to that synod.

Article 24

a. Matters within the jurisdiction of the Protests and Appeals Committee shall be referred to it at any time after its members have been appointed.

b. The Protests and Appeals Committee shall meet between synods as frequently as its business requires, and normally shall convene a week before synod to prepare its recommendations.

c. As to appeals from decisions of consistories and classes, the Protests and Appeals Committee shall permit complainants and respondents to present arguments before it.

d. As to other matters requiring formal adjudication which synod shall undertake, the Protests and Appeals Committee shall follow the hearing procedures described herein.

Article 25

Recommendation of the Protests and Appeals Committee shall be presented to the synod in writing, shall be accompanied with grounds, and shall be openly discussed in plenary session of synod.

Article 26

Synod may dispose of a judicial matter in one of the following ways:

a. By deciding the matter;

b. By referring it to one of its committees for settlement or reconciliation;

c. By remanding it with advice to the appropriate classis or consistory; or

d. By conducting its own hearing.

Article 27

If synod conducts its own hearing it shall follow the hearing procedures set forth herein.   (*Acts of Synod 1977,* pp. 48-54)

II. THE ASSEMBLIES OF THE CHURCH
A. GENERAL PROVISIONS (continued)

ARTICLE 31

REQUEST FOR REVISION OF A DECISION

A request for revision of a decision shall be submitted to the assembly which made the decision. Such a request shall be honored only if sufficient and new grounds for reconsideration are presented.

1. The Intent of This Article
   Article 31 deals with a request for revision of a decision of an assembly initiated *after* the meeting of the assembly. It refers only to decisions reached by previous assemblies of consistories, classes, or synods.

   a. Not to Be Confused with Appeals
      An *appeal* is an official procedure by which a case, or decision, is brought from a lower to a higher assembly for rehearing. A *request for revision* is a document addressed to the assembly making the decision on the basis of grounds which are new and sufficient for reconsideration.

      The procedure for making an *appeal* is dealt with in Article 30; the procedure for making a *request for revision* is dealt with here in Article 31.

   b. Not to Be Confused with Revisions during the Meeting
      Article 31 is not to be confused with the procedural course to be followed *during* the sessions of an assembly. Synod has adopted the following rules for altering a decision during the course of the meeting of synod (consistories and classes often follow the same procedure):
      "Motions to Bring Matters Once Decided Again Before Synod
      "If any member of synod for weighty reasons desires reconsideration of a matter once decided, the following course may be pursued:
      "1) A motion may be offered to *reconsider* the matter. The purpose of this motion is to propose a new discussion and a new vote.
      "2) A motion may be made to rescind a previous decision. The purpose of this motion is to annul or reverse such a previous decision. (Rescinding applies to decisions taken by the synod in session; it does not apply to decisions taken by previous synods. A succeeding synod may alter the stand of a previous synod; it may reach a conclusion which is at variance

140

with a conclusion reached by an earlier synod. In such cases the most recent decision invalidates all previous decisions in conflict with it.)"

(Rules for Synodical Procedure, VIII, H)

2. "The Assembly Which Made the Decision"
Article 31 preserves the right of decision for each assembly by stipulating that "a request for revision of a decision shall be submitted to the assembly which made the
decision."

Revisions of a decision of a consistory can be made only by the consistory which
made the decision, not by another consistory or classis or a synod. Likewise the decision of a classis can only be revised by that classis. Revisions of a decision made by
synod can only be made by a synod, not by any consistory or classis.

3. Revision of Decisions of Minor Assemblies
If an individual, or a consistory, wishes to have a minor assembly (consistory or
classis) alter or reverse its decision, a request for revision of the particular decision
may be submitted to that assembly. If the minor assembly does not believe that there
are new or sufficient grounds for reconsideration, or for any other reason does not
grant the request for revision, an appeal may be made to the major assembly (classis
or synod) in accord with the rules in Article 30.

4. Revision of Decisions of Major Assemblies
A request for revision of a decision of a major assembly is subject to all the rules pertaining to matters legally before that major assembly. One such requirement is that
decisions must be studied and processed as far as possible in the minor assemblies.
For example, a request for revision of a synodical decision must be studied and processed as far as possible in the consistory and classis before submission to the synod.

The reasons for processing requests for revision in the minor assemblies before
sending them on to the next major assembly are:

a. To Refine and Clarify the Matter
The minor assemblies serve to refine and clarify matters that are sent on to the
assembly next in order. This is true of overtures and appeals and is also true of requests for revisions of previous decisions. The processing of overtures, appeals,
and requests for revision serves to remove misunderstandings or problems and
helps to avoid unnecessary and ambiguous materials on the agenda of the major
assembly.

b. To Receive Further Information from the Delegates
Requests for revision of decisions of major assemblies should be presented to the
minor assemblies in order that further information and light on the matter may be
given by the consistorial or classical delegates who were present at the meeting of
the major assembly.

c. To Test the Validity and Weight of New Grounds
Article 31 states that "such a request shall be honored only if *sufficient and new
grounds for reconsideration* are presented." The requirement of Article 31 is that

141

a request for revision of a previous decision of a major assembly must contain new elements and bear sufficient weight. Just as overtures and appeals must be processed through the minor assemblies, so also requests for revision must be processed through the minor assemblies so that these assemblies may have opportunity to test the validity of the new elements and the weight of the grounds that are being presented. If errors or misconceptions can be eliminated by minor assemblies, the interest of the major assemblies will be served in accord with Article 28b which states that "a major assembly shall deal only with those matters...which could not be finished in the minor assemblies."

II. THE ASSEMBLIES OF THE CHURCH
A. GENERAL PROVISIONS (continued)

ARTICLE 32
PROCEDURE AND ORDER IN ASSEMBLIES

a. The sessions of all assemblies shall begin and end with prayer.

b. In every assembly there shall be a president whose duty it shall be to state and explain the business to be transacted, and to see to it that the stipulations of the Church Order are followed and that everyone observes due order and decorum in speaking. There shall also be a clerk whose task it shall be to keep an accurate record of the proceedings. In major assemblies the above named offices shall cease when the assembly adjourns.

c. Each assembly shall make proper provision for receiving communications, preparing agenda and acts, keeping files and archives, and conducting the financial transactions of the assembly.

d. Each assembly shall provide for safeguarding of its property through proper incorporation.

1. Prayer at Assemblies

The Church Order in Article 1 recognizes that Christ is the head of the Church. Article 32a emphasizes the dependence of the church on Christ. It stipulates that *each session* of every assembly "shall begin and end with prayer."

2. Officers of Assemblies

Article 32b mentions the two officers which all assemblies have in common, a president and a clerk.

a. The Responsibilities of the President
1) Presiding
a) The president serves as chairman of the assembly meetings. Each assembly should adopt its own rules for procedure, including rules of parliamentary order. The president shall see to it that all these rules are properly observed.
b) It is the responsibility of the president, and the vice-president when called upon, to be thoroughly versed in the Church Order, the assemblies' rules of procedure, and the rules of parliamentary order.
c) The chairman is called upon "to see to it that the stipulations of the Church Order are followed and that everyone observes due order and decorum in speaking."

2) Clarifying

The chairman must also "state and explain the business to be transacted." It is essential to good order that when any matter before the assembly is discussed, the motion on the floor be made clear. The president of the assembly should not accept any motion made by a member unless the member has clearly stated the motion and the entire assembly understands its precise meaning. After a motion has been made and supported and discussed, the president should once again state the motion very clearly before a vote is taken.

Nothing is more discouraging in terms of procedure than a meeting in which good order does not prevail. It is the president's responsibility to see that motions are properly placed before the assembly and that long discussions without motions are avoided. Meetings not properly chaired are apt to be unduly long and, worse still, inefficient and divisive.

b. The Responsibilities of the Clerk

The responsibilities of the clerk of the assembly is to keep "an accurate record of the proceedings." The clerk is responsible for recording the motions before the assembly and the precise action taken by the assembly with respect to these motions. The records of the proceedings of all the meetings of the assemblies are called *minutes*.

c. Termination of Office

Article 32b states that in major assemblies the offices of the president and the clerk "shall cease when the assembly adjourns." In the case of consistories the above rule does not hold. In consistories the president and the clerk along with other officers are generally chosen for a one-year term. The reference of Article 32b is to the clerk of particular sessions of the assembly and not to the stated clerks of classis or synod.

d. Other Officers

Other officers of the assemblies are dealt with in connection with the specific articles of the Church Order dealing with the various types of assemblies: the consistory (Art. 36), the classis (Art. 40), and the synod (Art. 46).

3. Proper Provision for Conducting Business

Article 32c specifies four matters which require the attention of each assembly for which proper provision must be made.

a. Receiving Communications

Each consistory has a responsibility to give careful consideration to every communication which is placed before it. All letters that are officially addressed to the consistory and are properly in order should be presented to the entire consistory either by the reading of the communication or, better still, by duplicating the material for the officebearers who are members.

A distinction must be observed between proper and official communications and those which may come as circulars or advertisements.

b. Preparing the Agenda

When an assembly meets it should have before it an agenda properly prepared by a designated person. This agenda should be printed, or written out, and should be in the hands of the office-bearers of the assembly and, if possible, in the hands of all members of the assembly.

Sample agendas for general consistory meetings, elders' meetings, and deacons' meetings are contained in Your Church in Action,'' the handbook for the consistories of the Christian Reformed Church. The format of an agenda should be adopted for each meeting of office-bearers, and blanks may well be left for the officers to fill in at each individual meeting, so that no matters are omitted.

c. Preparing Minutes or Acts

It has been noted in Article 32b that it is necessary to keep an accurate record of the proceedings of each assembly. After each meeting the records kept by the clerk must be accurately recorded or transcribed, and printed or written legibly so that an accurate file of all of the work of the assembly may be maintained. The minutes of each meeting must be approved at the next meeting. The minute book should be available for reference at every meeting.

d. Files and Archives

The Church Order calls for the careful retaining of files and archives by each assembly. This includes the careful filing of all matters pertaining to membership, previous decisions, communications and responses, and all other matters that may have bearing upon the future work of the assembly. The archives in every case should include the complete minutes of all of the assemblies with which a congregation is united: minutes of the consistory, the minutes of classis, and the *Acts of Synod.*

In order to keep the records, files, and archives of a consistory, study must be given by each consistory as to the kind of filing system that is to be set up. Someone should be appointed to retain this filing system in good order, and all the archives should be available to the members of the consistory when information is sought.

On a denominational level, synod has appointed a Historical Committee which collects and preserves a wide variety of documents and memorabilia of historical value. Minutes of consistories and classes are duplicated on microfilm and preserved in Heritage Hall at Calvin College. Synod urges "the united cooperation of all the churches and office-bearers with the committee and its representatives in the pursuit of its goals" *(Acts of Synod 1977,* p. 21).

e. Financial Transactions of Assemblies

1) Accurate Records

Each assembly is responsible for retaining an accurate record of all of its financial transactions. This record should include all income for the assembly as well as an accurate listing of the nature of every expenditure. In each

145

assembly a budget should be adopted and all expenditures should be made in accord with the rules adopted by the assembly within the framework of its budget.

2) Miscellaneous Decisions
Our churches through synod have adopted several decisions pertaining to the financial transactions of our assemblies. These are contained in the commentary on Article 62.

3) Bonding Policy
Synods from 1948 to 1953 instructed all of its agencies and committees to be properly bonded. The Synod of 1977 adopted "as policy that all denominational boards, agencies and committees which receive denominational funds and all accredited causes must give clear evidence that they are bonded in accordance with the guidelines" of synodically recommended amounts. Synod declared that " 'Honesty Bond Coverage' commensurate with each fund's potential for loss is simply good business practice and in keeping with the principles of good stewardship" *(Acts of Synod 1977,* p. 123).

4) Tax Exemption Certification
The Synods of 1975 and 1976 have urged all of our United States classes and congregations "to comply with the rules of the Internal Revenue Service by obtaining their own Federal Identification Number and giving written authorization requesting their inclusion under our denominational group exemption in accord with the rules of the United States Department of Internal Revenue" *(Acts of Synod 1975,* p. 85; see also *1976,* 46, B, 4, p. 43).

Federal Identification Numbers of our congregations in the United States and in Canada are listed in the annual Yearbook of the Christian Reformed Church.

In keeping with Church Order Article 32d every congregation should safeguard its status, its property, and the exemption privileges of its donors by compliance with the laws regarding tax exemption certification.

4. Incorporation of Assemblies
Church Order Article 32d provides that each assembly shall provide for the safeguarding of its property through proper incorporation.

a. Congregational Incorporation
1) Form for Incorporation of Congregations
The Synod of 1963 decided that certain basic articles should be included in a complete form of incorporation of congregations proper for their local state or province *(Acts of Synod 1963,* pp. 50-52.).

The decision of 1963 was reviewed, augmented, and amended in 1970 when synod adopted a form, including the basic elements which should appear in the incorporation of each congregation. This form should be used by each consistory and adapted by its attorney to meet the requirements of the state or province in which the congregation is located.

Copies of the form of incorporation are available in the office of the Stated Clerk of synod.

2) Church Visitors

Synod requested all classes "to instruct their Church Visitors to review the matter of proper incorporation with each church in harmony with the decisions above" (*Acts of Synod 1963*, p. 52).

3) Schism within a Local Congregation

The synodically approved Articles of Incorporation of Congregations of the Christian Reformed Church refer in Article 7 to "schism." The Synod of 1970 adopted the following definition of schism:

" 'A schism is deemed to exist when a dispute has arisen between two or more groups of members of the church with respect to the interpretation and application of the Bible, the official Creeds, and the Church Order of the Christian Reformed Church, which has resulted in:

a) a decision of synod, (in response to an appeal) followed by

b) the departure and withdrawal of membership of at least 15 percent or 25 (whichever is the least) of the confessing members of the church, who

c) cause the incorporation or other establishment in accordance with the laws of jurisdiction under which this church is incorporated as a church which continues in existence and is administered as a church for a period of one year after its incorporation or other establishment. (See *Acts of Synod 1967*, p. 668.)

"Grounds:

" 'a) The ruling adopted by the synod of 1963 leaves the decision as to which of the contending parties is true to the Creeds and the Church Order of the Christian Reformed Church to the judgment of the civil magistrates.

" 'b) When members of the Church of Christ challenge each other before the courts with respect to the ownership of temporal possessions, the name of Christ is dishonored on their account. (See I Cor. 6:1ff.)'

"Recent court decisions have declared that the civil courts cannot make decisions in regard to differences of opinion over doctrine and/or church government."

(Acts of Synod 1970, pp. 106, 476-483)

b. Denominational Incorporation

1) Christian Reformed Church Synod Trustees

In 1965 synod decided to incorporate itself or its Synodical Committee to serve as a depository for devolution of church assets in the event of dissolution. The Articles of Incorporation were adopted by the Synod of 1969 and the incorporation was completed in 1970.

The Synod of 1972 authorized the Synodical Interim Committee to make the necessary revisions in the Articles of Incorporation so that the entire

147

Synodical Interim Committee might serve as the Christian Reformed Church Synod Board of Trustees. The above change was effected and the Synod of 1973 noted that the entire Synodical Interim Committee now comprises the Christian Reformed Church Synod Board of Trustees.

The Articles of Incorporation and By-Laws of Christian Reformed Church Synod Trustees are contained in the *Acts of Synod 1969,* pp. 424-428.

2) Christian Reformed Church in North America

In 1974 the Synodical Interim Committee, as corporate trustees of the Christian Reformed Church Synod Trustees, reported to synod that the need for a blanket coverage for our congregations and classes, and the needs of our Pension Committee's status have made it imperative to restructure our incorporation status so that we will be fully recognized and meet the demands of the Internal Revenue Service for classification under Section 501 (c) (3) of the United States Revenue Code, as amended. Accordingly, synod approved the Articles of Association and the By-Laws of the Christian Reformed Church in North America and authorized the Synodical Interim Committee to complete the incorporation procedures and application for group exemption ruling. (See *Acts of Synod 1974,* pp. 49, 396, 407-410.)

The Christian Reformed Church was legally incorporated in the State of Michigan on July 29, 1974 *(Acts of Synod 1975,* pp. 85, 378, 379).

The Articles of Association and By-Laws of the Christian Reformed Church in North America, adopted in 1974, were amended in 1977. (See *Acts of Synod 1977,* pp. 124-125.)

ARTICLES OF ASSOCIATION
OF
THE CHRISTIAN REFORMED CHURCH IN NORTH AMERICA

We, the undersigned, desiring to become incorporated under the provisions of Act No. 327, Public Acts of 1931, as amended, do hereby make, execute, and adopt the following Articles of Association, to-wit:

First, The name assumed by this corporation and by which it will be known in law, is The Christian Reformed Church in North America.

Second, The location of said church or society shall be in the City of Grand Rapids, County of Kent, and State of Michigan.

The address of the initial registered office is:

2850 Kalamazoo Avenue, S.E., Grand Rapids, Michigan 49560

The name of the initial resident agent at the registered office is:

William P. Brink.

Third, The time for which said corporation shall be created shall be perpetual.

Fourth, The members of said church or society shall worship and labor together according to the discipline, rules, and usage of The Christian Reformed Church, as from time to time authorized and declared by synod.

Fifth, The Corporation is a nonprofit ecclesiastical corporation organized and operated exclusively for religious and charitable purposes within the meaning of Section 501 (c) (3) of the United States Internal Revenue Code of 1954, as amended.

The purposes of the corporation are the following:

A. To proclaim the gospel of the Lord Jesus Christ through the churches of the denomination, its agencies and boards.
B. To promote the principles and teachings of the Holy Bible, as interpreted by the Reformed Creeds, namely, The Belgic Confession, The Heidelberg Catechism, and The Canons of Dort, in the churches of the denomination.
C. To fulfill the scriptural mandate enunciated by Jesus Christ in Mark 16:15 to "go ye into all the world and preach the gospel to every creature," by actively supporting and promoting Christian missions through the churches of the denomination, classical home mission programs, and synodical agencies and boards for home missions and world missions.
D. To extend mercy and help to those in distress by reason of natural catastrophe and disaster, illness, old age, poverty, unemployment, and war, through synodical and classical agencies and the churches of the denomination.
E. To train members of the denomination to be ministers of the gospel, missionaries, and lay workers in the service of the church and society; to provide for the financial support and security of ordained and unordained personnel of the churches of the denomination, and synodical and classical agencies and boards.
F. To receive funds directly and/or through offerings in the churches for the support of the activities, agencies, functions, and programs of the denomination and/or for the purpose of supporting and contributing to religious, charitable, and educational organizations exempt from taxation under Section 501 (c) (3) of the United States Internal Revenue Code of 1954, as amended.
G. To conduct a literature ministry for the production and distribution of Christian periodicals and writings, Sunday school materials, and other publications needed to carry out the religious and charitable objectives and purposes of the corporation.
H. To do all other lawful acts and things necessary to fulfill the mandate and mission of the Christian Reformed Church in North America as determined by synod.

Sixth, In the event of termination, dissolution, or winding up of this corporation in any manner or for any reason whatsoever, its remaining assets, if any, shall be conveyed or distributed to, and only to, one or more organizations which qualify as exempt organizations under Section 501 (c) (3) of the Internal Revenue Code, as may be determined by synod.

IN WITNESS WHEREOF, we, the parties hereby associating for the purpose of giving legal effect to these Articles, hereunto sign our names and places of residence.

BY-LAWS OF
THE CHRISTIAN REFORMED CHURCH IN NORTH AMERICA
Preamble

Believing that all things should be done decently and in order, we hereby adopt the following By-Laws for the regulation, management, and government of this corporation, to-wit:

Article I
Objectives and Purposes of Corporation

The Corporation is organized and operated exclusively for religious and charitable objectives and purposes within the meaning of Section 501 (c) (3) of the United States Internal Revenue Code of 1954, as amended. The general religious and charitable objectives and purposes of the Corporation shall be those stated in the Fifth Paragraph of the Articles of Association of the Christian Reformed Church in North America.

Article II
The Basis

The basis of this corporation is the Holy Bible which we believe, confess, and declare to be the inspired and infallible Word of God, and our only rule for faith and practice.

Article III
Forms of Unity

The church, as an ecclesiastical organization and legal corporation, together with its members, and its supporting members and assemblies, accepts, believes, and is bound by the Form of Subscription to the following named Reformed Creeds as a true interpretation of the Holy Bible, to-wit:

The Belgic Confession
The Heidelberg Catechism
The Canons of Dort

Article IV
Church Government

The Ninety-Six Articles of the Church Order, adopted by the Synod of the Christian Reformed Church on June 16, 1965, and which are incorporated herein by reference, and any revision thereof, and synodical regulations and mandates, shall regulate the ecclesiastical organization and operation of the denomination in its corporate expression and form.

Article V
Members

The members of the corporation are the delegates duly elected from time to time to the synodical assembly of the church, pursuant to the Church Order and/or synodical regulations. Each delegate shall continue to hold the office of member of this corporation until his successor has been chosen and the next synodical assembly has been duly convened and constituted.

Article VI
Meetings of Members

The members of the corporation shall meet in annual session as the Synod of the Christian Reformed Church at a time and place designated by the previous synod.

Special meetings of the members may be called by the convening church with the approval of the Synodical Interim Committee, pursuant to the Church Order.

Article VII
Notice of Meetings

Notice of any annual and/or special meeting of the members of the corporation shall be given in the official publications of the church at least fifteen (15) days prior to the date of said meeting.

Article VIII
Supporting Members; Meetings

All members of the churches of the denomination are supporting members of the denomination and of this corporation.

All members of each church entitled to vote shall meet annually for the purpose of conducting such business as is presented by the consistory. Special meetings of the members may be called by the consistory.

Article IX
Supporting Assemblies; Their Jurisdiction and Meetings

The supporting assemblies of the denomination are the following: the consistory and the classis.

The jurisdiction of the consistory is exercised in the local church of which it is the governing body.

The jurisdiction of the classis is exercised in the geographical district in which its constituent churches and congregations are located and over which it has been appointed, pursuant to synodical regulations.

The consistory and the classis shall meet from time to time as prescribed by the Church Order.

Article X
Synodical Interim Committee

The Synodical Interim Committee shall have such authority, duties, and responsibilities as are prescribed by the Church Order and synodical regulations and decisions.

Whenever it is necessary that the denomination deal with or report to any governmental authority or agency, the Synodical Interim Committee shall be the Board of Trustees of the corporation for all legal purposes.

Article XI
Officers of Synodical Interim Committee

The Synodical Interim Committee at its first meeting following the adjournment of synod shall elect a president, vice president, and recording secretary.

The Denominational Stated Clerk shall be the secretary of the Synodical Interim Committee.

Article XII
Stated Clerk

The office of Stated Clerk of the denomination is hereby established.

Synod shall appoint the Stated Clerk.

The Stated Clerk shall have such authority, duties, and responsibilities as are prescribed by synod.

Article XIII
Denominational Financial Coordinator

The office of Denominational Financial Coordinator is hereby established.

Synod shall appoint the Denominational Financial Coordinator.

The Denominational Financial Coordinator shall have such authority, duties, and responsibilities as are prescribed by synod.

Article XIV
Operation Provisions

The fulfillment of the objectives and purposes of the corporation as stated in Article I shall be through the functioning of such agencies and divisions, to be composed of such members, staff, and directors, to perform such functions and to have such authority, duties, and responsibilities, all as provided and prescribed by synod from time to time.

Article XV
Corporate Property

All property of the corporation, real and personal, shall be devoted to the objectives and purposes of the corporation as stated in Article I, and shall be subject to the control, management, and supervision of synod when in session; when synod is not in session the Synodical Interim Committee shall act for synod, pursuant to synodical direction, with the assistance and cooperation of the Stated Clerk and Denominational Financial Coordinator.

Article XVI
Amendments to Articles of Association and By-Laws

The members of the corporation meeting in synodical assembly may alter, amend, or repeal the Articles of Association and/or the By-Laws, by majority vote in the manner provided by law. (*Acts of Synod 1974*, pp. 407-410; *1977*, pp. 124, 125)

II. THE ASSEMBLIES OF THE CHURCH
A. GENERAL PROVISIONS (continued)

ARTICLE 33
ASSEMBLY COMMITTEES

a. The assemblies may delegate to committees the execution of their decisions or the preparation of reports for future consideration. They shall give every committee a well-defined mandate, and shall require of them regular and complete reports of their work.

b. Each classis shall appoint a classical interim committee, and synod shall appoint a synodical interim committee, to act for them in matters which cannot wait action by the assemblies themselves. Such committees shall be given well-defined mandates and shall submit all their actions to the next meeting of the assembly for approval.

1. Committee Functions

Article 33a provides for the appointment of committees to assist the assemblies in two kinds of work:

a. "The Execution of Their Decisions"

Some decisions require continuing attention and are therefore assigned to permanent committees (customarily called "standing committees"). Other decisions require only temporary attention and are therefore assigned to temporary committees (usually called "study committees" or "ad hoc" committees).

Consistories often have standing committees for such functions as Worship, Education, Evangelism, Finance, Building, and other on-going projects of the congregation.

Classes also assign work to standing committees such as the Home Missions Committee, the Student Fund Committee, and others which may be necessary.

On the synodical level, the assembly appoints committees (Boards and Standing Committees) to carry out its decisions. These include such agencies as the Back to God Hour, the Board of Publications, the Board of Trustees of Calvin College and Seminary, the Board for World Missions, the Board of Home Missions, the World Relief Committee, the Chaplain Committee, the Church Help Committee, Interchurch Relations, and others (totaling twenty-one agencies in 1980). In addition, there are numerous synodical "study committees."

b. "The Preparation of Reports for Future Consideration"

Assembly committees exist to implement past decisions and to propose future action by the assembly. Both standing committees and study committees perform these functions.

2. Mandates and Reports
Article 33a also requires the assembly to "give every committee a well-defined mandate" and to "require of them regular and complete reports of their work."

   a. "Well-defined Mandates"
   Each committee should have, in writing, a clear and specific mandate, so that it will know exactly what it is authorized to do.

   b. "Regular and Complete Reports"
   The assembly retains responsibility for and supervision of the work assigned to committees, thus maintaining the system of representative control practiced in the Reformed system of church government. For this reason each committee is required to report regularly and completely, recognizing that its work is subject to the approval or disapproval of the assembly.

3. Committee Membership
   a. Synodical Rules for Study and Standing Committees
      1) All study committees shall be appointed by the Committee on Appointments for approval by synod.
      2) All administrative standing committees shall be elected from nominations presented to synod.
         Standing committees in which vacancies must be filled shall present multiple nominees for election rather than a single name for appointment.
      3) All secretaries of administrative standing committees as well as stated clerks of classes shall present their nominations by June 1 to the Stated Clerk, who will submit these nominations to the Committee on Appointments.
      4) The Committee on Appointments shall prepare a ballot of nominations for synod on which space is reserved for nominations from the floor *(Acts of Synod 1952,* p. 111).
      5) The Committee on Appointments shall report throughout the sessions of synod.
      6) A person whose work is regulated by a board shall not be delegated to that particular board *(Acts of Synod 1966,* p. 87).
      7) Synodical board and committee members who have served two three-year terms shall not be eligible for reelection.
      8) The terms of office of classical representatives to our denominational boards and committees begin and terminate on September 1 of the year of appointment or termination *(Acts of Synod 1972,* p. 14).
      9) Synod requests all classes, when nominating members of denominational boards or committees, to designate the term of the alternate to coincide with the term of the delegate. When an alternate replaces a delegate, or when a new delegate is nominated by a classis, the term of office shall begin the year a delegate assumes the office and shall terminate on September 1 three years later *(Acts of Synod 1973,* p. 19).

10) Synod has exempted the Bible Translation Committee from the six-year tenure rule listed above.

(Cf. Rules for Synodical Procedure, Section VI, B, 4.)

b. Synodical Advice to the Churches re Committee Membership
Synod urged the churches "to make all possible use, within biblical guidelines and the restrictions of the Church Order, of the talents and abilities of women in the work of the church" (*Acts of Synod 1976,* p. 47).

Synod encourages our classes "to make more use of the talents of their non-ministerial members by assigning them to various committees, boards and functions" (*Acts of Synod 1971,* p. 21).

4. Interim Committees
Article 33b requires that each classis, as well as synod, shall appoint an "interim committee." The general rules for these committees are:
a. They are "to act for them [classis, synod] in matters which cannot wait action by the assemblies themselves."
b. They "shall be given well-defined mandates."
c. They "shall submit all their actions to the next meeting of the assembly for approval."

5. Synodical Interim Committee
a. Corporate Board of Trustees
The Synodical Interim Committee also functions as the Corporate Board of Trustees of both the Christian Reformed Church in North America and the Christian Reformed Church Synod Trustees.

b. Liaison with Government
"Whenever it is necessary that the denomination deal with or report to any governmental authority and agency, the Synodical Interim Committee shall be the Board of Trustees of the corporation for all legal purposes" (Articles of Association, By-Laws, Article X).

c. Rules Governing the Synodical Interim Committee
The Synodical Interim Committee is governed by the following rules:

I. MEMBERSHIP
The Synodical Interim Committee shall be composed of fourteen (14) members, elected by synod from nominations submitted by the Synodical Interim Committee. Synod has the right to add to the nominations presented by the Synodical Interim Committee.
A. One-half of the Synodical Interim Committee shall be ministers and one-half non-ministers who are or who have previously served as office-bearers in the church. The terms shall conform to the synodical rules which apply.
B. The alternate member will take the place of the regular member when a member moves outside his area or is incapacitated. The terms of the alternate shall conform to the synodical rules which apply.

155

 C. Each of the following regions shall be represented as follows:
  1. Far West (United States)—two
  2. Western Canada—one
  3. Rocky Mountain to Mississippi River—two
  4. Central United States—six
  5. Eastern Canada—two
  6. East Coast—one

II. OFFICERS: The Synodical Interim Committee shall elect its own officers, with this exception: that the Stated Clerk shall function as general secretary of the Synodical Interim Committee.

III. MEETINGS: The Synodical Interim Committee shall meet at least three times a year: in October, February, and May.

IV. ORGANIZATION: The Synodical Interim Committee shall designate at least two subcommittees from within its membership (including alternates):
 A. Church Polity and Program
 B. Finance

V. CORPORATE FUNCTION
The Synodical Interim Committee shall function as the Corporate Trustees of Synod.
 A. Christian Reformed Church Synod Trustees—All members of the Synodical Interim Committee shall serve as the Christian Reformed Church Synod Trustees. (See *Acts of Synod 1972, Supplement*—Report 50, pp. 614-615, and Article 11, B and C, pp. 13-14.)
 B. The Christian Reformed Church in North America—The members of the Synodical Interim Committee shall serve as the Board of Trustees of the Christian Reformed Church in North America.
  1. The incorporation Christian Reformed Church in North America is certified by the State of Michigan, and group exemption under the Internal Revenue Code 501 (c) (3) is approved for the denomination and all of its boards and committees along with the classes and congregations in the United States who have obtained Federal Identification Numbers and have given written authorization requesting their inclusion (*Acts of Synod 1975,* Article 86, p. 85).
  2. The title of the Denominational Building is held by the Christian Reformed Church in North America. The trustees are also charged with the financing and management of the Denominational Building. (Cf. *Acts of Synod 1974,* Article 43, VII, pp. 38-39, 388-89; and *Acts of Synod 1975,* Article 86, pp. 85, 379-80, 395.)

VI. Mandate
 A. The Synodical Interim Committee shall execute all matters committed to it by definite instruction of synod.
 B. The Synodical Interim Committee shall execute all synodical matters which cannot be postponed until the next synod.
 C. The Synodical Interim Committee shall supervise the work of the Stated Clerk

and the Denominational Financial Coordinator, and advise them in respect to the discharge of their work.

D. The Synodical Interim Committee shall be responsible for expediting the work which synod does directly.

E. The Synodical Interim Committee shall be responsible for promoting the planning, coordinating, and the setting of priorities of programs by each of the synodical agencies and by all of them together, in keeping with synodical guidelines, and shall serve synod with periodic analyses and overall reviews of programs and resources of the denomination after consultation with the agencies.

F. The Synodical Interim Committee shall receive regular financial and program reports from the agencies of synod and approved by synod so that it can evaluate budget requests in the light of current projects and future goals and make appropriate recommendations to synod. Any new organization requesting support must first submit to the Synodical Interim Committee a statement of its aims and goals, and be approved as to program (*Acts of Synod 1973*, p. 20).

G. The Synodical Interim Committee shall be responsible for the preparation and distribution of the *Synodical Agenda,* the *Acts of Synod,* the *Yearbook,* and such other official publications as synod shall authorize.

H. The Synodical Interim Committee shall prepare for synod an annually updated survey of minister's compensation to be distributed to all consistories for their guidance as a supplement to the Guidelines for Ministers' Salaries adopted by the Synod of 1970.

I. The Synodical Interim Committee shall be responsible for administering the denominational master address list in keeping with the instructions of synod.

J. The Synodical Interim Committee shall be available for consultation with standing committees and denominational agencies.

K. The Synodical Interim Committee shall present a full report of its actions to each synod.

VII. PROGRAM PLANNING, COORDINATION, AND SETTING OF PRIORITIES

With respect to program planning, coordination, and setting of priorities by the synodical agencies, synod decided:

A. To instruct the SIC to formulate, in consultation with each of the agencies, a set of guidelines to be used by each agency for analyzing its own mandate and programs.

Grounds:

1. A common set of guidelines is necessary for pinpointing areas of overlapping and inefficiency.
2. The guidelines have to reflect the individuality and specific function of each agency.
3. The SIC is the logical instrument to formulate such guidelines.

B. To instruct each of the synodical agencies

1. To engage in a thorough analysis of its mandate, programs, finances, and

office operations, in keeping with the formulated guidelines and according to a mutually agreed upon schedule;

2. To keep the SIC regularly and fully informed on the progress of this analysis;

3. To engage, upon the completion of the analysis, in a joint evaluation of it with the SIC; and

4. To keep the SIC regularly and fully informed on both the need for and progress in program coordination with other agencies, and to seek the SIC's services whenever needed.

   Grounds:

   a. There is a continuing need for coordinating the work of the synodical agencies.

   b. The agencies themselves have the fundamental responsibility for such coordination.

   c. The required analysis can be carried out most efficiently by each of the agencies, since each is best acquainted with its own mandate and detailed programs.

   d. The SIC can promote coordination only when it is kept fully informed and is regularly consulted.

C. To instruct its agencies and the SIC to address themselves to long-range planning and the setting of priorities by each of the agencies and by all of them together, following the general pattern adopted for program coordination.

   Grounds:

   1. The denomination through synod should from time to time reflect on its priorities and examine its existing programs.

   2. Planning enables the denomination to develop programs for carrying out its many-sided task in a responsible and opportune way.

                                    (Acts of Synod 1971, pp. 74-75; *1976,* pp. 49-51)

6. The Denominational Clerk

Synod has adopted the following description and regulations for the position of the Stated Clerk:

I. QUALIFICATIONS

A. The Stated Clerk must be theologically trained.

B. The Stated Clerk shall have served as a pastor in at least one of the congregations of the denomination.

C. The Stated Clerk shall be well acquainted with the Christian Reformed denomination, its churches, ministers, lay-leaders, and agencies both in the Dominion of Canada and in the United States.

D. The Stated Clerk shall possess a thorough knowledge of the Church Order, and be competent in interpreting the same.

E. The Stated Clerk shall have the ability to write lucidly and succinctly. He should also be competent in public address.

F. The Stated Clerk shall possess administrative and organizational ability.

G. The Stated Clerk shall be broad in spirit, able to move with ease and dignity in the North American ecclesiastical circles. He should be congenial and able to cooperate with representatives of other churches as well as members of our own denomination.

II. ORGANIZATIONAL RELATIONSHIP

A. The Stated Clerk shall be the executive officer of synod.

B. The Stated Clerk shall be an *ex officio* member of the Synodical Interim Committee and shall serve as its general secretary. He shall also serve as the general secretary of the synod's incorporated entities, the Christian Reformed Church Synod Trustees, and the Christian Reformed Church in North America.

C. The Stated Clerk shall be an *ex officio* member of the Interchurch Relations Committee.

D. The Stated Clerk shall have the privilege of the floor at synodical meetings in all matters relating to the exercise of his office. He shall be present during all executive sessions of synod.

III. SUPERVISION: The Stated Clerk shall work under the supervision of the Synodical Interim Committee and shall be ultimately responsible to synod.

IV. APPOINTMENT

A. The Stated Clerk shall be appointed by synod (*Acts of Synod 1956,* Art. 143, pp. 104-05), from a nomination by the Synodical Interim Committee. Inasmuch as extensive evaluation is involved in making a nomination, any nominations from outside the Synodical Interim Committee shall be evaluated by the committee.

B. The term of appointment shall be four years after which the Stated Clerk shall be eligible for reappointment to additional four-year terms.

C. An alternate Stated Clerk shall be annually appointed by the Synodical Interim Committee, preferably from within its own membership, and shall function when the Stated Clerk is incapacitated due to illness, injury, or other extraordinary circumstances. He shall not automatically succeed to the office of Stated Clerk.

The alternate Stated Clerk should be:

1. Near at hand.
2. Kept informed at all times.
3. If the alternate Stated Clerk is not already a member of the Synodical Interim Committee he shall be an *ex officio* member of the Synodical Interim Committee.
4. When the alternate Stated Clerk serves as Stated Clerk, he shall be a nonvoting member of the committee during the time he serves.

V. DUTIES AND RESPONSIBILITIES

A. Responsibilities to Synod:

1. The Stated Clerk shall edit, and have suitably printed, such official publications as the synod or the Synodical Interim Committee shall authorize.
2. The Stated Clerk shall have synodical papers, including correspondence, surveys, questionnaires, materials, reports, minutes, etc., produced for the

synod and shall keep a file of synodical correspondence. He shall keep an accurate record of the proceedings of synod and the Synodical Interim Committee.

3. The Stated Clerk shall have surveillance over denominational archives and historical documents on behalf of the Synodical Interim Committee and shall be responsible for the right of access to such documents.

4. The Stated Clerk shall inform all persons who have been appointed by synod to serve on committees, and provide them with relevant data concerning their assignment.

5. The Stated Clerk shall receive progress reports and/or minutes from the committees appointed by synod.

6. The Stated Clerk shall serve synod with information and advice as requested regarding matters which come to the floor of synod.

7. The Stated Clerk shall perform such duties as synod or the Synodical Interim Committee shall direct.

B. Responsibilities to the Denomination:

1. The Stated Clerk shall handle the general correspondence of the denomination.

2. The Stated Clerk shall, when called upon, give advice and information regarding the provisions of the Church Order, and the decisions of synod. In matters of major proportions, this advice shall be given in consultation with the Synodical Interim Committee.

3. The Stated Clerk, in consultation with the Synodical Interim Committee, shall consult with denominational agencies and denominationally related agencies and alert synod regarding the coordination of effort and procedures for mutual cooperation.

4. The Stated Clerk on behalf of synod and the Synodical Interim Committee shall be a servant of the people, the churches, and the denominational agencies. To this end he shall respond to invitations, maintain liaison, and visit classes, as time and circumstances allow, or as the Synodical Interim Committee may direct.

C. Responsibilities on Behalf of the Denomination

1. The Stated Clerk shall represent the denomination or secure the proper representation of the denomination at civic and religious functions in keeping with its relationship to the governments of Canada and the United States. In all cases the Stated Clerk shall act in accordance with the approved policies of the Christian Reformed Church. In cases where there is a question, the Synodical Interim Committee should be consulted.

2. The Stated Clerk, as agent of the Synodical Interim Committee or synod, shall prepare news or information bulletins for the news media which will inform the public of the work and witness of the church.

3. The Stated Clerk shall, with the approval of the Synodical Interim Committee, perform services which will represent the position and extend the witness of the Christian Reformed Church.

D. In order that the Stated Clerk may be able to perform the foregoing duties and discharge his responsibilities, he shall be provided with the necessary personnel and equipment.   (*Acts of Synod 1971*, pp. 75-77)

7. The Denominational Financial Coordinator
Synod has adopted the following description and regulations for the position of the Denominational Financial Coordinator:

I. QUALIFICATIONS
A. The Financial Coordinator should be a Certified Public Accountant or have a broad accounting background.
B. The Financial Coordinator shall have had several years of experience in a financial administrative position.
C. The Financial Coordinator shall possess the ability to communicate effectively.
D. The Financial Coordinator shall be a member of and familiar with the Christian Reformed Church.

II. ORGANIZATIONAL RELATIONSHIPS
A. The Financial Coordinator shall be responsible to the Synodical Interim Committee through the denominational Stated Clerk but be ultimately responsible to synod.
B. The Financial Coordinator shall work closely with the Finance Committee of the Synodical Interim Committee.
C. The Financial Coordinator shall be an *ex officio* member of the Synodical Interim Committee.
D. The Financial Coordinator shall be present at all public meetings of synod and have the privilege of the floor in all matters relating to the exercise of his office.

III. DUTIES AND RESPONSIBILITIES
A. The Financial Coordinator shall exercise careful oversight of the administration of finances of the denomination with a view to the greatest possible economy and efficiency.
B. The Financial Coordinator shall examine the budgets of denominational agencies, analyze their requests for quotas or financial support, and assist the Finance Committee in making its recommendations through the Synodical Interim Committee to synod.
C. The Financial Coordinator shall receive and examine regular financial reports of all denominational agencies.
D. The Financial Coordinator shall determine that financial records of all denominational agencies have been audited by Certified Public Accountants.
E. The Financial Coordinator shall receive, examine, and analyze financial reports of all non-denominational agencies requesting financial support.
F. The Financial Coordinator shall advise, counsel, and assist the denominational agencies on matters such as size of reserves, fund management, financial reporting, and insurance, pension, and investment programs.
G. The Financial Coordinator shall systematically collect relevant economic and financial data that will assist his office, the Finance Committee, and the Synodical Interim Committee in completing their respective work.

H. The Financial Coordinator shall perform such duties as may be assigned by synod, the Synodical Interim Committee, the Finance Committee, or the Stated Clerk.

I. In order that the Financial Coordinator may be able to perform the foregoing duties and discharge his responsibilities, he shall be provided with the necessary personnel and equipment.

IV. APPOINTMENT

A. The Financial Coordinator shall be appointed by synod from a nomination(s), evaluated and approved by the Finance Committee, and submitted by the Synodical Interim Committee.

B. The term of appointment shall be four years, after which the Financial Coordinator shall be eligible for reappointment to additional four-year terms.

(Acts of Synod 1971, pp. 110-11)

II. THE ASSEMBLIES OF THE CHURCH
A. GENERAL PROVISIONS (continued)

ARTICLE 34

DELEGATION TO ASSEMBLIES

The major assemblies are composed of office-bearers who are delegated by the constituent minor assemblies. The minor assemblies shall provide their delegates with proper credentials which authorize them to deliberate and vote on matters brought before the major assemblies. A delegate shall not vote on any matter in which he himself or his church is particularly involved.

1. Composition of Major Assemblies

Article 34 states that "major assemblies are composed of office-bearers who are delegated by the constituent minor assemblies."

The office-bearers to be delegated to attend the meeting of a classis are designated in Article 40 of the Church Order, and the delegates designated to attend the synodical assembly are listed in Article 45 of the Church Order.

The point of Article 34 is that the major assemblies are representative of the congregations constituting the minor assemblies. Each minor assembly has representatives and a voice through these representatives in the major assemblies of the church. This representation binds the church together. Each minor assembly must be fully aware of the fact that it has had opportunity by way of overture, communication, appeal, and also through representatives to make its contribution to every decision adopted by the major assemblies.

2. Authorization of Delegates by Proper Credentials

Article 34 states that "the minor assemblies shall provide their delegates with proper credentials which authorize them to deliberate and vote on matters brought before the major assemblies."

Copies of credentials for delegates to classis and delegates to synod are available from the Christian Reformed Publishing House. Before each synod such credentials are furnished by the office of the Stated Clerk of synod to the stated clerks of classes.

Copies of classical and synodical credentials are contained in the Appendix (pp. 340 and 341).

3. The Responsibility and Freedom of Delegates to Deliberate

It should be noted that the credentials to major assemblies authorize delegates "to deliberate and vote on matters brought before the major assemblies." The nature of

163

the assemblies of the church, whether they be minor or major, is that they are *deliberative* assemblies. This means that the delegates shall carefully consider every matter before the assembly. Careful consideration includes the determination as to whether these decisions are in accord with the Word of God, the confessions of the church, and the Church Order. Serious consideration must be given to all of the matters presented to and discussed by the assembly, so that each delegate, being fully informed and convinced, may cast his vote in accord with his conscience.

While each assembly has the right to present its position to its major assembly, the provisions of Article 34 do not permit a minor assembly to bind the vote of any of its delegates. The instructions given to its delegates are general in nature and give him authorization to act after due deliberation. Each delegate must therefore use his best judgment on each issue and vote in accord with his conscience before the Lord.

If the minor assemblies were to bind upon their delegates the necessity of voting in one way, it would obviate the possibility of a deliberative discussion at the meeting of the major assembly, and it would nullify the influence and the conscience of the delegates.

4. Limitation of the Voting Privilege
Article 34 specifies one limitation upon the voting privilege: "A delegate shall not vote on any matter in which he himself or his church is particularly involved."

To vote under such a circumstance would be less than objective and prejudicial to any adjudicatory process.

II. THE ASSEMBLIES OF THE CHURCH

B. THE CONSISTORY

ARTICLE 35

COMPOSITION OF A CONSISTORY

a. In every church there shall be a consistory of the office-bearers. The consistory is responsible for the general government of the church.

b. Where the number of elders is at least four, a distinction may be made between the general consistory, to which all office-bearers belong, and the restricted consistory, in which the deacons do not participate.

c. When such a distinction is made, the supervision and discipline of the congregation shall be vested in the restricted consistory. The work of Christian mercy shall be the task of the deacons, who shall render account of their work to the general consistory. All other matters belong to the general consistory.

1. The General Nature and Function of the Consistory

Article 35a states that "in every church there shall be a consistory composed of the office-bearers." The office-bearers intended here are those which are listed in Church Order Article 2: the minister of the Word, the elder, and the deacon. These office-bearers form the congregational assembly we call the consistory.

The function of the consistory is spelled out in Article 35 in broad terms: the consistory is responsible for the general government of the church. If the injunction of Paul to the church that "all things are to be done decently and in order" is to be carried out, it follows that there must be some regulatory body. In the local church this body is the consistory.

2. General and Restricted Consistory

Article 35b provides that "where the number of elders is at least four, a distinction may be made between the general consistory. . .and the restricted consistory." (Cf. Arts. 39, 40.) As a matter of practice in most of our churches this distinction is made for the sake of efficiency, giving each of these two groups opportunity to specialize in their particular functions.

Note: The Belgic Confession, Article 30, speaks of the meeting of the ministers, elders, and deacons as the "council" of the church, a term sometimes employed in our churches in place of the term "general consistory." For a comment on this see *Acts of Synod 1961,* p. 445.

The general consistory is made up of all office-bearers of a local congregation whereas the restricted consistory meeting is generally called the elders' meeting.

In a smaller congregation where all office-bearers belong to the general consistory, the deacons as well as the elders perform presbyterial functions. For this reason synod stated that in cases where the deacons and elders together meet in one general consistory, the deacons "may function as elders,...to avoid the un-Reformed practice of oligarchic rule which would be the only alternative....Such deacons, in matters of church government, should naturally give due consideration to the judgment of the elders" (*Acts of Synod 1938*, p. 81; *1896*, p. 42). When a distinction is made between the general consistory and the restricted consistory, the latter body is one in which the deacons do not participate.

3. The Distinction of Functions
Article 35c indicates that when a distinction is made between the general consistory and the restricted consistory, these two assemblies assume their own specific functions.

a. Supervision and Discipline
"The supervision and discipline of the congregation shall be vested in the restricted consistory." This work includes such matters as family visiting, the teaching ministries of the church, counseling, and Christian discipline.

b. Christian Mercy
"The work of Christian mercy shall be the task of the deacons, who shall render account of their work to the general consistory." This involves the work of mercy in the congregation, the community, and the world. The broader ministries of the diaconate are carried out through deacons' conferences of the classes and through the general ministry of the Christian Reformed World Relief Committee. The Church Order indicates that the deacons should present an account of their work of mercy to the *general* consistory, that is, they should share with all their fellow office-bearers the perspectives of the church's ministry of mercy.

c. Other Matters for the General Consistory
"All other matters belong to the general consistory." These include such items as correspondence, committee reports, and all matters not specifically assigned to the elders or to the deacons.

All matters referred to the general consistory are matters in common, and, as such, are open for discussion and vote by all members of the general consistory.

Sample agenda for these three kinds of meetings may be found in "Your Church in Action," a handbook for consistories. Suggestions are also provided with respect to rules for the consistory and its committees.

II. THE ASSEMBLIES OF THE CHURCH
B. THE CONSISTORY (continued)

ARTICLE 36
FREQUENCY OF MEETINGS AND MUTUAL CENSURE

a. The consistory shall meet at least once a month, at a time and place announced to the congregation. Ordinarily the meeting shall be presided over by the minister, or in the absence of the minister by one of the elders.
b. The consistory, at least four times per year, shall exercise mutual censure, which concerns the performance of the official duties of the office-bearers.

(Amended—*Acts of Synod 1973,* p. 82)

1. Time and Place of Meeting
   Article 36a specifies that "the consistory shall meet at least once a month, at a time and place announced to the congregation."

   Such announcement enlists the prayer support of the membership and also provides opportunity for members to bring matters to the attention of the consistory for its consideration.

2. The Officers of the Consistory
   a. The President
   The consistory, as all assemblies, must have a presiding officer (see Art. 32b). Article 36a states that "ordinarily the meetings shall be presided over by the minister, or in the absence of the minister by one of the elders."

   The word *ordinarily* was inserted into Article 36a by the Synod of 1973. This synod appended the following grounds for the use of the word *ordinarily*:
   "1) The offices of minister and elders as rulers are equal.
   "2) There are experienced elders who are quite capable of chairing meetings of consistory.
   "3) In crucial times, such as when a congregation is without a pastor, elders preside over the meetings and have proven themselves capable to do so quite adequately."   *(Acts of Synod 1973,* p. 82)
   This decision indicates that Article 36a does not demand that in every case a minister should be the presiding officer of the consistory. Moreover, in congregations having more than one pastor, it is evident that a choice must be made with respect to the presiding officer of the consistory.

167

b. The Vice-President
In addition to a president, every consistory ordinarily elects a vice-president. He also functions as a member of the officers' committee and presides when the president is unable to do so.

c. The Clerk of the Consistory
In accord with the general rules for assemblies (see Art. 32b) there must be a clerk for each consistory. The responsibilities of the clerk are the keeping of the minutes, the care of the archives, and carrying on the correspondence of the consistory. In some of the larger consistories a minute clerk and a corresponding clerk are elected to carry on the functions of the consistory.
It is the responsibility of the clerk along with the president to plan the agenda for each meeting.

d. The Treasurer of the Consistory
For the financial work of the consistory each consistory must have its own general treasurer.

e. Other Officers
In addition to the officers above, in churches having a restricted consistory, officers must be chosen for the meeting of the deacons, including a president of the deacons, a clerk to record the minutes of the deacons, and a benevolence treasurer.

3. Mutual Censure
a. Its Frequency
Article 36b prescribes that "the consistory, at least four times per year, shall exercise mutual censure, which concerns the performance of the official duties of the office-bearers."
Mutual censure must be exercised *at least* four times per year. It ought to be apparent that there may be many more than four times a year when the consistory will want to discuss the work of its membership and ways and means by which they may be more effective in representing the Lord Jesus Christ in the leadership of the church.
In the earlier history of our church, there was the tendency to tie in the matter of mutual censure with the observance of the Lord's Supper. In churches where the Lord's Supper is observed four times per year, this often has led to the consideration of mutual censure during the meeting preceding the Lord's Supper. While there is no objection to exercising mutual censure at the meeting before the Lord's Supper, this is by no means necessitated by 36b of the Church Order. The article simply implies that a discussion of the performance of the official duties of the office-bearers shall take place with regularity, and at least four times per year.

b. Its Exercise
The purpose of mutual censure is to encourage consistories to discuss together the work which the Lord has committed to the church and its office-bearers. In some

consistories, mutual censure has become a mere form or an occasion to find fault with each other. This easily occurs when a chairman asks, "Does anyone have anything for mutual censure?" and office-bearers respond with no. Mutual censure demands a positive rather than a negative approach.

Mutual censure should be a time for fruitful discussion about the work of the Lord, the program of the congregation, ways and means to encourage the members of the congregation in their ministries, and the development of dynamic spiritual leadership by the office-bearers. With such discussions, prayers, and efforts we may expect development in our congregations of the ideals which Paul sets forth in Ephesians 4:11-16; namely, "the equipment of the saints, for the work of ministry."

Note: The Reformed Church in America, which shares the same tradition as our own Christian Reformed Church, has stated the requirement for mutual censure in a positive form as follows: "The board of elders shall make a faithful and solemn enquiry at least four times a year to ascertain whether any members of the congregation are in need of special help regarding their spiritual condition, and shall provide the means of extending Christian ministry to such persons."

II. THE ASSEMBLIES OF THE CHURCH
B. THE CONSISTORY (continued)

ARTICLE 37

CONGREGATIONAL MEETINGS

The consistory, besides seeking the cooperation of the congregation in the election of office-bearers, shall also invite its
judgment about other major matters, except those which
pertain to the supervision and discipline of the congregation. For this purpose the consistory shall call a meeting at
least annually of all members entitled to vote. Such a
meeting shall be conducted by the consistory, and only
those matters which it presents shall be considered. Although
full consideration shall be given to the judgment expressed
by the congregation, the authority for making and carrying
out final decisions remains with the consistory as the governing body of the church.

1. The Purpose of Congregational Meetings
Article 37 lists two purposes of congregational meetings: "the election of office-
bearers" and "judgment about other major matters."

a. Election of Office-bearers
In accord with Church Order Article 4 the consistory before the congregational
meeting must prepare nominations for office-bearers. Except for very unusual
circumstances (see Art. 4) the nomination(s) shall be at least twice the number to
be elected.

Prior to the making of these nominations the consistory may give the congregation an opportunity to direct attention to suitable persons (Art. 4).

A majority vote is required for election of office-bearers. A majority is a vote
of more than half of the legal votes cast. Blank or improper ballots do not count
as legal votes. (Cf. *Acts of Synod 1904*, p. 53.)

Before the election takes place, it should be stipulated by the consistory, or approved by the congregation, that if more than the required number obtain a majority of votes, those with the highest number of votes shall be elected.

b. The Judgment of the Congregation
The consistory "shall also invite its judgment about other major matters."

The congregational meeting gives the consistory opportunity to seek the judgment or advice of the members on various matters, such as the program of the
church, evangelistic outreach, community relations, and other matters.

It should be noted that only matters placed on the agenda by the consistory may be considered at a congregational meeting.

In matters pertaining to certain items of building and salaries, the consistory is required to seek the judgment of the congregation. As a corporate entity, the consistory serves as the board of trustees of the congregation. Article X of the synodically approved Articles of Association for our congregations provides the following:

> "Said trustees shall have the power and authority to bargain, sell, convey, mortgage, lease, or release any real estate belonging to said church or held by them as such trustees, and to erect churches, parsonages, schoolhouses, and other buildings for the direct and legitimate use of said church, and to alter and repair the same, and to fix the salary of its minister or ministers (if at any time there be more than one) or anyone in its employ:

> "Provided that no such purchases, sale or conveyance, mortgage, lease, or fixing of salaries shall be made unless the affirmative vote of a majority of the members of this church organization, of which said trustees are officers, shall be first obtained at a meeting of such members of this church or congregation present and entitled to vote, duly and specially called for that purpose by notice given for two successive Sundays at the usual place of meeting next preceding such meeting:

> "Provided, further, that no sale, mortgaging, or conveyance shall be made of any gift, grant, or donation, conveyance, device, or bequest which would be inconsistent with the express terms of plain intent of the grant, donation, gift, conveyance, device, or bequest."

c. Business Specifically Excluded

Article 37 makes it clear that matters "which pertain to the supervision and discipline of the congregation" must be excluded from the congregational meeting.

2. The Consistory's Role at Congregational Meetings

Article 37 indicates several responsibilities regarding congregational meetings which belong to the consistory:

a. Calling Annual and Special Meetings

"For this purpose the consistory shall call a meeting at least annually." Congregational meetings may or must be called more often when the occasion warrants it. Article 37 specifies that a congregational meeting must be held at least once a year.

b. Conducting the Meeting

Ordinarily the president of the consistory or an office-bearer designated by the consistory presides at the congregational meeting.

c. Setting the Agenda

"...only those matters which it [the consistory] presents shall be considered."

Matters which a member wishes to have considered must first be presented directly to the consistory, and the consistory will determine whether or not and in what form the matter will be presented to the congregation.

3. Participation in Congregational Meetings
   a. All Confessing Members
   The right to participate in congregational meetings belongs to the office of all believers. All members who have made profession of faith and are members in good standing are eligible participants for congregational meetings.

   b. Members under Discipline
   Synod has ruled that members under discipline have no right to vote at congregational meetings *(Acts of Synod 1892,* p. 23).

   c. Women in Congregational Meetings
   The Synod of 1957 decided that "women may participate in congregational meetings with the right to vote subject to the rules that govern the participation of men. The question as to whether and when the women members of any church shall be invited to participate in the activities of its congregational meetings is left to the judgment of each consistory" *(Acts of Synod 1957,* p. 90).
   In 1972 synod reaffirmed that decision as follows:
   "Synod reaffirms that it is the right of women members, as full members of Christ and his church and sharers in the office of believers, to participate in and vote at congregational meetings on a level of equality with men."
   "Synod commends to those churches, presently not granting suffrage to women members, the above stated recommendation for serious consideration and implementation." *(Acts of Synod 1972,* p. 103)

   d. Adopting and Implementing Decisions
   "Although full consideration shall be given to the judgment expressed by the congregation, the authority for making and carrying out final decisions remains with the consistory as the governing body of the church."
   In order for decisions made at a congregational meeting to become final, the consistory must adopt them as its own. If for any reason the consistory cannot do so, or feels it unwise to do so, it should defer action and seek a more appropriate course to be presented to the congregation at a later meeting. This may well be the wise course when an important decision is made by a bare majority.

II. THE ASSEMBLIES OF THE CHURCH
B. CONSISTORIES (continued)

ARTICLE 38

UNORGANIZED CHURCHES

a. Groups of believers among whom no consistory can as yet be constituted shall be under the care of a neighboring consistory, designated by classis.
b. When a consistory is being constituted for the first time the approval of classis is required.

1. The Care of Unorganized Churches

Article 38a states that "groups of believers among whom no consistory can as yet be constituted shall be under the care of a neighboring consistory, designated by classis." The care of unorganized churches involves the holding of memberships, supervision of worship services, the administration of the sacraments, and Christian discipline.

Groups of believers, although too small to be fully organized, do constitute the church and are entitled to the love and care of the church through the ministrations of a neighboring consistory. Article 38a prescribes that classis shall designate the consistory which is to care for such groups of believers.

When a missionary is provided by the Denominational Home Missions Board, the Home Mission order approved by synod provides that "membership papers shall be deposited with the missionary as the duly appointed office-bearer of the church which he represents" (*Acts of Synod 1959*, pp. 77, 207).

It should be observed that both Article 38 and the rule providing for the care of congregations by a home missionary, adopted in 1959, place the holding of memberships not in a person but in a duly constituted consistory.

The normal procedure *when an emerging church is within or near the confines of a classis* is that the classis shall designate a neighboring consistory to take the emerging church under its care, one of the aspects of such care being the holding and supervision of membership.

The regulation pertaining to home missions deals with a rule for *churches* which may be *far removed from the calling church.* In such cases the responsibility for assigning a church of the classis which is "a neighboring church" is not possible as a general rule.

It must be recognized that the credentials of the home missionary are often in a church that is somewhat removed from the church in which he works. Even though

173

the church may be at some distance, membership papers are deposited with the missionary "as the duly appointed office-bearer of the church which he represents."

The home missionary does not hold membership in his person, but he holds memberships as one who represents his calling church and the synod of the Christian Reformed Church through the assignments of the Christian Reformed Board of Home Missions. The home missionary reports regularly both to the Board of Home Missions and to his calling church with respect to the memberships and the supervision of the memberships in the church which he is serving.

Through the regulations of Article 38 of the Church Order and the regulations pertaining to the care given to a mission group through a home missionary as a representative of his calling church, the church is looking out for the care of all members in emerging churches: in some circumstances through a classically designated consistory; and in other circumstances through a calling consistory (and the Board of Home Missions) represented by its home missionary. (See *Acts of Synod 1980,* p. 22.)

The membership statistics of unorganized and organized churches are listed separately in the *Yearbook* of the denomination.

2. Assembly Approval for Organization
   a. When a new congregation is contemplated within the domain of an *existing congregation*, synod has ruled that permission shall be sought first from the consistory and then from the classis. In case of differing judgments an appeal may be made to the major assembly or assemblies (*Acts of Synod 1908*, p. 36).
   b. Article 38b states that "when a consistory is being constituted for the first time [that is, when the church is organized] the approval of classis is required." The responsibility of classis involves the consideration of the number of members, the presence of necessary leaders, proximity to neighboring congregations, financial ability to support the work, and other pertinent information.

3. Procedures for Organization
   Synod has adopted the following rules of procedure for the organization of new congregations:
   a. "Classis shall mandate a neighboring consistory to effect the organization of the new congregation."
   b. "This consistory which is so mandated shall meet with the petition-signers to arrange for the organizational meeting and the nomination of at least twice the number of office-bearers to be elected, or less than twice the number to be elected, giving reasons for this departure from the rule. Prior to making these nominations, the effecting consistory shall give the petition-signers an opportunity to direct attention to suitable persons. Nominations are to be announced two successive Sundays before the organizational meeting. Any objections to the nominations are to be heard by the consistory or representatives of the effecting consistory."
   c. "The consistory mandated to effect the organization shall accept and hold memberships of the petition-signers and present them at the organizational meeting."

d. "At the organizational meeting, the office-bearers shall be elected by the balloting of all confessing members whose letters of transfer or dismission have been accepted by the effecting consistory, and a majority is sufficient to elect. These office-bearers shall be ordained and shall sign the formula of subscription at the organizational meeting."
e. "No professions of faith shall be heard at the organizational meeting."
f. "The papers of incorporation shall be prepared with legal counsel at a meeting of the newly organized consistory and presented for approval of the new congregation as early as possible after their organization." (*Acts of Synod 1971*, p. 99)

4. Rules for Calling by Smaller Churches
   a. Synod has restricted the right of a church to call a minister in the case of a small or needy church seeking aid from the Fund for Needy Churches (*Acts of Synod 1957*, p. 38).
   b. Synod has also declared "that an organized church which cannot support itself should not ordinarily become a calling church until it has reached at least the level of thirty families" (*Acts of Synod 1971*, p. 23).

II. THE ASSEMBLIES OF THE CHURCH

C. THE CLASSIS

ARTICLE 39

CONSTITUENCY OF A CLASSIS

A classis shall consist of a group of neighboring churches. The organizing of a new classis and the redistricting of classes require the approval of synod.

1. Definition of a Classis
   Article 39 defines the classical assembly as "a group of neighboring churches."
   Every organized church must belong to a classis. Unorganized churches become members of a classis when a consistory is formally elected and installed (that is, when a church becomes organized).

2. Jurisdiction of a Classis
   "The jurisdiction of the classis is exercised in the geographical district in which its constituent churches and congregations are located and over which it has been appointed, pursuant to synodical regulations" (Articles of Association and By-laws of the Christian Reformed Church in North America, By-law IX).

3. Organizing New Classes
   Article 39 also requires that the organization of a new classis requires "the approval of synod."
   The desirability of organizing a new classis depends on the consideration of the number of families, the number of congregations, the geographical distances, the effectiveness of ministry, and other factors. Before a new classis is organized, the approval of synod is required.

4. Redistricting of Existing Classes
   The redistricting of two or more classes belongs properly to the classes involved as the agency to take the initiative, but their proposal for redistricting must also be submitted to synod for approval *(Acts of Synod 1930,* p. 39).

5. Transfer of a Congregation to Another Classis
   A congregation may obtain permission from synod to be transferred to another classis through the request to and approval of one or both of the classes *(Acts of Synod 1922,* p. 78).

II. ASSEMBLIES OF THE CHURCH
C. THE CLASSIS (continued)

ARTICLE 40
THE SESSIONS OF CLASSIS

a. The consistory of each church shall delegate a minister and an elder to the classis. If a church is without a minister, or the minister is prevented from attending, two elders shall be delegated. Office-bearers who are not delegated may also attend classis and may be given an advisory voice.
b. The classis shall meet at least every four months, unless great distances render this impractical, at such time and place as was determined by the previous classical meeting.
c. The ministers shall either preside in rotation, or one shall be chosen to preside; however, the same minister shall not be chosen twice in succession.

1. The Delegates to Classis

Article 40a stipulates that "the consistory of each church shall delegate a minister and an elder to the classis."

If a church is without a minister, or the minister is for any reason prevented from attending the meeting of classis, Article 40 provides that two elders shall be delegated.

Article 40a indicates that the meetings of a classis are not as a general rule a closed session. Classical sessions are open to the public, except for executive sessions. All office-bearers, although not delegated, may be given an advisory voice, if or when the classis so decides.

Concerning home missionaries, the Synod of 1957 delcared that "when a Home Missionary labors in an organized church—although officially not connected with this congregation, but with the church that called and commissioned him—he may with the approval of his calling church and at the request of the church in whose midst he labors, represent said church at major ecclesiastical assemblies" *(Acts of Synod 1957,* p. 84).

Concerning churches which have more than one minister, synod declared in 1964 that "only those ministers who have been officially delegated by organized churches shall be seated as members of a classical session. All other ministers of those churches shall have the right to attend classis with advisory voice... (cf. Art. 35). Any of the ministers who are officially connected with the organized churches of a classis may be chosen as delegates to Synod or used for functions and/or committee work at the discretion of classis" *(Acts of Synod 1964,* p. 57).

With respect to "the right to attend classes with advisory voice," the 1965 Church Order revision modified the decision above. Both nondelegated ministers and elders *may* attend classis and *may* be given an advisory voice. While such a privilege may be granted by a classis, nondelegated office-bearers may not claim such a privilege as their right.

2. The Meetings of Classis
Article 40b stipulates that each classis "shall meet at least every four months, unless great distances render this impractical."

The time and the place of each meeting of classis shall be determined at the previous classical meeting, and announcements should be published in the church papers and in the congregational bulletins.

The dates of classical meetings are also listed annually in the *Yearbook*.

3. The President of Classis
Article 40c provides that "the ministers shall either preside in rotation, or one shall be chosen to preside; however, the same minister shall not be chosen twice in succession."

The responsibilities of the president, as well as of the clerk, are explained in Article 32.

4. Other Offices of Classis
In addition to the president and the clerk of classis, every classis should have a stated clerk and a treasurer.

a. Stated Clerk of Classis
   1) The stated clerk, unlike the president and clerk of the assembly (cf. Art. 32b), continues to function after the session has ceased. He is elected by classis for a specific term of office.
   An alternate stated clerk is also elected by each classis to function if or when the stated clerk is incapacitated or moves from the classis.
   2) The stated clerk shall prepare the agenda, transcribe the minutes, maintain the files and archives, and attend to all official correspondence of classis *(Acts of Synod 1900,* p. 60).
   3) The stated clerk shall send notices of classical meetings to all consistories and the church papers.
   4) The stated clerk shall send agenda and minutes of the classis to all consistories. The number of copies sent to each consistory shall be determined by each classis.
   5) It is the duty of the stated clerk to transmit one copy of the advice of synodical deputies to the Stated Clerk of Synod. A second copy should be retained for the files of classis.
   6) The stated clerk should submit to the Stated Clerk of Synod all overtures, appeals, and communications endorsed by classis. Each overture, appeal, or communication should be addressed to synod and sent as a separate official communication.

7) The stated clerk shall submit to the Stated Clerk of Synod all classical nominations for election to denominational boards. Such nominations must be approved by synod, or by the Synodical Interim Committee between synods. Nominations of each classis should be sent to the Stated Clerk of Synod as a separate communication.

8) The stated clerk shall submit to the Stated Clerk of Synod all items to be considered by synod in time to meet the agenda deadline of the Rules for Synodical Procedure.

9) At the close of each year the stated clerk shall submit the classical statistics for the *Yearbook* in accord with the deadlines established.

10) The stated clerk shall send notices of all emeritations both to the Ministers' Pension Fund and to the Stated Clerk of Synod. Such notices should include effective date and ground for each emeritation.

11) Synod has established the following rules involving consistories and stated clerks of classes re notification about suspension, deposition, or resignation of a minister:

a) With respect to suspension, "the minor assemblies involved...can judge whether the publication of notice of suspension serves the best interests of the minister and of all the churches" *(Acts of Synod 1975,* p. 19).

b) "In the case of deposition, the stated clerk of the classis shall notify the stated clerks of all the other classes concerning the action, and these shall in turn notify each consistory within their classis" *(Acts of Synod 1972,* p. 26).

c) "In the case of resignation, the stated clerk of classis in which the resignation has taken place shall place an appropriate announcement in the denomination's periodicals" *(Acts of Synod 1972,* p. 26).

b. The Treasurer of Classis

Each classis shall elect a treasurer and an alternate treasurer.

Synod requested all treasurers "when remitting moneys to Synodical treasurers received for synodical funds to itemize very distinctly from which congregation or other sources these moneys were received. This is imperative for correct bookkeeping" *(Acts of Synod 1936,* p. 102).

The Synod of 1937 approved uniform "blanks for classical treasurers prepared at Synod's request" and recommended that "classical treasurers...use them faithfully in remitting moneys to synodical treasurers" *(Acts of Synod 1937,* p. 40).

The Synod of 1969 requested the treasurers of all classes to disburse their funds quarterly since delaying disbursements "causes financial hardship to denominational agencies and makes it difficult for them to meet their financial obligations on a consistent basis throughout the year" (*Acts of Synod 1969,* pp. 12-13). Monthly disbursements are still more desirable, and the Synodical Interim Committee, in behalf of synod and the denominational agencies, has urged all classical treasurers to make monthly remittances. Congregational treasurers should also make monthly remittances to the classical treasurer to insure an efficient and financially responsible flow of funds. Prompt remittances by all treasurers will insure a considerable saving of funds in the Lord's work.

Responsibilities of treasurers in the financial transactions of the assemblies are dealt with in the chapter on Article 32, 3, e.

II. THE ASSEMBLIES OF THE CHURCH
C. THE CLASSIS (continued)

ARTICLE 41

QUESTIONS TO EACH CONSISTORY AT CLASSIS

In order properly to assist the churches, the president, on behalf of classis, shall among other things present the following questions to the delegates of each church:

1. Are the consistory meetings regularly held in your church; and are they held according to the needs of the congregation? Is church discipline faithfully exercised?
2. Is church discipline faithfully exercised?
3. Are the needy adequately cared for?
4. Does the consistory diligently promote the cause of Christian education from elementary school through institutions of higher learning?
5. a. Have you submitted to the secretary of our Home Missions Board the names and addresses of all baptized and communicant members who have, since the last meeting of classis, moved to a place where no Christian Reformed churches are found?
   b. Have you informed other consistories or pastors about members who reside, even temporarily, in the vicinity of their church?
   c. Have you, having been informed yourself of such members in your own area, done all in your power to serve them with the ministry of your church?
6. Does the consistory diligently engage in and promote the work of evangelism in its community?

(Amended—*Acts of Synod 1966*, p. 87)

1. Presentation of the Questions

   Article 41 stipulates that "in order properly to assist the churches, the president, on behalf of classis, shall among other things present...questions to the delegates of each church."

   In 1942 synod affirmed the importance of Article 41 by declaring

   "that an inquiry on the part of the Classis into the spiritual state of its several congregations constitutes the central and principal task of Classis, and therefore should take precedence. Hence Article 41 should not be taken up at the end of Classical meetings but at the outset.

181

"Furthermore, Synod directs the attention of the churches to the fact that these questions should never be answered in a perfunctory manner, but should serve as a basis for further examination." *(Acts of Synod 1942,* p. 110)

The same synod (1942) approved the method of asking the questions under Church Order, Article 41 by the written questionnaire method as well as by the oral method. An excellent report on Article 41 appears in the Agenda I (only) of 1942. (See *Acts of Synod 1942,* pp. 109-111; Agenda I for Synod of 1942, pp. 26-35.)

The credentials for classis furnished by the Board of Publications of the Christian Reformed Church include the questions to be answered by each consistory. Having the consistory fill in these answers at its meetings assists the office-bearers in their joint appraisal of their work and the needs of their congregation.

2. Explanation of the Questions
   a. Question 1—*Are the consistory meetings regularly held in your church; and are they held according to the needs of the congregation?*
   Regulations for consistory meetings are explained in Articles 35-38.
   b. Question 2—*Is church discipline faithfully exercised?*
   Articles 78-94 contain the regulations for church discipline.
   c. Question 3—*Are the needy adequately cared for?*
   Synod "urges the classes earnestly to remind the delinquent congregations of their calling to extend the Christian hand of mercy to the poor, if necessary, also of other congregations and promote the development of the diaconate and mutual correspondence among diaconates" *(Acts of Synod 1919,* p. 63).

   Diaconal conferences and the Christian Reformed World Relief Committee are set up to enable every church to reach out with the mercy of Christ. Further discussion of the deacon's task is found in Article 25.
   d. Question 4—*Does the consistory diligently promote the cause of Christian education from elementary school through institutions of higher learning?*
   "The term 'schools'. . .in Article 41 refers to the Christian primary and grammar and high schools. . .where the bulk of our children get their general school education as distinguished from technical and professional schools, while the college would fall under the question of Article 41 in the measure in which it might become the common instrument of a general education.

   "The expression 'support the cause of Christian Schools' means that it is the duty of the consistory to use every proper means to the end that a Christian School may be established where it does not exist. . .and to give whole-hearted and unreserved moral backing to existing Christian schools and a measure of financial help in case of need." *(Acts of Synod 1936,* pp. 36-37)
   e. Question 5a—*Have you submitted to the secretary of our Home Mission Board the names and addresses of all baptized and communicant members who have, since the last meeting of classis, moved to a place where no Christian Reformed churches are found?*
   Question 5b—*Have you informed other consistories or pastors about members who reside, even temporarily, in the vicinity of their church?*

Question 5c—*Have you, having been informed yourself of such members in your own area, done all in your power to serve them with the ministry of your church?*

f. Question 6—*Does the consistory diligently engage in and promote the work of evangelism in its community?*

The Church Order regulations concerning missions are found in Articles 73-77.

3. Support of Our Mutual Responsibilities

Synod reminds the consistories of the urgent necessity of keeping before their congregations not only the privilege but also the sacred duty to contribute liberally toward the work of the Lord, which we have taken upon ourselves as the Christian Reformed Church.

"The Classes shall (may) consult with delinquent congregations through the Consistories and, if necessary, admonish them to become more abundant in manifesting their love for the Lord's cause" (*Acts of Synod 1939,* p. 72).

If churches are unable to meet their financial obligations, synod has urged classes to instruct their church visitors "in addition to their regular duties as church visitors to also delve into reasons for any church not meeting its denominational quotas. When a classis is convinced that a member church is unable to pay the quotas, the churches within a classis, if possible, through a combined effort [should] be requested to assist a church to meet its denominational obligations [in accordance with our duty] to bear one another's burdens (Gal. 6:2). (Cf. *Acts of Synod 1970,* p. 81.)

II. THE ASSEMBLIES OF THE CHURCH
C. THE CLASSIS (continued)

ARTICLE 42

CHURCH VISITORS

a. The classis shall appoint at least one committee composed of two of the more experienced and competent office-bearers, two ministers, or one minister and one elder, to visit all its churches once a year.

b. The church visitors shall ascertain whether the office-bearers faithfully perform their duties, adhere to sound doctrine, observe the provisions of the Church Order, and properly promote the edification of the congregation and the extension of God's kingdom. They shall fraternally admonish those who have been negligent, and help all with advice and assistance.

c. The churches are free to call on the church visitors whenever serious problems arise.

d. The church visitors shall render to classis a written report of their work.

(Amended—*Acts of Synod 1972*, p. 27)

1. Appointment of Church Visitors
   a. The Number of Church Visitor Teams
   Article 42a states that each classis "shall appoint at least one committee...to visit all its churches." The number of such committees is left to the discretion of classis and should be determined by local factors, such as the number of churches in the classis and the geographical location of the churches.

   b. Qualifications of Church Visitors
   Article 42a also states that these church visiting committees shall be "composed of two of the more experienced and competent office-bearers, two ministers, or one minister and one elder."

   Experience and competence are the two qualifications specified by the Church Order, and they are essential if the churches are to be well served.

   The appointment of competent elders should not be overlooked. The Synod of 1972 stated that "the work of church visiting is appropriate to the office of elder and within the competence of some of the experienced elders" (*Acts of Synod 1972*, p. 27).

c. Frequency of Church Visits
Article 42a also specifies that these committees shall visit all the churches of classis "once a year."

A proposal to change this rule from once every year to at least once every two years was rejected by the Synod of 1975.

2. Duties of Church Visitors
Article 42b specifies the following duties of church visitors with respect to the office-bearers of the churches:
a. They "shall ascertain whether the office-bearers:
   . . . faithfully perform their duties,
   . . . adhere to sound doctrine,
   . . . observe the provisions of the Church Order,
   . . . properly promote the edification of the congregation,
   . . . [properly promote] the extension of God's kingdom."
b. They "shall fraternally admonish those who have been negligent."
c. They shall "help all with advice and assistance."

Church visitors are required to make inquiry not only about office-bearers directly serving the local church, but also regarding office-bearers serving in special capacities, including all ministers of the Word whose credentials are held by a consistory and all evangelists appointed (or ordained) by the local church.

The Synod of 1978 ruled that church visitors shall inquire annually into the supervision of the calling church toward ministers of the Word in specialized ministerial tasks, noting the nature of the reporting of such ministers and of the consistorial supervision. Church visitors are required to inform classis of departure from the approved provisions for supervising and reporting. (Cf. *Acts of Synod 1978*, p. 48; and under Church Order Art. 12, section 4, of this manual.)

If the supervision of a consistory holding credentials of ministers of the Word is to be meaningful, the stipulations of the 1978 Synod above must be applicable to all such office-bearers, and church visitors should faithfully make inquiry into their work and its supervision.

The Synod of 1936 adopted the following statement in response to a communication from a classis (the reference to Article 44 uses the numbering of the former Church Order):

"Since Classis Pella, considering the importance of church visitation, gives expression to its fear that in our present-day practice the work is often performed in a perfunctory manner, and since the expressed purpose of church visitation as found in Article 44, Church Order, is that this work should be done for the upbuilding of the congregation, Synod urges upon all Classes to perform this work in a way most conducive to the churches, in full accord with the spirit of Article 44 which militates against all mechanization and requires a thorough discussion on all matters pertaining to the welfare of the church, particularly of the youth.

"As to a revision of the Rules for Church Visitation, Synod deems the present Rules adequate, provided they are used in the spirit of Article 44, the Church Visitors use their own discretion and individualize their task in every church visited."   (*Acts of Synod 1936*, p. 123)

185

3. Observations Regarding Church Visiting

"It is readily acknowledged that the practice of church visitation has not always been as effective or as meaningful as it might have been. In many instances church visitation has been conducted mechanically, hastily, and with relatively little profit. On the other hand, many have found church visitation to provide a meaningful setting for receiving genuinely helpful counsel and needed fraternal advice, as well as an opportunity for pastoral and consistorial growth.

"Since church visitation has the potential for providing significant benefits for every consistory, it is important that the practice of regular visitation be strengthened rather than weakened. Those churches which are at some distance from others within the classis surely need the stimulation and fellowship provided by church visitation as much as, or even more, than others. The expenditure of time and money which may be involved is surely justified by the potential results of a well-executed program of visiting. Consequently, rather than diminishing the number of visits which are to be made, the classis should diligently continue the practice of yearly visitation while seeking to make each visit a meaningful and spiritually enriching experience for all of those involved."

(*Acts of Synod 1975*, p. 17)

4. Guide for Conducting Church Visiting

In order to assist the church visitors synod has provided the following Guide for Conducting Church Visiting:

GUIDE FOR CONDUCTING CHURCH VISITING

The annual visit of the churches, as prescribed in Article 42 of the Church Order, must follow an orderly procedure. The following rules are intended to guide both the church visitors and the consistories so that the visit may be helpful.

Arrangements for the Visit

The annual visit shall be announced to both the consistory and the congregation.

The official records of the church are to be brought to the meeting.

Matters upon which the consistory seeks advice of the church visitors must have been agreed upon prior to the visit.

The questioning shall be conducted by the chairman of the committee, and the report to classis written by the secretary of the committee.

Guide for the Examination

Questions Regarding the Whole Consistory

1. Preaching Services
   a. Do you have preaching services at least twice on each Lord's day?
   b. Is one of the preaching services each Sunday devoted to the exposition of a Scripture passage, the choice of which is left free to the minister?
   c. At the other service does the minister ordinarily preach the Word as summarized in the Heidelberg Catechism, following its sequence? (C.O. Art. 54b)
   d. Is the "Lord's Day" which is to be considered read to the congregation before the sermon is preached? (*Acts of Synod 1950*, Art. 141, pp. 62, 441)

2. Reading Services and Guest Ministers
   a. Does the consistory approve the sermons that are read at reading services? (C.O. Art. 53c)
   b. When guest ministers or unordained men are invited to preach, does the consistory employ only persons who are of Reformed persuasion and who are properly licensed?
3. The Lord's Supper
   a. Is the Lord's Supper administered at least every three months and ordinarily preceded by a preparatory sermon and followed by an applicatory sermon? (C.O. Art. 60)
   b. Does the consistory properly guard the sanctity of the Lord's Table by admitting only those who give evidence of true faith and godliness? (C.O. Arts. 59, 85)
4. Church Music
   Do you observe the synodical regulations governing the content of hymns and anthems to be sung in worship services, and do you supervise the choice of choir anthems, solo anthems, and supplementary hymns according to these regulations and according to the statement and implications of the principles of music as found in the *Psalter Hymnal?* (C.O. Art. 52b)
5. Is catechetical instruction supervised by the consistory? (C.O. Arts. 63-64)
6. Are the members of the consistory elected according to the stipulations of the Church Order? (C.O. Arts. 3, 4, 23)
7. Have all the consistory members signed the Form of Subscription? (C.O. Art. 5)
8. Does the consistory meet at least once a month? (C.O. Art. 36a)
9. Does the consistory strive to become familiar with the Church Order and the *Acts of Synod* and act in accordance with the Church Order and the decisions of synod?
10. Are the minutes of the consistory accurately recorded and kept? (C.O. Art. 32b)
11. Do the members of the consistory, at least four times a year, exercise mutual supervision among themselves? (C.O. Art. 36b)
12. Is church discipline administered faithfully in accordance with the Word of God and the Church Order?
13. Is the consistory aware of any members who belong to secret societies or to other organizations, membership of which is incompatible with membership in our church?
14. Do the members of the consistory, as their office demands, regularly visit the families, the sick, and the poor? (C.O. Art. 65)
15. a. What is the spiritual condition of the church?
    b. Does the consistory promote and preserve peace, unity, and love among the members? (C.O. Arts. 65, 80)
16. Do the youth upon reaching maturity profess Christ as their Savior and Lord, and seek admission to the Lord's Table? If not, what does the consistory do to change this situation? (C.O. Art. 63)
17. Is the consistory diligent in promoting the cause of missions in the community, throughout the nation, and on the foreign field? (*Acts of Synod 1959,* Art. 94, p. 36)

18. Does the consistory show concern regarding the doctrine and conduct of those seeking admission into the church by transfer? (C.O. Art. 59c)
19. Does the consistory keep in contact with members who have moved away but have not requested transfer of membership? (C.O. Art. 67)
20. Does the consistory make proper provision for receiving communications, preparing agenda and acts, keeping files and archives, and conducting the financial transactions of the assembly, and for maintaining proper incorporation? (C.O. Art. 32)
21. Does the consistory diligently encourage the members of the congregation to establish and maintain good Christian schools? (C.O. Art. 71)
22. Are the offerings prescribed by classis and synod taken according to the respective regulations? (See comments under Church Order Article 41, section 3, of this manual.)

Questions Regarding the Minister
1. Is the minister faithful in administering the Word and the sacraments according to the Formulas of Unity and the Church Order? (C.O. Art. 11)
2. Are the prescribed Forms of the Church correctly used and honored in his ministry? (C.O. Art. 55)
3. Does he conduct public worship in an edifying manner?
4. Does he diligently instruct the children and youth of the church in the doctrine of salvation? (Form for Ordination)
5. Is he faithful in visiting the sick, the distressed, and the erring, and does he assist the elders in the work of annual family visiting? (C.O. Art. 65)
6. Does he with the elders engage in and promote the work of evangelism? (C.O. Art. 12)
7. Does his work as teacher and preacher give evidence of diligent study and of relevance to the needs of today?
8. Does he devote himself exclusively to the discharge of his official duties? Does he receive adequate time for spiritual and physical refreshment?
9. Does he receive an income proportionate to the needs of a well-ordered family and commensurate with his training and position? (C.O. Art. 15). Does the congregation strive to pay the pastor's total compensation as indicated by the cost of living indicator as shown in the current compensation guide for ministers? (*Acts of Synod 1978*, p. 92)
10. Does he set an example of godliness in his personal life, in his home life, and in his relations with his fellowmen? (Form for Ordination)

Questions Regarding the Elders
1. Do the elders faithfully attend the meetings of the church and of the consistory?
2. Do they supervise the instruction given in the catechism classes of the church, and do they, upon request, assist the minister in the catechizing? (C.O. Art. 64)
3. Do they exercise discipline and promote good order in the church? (C.O. Art. 24)
4. Do they faithfully visit the members of the congregation in regular family visiting, and also when there is a need for comfort, encouragement, or instruction? (C.O. Art. 65)
5. Do they promote within the congregation societies for the study of God's Word,

and do they serve the youth organizations with counsel and assistance? (C.O. Art. 72)

6. Do they set an example of godliness in their personal life, in their family life, and in their relations with their fellowmen? (Form for Ordination)

Questions Regarding the Deacons

1. Do the deacons faithfully attend the meetings of the church, of the consistory, and if such are held, of the deacons?

2. Are they faithful and diligent in the ingathering of offerings which God's people in gratitude make to their Lord? (Form for Ordination)

3. a. Are the collections counted by the deacons jointly, or, where there are very few deacons, in the presence of the pastor or one or more elders? (*Acts of Synod 1928,* p. 132)

   b. Do they keep a double record of receipts and disbursements?

4. In cases of need do they carefully investigate the actual situation and jointly decide on the nature and extent of help to be proffered?

5. Do they administer Christian mercy toward those who are in need, first of all toward those of the household of faith, but also toward the needy in general? (C.O. Art. 25a)

6. Do they serve the distressed in order to prevent their poverty? (Form for Ordination)

7. Do they minister to the distressed with kindly deeds and words of consolation from Scripture? (Form for Ordination)

8. Do they periodically render an account of their work to the general consistory? (C.O. Art. 35c)

9. Do they set an example of godliness in their personal life, in their home life, and in their relations with their fellowmen? (Form for Ordination)

(*Acts of Synod 1966*, pp. 20-22; *1975*, p. 47; *1978*, p. 92)

5. Availability of Church Visitors

Article 42c provides that "the churches are free to call on the church visitors whenever serious problems arise."

Whenever problems arise concerning which outside advice is desirable, the consistory should feel free to request a special meeting with the church visitors.

6. Reports of Church Visitors

Article 42d requires that "the church visitors shall render to classis a written report of their work."

In some classes these reports are preserved in notebooks which are turned over to new teams of church visitors when they are appointed. This practice contributes a measure of continuity and may be helpful both to the visitors and consistories.

II. THE ASSEMBLIES OF THE CHURCH
C. THE CLASSIS (continued)

ARTICLE 43

CLASSICAL LICENSURE TO EXHORT

The classis may grant the right to exhort within its bounds to men who are gifted, well-informed, consecrated, and able to edify the churches. When the urgent need for their services has been established, the classis shall examine such men and license them as exhorters for a limited period of time.

1. The Right to Exhort (Licensure)
Article 43 stipulates that "the classis may grant the right to exhort within its bounds...."

Synod has declared that with the exception of licensed students, no one has the right to speak in public worship unless he has received such right from his classis, after it has examined him relative to his orthodoxy, his godly walk, and his ability to address a congregation (cf. *Acts of Synod 1924*, p. 93).

This right is limited to the churches of the classis which grants the right to exhort. Whether a person who has been granted this right by one classis shall have the privilege of speaking in other classes must be determined by those classes, each for its own churches (cf. *Acts of Synod 1924*, p. 93).

2. Conditions for Granting the Right to Exhort
Article 43 specifies four conditions to be met when licensure is granted by a classis:
   a. Personal Qualifications
   Exhorters must be "men who are gifted, well-informed, consecrated, and able to edify the churches."
   b. Urgent Need
   It must be determined that there is "urgent need for their services."
   c. Classical Examination
   After the urgent need for their services has been established, "the classis shall examine such [a person]" to determine whether he has the necessary qualifications.
   d. Limited Period
   The right to exhort shall be given "for a limited period of time." The Church Order does not permit licensure for an unlimited period.

3. Theological Students
With respect to students preparing for the ministry of the Christian Reformed

190

Church, synod has declared that although the classes have the right to license persons in their respective domains, it is not in the interest of good order to license students other than those who have studied in our own seminary (cf. *Acts of Synod 1924*, p. 38).

Church Order Article 22 regulates the licensure of theological students and provides the relevant synodical regulations.

Church Order Articles 6 and 7 prescribe the way of admittance to the ministry in the Christian Reformed Church through Calvin Seminary and regular theological training, as well as for those who have not received the prescribed theological training.

4. List of Licensures Granted by Classes
The annual *Yearbook* of the Christian Reformed Church provides a list of all persons who have been licensed by various classes to conduct religious services in accordance with Article 43.

II. THE ASSEMBLIES OF THE CHURCH
C. THE CLASSIS (continued)

ARTICLE 44

JOINT ACTION OF NEIGHBORING CLASSES

A classis may take counsel or joint action with its neighboring
classis or classes in matters of mutual concern.

1. The Propriety of Joint Action
   Article 44 recognizes that "a classis may take counsel or joint action with a neighboring classis or classes in matters of mutual concern."
   Some classes band together to support an area-wide mission effort.
   Some classes also take counsel and joint action in supporting Christian educational or benevolent agencies, and contact the government on moral and other matters of mutual concern only to the classes involved.

2. Ecclesiastical Status of Joint Meetings of Classes
   It should be observed that meetings of neighboring classes do not constitute an ecclesiastical assembly. These extraordinary meetings should therefore be careful not to assume tasks assigned to the consistories, classes, or synods, and should refrain from setting up programs that duplicate those of the separate classes or other denominational programs.
   Matters clearly assigned to the regular ecclesiastical assemblies such as matters of doctrine or discipline, reports of classical and synodical committees, and other ecclesiastical procedures are not within the province of interclassical meetings.

3. Guidelines for Joint Action of Classes
   The decision of the Synod of 1966 re the Council of Christian Reformed Churches in Canada gives helpful insights into the provisions of Article 44 of the Church Order. The following is an analysis of this decision:
   a. Guidelines
      Synod adopted the following guidelines for those classes which desire to take "counsel" or "joint action" as proposed by the study committee on the Canadian Council:
      "1) That synod remind the congregations and classes of the Christian Reformed Churches in Canada that the first responsibility of dealing with matters peculiar to their situation resides with the local consistorial and classical assemblies in keeping with the principle of Article 28, a and b of the Church Order.

"2) That synod declare that in harmony with Article 44 of the Church Order, the Canadian classes may 'take counsel or joint action' as often as necessary on matters that are peculiar to the Christian Reformed Churches in Canada."

b. Definitions of Mutual Concerns
3) Synod declared "that the matters to be considered by the cooperating classes be confined to those matters that are of 'mutual concern' (Art. 44) and which cannot with equal effect be dealt with either by the local churches individually, or by the classes, or by the General Synod, or their respective committees. Examples of such matters of 'mutual concern' are:
   a) "Official contact with the Canadian government on such matters as: The Lord's Day Act, laws on incorporation and proposed legislation in which Biblical principles are involved.
   b) "Matters of public relations as: Canadian Centennial in 1967, government control of radio and television, and press releases.
   c) "Spiritual care for those in the Canadian armed forces.
   d) "Contacts with other churches and/or denominations in Canada.
   e) "Liaison with Canadian Christian institutions of mercy and social-cultural organizations."   (*Acts of Synod 1966,* pp. 53-54)

c. Limitations
4) Synod declared "that the inter-classical gathering, where 'counsel or joint action' is taken, shall in no wise be construed as a court of appeal in cases of discipline or protest against decisions of ecclesiastical assemblies."

d. Voluntary Character of Joint Action
5) Synod affirmed "the voluntary character of this inter-classical 'counsel or joint action' in that each invited classis remains free to join and to continue participation in such a cooperative effort."
                                        (*Acts of Synod 1978,* pp. 117-118)

II. THE ASSEMBLIES OF THE CHURCH
D. THE SYNOD

ARTICLE 45

THE CONSTITUENCY OF SYNOD

The synod is the assembly representing the churches of all
the classes. Each classis shall delegate two ministers and two
elders to the synod.

1. The Representative Nature of Synod
   Article 45 emphasizes the representative nature of synod: "The synod is the assembly
   representing the churches of all the classes."
      The authority of consistories is original, as Article 27 states, whereas that of major
   assemblies is delegated. When a classis meets, it represents every consistory of its
   churches. When synod meets, it represents the churches of all the classes.
      Synod is not, therefore, an assembly standing over and above the churches, but it
   is in the fullest sense an assembly representing all the churches of the denomination.
   When a decision is made by the synod, that decision is adopted by the delegates
   representing every classis and every church.

2. The Delegates to Synod
   a. Number of Delegates
      Article 45 also requires that "each classis shall delegate two ministers and two
      elders to the synod."

   b. Election of Delegates
      Synod does not stipulate for the classes a definite method of selecting delegates to
      synod, but "with a view to the welfare of the churches, it advises against the
      rotary [rotation] method of selecting Synodical delegates" (*Acts of Synod 1938,*
      pp. 80-81).

   c. Reimbursement for Loss of Wages
      Synod encourages classes to set up plans for the reimbursement of elder delegates
      to synod who feel that they need compensation for loss of wages (*Acts of Synod
      1965,* p. 21).

3. Preparation of Synodical Delegates
   The delegates to synod are usually chosen by the classes during their winter sessions.

Synodical rules require the following steps of preparation prior to the convening of the synod in June:

a. Submission of Credentials to Synod
   When each classis elects its synodical delegates, the classical stated clerk must send to the Stated Clerk of Synod the Credentials for Synod.

   The credential forms, provided to the classis by synod, provide spaces for the names of the ministers and elders chosen to represent the classis at synod and the names of alternate delegates who will attend if the first named delegate is unable to attend.

   The Credentials for Synod declare that the classis instructs and authorizes the delegates to take part in all the deliberations and transactions of synod regarding all matters legally coming before synod and transacted in agreement with the Word of God according to the conception of it embodied in the doctrinal standards of the Christian Reformed Church as well as in harmony with our Church Order.

   The credentials must be signed by the president and stated clerk of classis and forwarded to the Stated Clerk of Synod as soon as possible.

   Note: A copy of the Credentials for Synod is included in the Appendix, p. 341.

b. Submission of Information Questionnaire
   In addition to the synodical credentials each stated clerk must submit as soon as possible an information questionnaire which has been filled in by each synodical delegate. Early information with respect to each delegate is necessary for the proper functioning of the Program Committee of Synod which preappoints members of the advisory committees of the forthcoming synod. (See below, c-4.)

c. Preappointment of Advisory Committees (by the Program Committee)
   Synod has adopted the following rules pertaining to the Program Committee:
   1) Members
      a) The Program Committee shall be composed of the officers of the previous synod and the Stated Clerk of the Christian Reformed Church.
      b) In case of a vacancy on this committee, the Synodical Interim Committee shall appoint another member.
   2) The Appointment of Advisory Committees
      a) The Program Committee shall meet to make tentative preappointment of the various advisory committees prior to May 1.
      b) The Program Committee shall classify all the reports, overtures, and other communications into various groups, and advise which matters shall be laid directly before synod, and which shall be placed in the hands of advisory committees.
      c) In the event that a given delegate cannot attend synod, his alternate accepts the appointed assignment subject to revision by synod.
   3) The Stated Clerk shall:
      a) Receive and tabulate the information sheet on the synodical delegates.

b) Inform the delegates of their tentative assignments prior to May 15.

c) Suggest to chairmen and delegates sources of background information relative to their assignment.

d) Provide committee members with copies of background materials that are not readily available in previous *Acts of Synod.*

4) Information on Delegates

a) The stated clerk of every classis shall forward an information sheet on each synodical delegate to the Stated Clerk of the Christian Reformed Church before March 15.

b) These information sheets shall give answer to the following questions:
For the minister delegates:

(1) To which previous synod(s) were you delegated, if any?

(2) At such synod(s), on which committee(s) did you serve?

(3) Of what denominational boards, standing committees, or study committees are you or have you been a member?

(4) Of what classical and/or local committees are you or have you been a member?

(5) What are your areas of special interest in the work of synod?

(6) What other data do you wish to submit that will aid in being assigned to an advisory committee of synod?

For the elder delegates:

(1) through (6)—the same as for minister delegates.

(7) What is your present occupation?

(8) What have been your previous occupations, if any?

5) Report of the Program Committee

a) A written report of the Program Committee shall be mailed to all synodical delegates before May 25.

b) This report shall be submitted for possible change and adoption as one of the initial items of synodical business.

(Rules for Synodical Procedure, pp. 9-10)

II. THE ASSEMBLIES OF THE CHURCH
D. THE SYNOD (continued)

ARTICLE 46

MEETINGS OF SYNOD

a. Synod shall meet annually, at a time and place determined by the previous synod. Each synod shall designate a church to convene the following synod.

b. The convening church, with the approval of the Synodical Interim Committee, may call a special session of synod, but only in very extraordinary circumstances with the observance of synodical regulations.

c. The officers of synod shall be elected and shall function in accordance with the Rules for Synodical Procedure.

1. Convening of Synod
   a. Time and Place

   Synod meets annually "at a time and place determined by the previous synod." Since 1969 the set time for the annual meeting of synod has been the second Tuesday of the month of June. Every church is asked to remember the synodical assembly in prayer on the Sunday before it meets, and a special prayer service of the delegates and members of the churches is held on the Monday evening preceding the beginning of synod.

   b. The Convening Assembly

   Each synod designates "a church to convene the following synod."

   The responsibilities of the convening church are to conduct the pre-synodical worship service and to have its pastor serve as the president pro-tem for the first session of synod. Announcements re the assembly are made through the office of the Stated Clerk.

2. Special Sessions of Synod

   Article 46b provides a way by which synod may be convened for a special session. It specifies that this may be done "only in *very extraordinary circumstances* with the observance of synodical regulations."

   In emergency or very extraordinary circumstances "the convening church, with the approval of the Synodical Interim Committee, may call a special session of synod." It is well to observe in this connection that the Synodical Interim Committee is involved by its mandate to execute all synodical matters which cannot be postponed until the next synod, and constitutes the corporate Board of Trustees of the Christian Reformed Church in all legal matters.

3. The Officers of Synod

Article 46c specifies that "the officers of synod shall be elected and shall function in accordance with the Rules for Synodical Procedure."

The officers of each synod are elected by a free ballot of the delegates of synod.

The Rules for Synodical Procedure prescribe the following duties of the elected officers of synod:

A. The President
1. He shall request the members of synod and the advisory members of synod to arise, read the Public Declaration of Agreement with the Forms of Unity, and request them to express agreement in unison. A delegate who assumes his seat at a later time shall be requested to express his individual agreement.
2. He shall call the meeting to order at the appointed time, and shall see that each session is properly opened and closed.
3. He shall see to it that business is transacted in the proper order and expedited as much as possible, and that members observe the rules of order and decorum.
4. He shall welcome fraternal delegates, or other guests of synod, respond to greetings received, or appoint members of synod for this purpose.
5. He shall place before synod every motion that is made and seconded. He shall clearly state every question before a vote is taken.
6. In case he feels impelled to express himself on a pending question, he shall relinquish the chair to the vice-president while so doing. He may speak, while holding the chair, to state matters of fact or to inform synod regarding points of order.
7. He shall have, and duly exercise, the prerogative of declaring a motion or person out of order. In case his ruling is disputed, synod shall sustain or reject the ruling by majority vote.
8. When a vote is tie, the president may cast the deciding vote, if he has not already voted.
9. The president shall not preside in any matters that concern himself.
10. The president rules on all points of order. His ruling may be reversed by a majority of synod if any member is dissatisfied with the ruling of the chair and appeals to the floor.
11. The president shall close the synodical assembly with appropriate remarks and with prayer.

B. The Vice-President
1. In the absence of the president the vice-president shall assume all his duties and privileges.
2. The vice-president shall render all possible assistance to the president as circumstances may require.

C. The First Clerk and Second Clerk
   1. The first clerk shall each day call the roll immediately after the opening devotionals. Thereupon the minutes of the previous day shall be read.
   2. The clerk shall keep an exact record of the synodical proceedings. This record shall contain:
      a. opening and closing of sessions and roll call;
      b. all main motions whether carried or lost; all appeals whether sustained or lost;
      c. all reports of advisory committees and all decisions of synod;
      d. the names of fraternal delegates and others who address synod;
      e. any document, any phase of discussion on the floor of synod, or any address that synod by a majority vote decides to insert into the minutes.
   3. The record shall not contain:
      a. any rejected motion except it be a main motion;
      b. any motion that is withdrawn
   4. The second clerk shall serve in the absence of the first clerk. He shall render all possible assistance to the first clerk as circumstances may require.

4. Nondelegated Synodical Functionaries
   In addition to the elected officers the Rules for Synodical Procedure also define the role and duties at synod of several denominational appointed officials:

A. Seminary Professors
   1. At each synod one half of the seminary faculty shall be required to attend synod in an advisory capacity, with the exception of the president who shall be present at every synod.
   2. The seminary advisers shall serve on the advisory committees of synod.
   3. The seminary advisers shall be present at synod where they shall have the privilege of the floor for the purpose of advising synod on matters before it, subject to the accepted rules governing discussion. On important questions the chair, or any member of synod, may request their advice.

B. The Presidents of Calvin Seminary and of Calvin College
   1. The president of Calvin Seminary shall advise synod in matters pertaining to the seminary.
   2. The president of Calvin College shall advise synod in matters pertaining to Calvin College.

C. The Stated Clerk
   1. The Stated Clerk shall be the executive officer of synod.
   2. The Stated Clerk shall be an *ex-officio* member of the Synodical Interim Committee and shall serve as its general secretary. He shall also serve as the secretary of its incorporated entities, the Christian Reformed Church Synod Trustees.
   3. The Stated Clerk shall be an *ex-officio* member of the Inter-church Relations Committee.

4. The Stated Clerk shall have the privilege of the floor at synodical meetings in all matters relating to the exercise of his office. He shall be present during all executive sessions of synod.

5. The Stated Clerk shall serve synod with information and advice as requested regarding matters which come to the floor of synod.

6. The Stated Clerk shall edit and have suitably printed such official publications as the synod or the Synodical Interim Committee shall authorize.

7. The Stated Clerk, in consultation with the Synodical Interim Committee, shall consult with denominational agencies and denominationally related agencies and alert synod regarding the coordination of effort and procedures for mutual cooperation.

8. The term of appointment shall be four years after which the Stated Clerk shall be eligible for reappointment to additional four-year terms.

9. The Synodical Interim Committee, through the Stated Clerk, shall make arrangements for press representatives and releases for all meetings of synod. (For a complete description of the position of the Stated Clerk see commentary on Article 33, section 6, of this manual.)

D. Denominational Financial Coordinator

1. The Financial Coordinator shall be responsible to the Synodical Interim Committee through the denominational Stated Clerk but be ultimately responsible to synod.

2. The Financial Coordinator shall work closely with the Finance Committee of the Synodical Interim Committee.

3. The Financial Coordinator shall be an *ex-officio* member of the Synodical Interim Committee.

4. The Financial Coordinator shall be present at all public meetings of synod and have the privilege of the floor in all matters relating to the exercise of his office.

5. The Financial Coordinator shall exercise careful oversight of the administration of finances of the denomination with a view to the greatest possible economy and efficiency.

6. The term of appointment shall be four years, after which the Financial Coordinator shall be eligible for reappointment to additional four-year terms.
For a complete description of the Position of Denominational Financial Coordinator see manual under on Article 33, section 7.

E. The Synodical Treasurer
The synodical treasurer is appointed by synod for the term of two years. An alternate is appointed to serve when the treasurer is incapacitated or when other reasons make it necessary.

II. THE ASSEMBLIES OF THE CHURCH
D. THE SYNOD (continued)

ARTICLE 47

THE TASK OF SYNOD

The task of synod includes the adoption of the creeds, of the Church Order, of the liturgical forms, of the **Psalter Hymnal,** and of the principles and elements of the order of worship, as well as the designation of the Bible versions to be used in the worship services.
No substantial alterations shall be effected by synod in these matters unless the churches have had prior opportunity to consider the advisability of the proposed changes.

1. Specific Tasks
Article 47 identifies the six major functions assigned to synod. The task of synod includes:

a. The Adoption of the Creeds
   The creeds of the church express the church's interpretation of the Scripture and are basic to the unity and distinctiveness of the denomination. Since the creeds form our fundamental basis of unity in belief as a denomination, Article 47 mentions first, as one of the specific tasks of the synod, the adoption of its creeds.

b. The Adoption of the Church Order
   The second specific task of the synod is the adoption of the Church Order. As the creeds express the church's unity in the faith, the Church Order expresses our convictions as to how things are to be "done decently and in order" by means of the regulations of the church.

c. The Adoption of the Liturgical Forms
   Liturgical forms are used by the church to administer the sacraments, to install office-bearers, to receive persons into communicant membership by profession of faith, and to exercise discipline. The forms contain the scriptural basics for these aspects of worship and express them in ways which will enhance the worship of the church.
   Because the forms of the church are basic to its unity in doctrine and worship and belong to those essential elements which all our congregations have in common, the adoption and regulation of forms is the responsibility of synod as the broadest assembly of the church.

201

d. The Adoption of the *Psalter Hymnal*

In accord with Article 47 synod has prepared a common hymnal for the churches, containing the Psalms and a selection of scripturally sound hymns. The current Centennial Edition of the *Psalter Hymnal* has been in use since 1959. The Synod of 1977 appointed a committee to revise and improve the Centennial Edition. (Cf. *Acts of Synod 1977*, p. 139.)

In 1953 synod adopted a statement of principle for music in the church and recommended to the churches for study a series of ten implications. The principle and implications are printed in the front of the *Psalter Hymnal* (page v). (Also see Art. 52, section 4a of this manual.)

e. The Adoption of the Principles and Elements of the Order of Worship

Another of the common concerns of the churches committed to synod is the order of worship. Synod has on several occasions made declarations as to the order of worship. Complete orders of worship were adopted in 1928 and 1930. As a matter of practice, all of our churches are expected to maintain the essential elements of the worship prescribed by the Synod of 1930, although all the churches have followed various courses in their application and order. It should be noted that the Synod of 1930 left the introduction of the New Order of Worship entirely to the discretion of each local church (*Acts of Synod 1930*, p. 187).

In 1934 synod declared that the benediction and salutation is to be pronounced only when God's people are gathered for the specific purpose of corporate worship (*Acts of Synod 1934*, p. 136).

In 1968 the Liturgical Committee presented to synod a statement of the principles of liturgy and model services to be used in the churches. Synod commended this report to the churches for their study and consideration and authorized provisional use of an Order for Communion. These materials were reprinted by order of synod in the *Psalter Hymnal Supplement* of 1973. The above report is worthy of study, and defines the liturgy, worship, the history of liturgy, criteria for evaluating the liturgy and its components. (Cf. *Acts of Synod 1968*, pp. 64-65, 134-198; also see Art. 52, section 5, of this manual.)

f. The Designation of the Bible Versions to Be Used in the Worship Services (See also Art. 52, section 2, of this manual)

1) King James (Authorized) and American Standard Versions

In 1926 synod considered the adoption of the King James or the American Standard Version of the Bible as the *official version* of the Bible in our churches. Synod decided to refrain from adopting an official version. However, the synod recommended the American Standard Version to our churches on the grounds that they expected it to replace the King James Version and noted that "there is a closer similarity between the Holland Bible and the American Standard than there is between the Holland Bible and the Authorized Version" (*Acts of Synod 1926*, p. 47).

2) Revised Standard Version

In 1969, after the completion of a study by a committee of the Revised Standard Version of the Bible, synod designated this version as one of the versions acceptable for use in worship services. The grounds adopted by synod state:

"a) Though having its weaknesses, the RSV is, on the whole, superior to the King James Version and the American Standard Version, both of which are considered acceptable for use in the public worship of the Christian Reformed Church.

"b) The need for a modern translation for pulpit and other use in our churches is apparent. At present the RSV is the only modern translation available that is reasonably qualified to fill this need.

"c) The concern for a representative version expressed by the Synods of 1926 and 1966 supports this action." *(Acts of Synod 1969,* pp. 48-50)

The Synod of 1973 instructed the committee on the Heidelberg Catechism Translation "to quote biblical passages from the Revised Standard Version" *(Acts of Synod 1973,* p. 16).

This version is also used in all newly adopted forms and is used as the preferred version in all educational materials of the Christian Reformed Church.

The Synod of 1973 also authorized the sale of the Revised Standard Version by the Board of Publications of the Christian Reformed Church.

3) New International Version
The Synod of 1980 designated the New International Version (NIV) as one of the versions acceptable for use in worship services on the grounds that the NIV is textually acceptable, communicates effectively, is liturgically readable, and has potential for ecumenical acceptance. (See *Acts of Synod 1980,* pp. 70-71.)

2. Alteration of Materials
Article 47 declares that "no substantial alterations shall be effected by synod in these matters unless the churches have had prior opportunity to consider the advisability of the proposed changes."

3. Changes in the Creeds and Church Order
The Synod of 1979 made the following decisions:
a. "Whenever a recommendation is presented to synod which would require a change in the Creeds and/or in the Church Order, the proposal ought to specify the changes."
b. "Church Order Article 47 implies that whenever changes in the Creeds and/or substantial changes in the Church Order are made by synod, the churches shall be given adequate opportunity to consider the advisability of the changes before they are ratified by a following synod." *(Acts of Synod 1979,* pp. 89-90)
c. The synods of 1976 and 1979 rejected the adoption of a mandatory two-thirds vote for decisions that deal with matters related to the confessional standards and the Church Order. At the same time synod stated that the synod itself has the option to require a two-third majority vote for decisions dealing with our confessional standards and Church Order. *(Acts of Synod 1976,* p. 52; *1979,* p. 90)

II. THE ASSEMBLIES OF THE CHURCH
D. THE SYNOD (continued)

ARTICLE 48

SYNODICAL DEPUTIES

a. Upon the nomination of the classes, synod shall appoint ministers, one from each classis, to serve as synodical deputies for a term designated by synod.

b. When the cooperation of the synodical deputies is required as stipulated in the Church Order, the presence of at least three deputies from the nearest classes shall be prescribed.

c. Besides the duties elsewhere stipulated, the deputies shall, upon request, extend help to the classes in the event of difficulties in order that proper unity, order and sound doctrine may be maintained.

d. The synodical deputies shall submit a complete report of their actions to the next synod.

1. The Election of Synodical Deputies

Article 48a states, "Upon the nomination of the classes, synod shall appoint ministers, one from each classis, to serve as synodical deputies for a term designated by synod."

   a. The nomination of a synodical deputy (and an alternate) must be made by each classis.

   b. Synodical deputies are appointed by synod from the nominations made by the classis. They function in behalf of synod. Their terms of office conform to all the rules of synod pertaining to board and committee appointments (two three-year terms, effective and expiring on September 1).

2. Responsibilities Stipulated in the Church Order

Article 48b states that "when the cooperation of the synodical deputies is required as stipulated in the Church Order, the presence of at least three deputies from the nearest classes shall be prescribed."

Article 48 lists the general regulations for synodical deputies. Specific responsibilities of synodical deputies stipulated in the Church Order are described in the following articles:

   a. Responsibilities relating to admission to the ministry of the Word

     1) Article 7—admission to the ministry of the Word without prescribed theological training

2) Article 8—admission of ministers of other denominations to the ministry of the Word in the Christian Reformed Church

Synodical Deputies are mandated by synod to observe synodical regulations with respect to the "need" factor in the calling, or approving the calling, of ministers from other denominations. (See Church Order, Supplement to Article 8 found in this manual under Article 8.)

3) Article 10—admission of regular candidates to the ministry of the Word

b. Regulations regarding function and status of ministers of the Word
   1. Article 12—admission of a minister to specialized fields of ministerial work
   2. Article 13—loaning of a minister to serve as pastor of a congregation outside the Christian Reformed Church
   3. Article 14—release of a minister to assume a nonministerial vocation, as well as eligibility for call after release

c. Relationship of ministers to their congregations (severance and discipline)
   1. Article 17—severance of a minister from his congregation
   2. Article 90—the deposition of a minister
   3. Article 94—readmission of a deposed minister

Further information on these responsibilities is contained in the explanation of each of the above articles.

In connection with the work of the synodical deputies, synod has declared "that it is [the task of the synodical deputies either] to concur or not to concur in the action of Classis only *after* Classis has taken its decision in the matter at hand" (*Acts of Synod 1966*, p. 31). This assures that both the classis and the synodical deputies will reach their judgments independently and objectively.

3. Additional Responsibilities
   a. Advice to Classis
      The duties of synodical deputies are not limited to those specifically mentioned in the Church Order. Article 48c indicates a broader range of helpfulness: "Besides the duties elsewhere stipulated, the deputies shall, upon request, extend help to the classes in the event of difficulties in order that proper unity, order, and sound doctrine may be maintained."

      The synodical deputies are to be on call to give their help and advice as representatives of synod. With respect to such visits synod has made the following decisions:

      "Synod urges its deputies to insure that all synodical rules are observed in matters that concern their advice to a classis, and that when such rules are violated, explicit reason for the allowance of such deviation be given to synod.
      "Synod reminds its deputies of the high priority to be given to requests to serve as advisers to classes." *(Acts of Synod 1969, p. 30)*

   b. Duties re Specialized Ministerial Tasks
      See comments on Article 12, section 4.

4. Reports of Synodical Deputies
   a. Article 48d of the Church Order stipulates, "The synodical deputies shall submit a complete report of their actions to the next synod."
   b. "Synod informs its examiners that the reports must be signed by all the delegates. . . give the full name of the minister examined, the denomination from which he comes, and the congregation to which he has been called."
   (Acts of Synod 1959, p. 107)
   c. "The Synodical Examiners shall present their reports to the Classes in duplicate. It shall be the duty of the Stated Clerk of the Classis to transmit one copy of their advice to the Stated Clerk of Synod." *(Acts of Synod 1963,* p. 61)
   d. "Synod instructs the synodical deputies to file complete reports in accordance with the rules for such reports." *(Acts of Synod 1971,* p. 68)

   If decisions of synodical deputies are not carefully elaborated, the synod operates with insufficient information. In the event of any irregularities the deputies should outline the nature of such irregularities or problems involved in their judgment.

5. Synodical Action re Deputies' Reports
   a. All reports of synodical deputies are reviewed and adjudicated by synod.
   b. If a classis cannot concur with the advice of the deputies, the matter is automatically placed on the agenda of the next synod and rests in *status quo* until synod adjudicates the matter. (Cf. *Acts of Synod 1908,* pp. 36-37.)

II. THE ASSEMBLIES OF THE CHURCH
D. THE SYNOD (continued)

ARTICLE 49

INTERCHURCH RELATIONS

a. Synod shall appoint a committee to correspond with other Reformed churches so that the Christian Reformed Church may exercise Christian fellowship with other denominations and may promote the unity of the church of Jesus Christ.

b. Synod shall decide which denominations are to be received into ecclesiastical fellowship, and shall establish the rules which govern these relationships.

1. Interchurch Relations Committee

The Synod of 1977 adopted the following paragraphs, covering the Basic Mandate, the Scope of the Work, and the Specific Responsibilities of the Interchurch Relations Committee:

I. Basic Mandate
   A. The Interchurch Relations Committee is a standing committee of the Christian Reformed Church, authorized by Article 49 of the Church Order.
   B. The basic mandate of the committee is expressed in Church Order Article 49: namely, to serve as the official agency of liaison between the Christian Reformed Church and other churches throughout the world. As a committee of synod the Interchurch Relations Committee shall exercise only those powers which are assigned by synod.
   C. Synod of 1944 has adopted the following principles relating to the ecumenical responsibilities of the Christian Reformed Church (*Acts of Synod 1944,* pp. 83-85; 330-367):
      1. The Christian Reformed Church is closely related to other Christian churches as being with them a manifestation of the church, which is the one body of Christ.
      2. Though organizational unity is not the paramount interest of the church, its spiritual unity should come to expression as much as possible.
      3. Where organizational unity cannot be realized, churches should relate to each other in the spirit of Article 49 of the Church Order.
      4. For the purpose of implementing interchurch relations in the spirit of Church Order Article 49, the churches of Christ may be roughly classified

into four groups: Eastern Orthodox churches, the Roman Catholic Church, non-Reformed Protestant churches, and Reformed churches. Hence the Christian Reformed Church may maintain a variety of types of interchurch relations.

5. The Christian Reformed Church should seek unity in the truth with all churches of Christ but should attach priority to churches which are Reformed as to confession, polity, and liturgy, as determined not only by their formal standards but also by their actual practice.

6. The unity of those churches which are Reformed in confession, polity and liturgy should come to organizational expression as soon and as fully as possible.

7. In shaping this organizational unity, consideration should be given to such circumstances as language, distance, and non-essential differences in formal standards and practice.

II. Scope of the Work of the Interchurch Relations Committee

A. The Committee on Interchurch Relations shall actively seek to promote and maintain relations of the Christian Reformed Church:
1. with churches in ecclesiastical fellowship,
2. with other churches of Reformed persuasion,
3. with ecumenical organizations in which the Christian Reformed Church cooperates with other denominations of Reformed faith, in accord with Church Order Article 50.

B. Relationships of the Christian Reformed Church with other churches of Reformed practice shall be governed by the following regulations of synod (cf. *Acts of Synod 1974*, p. 57):
1. There shall be one relationship with other Reformed churches designated by synod as "Churches in Ecclesiastical Fellowship."
2. The receiving of churches into ecclesiastical fellowship implies, and where possible and desirable involves:
   a. exchange of fraternal delegates at major assemblies,
   b. occasional pulpit fellowship,
   c. intercommunion (i.e., fellowship at the table of the Lord),
   d. joint action in areas of common responsibility,
   e. communication on major issues of joint concern,
   f. the exercise of mutual concern and admonition with a view to promoting the fundamentals of Christian unity.

C. The committee shall maintain a broader interest in the church at large through study and contact with ecumenical organizations and other denominations.

III. Specific Responsibilities of the Interchurch Relations Committee

A. The Interchurch Relations Committee shall continue close relationships with the denominations which have been named by synod as churches in ecclesiastical fellowship.

B. The Interchurch Relations Committee shall recommend to synod which additional churches are to be received into ecclesiastical fellowship.

C. The Interchurch Relations Committee shall recommend which specific kinds of fellowship and cooperation shall apply to each church in ecclesiastical fellowship.

D. The Interchurch Relations Committee shall initiate and/or pursue contact and closer relationship with churches other than those referred to in A, B, C above in accord with the principles laid down in I, C above.

E. Ecumenical Organizations—The Interchurch Relations Committee shall serve as the agency of contact with ecumenical organizations.

1. It shall serve as the agency of liaison of the Christian Reformed Church with those ecumenical organizations with which the CRC is affiliated, such as the Reformed Ecumenical Synod and the North American Presbyterian and Reformed Council.

2. It shall welcome suggestions from the churches and present to synod names of nominees as delegates to the Reformed Ecumenical Synod and shall designate those who are to serve as delegates to NAPARC and its various committees.

3. It shall study the activities of the above two ecumenical organizations and present to synod reports on the work of these organizations and such recommendations as may be necessary.

4. It shall observe and study various other ecumenical organizations and report the results of such observations and studies to synod.

5. It shall maintain contact as circumstances warrant with ecumenical organizations with which the Christian Reformed Church has not affiliated.

F. The Interchurch Relations Committee shall annually present to synod in its printed agenda a report of its activities which shall include a resumé of all the interchurch relations comprehended in the mandate detailed above.

(Acts of Synod 1977, pp. 38-40)

2. Churches in Ecclesiastical Fellowship

Article 49b states: "Synod shall decide which denominations are to be received into ecclesiastical fellowship, and shall establish the rules which govern these relationships."

a. Processing of Relationships

The reception of churches in ecclesiastical fellowship is processed by the Interchurch Relations Committee in accord with its mandate above. However, the synod itself must make the final decisions with respect to receiving other denominations as churches in ecclesiastical fellowship.

Synod must also establish the rules pertaining to these relationships when they are established.

b. Churches Received into Ecclesiastical Fellowship and Dates of Reception:

1) Associate Reformed Presbyterian Church (1977)

2) Christian Church of Sumba (Indonesia) (1974)

    3) Christian Reformed Church of Nigeria (1974)

    4) Dutch Reformed Church in Africa (NGKA) (1979)

    5) Dutch Reformed Church of Ceylon (Sri Lanka) (1974)

    6) Evangelical Reformed Church of Brazil (1974)

    7) Gereformeerde Kerk in Suid Afrika (1974)

    8) Gereformeerde Kerken in Nederland (1974)

    9) Korean American Presbyterian Church (1979)

    10) Orthodox Presbyterian Church (1975)

    11) Presbyterian Church in America (1975)

    12) Reformed Church in America (1976)

    13) Reformed Church in Argentina (1974)

    14) Reformed Church of Japan (1974)

    15) Reformed Churches of Australia (1974)

    16) Reformed Churches of New Zealand (1974)

    17) Reformed Presbyterian Church of North America (1978)

    18) Tiv Church of Christ (1974)

c. Fraternal Delegates to Synod

The Stated Clerk of Synod is mandated "to invite those churches which are in ec-clesiastical fellowship with the CRC and those which are in North American Presbyterian and Reformed Council (NAPARC) to send fraternal delegates to the annual meetings of synod, while the IRC [Interchurch Relations Committee] is mandated to invite fraternal delegates from other churches with which it is work-ing, such delegates to be presented to synod by its Reception Committee for the purpose of extending the greetings of their churches" *(Acts of Synod 1976,* p. 28).

3. Ecumenical Organizations

a. Reformed Ecumenical Synod (RES)

The Christian Reformed Church was one of the constituting churches of the Reformed Ecumenical Synod. The first Reformed Ecumenical Synod was con-vened in Grand Rapids, Michigan, in 1946.

    The doctrinal basis of the RES was adopted by the Synod of 1951 *(Acts of Synod 1951,* p. 43). A revised constitution was proposed in 1972 *(Acts of Synod 1972,* pp. 294-299) and was approved by the synod of the Christian Reformed Church in 1974 *(Acts of Synod 1974,* pp. 31-33, 490).

    The RES was incorporated in 1978, the Synod of the Christian Reformed Church serving as one of the incorporating bodies *(Acts of Synod 1978,* pp. 109-110).

b. North American Presbyterian and Reformed Council (NAPARC)

In 1975 synod mandated the Interchurch Relations Committee "to formalize the membership of the Christian Reformed Church in the Council and provisionally approve the Constitution and By-Laws of the Council" (*Acts of Synod 1975,* p. 24), and the Christian Reformed Church became one of the charter members.

Other member churches of NAPARC are the Orthodox Presbyterian Church, the Presbyterian Church in America, the Reformed Presbyterian Church Evangelical Synod, and the Reformed Presbyterian Church of North America.

The constitution and by-laws of NAPARC are contained in the *Acts of Synod 1975,* pp. 353-355.

c. National Council of Churches (NCC)

Synod declared that it "does not approve of any consistory or congregation of our church identifying itself by membership with any local council or agency of the National Council of Churches, or a similar local organization, which includes 'churches' that deny the orthodox faith and scriptural teaching" (*Acts of Synod 1958,* pp. 92-93).

d. World Council of Churches (WCC)

Synod in 1967 declared "with regret that it is not permissible for the Christian Reformed Church to join the fellowship of the World Council of Churches because of its present nature, its inadequate basis, the maintenance and functioning of that basis, its sociopolitical activities and declarations, and the implications of membership in this Council." (The full decision of synod and its grounds appear in the *Acts of Synod 1967,* pp. 89-90.)

e. National Association of Evangelicals (NAE)

In 1943 synod approved membership in the National Association of Evangelicals. CRC membership in this organization was terminated in the year 1951.

Proposals to reaffiliate with NAE were presented to the synods of 1952 and 1961. The CRC has chosen not to reaffiliate, but some of its agencies have maintained membership and associations with NAE affiliated agencies. Observers of our denomination also attend NAE conventions with regularity.

II. THE ASSEMBLIES OF THE CHURCH
D. THE SYNOD (continued)

ARTICLE 50

REFORMED ECUMENICAL SYNODS

a. Synod shall send delegates to Reformed ecumenical synods in which the Christian Reformed Church cooperates with other denominations which confess and maintain the Reformed faith.
b. Synod may present to such gatherings matters on which it seeks the judgment of the Reformed churches throughout the world.
c. Decisions of Reformed ecumenical synods shall be binding upon the Christian Reformed Church only when they have been ratified by its synod.

1. Participation in Reformed Ecumenical Synods
   Church Order Article 50a is a commitment of the Christian Reformed Church to broader ecumenical relationships. It states that "synod shall send delegates to Reformed ecumenical synods in which the Christian Reformed Church cooperates with other denominations which confess and maintain the Reformed faith."
   Whereas the Church Order speaks in general of Reformed ecumenical synods, the Christian Reformed Church was the convener and a charter member of the organization called the Reformed Ecumenical Synod (RES). Reference to the Reformed Ecumenical Synod and its history may be traced in the *Index of Christian Reformed Church Synodical Decisions*.
   The Church Order speaks in broad terms to authorize our efforts toward cooperation with all Reformed churches. Membership in the North American Presbyterian and Reformed Council (NAPARC) represents another application of Article 50a.

2. Agenda for Reformed Ecumenical Synods
   Article 50b authorizes synod to present to Reformed ecumenical gatherings "matters on which it seeks the judgment of the Reformed churches throughout the world."

3. Decisions of Reformed Ecumenical Synods
   Article 50c states, that "decisions of Reformed ecumenical synods shall be binding upon the Christian Reformed Church only when they have been ratified by its synod."
   Such synods are not to be construed as superassemblies which adjudicate the business of the member denominations on the matters submitted by them. We are

not necessarily bound by their decisions. These decisions are not always acted upon by synod. Some may be received as information, others may be used for further study, but, in any case, decisions of Reformed ecumenical synods are binding only after they have been ratified and adopted as its own by the synod of the Christian Reformed Church.

III. THE TASK AND ACTIVITIES OF THE CHURCH
A. WORSHIP SERVICES

ARTICLE 51
THE ELEMENTS AND OCCASIONS FOR WORSHIP SERVICES

a. The congregation shall assemble for worship at least twice on the Lord's day to hear God's Word, to receive the sacraments, to engage in praise and prayer, and to present gifts of gratitude.

b. Worship services shall be held in observance of Christmas, Good Friday, Easter, Ascension Day, and Pentecost, and ordinarily on Old and New Year's Day, and annual days of prayer and thanksgiving.

c. Special worship services may be proclaimed in times of great stress or blessing for church, nation, or world.

Article 51 begins the third major division of the Church Order, dealing with the Task and Activities of the Church. This division is subdivided into four sections: A. Worship Services, B. Catechetical Instruction, C. Pastoral Care, and D. Missions.

1. Worship Services on the Lord's Day
   a. Frequency
      Article 51a requires that "the congregation shall assemble for worship at least twice on the Lord's day."

   b. Time and Number of Services
      The time of worship and the number of services (more than two) are within the discretion of the consistory to decide (*Acts of Synod 1908*, p. 35).

   c. Second Sunday Service
      Attention is called to the Liturgical Committee report on this subject found in the *Acts of Synod 1973*, pp. 505-512. This report was referred to the churches for their reflection and consideration. The same synod did remind the churches "that whatever practices are followed with respect to the second service, the consistories [must] exercise care to observe Articles 51-55 of the Church Order, particularly Article 54a which states: 'In the worship services the minister of the Word shall officially explain and apply Holy Scripture' " (*Act of Synod 1973*, p. 55).

   d. Elements Essential to the Worship Service
      1) The Church Order specifies the elements that are essential to a worship service.

214

It states these in such a way that the congregation is described as actively engaged in the worship. A worship service, therefore, is not an occasion where certain things are done for people (as, e.g., by a priest even though there is no congregation present), but by the congregation. The congregation assembles: "to hear God's Word, to receive the sacraments, to engage in praise and prayer, and to present gifts of gratitude."

2) In response to questions relating to Articles 51-55 such as: How are these articles to be interpreted? How mandatory are they? Do they lay down guidelines, or do they prescribe rules which are never to be broken? And in particular, do they prescribe that in every official worship service there be a sermon, and that this be monologic in character? the Synod of 1970 replied:

a) "The articles of the Church Order, as well as their official interpretation in the Guide Rules for church visiting, clearly and explicitly state that the consistory shall see to it that, in the worship services of the congregation, the Word of God be proclaimed in which, through the preaching service, the Holy Scriptures are both explained and applied by those authorized to preach."

b) "That synod expects the churches to observe the Church Order in its explicit statements with regard to worship services so as to maintain unity of liturgical policy. (Cf. Art. 96 of the Church Order.)"

(Acts of Synod 1970, p. 69)

e. Observance of the Lord's Day

The *Post Acta* of the Synod of Dort, 1618-19, the 164th session, record the following decisions regarding the observance of the Lord's day:

1) There is in the fourth commandment of the divine law a ceremonial and a moral element.

2) The ceremonial element is the rest of the seventh day after creation, and the strict observance of that day imposed especially on the Jewish people.

3) The moral element consists in the fact that a certain definite day is set aside for worship and so much rest as is needful for worship and hallowed meditation.

4) The Sabbath of the Jews having been abolished, the day of the Lord must be solemnly hallowed by Christians.

5) Since the times of the apostles this day has always been observed by the old Catholic Church.

6) This day must be so consecrated to worship that on that day we rest from all servile works, except those which charity and present necessity require; and also from all such recreations as interfere with worship.

These principles were adopted by the Synod of 1881 (*Acts of Synod 1881*, p. 19). A further clarification of the status of these "Six Points of 1881" was made by the Synod of 1926:

"1) Although... they are [ecclesiastical definitions], their nature determines their authority, inasmuch as it is self-evident that they are doctrinal in character. In that sense they are, therefore, [sure and binding];

"2)   They constitute an interpretation of Lord's Day 38, because the same fundamental idea that the divine imperative of the fourth commandment also applies to the New Testament Church, in its observance of the day of rest and worship, is found in Lord's Day 38, and elaborated in the six points;

"3)   The six points of 1881 are to be regarded. . . as an interpretation of our Confession. First, the Synod of 1881 did not add a new confession to the Forms of Unity, but accepted the six points as an interpretation of the confessional writings, insofar as they express the Reformed position relative to the fourth commandment. Secondly, that such an interpretation given by Synod must be regarded as the official interpretation, and is, therefore, binding for every officer and member of our denominational group. Thirdly, one cannot place his personal interpretation of the Confessions or a part thereof above the official interpretation of Synod. That would make void the significance and power of the Forms of Unity."

(Acts of Synod 1926, pp. 191-192)

f. Designation of Lord's Days for Special Purposes
In 1964 synod advised its denominational boards and committees to refrain from designating certain Lord's days by a specific name such as CRWRC Sunday. The following ground was adopted:
"This tends to detract from the fact that it is the Lord's day and a day for worship since it directs one's attention to a cause or an institution rather than to worship" *(Acts of Synod 1964, p. 26; cf. also Acts of Synod 1972, p. 24; 1980, pp. 69-70).*

g. Children's Services
Synod expressed its agreement with the position stated in an overture from a classis "warning against the practice of introducing so-called 'youth services' held while the regular services are in progress" *(Acts of Synod 1961, pp. 98-99).*

2. Special Days for Worship
Article 51b designates that "worship services shall be held in observance of Christmas, Good Friday, Easter, Ascension Day, and Pentecost, and ordinarily on Old and New Year's Day, and annual days of prayer and thanksgiving."

a. Ascension Day
In 1971 synod declared that the consistory has the right to exercise its judgment [whether] the annual commemoration of the ascension of Christ [is observed] on the first or second Sunday prior to Pentecost instead of on the designated "Ascension Day" if. . .the change of date would help the church in its celebration of the Lord's Ascension *(Acts of Synod 1971, p. 137)*. This was judged to be implicit in Church Order Article 51 which states that "worship services shall be held in observance of. . .Ascension Day."

b. Old Year's and New Year's Services
"New Year's Eve and New Year's Day, though without redemptive association, are significantly meaningful to warrant public worship. The word 'ordinarily' [in

216

Church Order Article 51b] allows for enough flexibility as to the observance or non-observance of New Year's Eve or New Year's Day or both." (*Acts of Synod 1971*, p. 26)

c. Annual Day of Prayer
The Synod of 1970 reaffirmed the annual Day of Prayer in the following declaration:
"Synod continue to maintain the second Wednesday in March as an annual Day of Prayer."
"Those churches which judge that the observance of the Annual Day of Prayer can be more meaningful for them if it is observed in conjunction with the World Day of Prayer have the right to change the date of the service."
"The Annual Day of Prayer is a day of prayer specifically set aside primarily for the purpose of requesting God's blessing upon crops and industry."
(*Acts of Synod 1970*, p. 54)

3. Special Worship Services
Article 51c states that "special worship services may be proclaimed in times of great stress or blessing for church, nation, or world."

National Day of Prayer
The Synod of 1969 removed the "National Day of Prayer" from the list of special days to be observed and urged our churches in the United States to observe faithfully any national day of prayer which the United States' president publicizes to the nation (*Acts of Synod 1969*, pp. 71-72).

Previously synod had instructed the churches to observe days of prayer proclaimed by the respective governments of Canada and the United States because "these are days of national significance. Our churches must be open to our congregations and our fellow-countrymen on such occasions, when God in His providence leads those in civil authority to call our citizenry to prayer. We must pray for and with our country" (*Acts of Synod 1958*, p. 27).

III. THE TASK AND ACTIVITIES OF THE CHURCH
A. WORSHIP SERVICES (continued)

ARTICLE 52

CONSISTORIAL REGULATION OF WORSHIP SERVICES

a. The consistory shall regulate the worship services.
b. The consistory shall see to it that the synodically approved Bible versions, liturgical forms, and songs are used, and that the principles and elements of the order of worship approved by synod are observed.
c. The consistory shall see to it that if choirs or others sing in the worship services, they observe the synodical regulations governing the content of the hymns and anthems sung. These regulations shall also apply when supplementary hymns are sung by the congregation.

(Amended—*Acts of Synod 1975,* p. 46)

1. Regulation of Worship Services
   In Article 52a the stance of Synod of 1908 is affirmed: "Although it is the congregation that assembles for worship, the consistory has the responsibility for the regulation of the worship services" *(Acts of Synod 1908,* p. 35).
   The consistory's responsibility includes such matters as the times and place of the worship service, the language(s) used in worship, as well as observance of synodical regulations regarding Bible versions, liturgical forms, songs, the principles and elements of the order of worship, and of the choir or other music used in worship.

2. Synodically Recommended Bible Versions
   The designation of the Bible versions to be used in the worship services is specified in Article 47 as the task of synod. Although the Church Order speaks of "synodically approved Bible versions," synods have consistently spoken of "recommended" versions, or versions that are "acceptable for use in worship services."

   a. Recommended Bible Versions
      Bible versions which have been synodically recommended for worship services are:
      1) English Versions
         See comments on Church Order Article 47, section 1f.

2) Dutch Versions
   a) Staten Vertaling
   b) Bijbel in het Nieuwe Vertaling (*Acts of Synod 1953,* p. 20)

b. Contemporary Bible Versions
   A standing committee on Bible translation was appointed by the Synod of 1969 "to advise synod concerning the designation of Bible versions to be used in worship services, and to inform the churches concerning the quality of new translations" (*Acts of Synod 1969,* p. 49).

   This committee has published its evaluations in the official church papers and has reviewed the following new translations:
   Today's English Version (*Acts of Synod 1971,* p. 376; *1972,* p. 258)
       Cf. *The Banner* (Nov. 26 and Dec. 3, 1971)
           De Wachter (Aug. 17, 1971)
   The Living Bible: Paraphrased (*Acts of Synod 1973,* p. 274)
       Cf. *The Banner* (Nov. 24 and Dec. 1, 1972)
           De Wachter (Sept. 12, 1972)
   New English Bible *(Acts of Synod 1974,* p. 308)
       Cf. *The Banner* (June 20 and 27, 1975)
   New International Version (N. T. only) (*Acts of Synod 1975,* p. 314; *1976,* p. 289)
       Cf. *De Wachter* (Aug. 27, 1974)
   New International Version (complete Bible) (*Acts of Synod 1980,* pp. 70-71, 252-71)

3. Synodically Approved Liturgical Forms
   Article 52b also requires the consistory to see to it that the synodically approved liturgical forms are used in worship services. The adoption of these forms is specified in Article 47 as the task of synod.

   Synod declared "that formally the Liturgy does not have the same binding force as the Forms of Unity...because by the nature of the case the Liturgy does not have the same character [as the Forms of Unity]. In the case of Baptism and the Lord's Supper the use of the prescribed forms is obligatory" (*Acts of Synod 1916,* pp. 30, 31; cf. also Church Order Art. 55).

   Current copies of all liturgical forms which have been adopted by synod are found in the most recent editions of the *Psalter Hymnal.*

   "Synod expects the churches to observe the Church Order in its explicit statements with regard to worship services so as to maintain unity of liturgical policy."

   (Acts of Synod 1970, p. 69)

4. Synodically Approved Songs
   Article 47 specifies that the adoption of the *Psalter Hymnal* is the task of synod; Article 52b requires the consistory to see to it that synodically approved songs are used in the worship services.

   a. Statement of Principle
   A statement of principle for the music of the church was adopted by the 1953

219

Synod together with a series of implications which were recommended to the churches for study (cf. *the Psalter Hymnal; Acts of Synod 1953*, pp. 24-25):

PRINCIPLE: THE MUSIC OF THE CHURCH SHOULD BE APPROPRIATE FOR WORSHIP

1.   The music of the church should be liturgical—In spirit, form, and content it must be a positive expression of scripturally religious thought and feeling. It should serve the ministry of the Word.

2. The music of the church should be beautiful—Its religious thought or spirit should be embodied appropriately in the poetry as poetry, in the music as music, and in the blending of these in song. It should satisfy the aesthetic laws of balance, unity, variety, harmony, design, rhythm, restraint, and fitness which are the conditions of all art.

The principles above were restated by the Synod of 1979 as follows:

The music of the church should be appropriate for worship—that is, it should be liturgical and have aesthetic integrity. The music of worship should serve the dialogue between God and his people. It must be true to the full message of the Scriptures and reflective of biblical Christian experience. Along with this biblical motif, the music of worship should give expression to the other motifs of liturgy: the catholic, the confessional, and the pastoral. The music of worship should satisfy the aesthetic laws that are conditions of good art, such as imaginative craftmanship and seriousness of expression. It should reflect the church at worship today and throughout the ages in ways that are relevant, enduring, festive, and dignified.   (*Acts of Synod 1979*, p. 20)

Implications

1. The music of the church should represent the full range of the revelation of God.

2. The minister of the Word, on the one hand, and the organist and the choir director on the other, should cooperate constantly, so that the service of music will contribute to the service of the Word.

3. The poetry of the songs should be good poetry; it should not have to rely upon the music to carry it. The music of the songs should be artistically defensible as good music; it should not have to rely upon the words to carry it.

4. Whenever Psalms or other portions of Scripture are involved, the poetry of the songs should be true to the inspired Word. Such poetry should at the same time be vital—free from the defects of artificiality and sentimentality.

5. Whenever songs other than versifications of portions of Scripture are involved, the poetry should be genuinely expressive of religious experience, but should also be in harmony with the whole counsel of God.

6. The music of the church should be suitable to the liturgical text to which it has been adapted. It should be free from association with the currently secular or with anything that does violence to our Reformed conception of worship.

7. The music of the church should not be borrowed from that of the dance nor

220

from concert or other music which suggests places and occasions other than the church and the worship service.

8. Such devices as extreme syncopation and extreme chromaticism (although on occasion these may be of value for special text settings) should generally be avoided.

9. Great care must be exercised by the organist and choir director in selecting organ music and anthems, lest a secular association with the music interfere with the worshiper's service.

10. The music of the church should be expressive of our Reformed tradition and, so far as possible, should make use of the Genevan Psalm tunes and other music of Calvinistic inspiration.

b. The *Psalter Hymnal*

The *Psalter Hymnal* is the official book of praise of the Christian Reformed Church. In 1930 synod affirmed the principle of the use of the Psalms in worship: "In the Churches only the 150 Psalms of David...and the collection of Hymns for Church use, approved and adopted by Synod, shall be sung. However, while the singing of the Psalms in divine worship is a requirement, the use of the approved Hymns is left to the freedom of the churches."

(Acts of Synod 1932, p. 135)

c. The *Psalter Hymnal Supplement*

The 1971 Synod approved the production of a supplement to the *Psalter Hymnal,* which was published in 1974. The Synod of 1972 adopted principles, guidelines, and a long-range program for this supplement:

1) Principles for the Selection of Songs

"1. The singing in the church should be united praise and prayer; it should be response to God's acts of revelation to his people. The songs should fit into the liturgy which is in the nature of a dialogue between God and his people.

"2. Music is not centrally significant in worship, but secondary. The central purpose for the gathering of God's people is to hear the Word of God. Music and singing serve a supportive role, enabling the people to respond with meaningful gratitude to God's revelation.

"3. Instrumental music and instrumental accompaniments are entirely supportive of the text, intended only to assist the congregation in the corporate response that worship requires.

"4. The texts of hymns used in worship should be God-centered and true to God's Word.

"5. Both heart and mind are exercised in singing, hence the worshippers must be informed. This requires an on-going education of the church members in matters of music and singing and an understanding of their place in worship.

"6. The very best possible craftsmanship, in the writing of music and songs, as well as in performance, should be sought. There should be no room for shoddy work.

"7. The appropriateness of specific details in the practice of music and singing should be judged by contemporary standards. That is to say, we cannot simply adopt the Old Testament or New Testament or Reformation
era musical standards as entirely normative for today.

"8. Worship is a corporate activity. The songs sung in the public worship service should reflect that corporate unity and not be too individualistic an
expression of spiritual experience."

2) Guidelines for the Selection of Songs
"Selections for the *Psalter Hymnal Supplement* must:
1. meet liturgical requirements and practices;
2. support the preaching of and the response to the Word;
3. not allow the music to obtrude upon the text;
4. be scriptural and confessional as to content of lyrics;
5. be worthy of the educational program we recommend and not merely a collection of old favorites or simply familiar tunes;
6. be well-crafted as to composition, and yet not difficult for execution;
7. be relevant to the idea-patterns of the time;
8. serve for corporate worship and reflect the church's universality."

3) The Long-range Program
The Synod of 1972 appointed a special committee with the following mandate:
"a. to continue the program of educating the church in the newer, yet excellent, song styles that are available as well as some older unknown or
untried styles;
"b. to continue to screen and submit for provisional use by means of a *Banner* pull-out insert existing hymns and psalms not now in current use in
the churches;
"c. to continue to solicit and judge original compositions, which would be
published periodically as a pull-out in *The Banner,* used experimentally in
the churches, and so finally approved or not as they deserve;
"d. to engage in a revision of some existing songs in the Psalter Hymnal,
altering the instrumentation, harmonic patterns, vocal range, texts, and
such other details as will encourage the most universal use of the existing
collection of psalms and hymns."

(Acts of Synod 1972, pp. 415-418; cf. also p. 49)

5. The Order of Worship
Article 52b also requires the consistory to see to it "that the principles and elements
of the order of worship approved by synod are observed." This entire section of the
Church Order (Arts. 51-62) deals with the various components of the worship service.

The Synod of 1930 recognized the right of local consistories to consult the best interests of their churches in devising an order of worship. Though synod affirmed
that all churches should conform to whatever decisions are made touching the order
of worship, it declined to prescribe a specific order of worship for all the churches.
"It is not to be sustained upon the grounds of Scripture and Church Order, that it

lies within the jurisdiction of synod to prescribe a specific order of worship and to enforce its introduction into the churches" (*Acts of Synod 1930,* p. 187).

The *Acts of Synod 1928* (Report pp. 276-302), the *Acts of Synod 1930* (Report pp. 335-353) and the *Acts of Synod 1968* (Report pp. 134-198) contain valuable studies on the subject of orders of worship, including principles of liturgy and model forms of liturgy.

"The right of the local consistories to consult the best interests of their churches with respect to the introduction of an Order of Worship was recognized; an open way is left open for synod to employ means to advise and educate our churches with a view to reaching as great a measure of uniformity as is possible and practicable."

(Acts of Synod 1930, p. 187)

The Doxology: "The place of the doxology in the order of worship shall be left to the discretion of the consistories" *(Acts of Synod 1928,* p. 54).

6. Choirs and Others Who Sing

Article 52c requires the consistory to "see to it that if choirs or others sing in the worship services, they observe the synodical regulations governing the content of the hymns and anthems sung." This requirement also applies to supplementary hymns sung by the congregation.

The basic regulations governing the use of choirs in the worship services were adopted by synod in 1930 and amended in 1944:

"Though the introduction of choir-singing is left to the discretion of the consistory, synod nevertheless discourages choir-singing as a distinct element of public worship on the following grounds:

"1) The danger exists that congregational singing shall be curtailed.

"2) If the choir sings separately there is the difficulty of maintaining the principle of [former] Article 69 of the Church Order." (*Acts of Synod 1930,* p. 101) "In cases where choirs exist or will be introduced, it is insisted that only those Psalms or hymns shall be sung which are approved by [former] Article 69 of the Church Order; or such anthems as contain only the exact words of portions of Scripture; or such anthems or hymns which have previous consistorial approval as to their Scriptural soundness."

(Acts of Synod 1944, pp. 27-28)

It should be noted that Article 69 of the Church Order of 1914 which provided that "in the churches only the 150 Psalms of David, the Ten Commandments, the Lord's Prayer, the Twelve Articles of Faith, the Songs of Mary, Zacharias and Simeon, the Morning and Evening Hymns and the Prayer before the Sermon shall be sung" (*Acts of Synod 1914,* p. 64) is no longer a part of the Church Order.

The Synod of 1975 added the following question to the Guide for Church Visiting: "Do you observe the synodical regulations governing the content of hymns and anthems to be sung in worship services, and do you supervise the choice of choir anthems, solo anthems and supplementary hymns according to these regulations and according to the statement and implications of the principles of music as found in the *Psalter Hymnal*?" *(Acts of Synod 1975,* p. 47)

III. THE TASK AND ACTIVITIES OF THE CHURCH
A. WORSHIP SERVICES (continued)

ARTICLE 53

THE CONDUCTING OF WORSHIP SERVICES

a. The ministers of the Word shall conduct the worship services.
b. Persons licensed to exhort and anyone appointed by the consistory to read a sermon may conduct worship services. They shall, however, refrain from all official acts of the ministry.
c. Only sermons approved by the consistory shall be read in the worship services.

1. The Ministers of the Word
Article 53a assigns the conduct of worship services to the ministers of the Word (cf. Art. 11).

Article 11 of the Church Order defines the task of the minister to include the conduct of public worship services. Article 53a becomes specific and assigns the conduct of worship services to the ministers of the Word. Others such as licensed persons and elders or others appointed by the consistory to read a sermon (Art. 53b) do so by way of exception to the general rule stated in Article 53a.

Ministers of other denominations are permitted to preach in the churches provided that the consistory is convinced that such a minister is committed to the Reformed confessions (*Acts of Synod 1904*, p. 39).

"The Benediction, like the Salutation, is, by common consent of the Christian Church of all ages, to be pronounced only upon those assemblies of God's people in which they, with their children, meet with God for the specific purpose of corporate worship." (*Acts of Synod 1934*, p. 136)

2. Licensed Persons and Appointed Persons
Article 53b authorizes "persons licensed to exhort" and "anyone appointed by the consistory to read a sermon" to conduct worship services.

For regulations governing theological students and those granted licensure by a classis, see Articles 22 and 43.

It is not required that persons appointed by a consistory to conduct a worship service be office-bearers. Such persons, however, may only read sermons approved by the consistory.

3. Official Acts of Ministry

   Article 53b requires licensed and appointed persons to "refrain from all official acts of the ministry."

   The phrase "official acts of ministry" is nowhere defined in the Church Order or in synodical regulations.

4. Sermons for Reading Services

   Article 53c states that "only sermons approved by the consistory shall be read in the worship services."

   Synod has recognized the need for Reformed sermons and has appointed "a permanent Committee to collect suitable sermons for reading service, and attend to their distribution, as need arises" (*Acts of Synod 1940*, p. 33; cf. also *Acts of Synod 1974*, p. 18).

   These sermons, called *Living Word,* may be obtained from:
   Rev. Peter Nicolai
   27 Dittmer Cres.
   Rexdale, ON, Canada M9W 497

   A book of sermons on the Heidelberg Catechism may be obtained from:
   Board of Publications
   2850 Kalamazoo Avenue, SE
   Grand Rapids, MI 49560

III. THE TASK AND ACTIVITIES OF THE CHURCH
A. WORSHIP SERVICES (continued)

ARTICLE 54
PREACHING

a. In the worship services the minister of the Word shall officially explain and apply Holy Scripture.
b. At one of the services each Lord's day, the minister shall ordinarily preach the Word as summarized in the Heidelberg Catechism, following its sequence.

1. Responsibility to Explain and Apply Holy Scripture
   In harmony with Article 11 the task of the minister of the Word is here defined as being the official explanation and application of Holy Scripture. This general principle also governs the use of the Heidelberg Catechism in one of the services each Lord's day. By virtue of his preparation, examination, and ordination the church commits this trust to the minister; he is certified by the church to speak on its behalf and in its name to proclaim the Scriptures.

   The "Form for the Ordination (or: Installation) of Ministers of the Word," included in the *Psalter Hymnal,* further defines this part of the task of the minister as follows:

   "The minister of the Word is called by the command of God to preach the Gospel of His kingdom. This preaching has the two-fold object of calling sinners to reconciliation with God through Jesus Christ, and nurturing believers in the faith and life of the kingdom of God. Ministers are called 'ambassadors for Christ,' as though God were pleading by them, 'Be reconciled to God' (II Corinthians 5:20). This preaching must be addressed to all men. The preaching of the Gospel must also be addressed to the gathered congregation for the nurturing of Christian faith and life and for strengthening them against all error. Paul charged Timothy 'in the presence of God and of Christ Jesus,' to 'preach the word, be urgent in season and out of season, convince, rebuke, and exhort, be unfailing in patience and in teaching' (II Timothy 4:1-2), and he charged Titus that a minister 'must hold firm to the sure word as taught, so that he may be able to give instruction in sound doctrine and also to confute those who contradict it' (Titus 1:9)."

2. Preach the Word as Summarized in the Heidelberg Catechism
   Article 54b requires that "at one of the services each Lord's day, the minister shall ordinarily preach the Word as summarized in the Heidelberg Catechism, following its sequence."

Preaching on the Heidelberg Catechism must remain preaching the Word of God. The word *ordinarily* allows for occasional interruptions, but the minister is required to follow the sequence of the Catechism from Sunday to Sunday.

The new translation of the Heidelberg Catechism adopted by synod in 1975 may be found in the latest editions of the *Psalter Hymnal.* A Harmony of the Heidelberg Catechism, the Belgic Confession, and the Canons of Dort may be found in the *Acts of Synod 1974,* pages 619-622, and also in the latest edition of the *Psalter Hymnal,* pages 65-68.

The Guide for Church Visiting describes the church's official understanding as to how the Heidelberg Catechism is to be used as follows:

"Do you have preaching services at least twice on each Lord's day, once from a text the choice of which is left free, and once after the order of the Heidelberg Catechism, so that no Lord's Day is omitted, and are the words of the Catechism division to be preached read to the congregation before the sermon is preached, and are these sermon explanations and applications of the materials contained in the Lord's Day under consideration?"

(Acts of Synod 1950, p. 441; cf. also p. 62)

3. Preaching from the Confessional Standards

The Synod of 1973, while retaining the statement of the Church Order, Article 54b, nevertheless encouraged "the use of the Belgic Confession and the Canons of Dort, as well as the Heidelberg Catechism, in preaching" *(Acts of Synod 1973,* p. 65).

III. THE TASK AND ACTIVITIES OF THE CHURCH
A. WORSHIP SERVICES (continued)

ARTICLE 55

THE ADMINISTRATION OF THE SACRAMENTS

The sacraments shall be administered upon the authority of
the consistory in the public worship service, by the minister of
the Word, with the use of the prescribed forms.

1. Upon the Authority of the Consistory
   Article 55 states that "the sacraments shall be administered upon the authority of the
   consistory." Ministers are not permitted to administer baptism or the Lord's Supper
   on their own authority.
   In unorganized churches the sacraments may be administered under the supervision of a neighboring consistory. This must be accompanied by the preaching of the
   Word and with suitable representation of the consistory (*Acts of Synod 1908*, p. 37).

2. In the Public Worship Service
   Article 55 also states that "the sacraments shall be administered. . .in the public worship service."
   "The word 'public' in Article 55. . .is to be defined in the historical sense as the
   opposite of 'private' and the expression 'public worship service' should be
   understood to mean any service in which God's people gather for worship at the call
   and upon the authority of the consistory. . . . This allows each consistory the freedom
   to exercise its full responsibility in the administration of the sacraments."
   (Acts of Synod 1971, pp. 131, 132)
   "The phrase in Article XXXV of the Confession of Faith, 'we receive this holy
   sacrament in the assembly of the people of God' and the phrase in the Revised
   Church Order, Article 55, 'in the public worship service,' refer to a congregational
   setting for the celebration of the Lord's Supper. Therefore, an appeal to the Confession of Faith does not open the way to non-congregational settings for the Lord's
   Supper." *(Acts of Synod 1971*, p. 130)

3. By the Minister of the Word
   Article 55 assigns the administration of the sacraments to "the minister of the
   Word." Synod also authorized the evangelist to administer baptism and the Lord's
   Supper in the emerging church to which he is called (*Acts of Synod 1979*, p. 17). It
   should be noted that such authorization of an evangelist pertains only to the particu-

228

lar emerging church in which he labors and is not a general authorization as in the case of ministers.

The relationship of the Word and the sacraments is stated as follows in the guidelines adopted by synod in 1973 with respect to the nature of ecclesiastical office and ordination:

"7. The tasks of the preaching of the Word and of the administration of the sacraments have been given by Christ to the church. Although in the Scriptures these tasks are not explicitly limited to special office-holders, historically they have been assigned to and carried out by those whom the church has appointed on Christ's authority.

"8. There is no valid biblical or doctrinal reason why a person whom the church has appointed to bring the Word may not also be appointed to administer the sacraments." (*Acts of Synod 1973*, p. 63)

The "Form for the Ordination (or: Installation) of Ministers of the Word," found in the *Psalter Hymnal,* defined this part of the task of the minister of the Word as follows:

"The minister of the Word is called to administer the sacraments which the Lord has instituted as signs and seals of His grace. Christ gave this charge to His apostles, and through them to all ministers of the Word, when He commanded them to 'make disciples of all nations, baptizing them in the name of the Father and of the Son and of the Holy Spirit' (Matthew 28:19); and when He said of the Lord's Supper: 'Do this in remembrance of me' (I Corinthians 11:24, 25)."

The question "whether a minister of the church may administer the sacraments outside of our denomination in non-Christian Reformed Churches" was answered in the negative. "If a special occasion should arise, the classis should be consulted" (*Acts of Synod 1886*, p. 35).

In 1957 Synod recognized "the authority of the missionary, in consultation with and by permission of those supervising his work, to receive professions of faith and to administer the sacraments to members of the church, though these have not yet been organized into self-governing congregations" (*Acts of Synod 1957*, p. 100).

4. With the Use of the Prescribed Forms
Article 55 states also that the sacraments shall be administered "with the use of the prescribed forms."

The synodically approved and prescribed formularies for the administration of the sacraments are printed in the *Psalter Hymnal.*

"The prescribing of obligatory formularies is not contrary to the Bible.
"*Grounds:*
"1. The Bible neither commands nor prohibits the use of formularies.
"2. Formularies are used by the church for the purpose of remaining faithful to her Lord." (*Acts of Synod 1971*, pp. 130-131)

III. THE TASK AND ACTIVITIES OF THE CHURCH
A. WORSHIP SERVICES (continued)

ARTICLE 56
ADMINISTRATION OF INFANT BAPTISM

The covenant of God shall be sealed to children of believers by holy baptism. The consistory shall see to it that baptism is requested and administered as soon as feasible.

1. The Covenant of God
   The covenantal doctrine upon which baptism is based is found in Article 34 of the Belgic Confession, in Lord's Days 26 and 27 of the Heidelberg Catechism, and in the baptismal forms in the *Psalter Hymnal.*
   The Synod of 1964 answered an appeal regarding the question whether persons who were not convinced of the truth of the doctrine of infant baptism could be admitted into church membership as follows:
   "1. Article 61 [now 59] of the Church Order does not deny the right and duty of a consistory to evaluate each case of admittance according to the special circumstances of the persons requesting such admittance [to membership].
   "2. In this case the couple agrees wholeheartedly with the Reformed religion, except on the point of direct biblical evidence for the doctrine of infant baptism, and is willing to be further instructed in the Reformed doctrine of baptism.
   "3. This couple also promised not to propagate any views conflicting with the doctrinal position of the church." (*Acts of Synod 1964*, p. 63)

   Note: A previous decision by the Synod of 1888 (*Acts of Synod 1888*, p. 19) declared that a consistory "might not accept anyone as a member of the church who *denies and opposes* infant baptism" [italics added to differentiate from the decision of 1964].

2. Children of Believers
   Article 56 requires that holy baptism shall be administered to "children of believers." Various synods have dealt with questions relating to this requirement:

   a. Children of Parents Who Have Not Professed Their Own Faith
      "Parents who present their children for baptism must, according to Holy Writ and the Church Order, both, or at least one of the two, have acknowledged their own baptism by personal profession of faith."

      (*Acts of Synod 1898*, p. 76; *1902*, p. 65)

b. Failure to Present Children for Baptism
"Members who, because of scruples of conscience, fail to present their children for baptism should be instructed and admonished patiently; and if this proves ineffective, they should be disciplined." *(Acts of Synod 1888*, p. 19)

c. Parents under Formal Discipline
Church Order Article 85 bans persons under discipline from responding to the baptismal questions.

d. Baptism of Adopted Children
A number of study committees have addressed this issue. Significant reports on this question can be found in the following *Acts of Synod*:

    1910, p. 139-148;
    1930: pp. 89-93; cf. Agenda Report 1, pp. 111-148;
    1932, pp. 102-110;
    1934: cf. Agenda Report, pp. 97-234;
    1936, pp. 53-57.

The basic decision re the baptism of adopted children was made by the Synod of 1930 which declared that "children who were not born of believing parents, but who are adopted by believers, may be baptized" *(Acts of Synod 1930*, p. 93).

"This 1930 decision in no way justifies the molestation of anyone who, whether as church member or in the specific capacity of office-bearer, may have conscientious scruples against the administration of [the sacrament of] baptism to such children." *(Acts of Synod 1936*, pp. 54-55)

"According to the decision of 1936, a consistory has the right to refuse permission to baptize adopted children." *(Acts of Synod 1954*, p. 84)

A decision was made in 1949 (cf. *Acts of Synod 1949*, p. 20) that "no adopted child should be baptized until the probation period is over and the adoption made final." This decision was rescinded by the Synod of 1968 which lifted "the restriction imposed by the Synod of 1949 and grant[ed] each consistory, in consultation with the adoptive parents, the freedom to decide when children placed in adoptive homes should be baptized" *(Acts of Synod 1968*, p. 17).

3. Request for and Administration of Infant Baptism
Article 56 states that "the consistory shall see to it that baptism is requested and administered as soon as feasible."

"Article 56 of the Church Order determines the time of baptism only on the basis of feasibility. Only the local consistory can determine that feasibility, which specifically includes the desires of the parents. Consistories ought to be willing to grant permission for early baptism where such is requested" (as opposed to waiting for a stated Sunday per month at which time baptism will be administered). *(Acts of Synod 1960*, p. 41)

Synod has ruled that baptism may not be administered without using the entire form for baptism *(Acts of Synod 1914*, p. 80).

4. Recording of Baptisms
Article 68 of the Church Order provides that "each church shall keep a complete record of all...baptisms."

5. Historical Note
The Synod of Dort 1618-19 determined that "baptism may be administered outside of the meeting of the congregation to children or adults who are sick, only in critical emergency, and with the consent of and in the presence of the consistory; and it shall not be administered to condemned criminals except with the advice of delegates of classis" (Synod of Dort 1618-19, Post Acta, Session 163).

III. THE TASK AND ACTIVITIES OF THE CHURCH
A. WORSHIP SERVICES (continued)

ARTICLE 57

ADMINISTRATION OF ADULT BAPTISM

Adults who have not been baptized shall receive holy baptism upon public profession of faith. The Form for the Baptism of Adults shall be used for such public professions.

1. Adult Baptism

Article 57 states that "adults who have not been baptized shall receive baptism upon public profession of faith." The preface to Form Number I for the Baptism of Adults contains the following instructions:

"When those who were not baptized in their youth, upon coming to the years of discretion, desire to receive Christian baptism, they shall first be thoroughly instructed in the fundamentals of the Christian religion. And when they have made a good profession thereof before the consistory, they shall be permitted to make public profession and receive holy baptism; in the administration of which the following form shall be used."

2. Rebaptism

Article 57 applies only to adults who have not previously been baptized, not to those who were baptized in infancy and wish to be rebaptized.

In 1971 synod dealt with an appeal from a person who "gradually became convinced that the believer's water baptism is the only water baptism which God teaches in the Bible," and who wished to be rebaptized. Synod denied the appeal "since that would mean approval of a teaching and practice which are not in accord with the teaching of Scripture and the confession of the Christian Reformed Church" (*Acts of Synod 1971*, p. 162).

In 1973 the synod dealt with the case of a person who was rebaptized (the same person whose appeal was denied in 1971). Synod adopted the following:

"1. The churches are urged to preach and to teach faithfully and explicitly the biblical doctrine of infant baptism as this is rooted in the covenant and the unity of the Testaments, and thus to avoid and correct tendencies toward an individualistic understanding of the workings of God's grace.

"Parents must be urged to live up to the vows made at the time of the baptism of their children, specifically to instruct their children with respect to the meaning and implications of infant baptism.

233

"2. Members who are attracted to the view of 'believers' baptism' should be urged to seek the counsel of the office-bearers of the church concerning the biblical teaching on infant baptism.

"3. Whenever a consistory is reliably informed that a member has been re-baptized, the consistory shall officially ask such a member whether he still considers himself a member of the Christian Reformed Church and is willing to submit to the teaching and discipline of the Christian Reformed Church.

"a. If the reply is in the affirmative, the consistory must faithfully and persistently admonish such an erring member.

"b. The consistory should bar such a member from the Lord's table only if it is necessary for the unity and well-being of the congregation.

"c. If such a member actively disturbs the unity and peace of the congregation, the regular steps of discipline should be followed.

"4. Since neither the Bible nor the Confessions nor the Church Order allow consistories simply to terminate membership in the church when such action is not requested by the member, such a member as mentioned above can be excluded from the church only if he is worthy of excommunication, which is the act of public declaration by the church that such a person has no part in Christ or in his church.

"5. Under no circumstances should members erring in this respect be allowed to hold office in the church." (*Acts of Synod 1973*, p. 78)

3. Form for Adult Baptism

Article 57 requires that "the Form for the Baptism of Adults shall be used for such public professions." The synodically approved forms are found in the *Psalter Hymnal.*

234

III. THE TASK AND ACTIVITIES OF THE CHURCH
A. WORSHIP SERVICES (continued)

ARTICLE 58

VALID BAPTISM

The baptism of one who comes from another Christian denomination shall be held valid if it has been administered in the name of the triune God, by someone authorized by that denomination.

1. Administered in the Name of the Triune God
   Article 58 mentions two criteria for determining the validity of the baptism of a person who comes from another Christian denomination. The first of these is "if it has been administered in the name of the triune God."
   Baptism, to be valid, must be administered according to the institution of Christ in Matthew 28:19, "baptizing them in the name of the Father and of the Son and of the Holy Spirit."

2. Administered by an Authorized Person
   The second criterion mentioned by Article 58 for determining the validity of baptism is if it has been administered "by someone authorized by that denomination."
   Baptisms administered by private persons who are not duly authorized by their denomination are not valid baptisms.
   A fuller definition of valid baptism was adopted by the Synod of 1906:
   "Baptism is valid when it has been administered:
   a. According to the institution of Christ.
   b. In a gathering which resembles a gathering of believers.
   c. By a leader who by this assembly was considered a legitimate minister."
   (Acts of Synod 1906, p. 17)

3. Baptism with the Holy Spirit
   a. The Synod of 1973 (*Acts of Synod,* pp. 71-79, 398-493) addressed the following counsel to the churches with respect to the question of baptism with the Holy Spirit:
      "In the face of the phenomenon known variously as the charismatic or neo-Pentecostal movement, synod declines to assume a detached and non-committal attitude. The Christian Reformed Church cannot ignore the challenge that has come to her from those who identify themselves with this

movement. For these persons commonly lay at her doorstep the charge that the church as they know it has failed them. They generally accuse that church of having neglected to preach to them and transmit to them the 'baptism with the Holy Spirit'—the overpowering experience of the presence of God as a blessing distinct from and in addition to the experience of conversion. They now tend to look not to the church and its corporate life but to a neo-Pentecostal fellowship for the vitality, the assurance, and the experience they crave. And in their desire to revitalize the church to which they belong, they now devote themselves to the spread of this movement's 'superior spirituality.' Neo-Pentecostalism confronts the church, therefore, with a fundamental challenge.

"It is synod's conviction, on the one hand, that the church must examine herself. She must do so particularly with regard to the painful lack of religious assurance exhibited by many of her members, the limited display of joy and power in the service of Jesus Christ, and the widespread lack of appreciation for a full-fledged covenantal life in Christ as the Bible speaks of it. She must re-emphasize, in terms of today's needs, that the Gospel with its wealth of teaching is intended to produce a salvation that is *experienced.* For that she will need to accent clearly that in both the proclamation and the reception of salvation the work of the Holy Spirit is indispensable.

"Synod is convinced on the other hand that the church must firmly reject such attitudes, practices and teachings of neo-Pentecostalism as the following:

"a. the teaching that baptism with the Holy Spirit is a second blessing distinct from and usually received after conversion;

"b. a yearning for and seeking after the extraordinary, spectacular gifts of the Spirit, viewing these as primary evidence of Spirit-baptism;..."

(Acts of Synod 1973, p. 73)

b. Synod also urged the churches "to accept in love and patience those members who claim to have been baptized with the Holy Spirit as a 'second blessing' distinct from and received after conversion, and to deal firmly with them in a pastoral way so that they will be corrected in their belief, and helped to show the fruit of the Spirit, and so that the peace and unity of the church be maintained" *(Acts of Synod 1973,* p. 75).

c. Synod addressed the following affirmation to those who hold to the neo-Pentecostal position:

"According to the Scriptures a believer receives the baptism in or with the Holy Spirit at the time of his regeneration-conversion, as the apostle Paul declares: 'For in one Spirit were we all baptized into one body—Jews or Greeks, slaves or free—and all were made to drink of one Spirit' (I Cor. 12:13, ASV), so that in Christ we all 'have access in one Spirit to the Father' (Eph. 2:18) and 'are builded together for a habitation of God in the Spirit' (Eph. 2:22, ASV). Compare John 3:5f.; Acts 2:39; Romans 8:1-17; 15:13; I Corinthians 3:16f.; 12:3; II Corinthians 1:21ff.; Galatians 3:2; 5:16-26; I John 2:20,

27; and see also *Heidelberg Catechism,* Questions 49, 51, 53, 55. Synod rejects, therefore, the teaching that the baptism with the Holy Spirit is a second blessing distinct from and usually received after conversion, and declares that this doctrine is not to be taught or propagated in the Christian Reformed Church."   *(Acts of Synod 1973,* p. 74)

III. THE TASK AND ACTIVITIES OF THE CHURCH
A. WORSHIP SERVICES (continued)

ARTICLE 59
ADMISSION TO COMMUNICANT MEMBERSHIP

a. Members by baptism shall be admitted to the Lord's Supper upon a public profession of Christ according to the Reformed creeds, with the use of the prescribed form. Before the profession of faith the consistory shall examine them concerning their motives, doctrine, and conduct. The names of those who are to be admitted to the Lord's Supper shall be announced to the congregation for approval at least one Sunday before the public profession of faith.

b. Confessing members coming from other Christian Reformed congregations shall be admitted to communicant membership on the presentation of certificates of membership attesting their soundness in doctrine and life.

c. Confessing members coming from churches in ecclesiastical fellowship shall be admitted to communicant membership upon presentation of certificates or statement of membership after the consistory has satisfied itself concerning the doctrine and conduct of the members. Persons coming from other denominations shall be admitted to communicant membership only after the consistory has examined them concerning doctrine and conduct. The consistory shall determine in each case whether to admit them directly or by public reaffirmation or profession of faith. Their names shall be announced to the congregation for approval.

(Amended—*Acts of Synod 1976,* p. 43)

Article 59 deals with four categories of persons to be admitted into communicant membership: members by baptism, confessing members coming from other Christian Reformed congregations, confessing members coming from churches in ecclesiastical fellowship, and persons coming from other denominations.

1. Admission of Baptized Members
   Article 59a specifies three steps in the admission of members by baptism into communicant membership.

   a. Examination by the Consistory
      Article 59a states that "before the profession of faith the consistory shall examine them concerning their motives, doctrine, and conduct."

238

In the examination of applicants who desire to be admitted to the Lord's Supper, use shall be made chiefly of the Compendium. It shall be required that the applicant be sound in faith and blameless in conduct. (General Rules 1881, Articles 56 and 57).

Every consistory must ask of everyone who makes confession of faith whether he or she is a member of any secret society. (*Acts of Synod 1900,* p. 50; *1970,* p. 103; *1974,* pp. 58-60.)

The Synod of 1979, in answering an overture, did not accede to the concept that a consistory has the freedom to admit to membership in the Christian Reformed Church persons who are members of fraternal organizations. (See *Acts of Synod 1979,* p. 75; and also *1977,* pp. 102-106; *1970,* pp. 103-104; *1980,* p. 50-51)

"Synod instructs consistories to inquire of those who ask to be examined previous to making public profession of their faith and partaking of the Lord's Supper as to their stand and conduct in the matter of worldly amusements, and, if it appears that they are not minded to lead the life of Christian separation and consecration, not to permit their public profession."

(Acts of Synod 1928, pp. 88-89; cf. *1966,* pp. 34-36)

b. Announcement to the Congregation

Article 59a also requires that "the names of those who are to be admitted to the Lord's Supper shall be announced to the congregation for approval at least one Sunday before the public profession of faith."

"The names of those whose examination resulted favorably shall be made known to the congregation at least one Sunday before the public confession, in order to give opportunity to the congregation to make objection."

(General Rules 1881, Article 56)

c. Public Profession

Article 59a states that "members by baptism shall be admitted to the Lord's Supper upon a public profession of Christ according to the Reformed creeds, with the use of the prescribed form."

A revised form for public profession of faith was adopted in 1976 (*Acts of Synod 1976,* p. 89). A copy is found in the *Psalter Hymnal* and in the *Acts of Synod 1976* (pp. 352-354).

Since confession of faith admits one to the Lord's Supper, persons who do not intend to partake may not be admitted into the church as communicant members (*Acts of Synod 1904,* p. 38).

In 1959 synod adopted a threefold statement regarding the problem "that the Christian Reformed Church requirements for communicant membership were virtually tantamount to the qualifications expected for office-bearers.

"a. The confession made by the candidate for communicant membership must not be construed on the assumption that a disjunction may properly be made between a Christian confession and a Reformed confession.

"b. There is, nevertheless, no stereotyped pattern of confession that may be applied by consistories and sessions in the reception of members. Allowance must be made for the diverse levels of understanding of the implications of a truly Christian confession on the part of those who may be deemed eligible, in accordance with Christ's institution, for communicant membership. A fixed pattern is not adequate to meet the diversity with which consistories and sessions are confronted in concrete cases. Each individual must be examined and dealt with specifically.

"c. Church membership does not carry with it the implications that all male members in full communion are thereby deemed eligible for office in the church. Office in the church presupposes spiritual gifts for the office and doctrinal understanding and competence which may not be imposed as a condition of church membership." *(Acts of Synod 1959,* p. 21-22)

2. Admission of Confessing Members from Other Christian Reformed Congregations
   Article 59b states that such persons "shall be admitted to communicant membership upon the presentation of certificates of membership attesting their soundness in doctrine and life."

   These certificates of membership are issued by the consistory of the church from which the new member comes. Regulations for issuing the certificates are found in Article 66 of the Church Order.

3. Admission of Confessing Members from Churches in Ecclesiastical Fellowship
   Article 59c prescribes three steps in receiving into communicant membership confessing members coming from churches in ecclesiastical fellowship (A list of "Denominations in Ecclesiastical Fellowship" is presented in this manual under Article 49.):
   a. Certificates or statements of membership must be presented.
   b. The consistory must satisfy itself concerning the doctrine and conduct of the members.
   c. Announcement must be made to the congregation for approval.

4. Admission of Persons from Other Denominations
   Article 59c specifies three steps in admitting persons from other denominations to communicant membership.

   a. Consistorial Examination
      Article 59c states that such persons "shall be admitted to communicant membership only after the consistory has examined them concerning doctrine and conduct."

   b. Procedure for Admission
      Article 59c gives the consistory three options as to the procedure for admission: "The consistory shall determine in each case whether to admit them directly or by public reaffirmation or profession of faith."

   c. Announcement
      Announcement must be made to the congregation for approval.

III. THE TASK AND ACTIVITIES OF THE CHURCH
A. WORSHIP SERVICES (continued)

ARTICLE 60
ADMINISTRATION OF THE LORD'S SUPPER

a. The Lord's Supper shall be administered at least once every three months.
b. The consistory shall provide for such administrations as it shall judge most conducive to edification. However, the ceremonies as prescribed in God's Word shall not be changed.
c. The Lord's Supper shall ordinarily be preceded by a preparatory sermon and followed by an applicatory sermon.

1. Frequency of Celebration
Article 60a requires that "the Lord's Supper shall be administered at least once every three months."

"The present wording [of Church Order Art. 60] not only allows for, but encourages, the churches to celebrate the supper more often than once every three months" *(Acts of Synod 1971,* p. 131).

2. Consistorial Responsibilities
Article 60b assigns to the consistory the responsibility of providing "such administrations as it shall judge most conducive to edification," with the qualification that "the ceremonies as prescribed in God's Word shall not be changed."

Various synods have clarified certain questions relating to the administration of the Lord's Supper:

a. Method and Supervision
"The choice of method and administration of supervision is determined by the consistory since the Church Order does not speak directly to this issue" *(Acts of Synod 1975,* p. 103).

b. Use of Forms
The synodically approved forms for the Lord's Supper are found in the *Psalter Hymnal.*

Whether that part of the form for the administration of the Lord's Supper which concerns self-examination is to be read a week before communion Sunday is left to the discretion of the consistories *(Acts of Synod 1936,* p. 11).

Note: Also see comments under Article 55 in this manual.

c. Guests at the Lord's Supper
In 1975 synod adopted the following guidelines for admitting guests to the Lord's Supper:

"a. It is the responsibility of the consistory to identify guests in order to supervise properly the Lord's Supper.

"b. It is the responsibility of the consistory to inform guests as to the requirements for participation in the Lord's Supper and as to the consequence of partaking in an unworthy manner (I Corinthians 11:27-29).

"c. It is the responsibility of the consistory to invite guests 'who are truly sorry for their sins, who sincerely believe in the Lord Jesus as their Savior, and who desire to live in obedience to him,' to come to the Lord's Supper (Form 3; Heidelberg Catechism, Lord's Day 30, Q & A 81).

"Grounds:

1) These guidelines safeguard the integrity of the church.
2) These guidelines address themselves to the relationship of the guest to Christ.
3) These guidelines preserve the sanctity of the table."

(Acts of Synod 1975, p. 103)

With respect to churches in ecclesiastical fellowship, synod declared that this relationship involves, where possible and desirable, intercommunion (i.e., fellowship at the table of the Lord) *(Acts of Synod 1974,* p. 57).

d. Administration to the Sick
In the case of persons who are sick for years in succession and who desire to observe the Lord's Supper, it is permitted to administer it to them in their homes provided the congregation is represented *(Acts of Synod 1914,* p. 17).

The Synod of 1978 declined to authorize a special form for the Lord's Supper for shut-ins, declaring that this need can be met locally by adapting excerpts from Scripture and existing forms within the guidelines of the Church Order *(Acts of Synod 1978,* p. 51).

e. Neglect of the Lord's Supper
"As to what shall be done with those who constantly neglect the Lord's Supper, it is said that the indissoluble connection between baptism, the making of confession of faith, and the Lord's Supper should be urged, if necessary, by ecclesiastical discipline, in order that in the case of perseverance in the wrong way exclusion from the church may be reached in course of time."

(Acts of Synod 1904, p. 38)

3. Preparatory and Applicatory Sermons
Article 60c states that "the Lord's Supper shall ordinarily be preceded by a preparatory sermon and followed by an applicatory sermon."

"Preparatory sermons and applicatory sermons are meant to reinforce the biblical relationship between Word and sacrament." *(Acts of Synod 1971,* p. 131)

242

4. Confessional References

   The confessional basis of the Lord's Supper is found in the Belgic Confession, Article 35, and in the Heidelberg Catechism, Lord's Days 28-30.

III. THE TASK AND ACTIVITIES OF THE CHURCH
A. WORSHIP SERVICES (continued)

ARTICLE 61

PRAYER IN PUBLIC WORSHIP SERVICES

a. The public prayers in the worship services shall include adoration, confession, thanksgiving, supplication, and intercession for all Christendom and all men.
b. In the ministry of prayer the approved liturgical prayers may be used.

1. The Elements of Public Prayer

Article 61a lists the elements of public prayer in the worship services: "adoration, confession, thanksgiving, supplication, and intercession." These shall be for "all Christendom and all men."

The synodically approved "Form for the Ordination (or: Installation) of Ministers of the Word" defines the duty of the minister in the service of prayer in the following way:

"The minister of the Word is called to the service of prayer. In speaking of their calling, the apostles say: 'We will devote ourselves to prayer and to the ministry of the word' (Acts 6:4). So, too, it is the calling of all God's ministers to lead the people of God in 'supplications, prayers, intercessions, and thanksgivings. . .for all men, for kings and all who are in high positions' (I Timothy 2:1, 2)."

(Acts of Synod 1971, p. 529)

2. Liturgical Prayers

Article 61b states that "in the ministry of prayer the approved liturgical prayers may be used."

"A Collection of Prayers for Church and Family and Individual Use" is included in the *Psalter Hymnal* as part of the synodically approved liturgy of the Christian Reformed Church. An explanatory note precedes these prayers:

"These prayers all date from the time of the Reformation. With exception of the last, which was added in the beginning of the seventeenth century, they were first published in the Netherlands in an edition of the Dutch Psalter by Petrus Dathenus in the year 1566. Some of these prayers seem to have been composed by him, while others were taken in whole or in part from Calvin's liturgy or other liturgies based upon that of Calvin. Although they gradually fell into disuse, they have to the present time always been printed in every edition of the Liturgy of the Reformed Churches in the Netherlands.

244

"...A committee was appointed by the synod of 1930 to translate these prayers into the English language. Their work was submitted to the synod of 1932, and with a few slight revisions adopted by the synod of 1934. One of the prayers, namely, the Prayer for all the Needs of Christendom, was considerably abridged, but all the others are faithful renderings of the original.

"These prayers are for voluntary use. Neither the Reformed Churches in the Netherlands nor the Christian Reformed Church in our country imposes the use of prescribed forms of public prayer in worship. They are offered here, partly because of their historical interest, and partly because of the profitable aid they can render to those who are called to lead in public prayer."

(Centennial Edition of the *Psalter Hymnal,* p. 74)

The Liturgical Committee presented to the Synod of 1980 a new collection of prayers. Synod referred this collection to the churches "for study and provisional use for a period of three years with a view to these replacing or supplementing the present collection" (*Acts of Synod 1980,* pp. 42, 43, 325-47).

III. THE TASK AND ACTIVITIES OF THE CHURCH
A. WORSHIP SERVICES (continued)

ARTICLE 62
OFFERINGS

In the worship services Christian alms shall be received regularly.

1. Christian Alms (Offerings)

   The task of gathering and distributing the alms given by God's people is part of the work of the deacons. The form for their ordination expresses this function in the following way:

   "The work of the deacons consists in the faithful and diligent ingathering of the offerings which God's people in gratitude make to their Lord, in the prevention of poverty, in the humble and cheerful distribution of gifts according to the need, and in the relief of the distressed both with kindly deeds and words of consolation and cheer from Scripture."

2. Distribution of Offerings
   a. The Quota System

   The Christian Reformed Church has developed a unique system of giving to support the cooperative ministries of the churches. Each year synod adopts the budgets of the denominational agencies and computes the per-family share. This per-family share is called a "quota."

   The quota for each congregation is intended not to set an exact amount which each family must contribute, but rather to specify the equitable amount which each congregation should contribute.

   The Bible teaches that believers should support the work of Christ's church in proportion to their income. Malachi writes, "Bring the full tithes into the storehouse, that there may be food in my house; and thereby put me to the test, says the Lord of hosts, if I will not open the windows of heaven for you and pour down for you an overflowing blessing" (Mal. 3:10).

   Paul also wrote of proportionate giving for God's storehouse as an aspect of worship. "On the first day of every week, each of you is to put something aside and store it up, as he may prosper" (I Cor. 16:2).

   Families or individuals will not contribute in the manner prescribed if they contribute only the per-family amount set by the assemblies. Each family and wage earner must give as the Lord has prospered.

Proportionate giving will sometimes mean that single persons who are employed should be contributing well over the per-family quota amount. Some families with dependents and a relatively low income should not be expected to give beyond the measure in which God has blessed them. Other families, who are richly blessed with material goods, would grieve the Lord if they contributed only the per-family quota amount into the storehouse of God's church.

Faithful stewardship in the use of goods and money should be promoted in Christ's church by preaching and teaching. Church members cannot consistently pledge to the Lord all of their love while they withhold from him a tithe or fair proportion of the goods they have received as gifts of his love.

While the quota share is a general guide for the total giving of a congregation, each local congregation may employ its own means of realizing the needed budgetary contributions and love offerings for missions, education, and benevolence. In recent years a variety of methods have been employed: the general budget of the church, faith-promise pledges, special offerings, etc.

In affirming the decisions of previous synods on the necessity of paying quotas, the Synod of 1972 judged that:

1) "The success of the programs of our denominational agencies depends on the receipt of funds.
2) "The synod annually, as the broadest official representative body of our denomination, reviews all agency programs and approves budgets and quotas for these programs.
3) "The failure of some congregations to supply their quota puts added responsibility on other congregations to make up the resulting deficit.
4) "The lack of sufficient quota money puts in jeopardy the jobs of many people employed by these agencies. *(Acts of Synod 1972*, pp. 85-86)

b. Effective Date for Quotas
   1) For Established Churches
   Quotas established by synod go into effect on January 1 of the following year *(Acts of Synod 1937*, p. 27).

   2) For Churches Organized during the Year
   In the case of churches organized during the year quotas are computed from the time of organization and a proportionate reduction of quotas is permitted *(Acts of Synod 1938*, p. 89).

c. Responsibility for Quotas
   "All requests from consistories for exemption from full quota responsibility because of unusual circumstances must be presented to classis for advice."
   (Acts of Synod 1968, p. 88)
   Synod has also urged all the classes:
   1) "To request their churches to pay denominational causes before making gifts to non-denominational organizations on the synod-approved accredited list. Our denominational causes should have priority in our giving."

247

2) "To instruct its church visitors in addition to their regular duties as church visitors to also delve into reasons for any church not meeting its denominational quotas. When a classis is convinced that a member church is unable to pay the quotas, the churches within a classis, if possible, through a combined effort [should] be requested to assist a church to meet its denominational obligations" in accordance with our duty to bear one another's burdens (Gal. 6:2). (*Acts of Synod 1970*, p. 81)

d. The Family Unit
All families in the Christian Reformed Church (in organized and nonorganized churches) must be tabulated according to existing rules (*Acts of Synod 1968*, p. 88).

The per-family share is based on the following definition of what constitutes a family unit:

1) A family in which husband and wife are confessing members.
2) A family in which husband or wife by confession of faith belongs to the congregation and the marriage partner is a member by baptism, or there are one or more baptized or communicant children.
3) A family in which a widow is the acting head. *See "acts" 1986 Page 708-209*
Note: See *Acts of Synod 1906*, p. 52; *1924*, p. 94; *1954*, p. 38.

e. Above-Quota Offerings
Synod declared that the churches should put a greater emphasis on freewill offerings (above-quota gifts) in supplying the budgets of the denominational agencies, because the denominational agencies operate in increasing measure both by quota money and freewill offerings (*Acts of Synod 1972*, p. 86).

3. Accredited Agencies
Recommendations are prepared for each synod which adopts the budgets and the per-family share for each synodical agency. Synod additionally makes recommendations with respect to a number of causes and organizations not under the control of the church. The guidelines which are followed in evaluating agencies seeking synodical accreditation are:

a. "The church as an organization (institution) should consider itself responsible for appraising the programs and agencies which are closely related to its integral work (works of mercy, of Christian education, of the distribution of the Word of God, and of such avenues as will serve to the furthering of the Gospel of our Lord Jesus Christ). While the church has an unlimited interest in the work of the Lord's kingdom, and every Christian is in a real sense doing the work of the Lord's kingdom, the church cannot and should not assume the responsibility of making judgment on the worth of every kind of kingdom activity, nor the responsibility of assuming the financing of the Lord's work in every sphere of life.

b. "Accreditation of causes which are within the scope of the above limitation (works of mercy, of Christian education, of the distribution of the Word of God, and of such avenues as will serve to the furthering of the Gospel of our

Lord Jesus Christ) and are local, or regional, should be carried on by the local or regional assemblies, unless their unique character or need make this impossible.

c. "In order to move in the direction of accrediting only such causes which are intimately related with the mandate of the church as an organization and to limit the support of the synodical assembly only to such causes as cannot be carried by local or regional assemblies, the Synodical Interim Committee stipulates that synod does not assume the responsibility for any additional causes unless they are clearly and closely allied with our ecclesiastical task and ought with good reason to be recommended to the entire denomination for support.

d. "The lines of procedure above are not only an indication as to procedure with respect to new causes, but should serve as well as guidelines for the review of all the causes that have in the past been placed upon the accreditation list of synod.

e. "Whereas the Synodical Interim Committee and the synod ought to live by the guidelines above, this in no way infringes upon the broad scope of the work of the Lord in every avenue of life. Such support ought to be given on an individual basis rather than by way of ecclesiastical offerings or recommendations." *(Acts of Synod 1974*, pp. 49-50)

The lists of recommended agencies may be found each year in the *Acts of Synod* and in the *Yearbook*.

4. Supplementary Contributions

"Synod request[ed] our churches and their members to respond wholeheartedly and with unbiased consideration to the appeals of our agencies via mail solicitation of funds with full confidence that such appeals are not solicited with the thought of competing for the denominational dollar, but rather from the ordinary and special needs of a kingdom cause that cannot operate or survive without the full support and confidence of all our churches and their members.

"Synod request[ed] the churches and their members to give first and primary consideration to the mail solicitation of our denominational agencies. Further, synod observed that, as today constituted, our combined agencies and causes, both denominational and accredited nondenominational, cover a sufficiently wide spectrum of religious outreach, evangelism, works of mercy, Christian education at all levels, and many other worthy endeavors, to utilize every dollar available from our own constituency, responsibly, fruitfully, and profitably in God's service."

(Acts of Synod 1975, p. 86)

III. THE TASK AND ACTIVITIES OF THE CHURCH
B. CATECHETICAL INSTRUCTION

ARTICLE 63

THE PURPOSE OF CATECHETICAL INSTRUCTION

Each church shall instruct its youth—and others who are interested—in the teaching of the Scriptures as formulated in
the creeds of the church, in order to prepare them to profess
their faith publicly and to assume their Christian responsibilities in the church and in the world.

Article 63 begins the second subdivision of this part of the Church Order:
Catechetical Instruction.

1. The Church's Responsibility for Instruction of Its Youth
   Article 63 requires that "each church shall instruct its youth."
   Besides the school, the family, and other educational agencies, the church has its
own unique responsibility for instructing its youth, called catechetical instruction
(catechesis).

   a. Definition of Catechesis
      The following definition of catechesis comes from a report to the Synod of 1951:
      "Catechesis is the ecclesiastical cultivation of the nascent covenant-born
      spiritual life of the junior members of the church by means of the administra-
      tion unto them of the Word of God as interpreted in the official doctrinal
      standards of our church, in a manner suited to their age and their correspond-
      ing condition and needs, with a view pedagogically to their attainment, at the
      close of adolescence, of spiritual maturity and ecclesiastical majority and the
      strengthening thereby of the institutional church and the consistent propaga-
      tion of the Kingdom of God in life and the world generally."
      (Acts of Synod 1951, p. 357)

   b. Scope of Catechesis
      Since 1968 synod has understood the term "catechetical instruction" to include
      all instruction which is rightfully within the scope of the church's responsibility.
      In its report to the Synod of 1968, the Committee on Education said, "Catecheti-
      cal instruction must embrace a range of educational concerns no broader than
      and no narrower than the rightful sphere of sovereignty which is entrusted to the
      church" (*Acts of Synod 1968,* p. 284).

Summarizing the report of its committee, that same synod adopted the following statement:

"Since catechism is a specific ecclesiastical form of instruction, it must be in harmony with, and expressive of, the divinely ordained authority and calling of the church." *(Acts of Synod 1968,* p. 23)

2. The Church's Responsibility for Instruction of Others
Article 63 extends the catechetical responsibility of the church also to "others who are interested."

a. Practice Prior to 1970
Prior to 1970 most Christian Reformed churches had two educational agencies for the instruction of youth: the catechism class and the Sunday school. Officially the catechism class (catechesis) was for the covenant youth (baptized members of the church), and Sunday school was for the evangelism of children outside the covenant. In 1951 synod defined the function of these agencies as follows:

"Catechesis is uniquely the official ecclesiastical pedagogy of the covenant youth.

"The Sunday School is in principle an agency for official ecclesiastical evangelistic pedagogy, with additional utility as a voluntary association for covenantal pedagogy supplementary to the home and under the supervision of the Consistory, to be employed as the local circumstances of each congregation may dictate (e.g., for additional training where there are no Christian schools, for the stimulation of love for and interest in missions, etc.)."

(Acts of Synod 1951, p. 57)

Note: See also the report on catechetical training, *Acts of Synod 1951,* pp. 353-368.

b. Integration of Catechism and Sunday School Curricula
Already in 1928 synod took note of the desirability of unifying the instruction given in the catechism class and in the Sunday school.

"Whatever differences may be conceived to exist in status and character between Sunday School and catechetical instruction, both are given under the auspices of the Church and both are given largely to the same children. In the one instance the educational material is found in Bible story and Bible history, and in the other the object is to acquaint the children with the great doctrines of Scripture. These are found to supplement each other. It would therefore seem to be the part of wisdom to coordinate these two branches of instruction in such a way that, instead of being entirely unrelated, as is now the case, one may be helpful to the other, and both may work together to form a unified program of instruction in scriptural truth." *(Acts of Synod 1928,* p. 38)

It was not until 1970, however, that this integration actually took place. Recognizing that previous attempts had not sufficiently integrated the two agencies, the Synod of 1970 adopted a document entitled, "Toward a Unified Church School Curriculum." Among other things, this document states:

"In order to attain a unified educational ministry in which the church aims to lead people to Christian maturity in the most effective way, a single unified curriculum must be developed which will serve as a core program for the educational task of the church. This single-track curriculum must seek to do justice to the two-track program current in our churches by way of Sunday school and catechism instruction.

"This core program, in communicating educationally the single comprehensive message of Scripture, shall seek to adapt this message to all kinds of people representing the highly diversified religious commitments confronting us in our contemporary pluralistic society, and accordingly shall seek to do justice to both the catechetical and evangelistic dimensions of gospel teaching as a single educational task, teaching all who come under the influence of the church's educational ministry the Word of God in its life-relatedness as a message to be believed and obeyed.

"This core program shall address itself to persons of all ages from childhood through adulthood." *(Acts of Synod 1970,* p. 210)
Note: See also *Acts of Synod 1970,* pp. 67-68, 206-211.

c. Unified Curriculum
Since 1970 the Education Department of the Board of Publications has sought to implement the decisions of synod by developing a core curriculum for the church school which combines the objectives of both the catechism class and the Sunday school. This curriculum is known as the BIBLE WAY curriculum.

An excellent survey of all the above matters is found in a pamphlet entitled "Church Education in the Christian Reformed Church," which is available from the Board of Publications.

3. The Content of Catechetical Instruction
Article 63 requires each church to provide instruction "in the teaching of the Scriptures as formulated in the creeds of the church."

In 1968 synod adopted the following principles to govern the production of catechetical materials:
"a. The Word of God is the very basis, center, and norm of catechetical instruction.
"b. Since catechism is a specific ecclesiastical form of instruction, it must be in harmony with, and expressive of, the divinely ordained authority and calling of the church.
"c. Because the church is a confessional (i.e., creedal) community, the catechetical program must be oriented to and governed by the confessions of the church."
(Acts of Synod 1968, pp. 23-24)
The Synod of 1970 reaffirmed these principles, stating that "the essential element in the church's educational program is the administration of God's Word." Accordingly, it directed the church to "produce confessionally oriented materials and conduct a confessionally united educational ministry that does justice to the historic creeds of the church" *(Acts of Synod 1970,* pp. 208, 209).

4. The Purposes of Catechetical Instruction
Article 63 specifies two purposes of catechetical instruction: "in order to prepare them to profess their faith publicly and to assume their Christian responsibilities in the church and in the world."

The Synod of 1968 confirmed these purposes as follows:

"Because the church is a confessing community, the curriculum materials and the pedagogical methods employed in the catechetical program aim to lead catechumens to a believing response to the gospel, a meaningful confession of Christ, and an effective translation of this confession into God-centered living and witness in the world.

"Catechism instruction aims to bring the catechumen to spiritual and ecclesiastical maturity, so that he may share fully and serve fruitfully in the life and work of the church."   *(Acts of Synod 1968, p. 24)*

The Synod of 1970 likewise confirmed these purposes in the following decision:

"The goal of the educational curriculum of the church, as it administers the Word of God, is to impart to all who come under its nurture a saving knowledge of Jesus Christ and to direct them to the power which He dispenses to His servants through His Spirit for living the life of faith and obedience. In seeking to achieve this basic goal, the educational ministry of the church should strive for:

"1. a meaningful profession of faith and full participation in the life and work of the church.

"2. a broader expression of Christian discipleship in the service of God and man and in a wholesome and effective witnessing in every area of life, for the promotion of the Kingdom of God."

(Acts of Synod 1970, pp. 209-210)

III. THE TASK AND ACTIVITIES OF THE CHURCH
B. CATECHETICAL INSTRUCTION (continued)

ARTICLE 64

THE IMPLEMENTATION OF CATECHETICAL INSTRUCTION

a. Catechetical instruction shall be supervised by the consistory.
b. The instruction shall be given by the minister of the Word with the help, if necessary, of the elders and others appointed by the consistory.
c. The Heidelberg Catechism and its Compendium shall be the basis of instruction. Selection of additional instructional helps shall be made by the minister in consultation with the consistory.

Note: Refer to the comments on Article 63 in this manual for additional important information about catechetical instruction.

1. Supervision by the Consistory
   Article 64a states that "catechetical instruction shall be supervised by the consistory."
   The Synod of 1968 interpreted the term "catechetical instruction" to "embrace a range of educational concerns no broader than and no narrower than the rightful sphere of sovereignty which is entrusted to the church" (*Acts of Synod 1968*, p. 284). As such, catechetical instruction includes the entire program of the congregation.
   Already prior to the 1970 decision to integrate the catechism class and the Sunday school (see Art. 63), synod in 1951 specified the following agencies as being under consistorial supervision:

   a. The Catechism Class
   "Catechesis is uniquely the official ecclesiastical pedagogy of the covenant youth."

   b. The Sunday School
   "The Sunday School is in principle an agency for official ecclesiastical evangelistic pedagogy, with additional utility as a voluntary association for covenantal pedagogy supplementary to the home and under the supervision of the Consistory, to be employed as the local circumstances of each congregation may dictate (e.g., for additional training where there are no Christian schools, for the stimulation of love for and interest in missions, etc.)."(*Acts of Synod 1951*, p. 57)

c. The Home, the School, and Voluntary Societies
   "The church exercises supervision over the teaching of the Word of God in the other covenantal relationships of the home, the school, and voluntary societies. It does this by the use of the keys of the kingdom, i.e., the official administration of the Word of God and the exercise of discipline."

   (Acts of Synod 1951, p. 357)

2. Instruction by the Minister of the Word
   Article 64b requires that "the instruction shall be given by the minister of the Word with the help, if necessary, of the elders and others appointed by the consistory."
   In 1947 synod stressed the importance of having the minister of the Word teach the children:
   "Wherever feasible, this work too shall be done by the pastor of the church. If need be, the consistory should free him of less important labors. ... The greatest need of any church is the spiritual instruction of its future generation."

   (Acts of Synod 1947, p. 57)

   The synodical Committee on Catechetical Training explained the importance of ministerial instruction thus:
   "Catechesis is part of the ministry of the Word. That gives it high standing. There are four specific phases of the administration of the Word which are mentioned in the call extended to a minister: preaching, catechetical instruction, family visiting, and ministering to the sick. Thus, although it is usually not so honored, catechesis has a place on a par with preaching. It is no less important. It belongs just as integrally to the work of the minister. It is work for which he is specifically educated and ordained." *(Acts of Synod 1951*, pp. 357-358)

   After the adoption of the mandate for the Unified Church School Curriculum in 1970 (see comments in this manual on Art. 63), it is unlikely that the minister will teach all the classes. Article 64b states that the consistory should appoint "elders and others" to help the minister.

3. The Heidelberg Catechism and Its Compendium
   Article 64c requires that "the Heidelberg Catechism and its Compendium shall be the basis of instruction."

   a. The Heidelberg Catechism
      Originally written in 1563, the Heidelberg Catechism has been adopted as one of three Reformation confessions by the Christian Reformed Church. The latest English translation was approved by synod in 1975, and is included in the latest edition of the *Psalter Hymnal.* Appended to that translation is a harmony (cross-reference) of the Confessions of the Christian Reformed Church.

   b. The Compendium
      "The Compendium of the Christian Religion" is an abbreviation and adaptation of the Heidelberg Catechism for the instruction of those desiring to partake of the Lord's Supper. The Dutch version of the Compendium goes back to 1620, the Christian Reformed version to 1943, and the latest official revision dates from 1957.

MANUAL OF CHRISTIAN REFORMED CHURCH GOVERNMENT

c. The Basis of Instruction

There have been three different ways in which catechetical instruction given in the Christian Reformed Church has utilized the Heidelberg Catechism and its Compendium as the basis of instruction:

1) Prior to 1962

Prior to 1962 many Christian Reformed churches used the Compendium and/or numerous other catechetical booklets as the actual textbooks for instruction.

2) From 1962 to 1972

During this decade the church published a series of seven doctrinal textbooks geared to the maturity level of students from eight to twenty years old (grades 3-12). Each of these books incorporated eighteen doctrinal concepts drawn from the Heidelberg Catechism.

3) Since 1972

Although some churches continue to use the materials described above, the Synod of 1970 committed the denomination to an educational program which combines the catechism class and the Sunday school (see comments in this manual on Art. 63), and used the term "church school" to designate the program. The unified curriculum produced since 1972 contains doctrinal teaching in all its courses, and includes specific studies of the Heidelberg Catechism.

4. Additional Instructional Helps

Article 64c also indicates that "selection of additional instructional helps shall be made by the minister in consultation with the consistory."

When it becomes apparent that additional instructional materials will be useful in the church's instructional program, these should be selected by the minister of the Word in consultation with the consistory.

III. THE TASK AND ACTIVITIES OF THE CHURCH
C. PASTORAL CARE

ARTICLE 65
THE EXERCISE OF PASTORAL CARE

Pastoral care shall be exercised over all the members of the congregation. The minister of the Word and the elders shall conduct annual home visitation, and faithfully visit the sick, the distressed, the shut-ins, and the erring. They shall encourage the members to live by faith, comfort them in adversity, and warn them against errors in doctrine and life.

Article 65 begins the third subdivision of this part of the Church Order: Pastoral Care.

1. Pastoral Care over the Congregation
Article 65 states that "pastoral care shall be exercised over all the members of the congregation."

Although this article only speaks of the responsibility of the consistory to provide pastoral care to the members of the congregation, consistories and pastors should be ready to provide appropriate care for others as well whenever the occasion arises.

2. Responsibility for Pastoral Care
Article 65 assigns the responsibility for pastoral care to the "minister of the Word and the elders."

This provision conforms to Articles 12a and 24 which define the duties of the minister of the Word and the elders respectively. The "Form for the Ordination (or: Installation) of Ministers of the Word" describes the pastoral function of both ministers of the Word and elders as follows:

"The minister of the Word is called, together with the elders, to shepherd the people of God in the Christian life, giving guidance and counsel in all things needful, exhorting them to contend earnestly for the faith once for all delivered to the saints (Jude 3), and keeping the church of God in good order and discipline. They are pastors, appointed to shepherd the church of Christ which he purchased with his own blood, in keeping with the Lord's command: 'Feed my sheep!' 'Feed my lambs!' They, together with the elders, watch over the house of God for the right and fruitful ordering of the faith and life and worship of the people of God. In their exercise of the keys of the kingdom, what they bind on earth shall be bound in heaven, and what they loose on earth shall be loosed in heaven (Matthew 18:18)."
(*Acts of Synod 1971*, p. 529)

3. Pastoral Tasks

Article 65 requires the minister of the Word and the elders to "conduct annual home visitation, and faithfully visit the sick, the distressed, the shut-ins, and the erring."

a. Home Visiting

Each home in the congregation should receive an official visit from the consistory once a year. The Guide for Church Visiting (cf. comments in this manual on Art. 42) includes the following questions:

"Is the minister of the Word faithful in visiting the sick, the distressed, and the erring, and does he assist the elders in the work of annual family visiting?"

"Do the elders faithfully visit the members of the congregation in regular family visiting, and also when there is a need for comfort, encouragement, or instruction?"

b. Pastoral Visiting

Both the minister of the Word and the elders are expected to visit the sick, the shut-ins, and the erring. The Guide for Church Visiting includes this question regarding the entire consistory:

"Do the members of the consistory, as their office demands, regularly visit the families, the sick, and the poor?"

4. The Purpose of Pastoral Care

Article 64 states that there are three components in pastoral care which ministers of the Word and the elders must exercise. They shall:

a. "*Encourage* the members to live by faith"

b. "*Comfort* them in adversity"

c. "*Warn* them against errors in doctrine and life"

The Guide for Church Visiting asks these questions of the entire consistory:

"What is the spiritual condition of the church?"

"Does the consistory promote and preserve peace, unity, and love among the members?"

5. Pastoral Declarations by Synod

On a number of occasions various synods have spoken pastorally to the churches with respect to matters of conduct, societal responsibilities, as well as ethical and doctrinal issues. These are published separately in a special volume entitled "Synodical Decisions on Doctrinal and Ethical Matters." This pamphlet is obtainable from the Board of Publications and contains statements on the following topics:

DOCTRINAL MATTERS

1. The Bible
2. Common Grace
3. Conclusions of Utrecht
4. Creation and Evolution
5. Interchurch Relations
6. Eschatology
7. Neo-Pentecostalism

ETHICAL MATTERS
8. Abortion and Birth Control
9. Amusements and Film Arts
10. Christian Education
11. Labor Organizations and Corporate Responsibility
12. Church and State
13. Homosexuality
14. Liquor Problem
15. Lodge and Church Membership
16. Lord's Day
17. Marital Matters
18. Race Relations
19. War, Pacifism, and Amnesty
(Cf. *Acts of Synod 1975*, pp. 602-603.)

The Synodical Interim Committee provides updated copies of "Synodical Decisions on Doctrinal Matters, Ethical Matters, and Ecclesiastical Matters" in the handbook for consistories, "Your Church in Action." These materials are available in notebook form from the Synodical Office.

The updated materials for the handbook include Guidelines for Ethical Decisions about War, Guidelines for Understanding the Nature of Ecclesiastical Office and Ordination, An Evangelism Manifesto, A Statement of Mission Principles, and the Judicial Code of Rights and Procedures.

III. THE TASK AND ACTIVITIES OF THE CHURCH
C. PASTORAL CARE (continued)

ARTICLE 66
MEMBERSHIP TRANSFERS

a. Confessing members who remove to another Christian Reformed church are entitled to a certificate, issued by the consistory, concerning their doctrine and life. When such certificates of membership are requested, they shall ordinarily be mailed to the church of their new residence.
b. Members by baptism who remove to another Christian Reformed church shall upon proper request be granted a certificate of baptism, to which such notations as are necessary shall be attached. Such certificates shall as a rule be mailed to the church of their new residence.
c. Ecclesiastical certificates shall be signed by the president and clerk of the consistory.

1. The Issuing of Certificates of Membership
   Article 66a stipulates that "confessing members who remove to another Christian Reformed church *are entitled to* a certificate, issued by the consistory, concerning their doctrine and life." It is to be noted that this provision deals only with *confessing members* (members by baptism are dealt with in Art. 66b) *who remove to another Christian Reformed church*. (Those who remove to another denomination are dealt with by synodical regulation; see section 4 below.)
   Various regulations concerning membership transfers have been adopted from time to time:
   "A certificate of membership may never be given to anyone who requests it because of difficulties one has with other members of the congregation, but these matters must be settled in the congregation where one is a member according to the instruction which Jesus Christ has given us." (*Acts of Synod 1898*, p. 72)
   A membership transfer must be granted to a member, even though it is evident, according to the judgment of the consistory, that it is requested in order to escape discipline (*Acts of Synod 1916*, pp. 48-49).

2. The Transmitting of Certificates of Membership
   Article 66a also stipulates that "when such certificates of membership are requested, they shall ordinarily be mailed to the church of their new residence."
   Requests for transfer of membership should be made as soon as it is known to which church the member is transferring.

The provision for mailing membership certificates is in contrast to the earlier custom of immigrants carrying their letter with them when they moved. In similar extraordinary circumstances members may deliver their own certificates.

There are several synodical regulations concerning the reception of membership certificates by the new consistory:

A member who moves shall not be admitted as a member into another congregation until his membership transfer has been received there (*Acts of Synod 1914*, p. 69).

"A member having requested his consistory to give him a testimony as to his membership remains a member of his church until his letter of membership has been accepted by the consistory of the church with which he desires to affiliate himself." (*Acts of Synod 1936*, p. 51)

Membership transfers containing information about conduct or discipline shall generally be accepted with the understanding that the proper ecclesiastical course is to be pursued. In exceptional cases consistories shall act according to their best judgment (General Rules of 1881, Art. 64).

The Synod of 1980 adopted a single certificate of membership to replace previous tranfer forms for baptismal and communicant members. This form provides adequate membership information for the transfer of baptized members, communicant members, single members, and families. Synod adopted this statement for use in transferring members within the denomination and to churches in ecclesiastical fellowship (*Acts of Synod 1980*, p. 22; see also Appendix of this manual, p. 342).

3. Certificates for Members by Baptism
Article 66b provides that "members by baptism who remove to another Christian Reformed church shall upon proper request be granted a certificate of baptism, to which such notations as are necessary shall be attached."

4. Members Who Remove to Other Denominations
   a. Churches in Ecclesiastical Fellowship
   Synod advised "consistories, under normal circumstances, to grant transfer of membership. . .to members seeking to affiliate with a church in ecclesiastical fellowship" (*Acts of Synod 1977*, p. 33).

   Note: A list of churches in ecclesiastical fellowship can be found in this manual under Article 49.

   b. Churches Not in Ecclesiastical Fellowship
   The Church Order does not contain regulations governing members who remove to denominations which are not in ecclesiastical fellowship. However, in 1959 synod approved an official Statement of Dismission of members to other denominations. Its use is not required, but it may be used at the discretion of the consistory (*Acts of Synod 1959*, p. 37).
   The Synod of 1980 decided that "when members choose to affiliate with a church not in ecclesiastical fellowship, the sending consistory may use the state-

ment of membership form, or should provide an appropriate statement of membership for that specific situation" (*Acts of Synod 1980,* p. 22).

5. Signatures for Ecclesiastical Certificates
Article 66c requires that "ecclesiastical certificates shall be signed by the president and clerk of the consistory."
   The dual signature is required to ensure that the certificate is issued by the official authority of the consistory.
   Consistories may obtain Certificate of Membership forms or Statement of Dismission Cards from the Board of Publications.

Note: A copy is included in the Appendix, p. 342)

6. Membership of Separated Mates
The Synod of 1908 ruled that "the membership of a wife who lives apart from her husband should remain in the church where he is a member" (*Acts of Synod 1908*, p. 42). This rule was rescinded in 1976 on the grounds that:
"a. The rule prejudices against the wife.
"b. The rule often removes the wife—and the children—from effective pastoral care and excludes her for quite some time from a real belonging to a local church fellowship."   (*Acts of Synod 1976*, p. 39)

7. Confessional Reference
The theology of church membership upon which Article 66 is based may be found in the Belgic Confession, Article 28:

EVERY ONE IS BOUND TO JOIN
HIMSELF TO THE TRUE CHURCH

"We believe, since this holy congregation is an assembly of those who are saved, and outside of it there is no salvation, that no person of whatsoever state or condition he may be, ought to withdraw from it, content to be by himself; but that all men are in duty bound to join and unite themselves with it; maintaining the unity of the church; submitting themselves to the doctrine and discipline thereof; bowing their necks under the yoke of Jesus Christ; and as mutual members of the same body, serving to the edification of the brethren, according to the talents God has given them.... Therefore all those who separate themselves from the same or do not join themselves to it act contrary to the ordinance of God."

III. THE TASK AND ACTIVITIES OF THE CHURCH
C. PASTORAL CARE (continued)

ARTICLE 67
ABSENTEE MEMBERS

Members who move to localities where there is no Christian
Reformed church may, upon their request, either retain their
membership in the church of their former residence, or have
their certificates sent to the nearest Christian Reformed
church.

1. Retention of Membership
   Article 67 provides two options for "members who move to localities where there is
   no Christian Reformed church." They may "either retain their membership in the
   church of their former residence, or have their certificate sent to the nearest Christian Reformed church." They must make request to the consistory for either of
   these.

2. Lapsing of Membership (Supplement, Art. 67)
   a. Persons Who Move Away from the Area of Their Church
      In 1974 synod decided that if members fail to request either of the above options,
      the consistory has the authority to declare their membership lapsed after two
      years.
        Synod declared that "baptized or confessing members who move away from
      the area of their church so that a meaningful church relationship is no longer
      possible, may retain their membership in their home church at their request and
      with the consent of the consistory. If they fail to make such a request, and do not
      transfer to a church near them, the consistory, having made serious attempts to
      rectify the situation, may declare their membership lapsed after a period of two
      years from the date of their departure. The member concerned shall be notified
      by the consistory of its action if at all possible."
        This rule does not apply to those whose absence from their home church is tem-
      porary.
      Grounds:
      1) "This recommendation removes the inconsistency between the decisions of
         synod in 1881 and 1910.
      2) "The primary responsibility for church membership rests with the members,
         but this does not exclude a certain responsibility of the home church and its
         consistory.

263

3) "The lapsing of membership should be by the action of the consistory in each individual case and not by automatic application of a rule, if proper pastoral work is to be carried out.

4) "No delinquency should be assumed on the part of those who are absent from their home church temporarily, as for reasons of education, military service or comparable circumstances.

5) "Pastoral concern for the well-being of the members warrants extending the time element from one year and six weeks to two years."

"This regulation supersedes the rules of 1881 and 1910."

(Acts of Synod 1974, pp. 81-82)

b. Persons Who Fail to Attend and Support Their Church

Synod decided that "with respect to a baptized or confessing member who, for a period of at least two years, has not moved but fails to attend and support the congregation that holds his membership, the consistory may declare that his membership has lapsed. This may be done when all the following conditions are present:

1) He claims to be still committed to the Christian faith.

2) He claims to be worshiping elsewhere.

3) The consistory is not aware of any public sin requiring discipline.

"Grounds:

"a) Since membership involves both rights and obligations, the right of membership may be forfeited when the obligations of membership in a local congregation are refused.

"b) After an adequate period during which the elders instruct the member in his responsibilities as a member of the congregation, his membership has become meaningless, and the action of declaring the membership lapsed is simply an acknowledgment of an already existing rupture between the member and the congregation.

"c) This provision has become necessary because of the increasing trend on the part of many churches and fellowships to ignore or reject the significance of membership in the visible church.

"d) This is consistent with the decision of synod that one who has separated himself from the fellowship of the congregation by moving away and takes no action to become a member of another church may also lose his membership by consistorial action.

"e) This will assist consistories, who at present face the alternative of taking no effective action with such a member or proceeding to erase or excommunicate him from the body of Christ, by providing a way of removing his name from the membership rolls without being required to pass judgment on his relationship to the church universal.

"Appropriate announcements [must] be made by the consistory to the congregation regarding such lapsed memberships and the person involved be notified."

(Acts of Synod 1976, p. 25)

3. Church Membership of Foreign Missionaries
   The Mission Order of the Board for Christian Reformed World Missions provides that missionaries "shall become members of the national church with which they labor if this is feasible and also retain membership in the Christian Reformed Church" *(Acts of Synod 1976,* p. 181 [Mission Order Art. VII. 5]).

III. THE TASK AND ACTIVITIES OF THE CHURCH
C. PASTORAL CARE (continued)

ARTICLE 68

MEMBERSHIP RECORDS

Each church shall keep a complete record of all births, deaths, baptisms, professions of faith, receptions and dismissals of members, and excommunications and other terminations of membership.

1. Church Records
   Article 68 requires that "each church shall keep a complete record" of the membership, and specifies the items to be included.

   Although there is no official form for maintaining the records of a congregation, useful forms are available from the Board of Publications. These are provided in either Membership Record Binders or Membership Record Cards.

   A commendable practice is followed by some consistories which conduct an annual review of the membership records to see whether all information has been accurately and fully recorded. This is frequently done when statistics are prepared for the denominational *Yearbook*.

2. Denominational Statistics
   Denominational, classical, and congregational statistics are published annually in the *Yearbook* of the Christian Reformed Church, available from the Board of Publications.

   Synod, recognizing the importance of the *Yearbook* and our denominational statistics, has mandated the Synodical Interim Committee with responsibility for the preparation of the *Yearbook* and has named the Stated Clerk the editor of this official publication. The Christian Reformed Board of Publications compiles, prints, and distributes the *Yearbook* on behalf of synod *(Acts of Synod 1971,* pp. 75-76).

   Synod requires that consistories, classes, and denominational agencies must report their statistics each year to the office of Stated Clerk. Synod has adopted several regulations pertaining to denominational statistics and has repeatedly urged the clerks of consistories and classes to submit the required information accurately and to meet the necessary deadlines promptly.

   The Synod of 1979 urged "our consistories to take special care that the statistics submitted for the *Yearbook* are up to date, accurate and fully in accord with the rules of synod" *(Acts of Synod 1979,* p. 30).

III. THE TASK AND ACTIVITIES OF THE CHURCH
C. PASTORAL CARE (continued)

ARTICLE 69
SOLEMNIZATION OF MARRIAGE

a. Consistories shall instruct and admonish those under their spiritual care to marry only in the Lord.
b. Christian marriages should be solemnized with appropriate admonitions, promises, and prayers, as provided for in the official form. Marriages may be solemnized either in a worship service, or in private gatherings of relatives and friends.
c. Ministers shall not solemnize marriages which would be in conflict with the Word of God.

1. Instruction Concerning Marriage in the Lord
   Article 69a requires that "consistories shall instruct and admonish those under their spiritual care to marry only in the Lord."
   To marry "in the Lord" means to marry a person who is a Christian. Consistories have the responsibility to provide such instruction and admonition to those under its spiritual care.

2. Solemnization of Marriage
   a. The Form for Marriage
      Article 69a requires that "Christian marriages should be solemnized with appropriate admonitions, promises, and prayers, as provided for in the official form."
      The approved "Form for the Solemnization of Marriage" was adopted by the Synod of 1934 (cf. *Acts of Synod 1934,* pp. 109, 295-297) and is printed in the *Psalter Hymnal.*
      A translation of this English form into the Dutch language was approved in 1953. (Cf. *Acts of Synod 1953,* pp. 45-48, where a copy can be found.)
      Additional forms were adopted by synod in 1977 and 1979. (Cf. *Acts of Synod 1977,* pp. 87, 406-409; *1979,* pp. 73, 367-370.)

   b. The Marriage Ceremony
      Article 69b also provides the option that "marriages may be solemnized either in a worship service, or in private gatherings of relatives and friends."
      Wedding customs in the Netherlands required two ceremonies, a legal ceremony performed by the state, and an ecclesiastical ceremony of confirmation

performed by the church. Since customs in Canada and the United States require only one ceremony, our present Church Order offers the option of conducting the ceremony either in a regular worship service or in a private gathering.

The following announcement must be made on the previous Sunday if the wedding takes place in a regular (or special) worship service:

"_____and_____ have signified their desire to be united in marriage in this church on _____. If there are no lawful objections, the ceremony will take place on that date." *(Acts of Synod 1934, p. 295)*

3. Marriages in Conflict with God's Word
Article 69c insists that "ministers shall not solemnize marriages which would be in conflict with the Word of God."

Significant reports concerning marriage have been prepared in recent years, and although they have not all been adopted by synod, they have been submitted to the churches for comments. These reports can be found in the following *Acts of Synod:*
1961, pp. 25-26, 134-140 (The report of the Reformed Ecumenical Synod);
1975, Report 38, pp. 488-514;
1976, Report 35, pp. 458-496;
1977, Report 35, pp. 510-548.

4. Divorce and Remarriage
The Church Order does not deal specifically with the questions relating to divorce and remarriage. There are, however, important synodical decisions regarding them.

a. The Sanctity of Marriage
"1. The consistories are urged most earnestly to guard the sanctity of marriage, and warn unceasingly against every violation of the marriage bond through unbiblical divorce or through adultery, keeping in mind the need for true repentance on the part of all who seek admission to the Church..
"2. The consistories are advised that people who are guilty of unbiblical divorce, or who are divorced as the result of their own adultery and having remarried, seek entrance or reentrance into the Church, shall be expected to show their sorrow and genuine repentance during an adequate period of probation. Such cases shall not be settled without the advice of Classis.
(Acts of Synod 1956, pp. 59, 118)

Note: the Synod of 1968 decided to drop the last sentence of the above, namely, "Such...Classis." Synod did state that it becomes the responsibility of classis in case of appeal (see *Acts of Synod 1968,* pp. 60-61).

"3. These declarations are referred to the consistories for their guidance so that they may deal with the concrete cases which come before them in accordance with the given situations, the demonstrable teaching of Scripture on marriage, divorce, repentance, and forgiveness, and the general provisions of the Church Order." *(Acts of Synod 1975, pp. 490-491)*

b. Remarriage after Divorce
"1. No substantial and conclusive Scriptural evidence has been produced to

establish the thesis that parties remarried after being divorced on the ground of their own adultery, or divorced on non-Biblical grounds, are living in continual adultery.

"2. No substantial and conclusive Scriptural evidence has been produced to warrant the demand that a person remarried after being divorced on the ground of his own adultery, or divorced on non-Biblical grounds, must, in order to prove the sincerity of his repentance, cease living in the ordinary marriage relationship with his present spouse."

(Acts of Synod 1956, pp. 59, 117-118)

c. Church Membership
Synod declared that admitting or readmitting to membership in the church persons who have been divorced on unbiblical grounds, and have remarried, or who are divorced as a result of their own adultery and have remarried, is the task of the consistory and is the responsibility of classis only in the case of appeal.
Grounds:
1. This is in harmony with the Church Order which designates the authority of the assemblies of the church as follows: "Each assembly exercises, in keeping with its own character and domain, the ecclesiastical authority entrusted to the church by Christ; the authority of consistories being original, that of major assemblies being delegated" (Art. 27a).
2. This is in harmony with the Church Order which stipulates with respect to the discipline of members as follows: "Confessing members who have offended in doctrine or in life and who have responded favorably to the admonitions of the consistory shall be reconciled to the church upon sufficient evidence of repentance. The method of reconciliation is to be determined by the consistory" (Art. 84).
3. Even in the matter of the readmission of excommunicated persons, the Church Order specifies that the consistory with the approbation of the congregation is empowered to readmit to the fellowship of the church (Art. 87).
4. This change in procedure does not diminish the force of the synodical admonition, "The consistories are advised that people who are guilty of unbiblical divorce, or who are divorced as the result of their own adultery and having remarried, seek entrance or reentrance into the Church, shall be expected to show their sorrow and genuine repentance during an adequate period of probation..." *(Acts of Synod 1956, p. 118; 1968, p. 61).*

5. Guidelines for the Ministry of the Church in Matters of Marriage, Divorce, and Remarriage
The Synod of 1980 (*Acts of Synod 1980*, pp. 480-485) adopted a set of "Guidelines for the Ministry of the Church" and referred "the same to pastors, consistories, and the church for guidance in handling the important matters of marriage, divorce, and remarriage":
"The church has a special interest in marriage and the family, for the Christian family is an important witness to the unity Christ creates. The unified Christian family, which is open toward the body of Christ, enriches this body, and contributes

269

to the unity of the family of God. Thus the church must develop a full-orbed ministry to strengthen marriage and family relationships, and to heal the brokenness that destroys the unity Christ gives.

"The ministry of the church is a corporate ministry of the entire body. Although the official teaching, preaching, and pastoral ministries of the church are of great importance, the mutual ministry and witness of Christian families and persons to each other is equally important. It is part of the responsibility we assume for one another. Thus the guidelines for ministry are guidelines for the entire church.

"a. The Educative Ministry

"Instruction is especially important in an age when the Christian view of marriage is not understood and often under attack. Therefore, the church must proclaim and teach the biblical doctrine of marriage, including both the creation ordinance and/or the law of marriage, as well as the significance of sin, grace, and redemption for marriage.

"To achieve this, the church must:

"1. Emphasize the sovereign claim of God on all of life so that also in the marriage relationship the first consideration is to please God by doing his will.

"2. Stress the God-willed permanence of marriage and counsel against violation of the marriage bond.

"3. Proclaim that Christian marriage is a relationship in which the grace of God in Christ enables one to live within the unity God demands.

"4. Teach that both partners in marriage fail in various ways to keep the covenant they make. Such failure is sin and such sin tends to separate those whom God has joined.

"5. Teach that in Christ husbands and wives are called to be reconciled to each other. They are to confess their sins, forgive one another, make restitution, and again live faithfully to their vows to love, honor, and cherish.

"6. Teach that we do not possess within ourselves the power to keep covenant. No one is able to keep the promise to be a husband or wife to the other and to love, honor, and cherish no matter what the circumstances of life, or what the other does to us or fails to do. Only the powerful grace of God can make each able so to keep covenant. Therefore, husband and wife must seek from God what they need in order to be faithful. The church must teach without ambiguity that God will give what each needs in order to keep covenant.

"7. Teach that marriage is not an end in itself but finds its fulfillment and ultimate purpose in the family of God, and, therefore, that Christian marriage must pattern itself after the relationship of Christ and his church.

"8. Promote a forgiving, sympathetic, and open church fellowship in which concern, compassion, and help can be freely offered and freely received.

"9. Challenge the heresies of our day which destroy marriage, e.g., the heresies of selfism, individualism, and humanistic secularism.

"b. The Ministry to Those Whose Marriages Are in Crisis

Sin disrupts the unity we have in Christ. Therefore, besides teaching and proclaiming the biblical doctrine of marriage, the church has a special ministry to those whose marriages are in crisis and to those who may be contemplating divorce.

"For such the church must:

"1. *Communicate hope to those who are losing hope.* The ground of such hope is not themselves, but God; not their good intentions nor the willingness or capacity of either to change, but the promise of God that he will bless those who seek him.

"Those who would have a well-grounded hope must begin by seeking for themselves the forgiving, restoring, and cleansing power of God. They must seek the grace of God in Christ so that they live in obedience to their vows regardless of the responses of their spouses.

"Persons who have experienced the power of the resurrection in their own marriages which once were dead but are now alive, can become powerful witnesses to such hope.

"2. *Exercise a ministry of reconciliation.* The church must call the marriage partners to confession, forgiveness, reconciliation, and renewed obedience. To achieve this the church must listen so that she understands the attitudes and behaviors of each spouse toward the other, how these affect the marriage relationship, and what God teaches concerning these attitudes and behaviors.

"But the church must not only listen, she must also speak in confrontation and with promise. Where overt sinful conduct is present, the church must address the Word of God in rebuke. Where separation is contemplated, the church must warn concerning the seriousness of such action. God declared to Old Testament Israel that he hated the breaking of the marriage covenant (Mal. 2:14-16). This will of God in favor of the permanence of marriage must be declared, for it is a primary motivation for reconciliation—and the grace of God makes reconciliation attainable.

"When one or both spouses refuse reconciliation or refuse to begin to live again in covenant faithfulness, the church must remind them of the sacredness of vows once taken and of the biblical demand for forgiveness and reconciliation. Recognizing, however, the complexities created by the deeply intimate relationships that marriage entails, the church must also encourage both partners to exhibit a patience like that of our Father in heaven. Where children are involved, parents should be encouraged to consider also the needs of the children as members of their family and of the family of God. The church must continue to encourage, sustain, and support so that hope does not die.

"3. *Develop a corporate ministry of reconciliation.* Friends, fellow Christians, and family must respond promptly with a ministry of hope and reconciliation to those whose marriage is in crisis. Such ministry may begin with one person but the gifts of many must be exercised. The prompt corporate response of fellow believers is necessary for healing to take place within the body of Christ. To develop such a corporate ministry of reconciliation, the church must encourage those whose marriage is in crisis to seek help and assistance, and the church in response must develop an appropriate ministry of support.

"4. *Consider the purpose of discipline:* namely whether formal discipline might not be a helpful or necessary means to achieve the repentance of persons involved in marital crisis, when one or both partners by word or deed refuse to hear the word of God, refuse the call to repentance and forgiveness, and appear to have closed their hearts to the hope of possible reconciliation.

"c. The Ministry to Those Who Are Divorced

Divorce is a traumatic experience and is often the occasion for deep grief with its constituent elements of guilt, anger, loneliness, and feelings of failure. A sense of shame experienced by divorced persons, by others toward them, and by parents or children of the divorced, frequently results in the divorced and their families feeling ostracized from even minimal fellowship. In addition, the many readjustments and the reorganization of many aspects of life contribute to the trauma that is divorce.

"Therefore, the church must:

"1. Continue to minister with special concern for those involved in this traumatic experience. Divorced persons need to be supported pastorally in a way similar to the manner in which other members involved in other personal difficulties are supported. Even where there is great guilt in divorce with no apparent repentance, the church must continue to minister persistently and patiently.

"2. Speak with clarity where sinful conduct is overt and apparent. However, recognizing the limits of human ability to discern the subtlety and intricacy of human motivation, the church must recognize the limits of its ability to assess guilt and blame in the intimate and private turmoil of marital distress.

"3. Understand that marital breakdown and divorce requires pastoral attention which emphasizes repentance, forgiveness, and reconciliation. As long as there is openness to the Word and to the pastoral counsel and admonition of the consistory, participation in the sacraments, which are a means of grace, should not be denied.

"4. Exercise formal discipline only when there is disdain for the biblical teachings and when unrepentance is beyond doubt. Marital breakdown and divorce does not by itself mean the loss of church membership.

"5. Maintain within the life and work of the church a place of acceptance and appreciation for those who by divorce are living the single life so that they may experience the vital spiritual, moral, and social support they need. The church must take special care to supply what is needed by the children of divorced members so that they may receive what is essential for their development as persons and members of the family of God.

"d. The Ministry to Those Contemplating Remarriage

The permanence of the marriage relationship lies at the heart of the biblical teaching on marriage. God wills a lifelong unity of husband and wife in marriage. Consequently, the basic declaration of Scripture is that divorce and remarriage while one's spouse is alive constitutes adultery (cf. Matt. 5:32; Mark 10:11-12; Rom. 7:2-3).

"The Bible also indicates that there can be circumstances involving unchastity (*porneia*) where the judgment of adultery does not fall upon a person who remarries after a divorce. However, the exceptive clause by itself does not fully inform us concerning all the relevant circumstances. Thus the two passages containing the exceptive clause (Matt. 5:32; 19:9), when taken in isolation from the rest of Scripture, are not as clear as they may seem to be. Certainly, they provide no simple law by which to regulate divorce and remarriage. In addition, I Corinthians 7:12-16 allows divorce under certain circumstances. However, since it does not explicitly address the matter of remarriage, it is impossible to prove conclusively that remarriage is either forbidden or permitted under the circumstances mentioned.

"Thus, on the one hand, Scripture states the principle or law governing marriage with such clarity that no one should be mistaken concerning God's will for the marriage relationship. The church must constantly reaffirm this biblical teaching both as God's will for its corporate life and in its proclamation to a society in which moral anarchy is destroying marriage and family life. However, on the other hand, the Scripture also considers cases where marriage does not attain the biblical norm. Although the cases considered are essentially only two, in those two cases the Scripture acknowledges the necessity of considering certain actions and attitudes which occur in a sinful world, which conflict with God's will for marriage, and which can destroy a marriage relationship.

"The church must exercise its pastoral ministry in the midst of this tension which exists between God's will for marriage and the multiplicity of personal factors which surround particular cases of divorce and remarriage. The church should neither issue a clear prohibition of remarriage in those cases where Scripture is unclear, nor should it attempt to list with legal precision the circumstances under which any particular remarriage does not conflict with biblical teaching. This is neither possible nor desirable. For example, even when unchastity has been a factor in the divorce, the legitimacy of the remarriage is not to be taken for granted. Other factors in the biblical teaching must be considered, such as repentance for personal failure in the breakdown of the previous marriage, forgiveness of others, understanding of the divinely intended permanence of marriage, and a renewed dependence on the grace of God for the success of the remarriage.

"Hence, the church must apply these biblical principles to concrete situations in the light of its best understanding of what happened in the divorce and what is being planned for the remarriage. The major part of the burden in making this application necessarily rests on the local consistory, for it has the most intimate and accurate knowledge of the situation of divorce and contemplated remarriage.

"Therefore, the church must:

"1. Reaffirm the general biblical principle that divorce and remarriage constitute adultery.

"2. Deal pastorally with those who have failed to keep the biblical principle by

"a. Refraining from a strictly legal approach to remarriage that tries to provide a basis for judgment that certain categories of remarriage are always compatible or incompatible with the teachings of Scripture.

"b. Seeking to bring persons contemplating remarriage to a genuine awareness of what is involved in the covenant of marriage. The teaching of Scripture concerning marriage, grace, love, loyalty, vows, forgiveness, hope, and promise should be openly discussed.

"c. Calling persons contemplating remarriage to an examination of their intentions in the light of the biblical teaching concerning reconciliation with the former spouse, the possibility of the single life, and remarriage.

"d. Counseling firmly and compassionately against any remarriage that conflicts with the biblical teaching concerning marriage and divorce.

"e. Exercising formal discipline when persons in hardness of heart refuse to heed the admonitions of the consistory and do not acknowledge and repent of their sins involved in divorce and remarriage."

(Acts of Synod 1980, pp. 480-485)

III. THE TASK AND ACTIVITIES OF THE CHURCH
C. PASTORAL CARE (continued)

ARTICLE 70

FUNERALS

Funerals are not ecclesiastical but family affairs, and should be conducted accordingly.

1. Funeral Services

   The basic principle of Article 70 is that "funerals are not *ecclesiastical* but *family* affairs."

   There is no synodically approved form for funerals, so that the family of the deceased has complete freedom to arrange the funeral service according to its own wishes. Local consistories may, however, adopt certain rules regarding the use of church facilities for funerals.

2. Synodical Judgments

   Because funerals are not ecclesiastical affairs, synodical judgments are rare and made only in response to specific requests for advice:

   a. "To bring a corpse into a church building and to have an appropriate discourse at that time is an indifferent matter." *(Acts of Synod 1886,* p. 22)

   b. "A consistory has the right to refuse to allow a corpse to be brought into the church building if it considers such refusal the best thing to do."

   (Acts of Synod 1888, p. 14)

III. THE TASK AND ACTIVITIES OF THE CHURCH
C. PASTORAL CARE (continued)

ARTICLE 71

CHRISTIAN SCHOOLS

The consistory shall diligently encourage the members of the congregation to establish and maintain good Christian schools, and shall urge parents to have their children instructed in these schools according to the demands of the covenant.

1. Establishing Christian Schools
   a. By Members of the Congregation
      Article 71 requires the consistory to "diligently encourage the members of the congregation to establish and maintain good Christian schools."
      The Christian Reformed Church shares a strong commitment to the necessity of covenantal, Christian education with Reformed churches throughout the world.
      It is to be noted that the Church Order does not require the *consistory* itself to establish Christian schools. Rather, the consistory's responsibility is to encourage the *members of the congregation* to do so. Such schools are, therefore, private, not ecclesiastical, schools.
      In 1898 synod affirmed the necessity of Christian education:
      Not a general, but a specifically Reformed instruction is the requirement for our children. Indeed, no educational system is satisfactory, but the acknowledgement of the necessity of regeneration, and additionally the acknowledgement of the covenant relationship in which God has placed our children, are the principles from which education must proceed.
      Christian education according to Reformed principles is the incontrovertible duty of Reformed Christians. All ministers and elders must labor to the utmost of their power in the promotion of Christian education wherever and whenever possible.
      The grounds for these declarations are:
      a. God's Word requires that children be trained in the fear and admonition of the Lord.
      b. Parents at the time of the baptism of the children have promised before the Lord and the congregation to do this.
      c. There may be no separation between civil, social and religious life, education, and nurture.

276

d. Christian education promotes the honor of our King who has been given all dominion in heaven and on earth, including the realms of education and nurture. *(Acts of Synod 1898,* p. 38)

b. Taxation and Christian Schools
A report and decisions on the subject of taxation of Christian schools can be found in the *Acts of Synod 1975,* pp. 64-70, 609-616.

2. Principles of Christian Education
Article 71 also requires the consistory to "urge parents to have their children instructed in these schools according to the demands of the covenant."

In 1955 synod recommended to the churches a report entitled "Basic Commitments in Christian Education." The main points of this report are as follows:
a. Christian education has its foundation in the Creator-creature relationship taught in Scripture.
b. The Creator-creature relationship continued though man fell in sin, but man lost true knowledge, righteousness, and holiness.
c. God gathers from a ruined human race, groping in the darkness of sin, a chosen people that they as sons by adoption may show forth "the praise of the glory of his grace." Christian education is education of the man in Christ.
d. Man is a religious being. His deepest needs are spiritual in character. Christian education is education of the religious being in the truth in order that he may commit himself to the truth, and the truth may make him free.
e. True education has its inception in the fear of the Lord which is the beginning of wisdom.
f. Education is the nurture or bringing up of the whole man and comprises all of life.
g. Children born of Christian parents are members of the church of Christ.
h. The responsibility for education rests upon the parents. Parents have the right and duty to avail themselves of assistance of social institutions which are able and willing to carry forward their God-given tasks. To entrust their children's education to agencies which violate their divinely ordained task represents, on the part of parents, a flagrant violation of their stewardship.
(Acts of Synod 1955, pp. 193-200)

Note: Cf. also the *Acts of Synod 1951,* p. 44, for a statement of "Principles of Christian Education" prepared by the Reformed Ecumenical Synod of 1949 and recommended to the members and congregations (Acts of Reformed Ecumenical Synod 1949, pp. 51ff.)

3. Higher Education
a. Calvin College
Synod in 1957 affirmed the right and duty of the church regarding ownership of a college (Calvin College):
1) "Scripture is abundantly clear in defining the primary task of the Church as Preaching and Teaching the Word, Administering the Sacraments, Exercising Discipline, and Collecting and distributing Alms.

277

2) "The Church cannot own and operate a general liberal arts college within the definition of this primary task of the Church as institute.

3) "Scripture neither *directly* affirms nor *directly* denies the right of the Church to perform other functions which are related to her primary task.

4) "The Church has, however, the derived (not inherent) right, and even duty, to perform functions related to, but not of the essence of, the primary task of the Church, whenever the well-being of the Church and her members demands it. Times, places, conditions, and circumstances determine this right.

5) "The Church possesses the derived, though not inherent, right to exercise ownership and control of a college. This derived right is based upon the following concerns, each of which is Scripturally orientated:

   a) "The responsibility of the Church for the spiritual nurture of its youth.

   b) "The grave responsibility of the Church to the Kingdom of God.

   c) "The close association of Church and education in the area of normative truth, which is especially a matter of importance in the relation of the college to the Church.

   d) "The demands upon the modern Church to assert its distinctive positions in a world of factionalism, sectarianism, and denominationalism."

(Acts of Synod 1957, p. 45)

b. Area Colleges

Area colleges are not supported directly by synodical quotas. Provision has been made, however, for a reduction in the amount of the contribution to Calvin College. This amount must be given to the area college *(Acts of Synod 1962, pp. 53-54)*.

III. THE TASK AND ACTIVITIES OF THE CHURCH
C. PASTORAL CARE (continued)

ARTICLE 72
CONGREGATIONAL SOCIETIES

The consistory shall promote societies within the congregation for the study of God's Word and shall serve especially the
youth organizations with counsel and assistance. All such
societies are under the supervision of the consistory.

1. Societies for the Study of God's Word
   Article 72 requires that "the consistory shall promote societies within the congregation for the study of God's Word."
   The consistory is responsible for promoting the study of God's Word in the congregation. In 1970 synod adopted far-reaching decisions designed to assist the consistories in developing their total educational programs in the church. These decisions require a denominational program of education based on Scripture, designed
   to promote a broader expression of Christian discipleship, and including persons of
   all ages through adulthood.

   a. Scripturally Directed Church Education
      "In responding to the Word of God in our educational ministry, we should
      recognize that God's revelation comes to us as the inscripturated Word (Bible),
      the incarnate Word (Jesus Christ), and the Word establishing order in creation
      (General Revelation). Through the power of the Spirit we must call all men to re-
      spond to this full-orbed Word as it confronts us today in the church and in the
      world, summoning them to faith and obedience through proclamation, service,
      and fellowship. Since the Scriptures speak comprehensively to man's heart, the
      center of his being, and thus to the whole man in his total life situation, we should
      strive for a truly scripturally directed church education and in our entire educa-
      tional enterprise we should seek to elicit a hearty response to the biblical
      message."   (*Acts of Synod 1970*, pp. 206-07)

   b. Broader Expression of Christian Discipleship
      "The goal of the educational curriculum of the church, as it administers the
      Word of God, is to impart to all who come under its nurture a saving knowledge
      of Jesus Christ and to direct them to the power which He dispenses to His ser-
      vants through His Spirit for living the life of faith and obedience. In seeking to
      achieve this basic goal, the educational ministry of the church should strive for:

"1. a meaningful profession of faith and full participation in the life and work of the church.

"2. a broader expression of Christian discipleship in the service of God and man and in a wholesome and effective witnessing in every area of life, for the promotion of the Kingdom of God."

c. Unified Educational Curriculum
"In order to attain a unified educational ministry in which the church aims to lead people to Christian maturity in the most effective way, a single unified curriculum must be developed which will serve as a core program for the educational task of the church. This single-track curriculum must seek to do justice to the two-track program current in our churches by way of Sunday school and catechism instruction."

d. Adult Education
"This core program shall address itself to persons of all ages from childhood through adulthood."

("Toward a Unified Church School Curriculum,"
Acts of Synod 1970, pp. 209-10.)

2. Youth Organizations
Article 72 also requires that the consistory "shall serve especially the youth organizations with counsel and assistance."

Youth organizations (such as those affiliated with United Calvinist Youth) are recognized as nonecclesiastical organizations and therefore outside of the direct supervision and control of synod *(Acts of Synod 1952,* p. 69). Synod, however, continues to recommend the youth organizations to the churches for support, appoints liaison persons to these organizations, and receives annual reports of their activities.

3. Supervision
Article 72 stipulates that "all such societies are under the supervision of the consistory."

Though membership in societies for the study of God's Word is voluntary, responsibility for their supervision rests in the consistory. The Guide for Church Visiting, echoing the provisions of this article, asks the following question of the elders: "Do they promote within the congregation societies for the study of God's Word, and do they serve the youth organizations with counsel and assistance?"

III. THE TASK AND ACTIVITIES OF THE CHURCH
D. MISSIONS

ARTICLE 73
THE CHURCH'S MANDATE TO MISSIONS

a. In obedience to Christ's great commission, the churches must bring the gospel to all men at home and abroad, in order to lead into fellowship with Christ and his church.
b. In fulfilling this mandate, each consistory shall stimulate the members of the congregation to be witnesses for Christ in word and deed, and to support the work of home and foreign missions by their interest, prayers, and gifts.

1. Christ's Great Commission
Article 73 insists that "in obedience to Christ's great commission, the churches must bring the gospel to all men at home and abroad."

a. Biblical and Confessional References
Christ's mandate to the church is found in Matthew 28:19, 20: "Go therefore and make disciples of all nations, baptizing them in the name of the Father and of the Son and of the Holy Spirit, teaching them to observe all that I have commanded you." (Cf. also Mark 16:15-18; Luke 24:46-49; John 20:21; Acts 1:8.)

The Heidelberg Catechism reminds us in Question and Answer 54 that the church's mission is Christ's mission and work:

"The Son of God, through his Spirit and Word, out of the entire human race, from the beginning of the world to its end, gathers...a community chosen for eternal life and united in true faith."

The Canons of Dort, I:3, remind us that it is God who sends his messengers:

"That men may be brought to believe, God mercifully sends the messengers of these most joyful tidings to whom he will and at what time he pleases; by whose ministry men are called to repentance and faith in Christ crucified."

b. Mission Principles
Significant study reports developing and defining principles of mission have been submitted to and adopted by synod in recent years. Copies of these reports are found in the following *Acts of Synod*:
a. Mission Principles—*1952*, pp. 63-67, 188-231.
b. Mission Principles—*1953*, pp. 84-87, 265-285.
c. Mission Principles—*1977*, pp. 92-93, 614-637.
d. Evangelism Manifesto—*1977*, pp. 639-641.

2. The Goal of Mission

Article 73a defines the goal of mission as being "to lead...into fellowship with Christ and his church."

The Synod of 1954 adopted the following statement of the goal of the church's mission:

a. "The objective of evangelization work is to bring into being the manifestation of the body of Christ in the establishment of the organized Church.

b. "As soon as possible the local group of believers shall become an organized church—self-governing, self-supporting, and self-propagating."

(Acts of Synod 1954, pp. 52, 215)

3. Stimulation of Members of the Church to Mission

Article 73b states that "each consistory shall stimulate the members of the congregation to be witnesses for Christ in word and deed."

a. Statement of Policy re Mission Promotion

In 1959 synod declared the following to be its policy concerning responsibility for ecclesiastical mission promotion:

1) "Primary responsibility rests upon the local consistory. It is the consistory's responsibility to stimulate and instruct the congregation in mission work.

2) "The local minister is to be recognized as the key man in mission promotion. He can best stimulate the consistory and through it the congregation.

3) "The denominational effort in mission promotion is primarily to assist the local congregation in carrying out its responsibility."

(Acts of Synod 1959, p. 34)

With respect to the promotion of denominational mission work synod declared:

"Synodical boards and committees, consistories, and classes should do the work of mission promotion consistent with their missionary responsibilities."

(Acts of Synod 1959, p. 36)

The same synod (1959) affirmed that "organizations such as the women's missionary unions may render valuable service in missions promotion," and adopted the following policy concerning mission promotion organizations:

1) All such organizations should be under the general supervision of the church as an institution.

2) Such organizations are not to engage in organized, properly ecclesiastical, missionary work.

3) The purpose of such organizations is that of study, prayer, fellowship, and the stimulation of missionary interest, activity and giving, and auxiliary tasks such as Bible and tract distribution.

4) "When such organizations receive funds, these funds should be distributed only to ecclesiastically approved causes." *(Acts of Synod 1959*, p. 34)

b. Promotion of Missions in the Local Churches
The synod of 1910 listed the following ways in which mission work may be promoted in the local churches:
1) That mission sermons be preached repeatedly to the congregation.
2) That the subject of missions be taught in the catechism classes as much as possible.
3) That a lesson on missions be taught quarterly in the Sunday school.
4) That existing societies make a systematic study of missions.
5) That the cause of missions be presented at public gatherings.
6) That mission fests be held annually as much as possible.
7) That each local church strive to support a missionary.
8) That systematic weekly offerings be taken for missions.

(Acts of Synod 1910, p. 24)

The Church Order in Articles 12 and 24 states that the task of the ministers and the elders includes that they shall "engage in and *promote* the work of evangelism."

c. The Guide for Church Visiting
The Guide for Conducting Church Visiting asks the following question of the whole consistory:
"Is the Consistory diligent in promoting the cause of missions in its community, throughout the nation, and on the foreign field?"

(Acts of Synod 1959, p. 36)

4. Support of Home and Foreign Missions
Article 73b also urges consistories to stimulate the members of the congregation "to support the work of home and foreign missions by their interest, prayers, and gifts."
The 1937 Synod urged the churches and people to limit their responsibility to mission work that has synodical approval:
"Our churches and our people are urged to unite strongly in their devotion to such missionary endeavors which are conducted by our churches or have synodical approval, and therefore [are encouraged] to assume responsibility, financial or otherwise, only for mission work that enjoys synodical approval."

(Acts of Synod 1937, p. 99)

III. TASK AND ACTIVITIES OF THE CHURCH
D. MISSIONS (continued)

ARTICLE 74
CONGREGATIONAL EVANGELISM

a. Each church shall bring the gospel to unbelievers in its own community. This task shall be sponsored and governed by the consistory.
b. This task may be executed, when conditions warrant, in cooperation with one or more neighboring churches.

1. Community Evangelism
   Article 74 requires that "each church shall bring the gospel to unbelievers in its own community."
   In 1954 synod adopted a Guide for Neighborhood Evangelization which presents its past decisions and advice to our consistories to guide them in this work (*Acts of Synod 1954*, pp. 52-53, 211-215). This guide affirms that:
   "The church has a special obligation to bring the Gospel to those neighbors whom God in His providence has placed in close proximity" (p. 213).
   Also that:
   "Every local church is expected to carry on mission work in its community, with the object of bringing converted mission subjects into its membership, or establishing a new congregation where feasible or desirable" (p. 212).
   And that:
   "The covenant conception of the work of neighborhood evangelism has also its practical significance; that, we should stress working with the family as a unit. God has not merely included a disconnected multitude of individual believers in the covenant, but as a rule He has included the parents and their children's children. 'I am thy God and the God of thy seed after thee' (Genesis 17:7). According to this plan God adds unto the church those that should be saved. Consequently, when we read of specific conversions to Christianity in the New Testament, we often read that the family of the convert shared his blessing (cf. Acts of the Apostles, Chapters 10-16)" (p. 213).

2. Consistorial Responsibility for Evangelism
   Article 74a also requires that "this task shall be sponsored and governed by the consistory."
   The Guide for Neighborhood Evangelization affirms consistorial responsibility for evangelism in the following statements:

284

"Though it is the duty of every Christian to evangelize, yet, the formal work of evangelization ought to be carried on under the direction of the consistory, which can utilize the gifts and talents with which God has adorned and equipped the membership....

"Evangelization in its technical sense as a department of the general missionary commission of the Church of Christ is the task of the instituted church. Therefore, evangelization work must be conducted either by the consistory, classis, or synod, and not by individuals, or groups of individuals, such as mission societies."   (*Acts of Synod 1954*, p. 211)

The guide also provides the following directives for consistories in the prosecution of neighborhood evangelization:

a. "Every consistory sponsoring neighborhood evangelism should appoint a consistorial committee on evangelism which shall report regularly to the consistory.

b. "This committee should enlist all qualified members of the church in the work of evangelization.

c. "The consistorial committee and the workers should carry out the work of evangelization on behalf of the consistory.

d. "In view of the magnitude of the task and the need for direction, a full-time worker, ordained or unordained, should be employed as soon as possible."

                                                    (*Acts of Synod 1954*, p. 52)

3. Cooperation with Neighboring Churches

Article 74b permits this task to be "executed, when conditions warrant, in cooperation with one or more neighboring churches."

"In any community where there are more than one of our churches, these churches may, when the situation demands it, carry on mission work jointly, including such endeavors as building a chapel, procuring an ordained missionary or lay-worker."   (*Acts of Synod 1954*, p. 212)

4. The Minister of Evangelism

The 1932 Synod adopted the following resolution:

"Synod resolve[d] that the rampant neo-paganism of our day and land requires that every one of our churches, whether alone or in collaboration with a neighboring church or churches, enter upon evangelistic activities. It also requires that, if possible, in addition to the regular pastor, the church or churches engage an ordained minister especially for this evangelistic work."

                                                    (*Acts of Synod 1932*, p. 20)

In recent years Calvin Seminary has introduced a special, two-year degree program leading to the Master of Church Education degree. This course of study is intended to prepare men and women for service as directors of evangelism and/or church education in our congregations. Complete information on this program can be obtained from the Registrar of Calvin Seminary.

5. The Office of Evangelist

In the early 1940s many of our churches began to appoint evangelists to assist the churches in neighborhood evangelism. A study committee was appointed by the

Synod of 1952 to formulate "a set of rules, according to which our consistories (and/or Classes) may regulate their work of neighborhood or city evangelism" (*Acts of Synod 1952*, pp. 69-70).

In 1954 synod adopted the Guide for Neighborhood Evangelism referred to above. Synod also adopted the following rules for the appointment of unordained evangelists:

"a. Synod instructs the sponsoring agencies when engaging a nonordained mission worker to first examine him in the following matters: the Bible, the Standards, subscription to the Standards, personal piety, and attitude to the work in question. (*Acts of Synod 1954*, p. 214)

"b. Synod declares that the unordained worker performs his labors by virtue of the fact that he shares the office of all believers and has been asked by the church to labor as an evangelistic teacher and exhorter."

(*Acts of Synod 1954*, p. 53)

Synod did not act on a recommendation of its study committee "that a committee be appointed to define the meaning of ordination and the status of the lay-workers of our denomination." As its grounds synod stated:

"a. The meaning of ordination is well-known among us.

"b. The status of the lay-worker is defined above," namely in statement b in the preceding paragraph. (*Acts of Synod 1954*, p. 53; see also p. 215)

The subsequent history of this matter is that after many requests to clarify the status of lay-evangelists, synod appointed in 1969 "a committee to study the nature of ecclesiastical office and the meaning of ordination as taught in the Scripture and exhibited in the history of the church of Christ" (*Acts of Synod 1969*, p. 85).

The above committee presented a report in 1972 and a final report in 1973 defining the nature of office and ordination. Its proposed "Guidelines for Understanding the Nature of Ecclesiastical Office and Ordination" were adopted in 1973 and appear in this manual in the section on Article 2.

Provisions were made for the ordination of evangelists by the Synods of 1978 and 1979 and appear in this manual under Church Order Articles 2, 23, and 24.

III. THE TASK AND ACTIVITIES OF THE CHURCH
D. MISSIONS (continued)

ARTICLE 75

CLASSIS MISSION WORK

The classes shall, whenever necessary, assist the churches in their local evangelistic programs. The classes themselves may perform this work of evangelism when it is beyond the scope and resources of the local churches. To administer these tasks each classis shall have a classical home missions committee.

1. The Task of Classis
   a. Assist the Churches
      In harmony with Article 75 which states that "the classes shall, whenever necessary, assist the churches in their local evangelistic programs," synod called on the churches as follows:
      "Our churches and our people [are urged] to unite strongly in their devotion to such missionary endeavors which are conducted by our churches or have synodical approval, and therefore are encouraged to assume responsibility, financial or otherwise, only for mission work that enjoys synodical approval."
      (*Acts of Synod 1937*, p. 99)

   b. Perform the Work of Evangelism
      Article 75 also provides that "the classes may perform this work of evangelism when it is beyond the scope and resources of the local churches."
      "City Mission work may properly be conducted by a Classis as a whole, as well as by a local church" (*Acts of Synod 1932*, p. 30).
      "When this work [evangelism] is conducted entirely by local initiative of Consistories or Classes without financial aid from the Church as a whole, . . . this work is not placed under the supervision and control of the Executive Committee for Home Missions." Consistories or classes conducting such work "should raise money for this purpose over and above the synodical quotas" for home missions (*Acts of Synod 1937*, pp. 74-75).

   c. Appoint a Classical Home Missions Committee
      Article 75 requires also that "each classis shall have a classical home missions committee" to administer these tasks.

287

MANUAL OF CHRISTIAN REFORMED CHURCH GOVERNMENT

"When the local churches are aware of mission opportunities and needs which they are unable to meet, it is suggested that they give such information and advice as is at their disposal to the Classical Home Missions Committee."

(Acts of Synod 1954, p. 212)

2. The Relationship of the Classis and Denominational Home Missions Committees
   This is specified in the Home Missions Order (Article 3) as follows:
   "Section 6— Relationship to Classes and Local Churches
   "The board shall work closely with classes and local churches in all its activities. The prior rights and responsibilities of classes and churches shall be respected. When requested the board shall function as consultant for local evangelism and mission programs and shall give assistance in investigating new opportunities.

   "The board shall promote local initiative and encourage classes and churches to assume full administrative and financial responsibility for home mission activity within their own areas. When necessary the board shall assist by providing counsel and funds through the Grant-in-Aid program.

   "When a mission project is beyond the resources or scope of a classis or a local church, the board may assume responsibility for the work upon the request or with the concurrence of the appropriate classis.

   "Joint supervision of the work on home missions fields shall be arranged by the board with classical home missions committees in a manner which best reflects the interest of all parties involved and does not conflict with the Church Order or the Home Missions Order.

   "The board shall keep the classes and churches informed of its activities by sending copies of the minutes of board and executive committee to board members and their alternates, through correspondence and through the involvement of the regional home missionary." *(Acts of Synod 1979*, pp. 249-50)

III. THE TASK AND ACTIVITIES OF THE CHURCH
D. MISSIONS (continued)

ARITCLE 76
DENOMINATIONAL HOME MISSIONS

a. Synod shall encourage and assist the congregations and classes in their work of evangelism, and shall carry on such home mission activities as are beyond the scope and resources of minor assemblies.

b. To administer these activities synod shall appoint a denominational home missions committee, whose work shall be controlled by synodical regulations.

1. The Task of Synod
   a. Encourage and Assist the Congregations and Classes
   Article 76a stipulates that "synod shall encourage and assist congregations and classes in their work of evangelism."

   1) The Board of Home Missions
   The Synod of the Christian Reformed Church has assigned the administration of the home mission work of the church to the Board of Home Missions, whose responsibility includes the work of encouraging and assisting the congregations and classes in their programs. On behalf of synod, therefore, the board provides leadership to the entire denomination as the church seeks to be obedient to Christ's great commission to bring the gospel to the people of Canada and the United States in order to lead them into fellowship with Christ and his church.

   Synod regulates the program of denominational home missions by means of the Home Mission Order. A revision of this Home Mission Order was adopted by the Synod of 1979 (*Acts of Synod 1979*, pp. 44-45, 247-252).

   2) The Prior Rights of Local Congregations and Classes
   The work of the Board of Home Missions is governed by a synodically adopted Mission Order which states:
   "The Board shall work closely with classes and local churches in all its activities. The prior rights and responsibilities of classes and churches shall be respected. When requested, the board shall function as consultant for local evangelism and mission programs and shall give assistance in investigating new opportunities" (*Acts of Synod 1979*, p. 249).

289

The Mission Order also outlines procedures which safeguard these rights and responsibilities of the local churches.

3) The Minister of Evangelism
One of the ways in which the board and synod carry out the responsibility for assisting congregations and classes in their work of evangelism is through the appointment and work of the Minister of Evangelism, recognizing that "although the work of neighborhood evangelism is performed by our Consistories and/or Classes, there should be denominational unity of procedure in such a rapidly expanding work" (*Acts of Synod 1952*, pp. 69-70).

The Minister of Evangelism serves as a consultant for local evangelism and mission programs, and may be called upon to give assistance in training the members of the church in more effective witnessing. Every effort is made to help the churches employ the gifts of the members to minister in word and deed to the people of the community, to call them to repentance and faith, to receive new believers into fellowship, and to teach them all that Christ has commanded.

4) Grant-in-Aid Program
While promoting local initiative and encouraging classes and congregations to assume full administrative and financial responsibility for home mission activity in their own areas, the board also administers a Grant-in-Aid program which provides subsidy to local churches and classes in carrying out their work. The synod annually reviews the requests submitted to the board and approves the allocation of funds. (Cf. *Acts of Synod 1973*, pp. 29-31.)

When assistance is received in the form of a Grant-in-Aid, the church, group of churches, or classis is the employer of the missionary and has the primary responsibility for the direction of the work while receiving such assistance.

The policies that regulate the Grant-in-Aid program are defined in the *Acts of Synod 1979*, pp. 228-231.

b. Carry on Home Mission Activity
Article 76a also stipulates that synod "shall carry on such home mission activities as are beyond the scope and resources of minor assemblies."

1) The Board of Home Missions
In addition to assisting the churches, the Board of Home Missions carries on home mission activities where our congregations do not exist or the work exceeds the scope and resources of a local church or group of churches. In doing so it carries out a variety of ministries.

2) Kinds of Ministries
a) Church Planting Ministries
Ministries are initiated and developed in strategic places where there is need

for a Christian Reformed church, opportunity to do evangelism, and potential for organizing believers into new congregations.

There are four stages of organizational development:

Stage 1: A missionary is working on the field, worship services are being held, a program of ministry is begun, a steering committee has been appointed, and worship services are initiated.

Stage 2: The congregation has been organized as a church within a classis and a consistory has been elected.

Stage 3: The church calls its own pastor while still financially dependent upon the board and under its supervision.

Stage 4: The church and its pastor become independent of the board.

b) Specialized Ministries

Ministries are initiated and developed where there are strategic opportunities to address the needs of students, military personnel, seafarers, or other groups. The goal of such mission activity is the extension of the church of Jesus Christ though the organization of a new Christian Reformed congregation is not anticipated.

c) Home Mission Fields

(1) Selection

Potential new fields are thoroughly investigated as to need and opportunity for ministry. The appropriate congregation and/or classis is consulted. The board decides to open a new field when it is convinced that a significant ministry is possible and denominational resources are necessary.

(2) Opening

No field is opened without the assurance of a continuing gospel ministry. Ordinarily a field is considered open when a resident home missionary arrives.

2. The Administration of Synodical Home Mission Work

Article 76b requires that "to administer these activities synod shall appoint a denominational home missions committee, whose work shall be controlled by synodical regulations."

a. Constitution of the Board of Home Missions

The Christian Reformed Board of Home Missions is composed of one member from each classis, preferably a member of the Classical Home Mission Committee. The names of these members and their alternates are proposed by their respective classes and elected by synod. Synod also elects a number of lay-members-at-large from a nomination presented by the board.

In a specific case involving the nomination by a classis of a home missionary as member of the board, synod ruled that "a person whose work is regulated by a [denominational] board should not be delegated to that particular board" (*Acts of Synod 1966*, p. 87).

b. Decentralization of Home Missions

The Synod of 1973 adopted the concept of decentralization in home missions and defined this as "an adjustment in present home missions policy to allow congregations and classes a greater share and involvement in the initiation, development, and administration of home mission work in their areas. [Decentralization] is a process already operative in various degrees throughout the denomination, which must be continued in a manner that builds the unity of the denomination and allows for maximum expression of local involvement and activity."

The Home Missionaries on General Assignment and the Grant-in-Aid program were judged by synod to be significant contributions to the process of decentralization.

(See *Acts of Synod 1973*, pp. 29-30, 203-211.)

c. Staff Personnel

The staff of the Board of Home Missions is elected by synod from a nomination presented by the board, and comprises:

1) The Executive Secretary

The Executive Secretary is responsible for the execution of the policies and decisions of the Board of Home Missions. He provides the leadership (supervision and coordination) for the attainment of the overall objectives of the Board of Home Missions.

2) The Treasurer

The Treasurer is responsible for receiving and handling all funds, advising the fields in matters of physical and financial development and supplying financial information to the board which will assist it in making its decisions.

3) The Minister of Evangelism

The Minister of Evangelism is responsible for promoting evangelism in all churches of the denomination and assisting the churches in meeting the challenge of reaching out in their own communities.

4) The Personnel Secretary

The Personnel Secretary is responsible for recruiting and training home missionaries.

5) The Field Secretary

The Field Secretary is responsible for the programs and activities on all home mission fields.

6) The Regional Home Missionaries

Canada and the United States are divided into six regions and each region is served by a regional home missionary. The regional home missionary functions as an enabler in the home missions effort of the denomination. As the first point of contact between the board and its fields and personnel, he works at improving the effectiveness of each ministry in his region. As liaison between the board and classical home missions committees, he assists in the development of mutual concerns and joint supervision. As one who has expertise in missions and evangelism, he provides counsel and instruction to the classes and the churches of his region.

3. Home Missionaries

Those persons who serve as home missionaries are an essential part of the home mission program. They are appointed by the board and called by a local congregation. The board determines their qualifications and provides orientation and training.

In order for the home missionaries to function productively, the board adopted and synod endorsed an appropriate policy which provides for regular, systematic assessment of each missionary. This "Policy for Personnel Assessment" can be found in the *Acts of Synod 1976*, pp. 35-36, 220-222.

4. Significant Guidelines and Decisions

The board has demonstrated leadership in guiding and challenging the churches to engage in various ministries by presenting to synod reports and recommendations which call attention to areas of evangelism in which the churches may be engaged and by formulating guidelines and principles for such work. The following are noted:

a. Campus Ministries

Churches in the areas of college and university campuses are confronted with unique challenges to carry out an evangelism program. (Specific and helpful guidelines can be found in the *Acts of Synod 1967*, pp. 79, 279-280.)

b. Inner City Missions

The Christian Reformed Church is concerned that the gospel of God's sovereign grace in Jesus Christ be presented in the context of the inner city as well as in the growing suburbs of our cities. A report, "Inner City Policy," was adopted as a guide for the churches. (Cf. *Acts of Synod 1966*, pp. 83-84, 409-10.)

c. Jewish Missions

Principles and guidelines were adopted by the Synod of 1971 to assist the churches in their concern for mission to the Jews. (These can be found in the *Acts of Synod 1971*, pp. 59, 290-91.)

d. Youth Evangelism

Out of concern that the youth of our communities be reached with the gospel, the Synod of 1971 also adopted a series of "Principles and Guidelines for Youth Evangelism." (Cf. *Acts of Synod 1971*, pp. 60, 291-302.)

5. List of Fields and Missionaries

A list of home missionaries and their fields of labor is included in the *Yearbook* of the Christian Reformed Church and in the annual reports of the Board of Home Missions in the *Acts of Synod*.

III. THE TASK AND ACTIVITIES OF THE CHURCH
D. MISSIONS (continued)

ARTICLE 77

DENOMINATIONAL WORLD MISSIONS

a. Synod shall determine the field in which the joint foreign mission work of the churches is to be carried on, regulate the manner in which this task is to be performed, provide for its cooperative support, and encourage the congregations to call and support missionaries.

b. To administer these activities synod shall appoint a denominational foreign missions committee, whose work shall be controlled by synodical regulations.

1. Synodical Responsibilities for World Missions
Article 77a lists four responsibilities to be exercised directly by synod in the task of world missions:

a. Determine the Fields
"Synod shall determine the field in which the joint foreign mission work of the churches is to be carried on."

A list of mission fields and missionaries is included in the annual report of the Board for World Missions in the *Acts of Synod* as well as in the *Yearbook* of the Christian Reformed Church.

b. Regulate the Performance
"Synod shall. . . regulate the manner in which this task is to be performed."

Synod regulates the performance of world missions by the "Mission Order of the Board for Christian Reformed World Missions," adopted by the Synod of 1976 *(Acts of Synod 1976,* pp. 17, 177-182) and amended by the Synod of 1977 *(Acts of Synod 1977,* pp. 18-19, 231).

This Mission Order defines the responsibilities of synod as follows:

Synod, being responsible for the joint foreign mission work of the church, is committed to regulate the work in accordance with the Word of God and in fulfillment of its mandate in Article 77 of the Church Order. Specifically, synod:

Section 1. Establishes and maintains a foreign mission program in which every aspect of the work undertaken is controlled by the standards of the Word of God for the attainment of the goal of carrying the gospel to the world.

Section 2. Exercises jurisdiction over the foreign mission program and determines the fields in which work is carried on.

Section 3. Adopts the Mission Order for the regulation of the foreign mission program.

Section 4. Establishes the Board for Christian Reformed World Missions in order to administer the joint foreign mission work of the churches. (Hereafter the Board for Christian Reformed World Missions is called "the board.")

Section 5. Appoints the members and alternates of the board.

Section 6. Appoints the Executive Secretary of Missions and the Area Secretaries upon recommendation of the board and arranges for their call and installation.

Section 7. Provides for the collective support of denominational foreign missions by stimulating interest, encouraging prayer, and authorizing the procurement and expenditure of funds.

Section 8. Encourages the churches to call and/or commission and to support missionaries appointed by the board.

c. Provide for Support
"Synod shall...provide for its cooperative support."
Synod provides for the support of the foreign mission program by means of the quota system (see this manual under Article 62).

d. Encourage the Calling and Support of Missionaries
"Synod shall...encourage the congregations to call and support missionaries."
Article VI of the Mission Order contains the following:

The Sending Churches

Section 1. While all churches of the denomination participate in the support of the denominational foreign missions, the individual churches may become specifically involved as sending churches by either calling, commissioning, or supporting one or more missionaries.

Section 2. There shall be a sending church for each missionary which shall call and/or commission in behalf of synod and the board.

Section 3. The calling or commissioning church shall have supervision of the missionary's doctrine and life, consonant with Article 12 of the Church Order.

Section 4. The sending churches shall be encouraged to sustain their missionaries through prayers, offerings, and personal contacts.

2. Administration of World Missions
Article 77b requires that "to administer these activities synod shall appoint a denominational foreign missions committee, whose work shall be controlled by synodical regulations."

The official name of the committee appointed by synod is the "Board for Christian Reformed World Missions." Its work is regulated by the "Mission Order of the Board for Christian Reformed World Missions," which defines the specific duties of the board as follows:

ARTICLE II
The Board for Christian Reformed World Missions

The synodically established Board for Christian Reformed World Missions shall:

Section 1. Administer the joint foreign mission work of the churches as the agent of synod in such a manner that scriptural standards for all aspects of the work are maintained and the Mission Order is observed. The board may adopt and/or amend such by-laws and regulations which are needed for the fulfillment of its assignment and are in accordance with synodical decisions.

Section 2. Be legally incorporated and be known as the Board for Christian Reformed World Missions.

Section 3. Consist of a nominee from each classis and members-at-large whose appointment and term of service are regulated by synodical rules. The members-at-large shall ordinarily be lay persons and eight (8) in number, as follows:

United States:	Eastern District (1)
	Central District (3)
	Mid-west District (1)
	Far West District (1)
Canada:	Eastern District (1)
	Western District (1)

Section 4. Have the following officers who are elected at the annual board meeting: president, vice-president, recording secretary, and treasurer.

Section 5. Be authorized by synod to acquire, possess, hold and convey property, and administer all funds relating to tasks assigned to it by synod.

Section 6. Recruit, appoint, and supervise all personnel, and make adequate provision for their needs and for the performance of their work.

Section 7. Designate calling and/or commissioning churches, present to them nominations, supply information and guidance to the churches, and jointly sign the letter of call or commission.

Section 8. Meet at least annually to administer the work entrusted to it by synod.

Section 9. Present an annual report to synod regarding the status and progress of the work on the various fields, together with a proposed budget and recommendations concerning the fields, personnel, and work.

Section 10. Provide for periodic visits to the fields by board representatives in order to encourage the missionaries and the national churches, keep abreast of current developments, and cultivate mutual understanding. These representatives shall submit a report of their visit to the board.

Section 11. Provide counsel and encouragement to all missionary personnel, which shall be supplemental to the primary care of the church where the missionary's membership resides.

Section 12. Elect annually from its membership an executive committee to exercise between the meetings of the board such of the board's responsibilities as the continuing and effective performance of the foreign mission task requires.

a. The executive committee shall be accountable to the board for all its actions.

b. The executive committee shall consist of eighteen (18) members, three of whom shall be members-at-large. The term of all executive committee members shall begin at the close of the annual board meeting.

c. The officers of the board shall be the officers of the executive committee.

Section 13.   Record the decisions and actions of all meetings of the board and its executive committee, and send copies of its minutes to all board members.

IV. THE ADMONITION AND DISCIPLINE OF THE CHURCH
A. GENERAL PROVISIONS

ARTICLE 78

THE NATURE OF AND RESPONSIBILITY FOR DISCIPLINE

a. The admonition and discipline of the church are spiritual in character and therefore require the use of spiritual means.
b. The exercise of admonition and discipline by the consistory does not preclude the responsibility of the believers to watch over and to admonish one another in love.

Article 78 begins the fourth major section of the Church Order, that dealing with the admonition and discipline of the church.

1. The Spiritual Character of Discipline
   Article 78 affirms that the "admonition and discipline of the church are spiritual in character and therefore require the use of spiritual means."

   a. Scriptural References
   Among the scriptural references which directly or indirectly enjoin church discipline are the following:
   "I will give you the keys of the kingdom of heaven, and whatever you bind on earth shall be bound in heaven, and whatever you loose on earth shall be loosed in heaven." (Matt. 16:19)
   "If your brother sins against you, go and tell him his fault, between you and him alone. If he listens to you, you have gained your brother. But if he does not listen, take one or two others along with you, that every word may be confirmed by the evidence of two or three witnesses. If he refuses to listen to them, tell it to the church, and if he refuses to listen even to the church, let him be to you as a Gentile and a tax collector." (Matt. 18:15-17)
   "For what have I to do with judging outsiders? Is it not those inside the church whom you are to judge? God judges those outside. 'Drive out the wicked person from among you.' " (I Cor. 5:12-13)
   "Do not be mismated with unbelievers. For what partnership have righteousness and iniquity? Or what fellowship has light with darkness? What accord has Christ with Belial? Or what has a believer in common with an unbeliever? What agreement has the temple of God with idols?" (II Cor. 6:14-16)

b. Confessional References

Important statements regarding church discipline are found in our confessions:

1) The Belgic Confession, Article 29:

"The marks by which the true church is known are these: if the pure doctrine of the gospel is preached therein; if it maintains the pure administration of the sacraments as instituted by Christ; if church discipline is exercised in punishing of sin; in short, if all things are managed according to the pure Word of God, all things contrary thereto rejected, and Jesus Christ acknowledged as the only head of the church. Hereby the true church may certainly be known, from which no man has a right to separate himself."

2) The Belgic Confession, Article 30:

"We believe that this true church must be governed by that spiritual polity which our Lord has taught us in his Word; namely, that there must be ministers to preach the Word of God and to administer the sacraments; also elders and deacons, who, together with the pastors, form the council of the church; that by these means the true religion may be preserved, and the true doctrine everywhere propagated, likewise transgressors punished and restrained by spiritual means; also that the poor and distressed may be relieved and comforted, according to their necessities. By these means everything will be carried on in the church with good order and decency, when faithful men are chosen, according to the rule prescribed by St. Paul in his Epistle to Timothy."

3) The Belgic Confession, Article 32:

"In the meantime we believe, though it is useful and beneficial that those who are rulers of the church institute and establish certain ordinances among themselves for maintaining the body of the church, yet that they ought studiously to take care that they do not depart from those things which Christ, our only Master, has instituted. And therefore we reject all human inventions, and all laws which man would introduce into the worship of God, thereby to bind and compel the conscience in any manner whatever. Therefore we admit only of that which tends to nourish and preserve concord and unity, and to keep all men in obedience to God. For this purpose, excommunication or church discipline is requisite, with all that pertains to it, according to the Word of God."

4) The Heidelberg Catechism, Question and Answer 82:

"Q. Are those to be admitted to the Lord's Supper who show by what they say and do that they are unbelieving and ungodly?

"A. No, that would dishonor God's covenant and bring down God's anger upon the entire congregation. Therefore, according to the instruction of Christ and his apostles, the Christian church is duty-bound to exclude such people, by the official use of the keys of the kingdom, until they reform their lives."

5) The Heidelberg Catechism, Question and Answer 84:

"Q. How does preaching the gospel open and close the kingdom of heaven?

"A. According to the command of Christ: The kingdom of heaven is opened by proclaiming and publicly declaring to each and every believer that, as often as he accepts the gospel promise in true faith, God, because of what Christ has done, truly forgives all his sins.

"The kingdom of heaven is closed, however, by proclaiming and publicly declaring to unbelievers and hypocrites that, as long as they do not repent, the anger of God and eternal condemnation rest on them.

"God's judgment, both in this life and in the life to come, is based on this gospel testimony."

6) The Heidelberg Catechism, Question and Answer 85:

"Q. How is the kingdom of heaven closed and opened by Christian discipline?

"A. According to the command of Christ: If anyone, though called a Christian, professes unchristian teachings or lives an unchristian life, if after repeated brotherly counsel, he refuses to abandon his errors and wickedness, and, if after being reported to the church, that is, to its officers, he fails to respond also to their admonition—such a one the officers exclude from the Christian fellowship by withholding the sacraments from him, and God himself excludes him from the kingdom of Christ.

"Such a person, when he promises and demonstrates genuine reform, is received again as a member of Christ and of his church."

2. Mutual Discipline

Article 78b affirms that "the exercise of admonition and discipline by the consistory does not preclude the responsibility of the believers to watch over and to admonish one another in love."

In 1976 synod urged the churches "faithfully to teach and preach the importance of self-discipline, mutual discipline, and ecclesiastical discipline as taught in God's Word" *(Acts of Synod 1976, p. 53).*

A lengthy and valuable study of church discipline, which synod said "deserves the special attention of the churches," may be found in the *Acts of Synod 1976* (pp. 631-66). This report covers the history, the biblical and creedal foundations, the official practice in our denomination, together with recommendations as to how discipline may be carried out. It should be noted, however, that synod did not adopt or approve this study and its recommendations.

IV. THE ADMONITION AND DISCIPLINE OF THE CHURCH
A. GENERAL PROVISIONS (continued)

ARTICLE 79

THE PURPOSE OF ADMONITION AND DISCIPLINE

The purpose of the admonition and discipline of the church is to maintain the honor of God, to restore the sinner, and to remove offense from the church of Christ.

1. The Purposes of Church Discipline
   Article 79 stipulates a three-fold purpose of church discipline:
   a. With respect to God—"to maintain the honor of God."
   b. With respect to the individual—"to restore the sinner."
   c. With respect to the church—"to remove offense from the church of Christ."

2. The Previous Church Order
   Prior to the adoption of the present Church Order by the Synod of 1965, the comparable article in the previous Church Order provided the following in Article 71:
   "As Christian discipline is of a spiritual nature, and exempts no one from civil trial or punishment by the authorities, so also besides civil punishment there is need of ecclesiastical censures, to reconcile the sinner with the Church and his neighbor and to remove the offense out of the Church of Christ."

IV. THE ADMONITION AND DISCIPLINE OF THE CHURCH

A. GENERAL PROVISIONS (continued)

ARTICLE 80

THE SUBJECTS OF ADMONITION AND DISCIPLINE

All members of the congregation are subject in both doctrine and life to the admonition and discipline of the church.

1. The Inclusive Character of Church Discipline

Article 80 uses the words "subject to" when it speaks of the admonition and
discipline of the church and specifies that admonition and discipline include all
members of the congregation. The scope of admonition and discipline includes the
doctrine and the life of all the members.

The committee for the revision of the Church Order used a different expression in
its report to the Synod of 1962. It spoke more positively than the statement proposed
to and adopted by the synod: "All members of the church are happily not deserving
of ecclesiastical discipline, but when they sin in any way they are *entitled* to the
church's correction" *(Acts of Synod 1962,* p. 407).

In view of the pastoral responsibility which all members must show to each other
(note Art. 78), the official discipline of the church must be based upon and be done
pastorally as the complement to the privilege the members have of serving each
other. Unless official discipline has as its basis this mutual concern and care, it will
seldom meet the purpose of restoring the sinner and promoting his own self-
discipline.

2. Promises Required by the Ecclesiastical Forms

a. Forms for Profession of Faith

Persons making a public profession of faith are required to answer affirmatively
the following question:

Form Number 1—"Do you promise to submit to the government of the church
and also, if you should become delinquent either in doctrine or in life, to submit
to its admonition and discipline?"

Form Number 2—"Do you promise to do all you can, with the help of the Holy Spirit, to strengthen your love and commitment to Christ by sharing faithfully
in the life of the church, honoring and submitting to its authority; and do you
join with the people of God in doing the work of the Lord everywhere?"

b. Forms for Adult Baptism

Adult baptism is the occasion at which the person to be baptized makes public profession of faith. He is asked to respond affirmatively to the following question:

Form Number 1—"Do you firmly resolve to lead a Christian life, to forsake the world and its evil lusts, as is becoming to the members of Christ and of His Church, and to submit cheerfully to all Christian admonitions?"

Form Number 2—"Do you promise to do all you can, with the help of the Holy Spirit, to strengthen your love and commitment to Christ by sharing faithfully in the life of the church, honoring and submitting to its authority; and do you join with the people of God in doing the work of the Lord everywhere?"

IV. THE ADMONITION AND DISCIPLINE OF THE CHURCH
A. GENERAL PROVISIONS (continued)

ARTICLE 81

OCCASIONS FOR DISCIPLINE

Commission of sins which give public offense or which are brought to the attention of the consistory according to the rule of Matthew 18:15-17 shall make one liable to the discipline of the church.

1. Initiation of Discipline
   Article 81 provides that official church discipline may be initiated for two reasons:
   a. The Committing of Sins That Give Public Offense
   Official church discipline may be initiated directly by the consistory when the committing of the sin has given public offense.
   b. According to the Rule of Matthew 18:15-17
   Official discipline may also be initiated when matters are brought to the attention of the consistory according to the rule of Matthew 18:15-17. In such instances the mutual concern of the members for each other must first have been carried as far as possible.
   > "If your brother sins against you, go and tell him his fault, between you and him alone. If he listens to you, you have gained your brother. But if he does not listen, take one or two others along with you, that every word may be confirmed by the evidence of two or three witnesses. If he refuses to listen to them, tell it to the church; and if he refuses to listen even to the church, let him be to you as a Gentile and a tax collector."

   In both instances cited above the Church Order only specifies that one is made "liable to the discipline of the church." Whether or not official discipline will be followed depends upon the circumstances, e.g., whether the person confesses and repents, in which case discipline would no longer be applicable or necessary.

2. Specific Cases
   Although Reformed churches have historically avoided cataloging sins, appeals to synod throughout the years have resulted in a lengthy series of judgments of specific cases. The synods have generally refrained from generalizing on such matters.

   a. Neglect of Infant Baptism
   "Members who, because of scruples of conscience, fail to present their children

304

for baptism, should be instructed and admonished patiently; and if this proves ineffective, they should be disciplined." *(Acts of Synod 1888,* p. 19)

b. Neglect of the Lord's Supper
As to what shall be done with those who constantly neglect the Lord's Supper, it is said that the "indissoluble connection between baptism, the making of confession of faith, and the Lord's Supper should be urged, if necessary, by ecclesiastical discipline, in order that, in the case of perseverance in the wrong way, exclusion from the church may be reached in course of time" *(Acts of Synod 1904,* p. 38).
A person becomes subject to official discipline for "neglect of the Lord's Supper for three years while unwilling to make any attempt at reconciliation" *(Acts of Synod 1924,* p. 61).

c. Neglect of Profession of Faith
"Those baptized who arrive at maturity but who do not make confession of faith, regardless of their conduct otherwise, become as unfaithful baptized members the objects of discipline; and, if they persist in their sin, they shall be excluded from the church." *(Acts of Synod 1918,* pp. 58, 180)
"Although the age limit is left to the discretion of the consistories, the need of eventual erasure is however urged" *(Acts of Synod 1910,* p. 58; *1912,* pp. 50-51; see also Art. 83 of the Church Order).

d. Neglect of Catechism Training
"If parents do not send their minor children to attend catechism sufficiently, they shall be admonished; if they persist in their neglect, they shall be disciplined; and if this be of no avail, they shall be excommunicated."
(General Rules of 1881, Art. 62A)

e. Violation of the Lord's Day
Consistories are urged "to take a firm stand in dealing with concrete cases of what they regard as transgressions of the Fourth Commandment" (*Acts of Synod 1939,* p. 77).

f. Unchristian Relations with Other Members
1) Living in an unreconciled attitude toward other members (*Acts of Synod 1924,* p. 61).
2) Unwillingness to act according to Matthew 18 (*Acts of Synod 1924,* p. 61).
3) In concrete cases it is judged that discipline should be applied if husband and wife are constantly quarreling and in disharmony (Minutes of April 5, 1865, article 20; October 2-3, 1867, article 19).
4) Synod approved the excommunication of a husband and wife for the following reasons:
"a) Living in an unreconciled relationship with other members of the church;
"b) Unwillingness to act according to Matthew 18 in the difficulties with these members;

305

"c) Neglect of the Lord's Supper for three years while making no attempts toward reconciliation." *(Acts of Synod 1924,* p. 61)

g. Withholding of Financial Support
"Members able but unwilling to contribute to the support of the church and the poor are to be admonished; and, upon continued delinquency, to be ecclesiastically disciplined." (Minutes of June 1, 1864, article 12)

h. Membership in Secret Oath-bound Societies
"The lodge member who desires to become a member of the church must be kindly but firmly shown that his lodge membership is contrary to the will of God and that membership in the lodge and in the church of Jesus Christ involves a double commitment which our Lord himself does not tolerate. Those in the church who affiliate with the lodge must be shown the error of their way and, if they refuse to repent, must be placed under the censure of the church."
(Acts of Synod 1974, pp. 59-60; see also 504-67)
The Synod of 1977 reaffirmed this decision:
"Synod maintain[s] its position that a member of the Christian Reformed Church who becomes a member of a lodge will be subject to admonition and discipline *(Acts of Synod 1974,* Art. 65)." *(Acts of Synod 1977,* p. 105)

i. Worldliness
"Synod urges consistories to deal in the spirit of love, yet also, in view of the strong tide of worldliness which is threatening our churches, very firmly with all cases of misdemeanor and offensive conduct in the matter of amusements, and where repeated admonitions by the consistory are left unheeded, to apply discipline as a last resort." *(Acts of Synod 1928,* pp. 86 ff.)
In 1951 synod reaffirmed and explained this decision:
"That in accordance with the principles of Reformed Church polity it is left to the judgment of the Consistory to determine in each particular case just what constitutes 'misdemeanor and offensive conduct' which call for admonition and eventual discipline." *(Acts of Synod 1951,* p. 66)

j. Corporate Responsibility
"Active participation in the sinful practices of an organization to which one belongs not only renders one guilty before God but may even make one an object of ecclesiastical discipline." *(Acts of Synod 1945,* pp. 103, 314-26)
"The full recognition of corporate responsibility is quite consistent with the position that mere passive corporate responsibility does not yet make one an object of censure, but that one becomes an object of church censure (as distinguished from discipline of the Word) only by the performance of censurable acts. Active participation in censurable acts may make one an object of ecclesiastical discipline. But even so the degree of participation may be so slight that the church would not think of applying censure." *(Acts of Synod 1943,* p. 105)

k. Rebaptism
"Whenever a consistory is reliably informed that a member has been re-baptized,

the consistory shall officially ask such a member whether he still considers himself a member of the Christian Reformed Church and is willing to submit to the teaching and discipline of the Christian Reformed Church.

1) "If the reply is in the affirmative, the consistory must faithfully and persistently admonish such an erring member.

2) "The consistory should bar such a member from the Lord's table only if it is necessary for the unity and well-being of the congregation.

3) "If such a member actively disturbs the unity and peace of the congregation, the regular steps of discipline should be followed.

"Since neither the Bible nor the Confessions nor the Church Order allow consistories simply to terminate membership in the church when such action is not requested by the member, such a member as mentioned above can be excluded from the church only if he is worthy of excommunication, which is the act of public declaration by the church that such a person has no part in Christ or in his church.

"Under no circumstances should members erring in this respect be allowed to hold office in the church." *(Acts of Synod 1973,* p. 78)

1. Racial Prejudice

   1) "Members of the Christian Reformed Church ought freely to receive as brethren, regardless of race or color, all who repent of their sins and who profess their faith in Jesus Christ as Savior and Lord; that exclusion from full Christian fellowship on account of race or color is sinful; and that if members are judged responsible for such exclusion they must be dealt with according to the provisions of the Church Order regarding Admonition and Discipline.

   2) "Fear of persecution or of disadvantage to self or our institutions arising out of obedience to Christ does not warrant denial to anyone, for reasons of race or color, of full Christian fellowship and privilege in the church or in related organizations, such as Christian colleges and schools, institutions of mercy and recreational associations: and that if members of the Christian Reformed Church advocate such denial, by whatever means, they must be reckoned as disobedient to Christ and be dealt with according to the provision of the Church Order regarding Admonition and Discipline."

(Acts of Synod 1968, p.19)

IV. THE ADMONITION AND DISCIPLINE OF THE CHURCH
A. GENERAL PROVISIONS (continued)

ARTICLE 82

PRELIMINARY REQUIREMENTS

Disciplinary measures shall be applied only after an adequate investigation has been made and the member involved has had ample opportunity to present his case.

The Church Order specifies two conditions that must be met *before* disciplinary measures may be applied:

1. An Adequate Investigation Must Be Made

   Article 82 requires that "disciplinary measures shall be applied only after an adequate investigation has been made."

   The "Judicial Code of Rights and Procedures" adopted by the Synod of 1977 ensures that proper procedures shall be used in cases where written charges requiring formal adjudication are filed.

Article 1

"a. These provisions apply to judicial hearings before a consistory, classis or synod occasioned by the bringing of written charges requiring formal adjudication. Such admonition and discipline of the church as does not involve the hearing of written charges requiring formal adjudication are not governed by these provisions.

"b. Written charges requiring formal adjudication, whether brought by an individual against an individual or an assembly, or by an assembly against an individual or an assembly, may refer only to alleged offenses in profession or practice against the Word of God, the confessions of the church, or the Church Order." *(Acts of Synod 1977,* p. 49; see comments in this manual on Art. 30b)

2. Ample Opportunity Must Be Given to the Member

   Article 82 also requires that "disciplinary measures shall be applied only after...the member involved has had ample opportunity to present his case."

   "In response to a question whether it is permissible for a minister or a consistory member from one congregation to support or justify a member of another congregation who seeks advice without hearing the accused party, synod declared that this may not be done under any circumstances."

(Acts of Synod 1874, p. 151)

IV. THE ADMONITION AND DISCIPLINE OF THE CHURCH
B. THE ADMONITION AND DISCIPLINE OF MEMBERS

ARTICLE 83

DISCIPLINE OF BAPTIZED MEMBERS

a. Members by baptism who willfully neglect to make public profession of faith, or are delinquent in doctrine or life, and do not heed the admonitions of the consistory shall be dealt with in accordance with the regulations of synod and, if they persist in their sin, shall be excluded from the church of Christ.

b. Members by baptism who have been excluded from the church and who later repent of their sin shall be received again into the church only upon public profession of faith.

note change ✗

1. Exclusion from the Church
   a. Article 83a states a number of reasons for which members may be excluded from the church of Christ:
      1) "Willfully neglect to make public profession of faith."
      2) "Delinquent in doctrine or life."
      3) "Do not heed the admonitions of the consistory."
      4) "Persist in their sin."
      (Cf. also manual under Art. 81, section 2c; *Acts of Synod 1918,* pp. 58, 180-81; *1910,* pp. 58-59; *1912,* pp. 50-51.)

   b. Exclusion of Unfaithful Baptized Members (Church Order Supplement, Art. 83)
      The Synod of 1918 defined the procedure to be followed regarding members by baptism (amended in 1974):
      1) "Baptized members having reached the years of maturity, but having failed to make profession of faith—aside from their conduct of life in other respects—being unfaithful covenant members, become the objects of ecclesiastical discipline, and when they persist in their sin, should be excluded from the church;
      2) "When such unfaithful covenant members move elsewhere, they should not be given a certificate, but at best a testimony of baptism with a notation as to their conduct;
      3) "Before a consistory proceeds to exclude unfaithful covenant members,
         a) An announcement, ordinarily without mentioning names, shall be made to the congregation with a request for prayer on behalf of them.

b) Thereupon the advice of classis shall be asked.
c) After the advice of classis has been received and before the final announcement of exclusion from the church is made, another request for the prayers of the congregation be made, this time mentioning their names. (As amended, *Acts of Synod 1974,* p. 110.)

4) "The exclusion of unfaithful covenant members is to take place by officially informing the congregation, notifying the parties involved that they, due to their persistent unfaithfulness as covenant members, notwithstanding all ecclesiastical admonitions, will henceforth not be regarded as belonging to the church;

5) "Excluded unfaithful covenant members who return with sorrow and repentance, cannot be received back into the church except through profession of faith, while the consistory judges concerning every individual case whether or not a separate confession of sin shall be required."
(Acts of Synod 1918, pp. 180-81; *1974,* p. 110)
"There can be no determined age for erasure of baptized members because circumstances vary greatly." *(Acts of Synod 1910,* p. 59)
"If upon being censured the disciplined member becomes insane, the case remains in status quo as long as the insanity lasts."
(Acts of Synod 1898, p. 67)

c. Exclusion of Members Who Fail to Attend and Support the Congregation
(See this manual under Article 67, section 2; *Acts of Synod 1976,* p. 25.)

d. Exclusion of Members Who Move Away
(See this manual under Article 67, section 2; *Acts of Synod 1974,* pp. 81-82.)

2. Readmission to Church Membership
Article 83b provides that "members by baptism who have been excluded from the church and who later repent of their sin shall be received again into the church only upon public profession of faith."

"Excluded unfaithful covenant members who return with sorrow and repentance, cannot be received back into the church except through profession of faith, while the consistory judges concerning every individual case whether or not a separate confession of sin shall be required." *(Acts of Synod 1918,* p. 58)

3. Concern for Family Members
Consistories must deal pastorally, not only with the person involved but also with the members of his/her family since they are often in need of pastoral care and help when a member is under discipline. This is especially true at the time of exclusion from membership. Before proceeding the consistory should inform such family members of contemplated announcements. (See also Art. 86 of this manual.)

IV. THE ADMONITION AND DISCIPLINE OF THE CHURCH
B. THE ADMONITION AND DISCIPLINE OF MEMBERS (continued)

ARTICLE 84

RECONCILIATION OF DISCIPLINED MEMBERS

Confessing members who have offended in doctrine or in life and who have responded favorably to the admonitions of the consistory shall be reconciled to the church upon sufficient evidence of repentance. The method of reconciliation is to be determined by the consistory.

1. Sufficient Evidence of Repentance
   Article 84 provides that "confessing members who have offended in doctrine or in life and who have responded favorably to the admonitions of the consistory shall be reconciled to the church upon sufficient evidence of repentance."
   It is the responsibility of the consistory to determine whether or not persons under discipline show adequate evidence of repentance.

2. Method of Reconciliation
   Article 84 also provides that "the method of reconciliation is to be determined by the consistory."
   Ordinarily sins which have given public offense should be reconciled publicly, and sins of a private nature may be reconciled privately.
   "In the case of transgression of the seventh commandment before marriage confession must be made before the consistory. The advisability of announcing the names to the congregation shall be determined by the consistory in each case" (*Acts of Synod 1908*, p. 38; amended: *1930*, p. 47; reaffirmed *1961*, p. 96).

IV. THE ADMONITION AND DISCIPLINE OF THE CHURCH
B. THE ADMONITION AND DISCIPLINE OF MEMBERS (continued)

ARTICLE 85

DISCIPLINE OF CONFESSING MEMBERS

Confessing members who have offended in doctrine or in life and who obstinately reject the admonitions of the consistory shall be barred from partaking of the Lord's Supper, responding to the baptismal questions, and exercising any other rights of membership.

1. "Silent Censure"
   In common usage the provisions of Article 85 are generally referred to as "silent censure." The meaning of this is that the consistory restricts the person from exercising the rights granted him as a confessing member of the church. This action is known only to the consistory and the offending party. Included in these rights, in addition to debarment from the use of the sacraments, would be all such privileges as are reserved for members by confession only. Some of these are specified in the Church Order:
   -Article 3: eligibility to be nominated for and hold office in the church.
   -Articles 4 and 37: the right to vote at congregational meetings.
   Each local consistory may have other specific areas of participation reserved for professing members only.
   Ultimately the question will need to be faced whether the offending party will be excommunicated (Art. 86) or reconciled (Art. 84). The status of "silent censure" cannot be retained permanently.

2. Classical Cooperation
   When requested and necessary, "in dealing with censured persons in a congregation, a committee of classis must labor in conjunction with the local consistory" (*Acts of Synod 1924*, p. 60).

312

IV. THE ADMONITION AND DISCIPLINE OF THE CHURCH
B. THE ADMONITION AND DISCIPLINE OF MEMBERS (continued)

ARTICLE 86
EXCOMMUNICATION

a. Confessing members who have have been barred from the Lord's Supper and who after repeated admonitions show no signs of repentance shall be excommunicated from the church of Christ. The Form for Excommunication shall be used for this purpose.

b. The consistory, before excommunicating anyone, shall make three announcements in which the nature of the offense and the obstinacy of the sinner are explained and the congregation is urged to pray for him and to admonish him. In the first announcement the name of the sinner shall ordinarily be withheld but may be mentioned at the discretion of the consistory. In the second, after the classis has given its approval to proceed with further discipline, his name shall be mentioned. In the third, the congregation shall be informed that unless the sinner repents he will be excommunicated on a specified date.

(Amended—*Acts of Synod 1974*, p. 77)

1. Conditions Requiring Excommunication

Article 86a requires that "confessing members who have been barred from the Lord's Supper and who after repeated admonitions show no signs of repentance shall be excommunicated from the church of Christ. The Form for Excommunication shall be used for this purpose."

As to the question "how to deal with members who deviated from the doctrinal position of our Standards so that they cannot be admitted to Holy Communion, but whom the consistory might hesitate to excommunicate by using the established Form since this involves the declaration that those excommunicated are outside the Kingdom of heaven," it is declared that (1)"our Church Order makes adequate provision for appropriate ecclesiastical action in the case of members who deviate from our doctrinal standards," and that (2) "in case a Consistory, after denying the Lord's Supper to a member who errs in doctrine, feels the need of guidance as to further procedure, the advice of Classis can be sought" (*Acts of Synod 1939*, p. 75; see also the report on this question in the *Agenda for Synod 1939*, Part I, pp. 11-18).

313

2. Procedures for Excommunication

Article 86b requires three announcements after "silent censure" (cf. Art. 85) leading to excommunication. Each announcement must explain the "nature of the offense and the obstinacy of the sinner" and the congregation must be "urged to pray for him and to admonish him":

a. "In the first announcement the name of the sinner shall ordinarily be withheld but may be mentioned at the discretion of the consistory."

b. "In the second, after the classis has given its approval to proceed with further discipline, his name shall be mentioned."

c. "In the third, the congregation shall be informed that unless the sinner repents he will be excommunicated on a specified date."

A copy of the Form for Excommunication is included in the liturgical section of the *Psalter Hymnal.*

The Synod of 1974 adopted the present wording of Article 86b by amending the article to include the provision that "in the first announcement the name of the sinner shall *ordinarily* be withheld *but may be mentioned at the discretion of the consistory*" (italics indicate the addition to the original form of the article). Synod made this change on the ground that "this would allow the consistory to determine whether, in its judgment, in a specific situation the earlier announcement of the sinner's name would be more effective in the administration of discipline." (Cf. *Acts of Synod 1974*, pp. 77-78.) The overture which gave occasion for this amendment presented two other considerations favoring this procedure, stating:

"a. This would enable consistories to determine which procedure would be more meaningful and helpful in a given situation.

"b. In some cases the earlier announcement would reduce the possibility of unhealthy speculation within the congregation as to the identity of the person involved." *(Acts of Synod 1974*, p. 626)

The Synod of 1979 adopted a new provisional Form for Excommunication and the required three announcements. (See *Acts of Synod 1979,* pp. 125, 370-373.)

3. Resignation under Discipline

a. Withdrawal from Discipline

The Synod of 1918 adopted the following policy with respect to a person who persists in resigning his membership:

"Synod, considering that the withdrawal from discipline, to which one has freely subjected himself, and the breaking off of the fellowship with the church to which one belongs, for reasons which cannot stand the test of God's Word, is a sin which should not be taken lightly, and that those who do so should be supplicated continuously and earnestly that they return from their erroneous way, and that they should not be released hastily; but considering also that one's affiliation with the church as an organization as well as one's continuation in the organized church should remain according to church government principles an act of each one's own personal choice, therefore synod judges that no one can continue to be an object of church discipline if he persists in resigning his membership." *(Acts of Synod 1918*, p. 66)

314

b. Announcement of Resignation

The Synod of 1936 insisted that a public announcement must be made when a member resigns:

"When a member persistently breaks the tie that binds him to the congregation, [the consistory must make a public announcement.]...Each...case must be judged on its own merits.

"In such announcements it should be plainly stated that the person who resigned his membership, in the manner indicated in the decision of 1918, by that very act has committed a grievous sin, and that he obstinately refused to listen to the admonition of the Consistory, though admonished repeatedly and seriously not to commit this sin. It stands to reason that expressions like 'accepting the resignation' should not be used in the announcement, because the full responsibility for his sinful act must remain with the person who withdraws himself from the church." *(Acts of Synod 1936*, p. 121)

A further elaboration of the content of this announcement was adopted in 1951:

"Synod calls the attention of the Churches to the necessity of a suitable announcement in such a case, in order that others may be warned against this sin. Such an announcement, already adopted by a previous Synod, includes the statement that the person who resigned his membership by that very act has committed a grievous sin, and that he has refused to heed the repeated admonitions of the Consistory not to commit this sin, and warns against such expressions as 'accepting the resignation' since the responsibility for his sinful act must remain with the person who withdraws himself from the Church." *(Acts of Synod 1951*, p. 17; cf. also pp. 274-278)

4. Status of Children of Parents Who Have Resigned for Themselves and Their Minor Children

In a specific case of parents, not under discipline, who resigned as members of the Christian Reformed Church for themselves and their minor children, the Synod of 1948 declared that "the resignation of the parents in this case involved the discontinuance of the membership of the children."

Grounds:

"1. These parents are the God-ordained representatives of these minor children and when they resigned they resigned not only for themselves, but also for their children who by laws both of nature and of grace were under their charge.

"2. Membership in the covenant and membership in the instituted church are closely related and normally overlap, yet they are not identical. Termination of membership in the church does not in all cases involve suspension in the covenant of grace."

(Acts of Synod 1948, pp. 66-67; see also *Acts of Synod 1947*, pp. 48-50; *1948*, Supplement 6, pp. 138-145.)

5. Concern for Family Members

In all cases of announcements such as are required by the above procedures, consistories should be aware of the need to exercise pastoral concern and care for the family of the person who is to be excluded or has resigned. This implies that they be informed of contemplated announcements. (See also Art. 83 of this manual.)

IV. THE ADMONITION AND DISCIPLINE OF THE CHURCH
B. THE ADMONITION AND DISCIPLINE OF MEMBERS (continued)

ARTICLE 87

RESTORATION OF EXCOMMUNICATED PERSONS

When anyone who has been excommunicated desires to become reconciled to the church, the consistory, having satisfied itself as to the sincerity of his repentance, shall announce these developments to the congregation. If no valid objections are presented, he shall be restored to the fellowship of the church of Christ. The Form for Readmission shall be used for this purpose.

1. Procedure for Restoration
   Article 87 specifies the following steps for the restoration of excommunicated persons:
   a. Expression of Desire for Reconciliation
      "When anyone who has been excommunicated desires to become reconciled to the church..."
   b. Determination of Sincerity
      "...the consistory, having satisfied itself as to the sincerity of his repentance..."
   c. Announcement to the Congregation
      "...shall announce these developments to the congregation...."
   d. Restoration to Fellowship
      "...If no valid objections are presented, he shall be restored to the fellowship of the church of Christ. The Form for Readmission shall be used for this purpose."
   A copy of the Form for Readmission is contained in the liturgical section of the *Psalter Hymnal.* The Synod of 1980 approved a new Form for Readmission for two years' trial use.

Note: It should be noted that whereas in matters of discipline involving excommunication and erasure the churches have agreed to seek the advice and approval of neighboring churches (classis) before terminating an individual's membership, the readmission of such members is the sole prerogative of the consistory, acting in accordance with the regulations of the Church Order and the approbation of the congregation.

317

2. Restoration of Persons Who Are Divorced

The Synod of 1980 adopted guidelines for pastors, consistories, and the church in handling important matters of marriage, divorce, and remarriage. These guidelines are helpful for all consistories. They are found in this manual, Article 69, sections 4 and 5.

IV. THE ADMONITION AND DISCIPLINE OF THE CHURCH
C. THE ADMONITION AND DISCIPLINE OF OFFICE-BEARERS

ARTICLE 88

THE RELATIONSHIP OF GENERAL AND SPECIAL DISCIPLINE

a. Ministers, elders, deacons, and evangelists, besides being subject to general discipline, are also subject to special discipline, which consists of suspension and deposition from office.

b. General discipline shall not be applied to an office-bearer unless he has first been suspended from office.

(Amended—*Acts of Synod 1979*, p. 67)

1. Suspension and Deposition

Article 88a affirms that office-bearers are subject to two kinds of discipline: general (which applies to all members of the church as detailed in Articles 83-87 of the Church Order) as well as special discipline (which applies only to office-bearers and is described in Articles 88-94 of the Church Order).

The term *suspension* means temporary debarment of an officebearer from exercising the duties of his office. The term *deposition* means removal of an office-bearer from his office.

2. Priority of Special Discipline

Article 88b assigns a priority to special discipline in the case of those who hold office in the church and specifies that "general discipline shall not be applied to an office-bearer unless he has first been suspended from office."

Prior to the adoption of our present Church Order in 1965, the Committee for the Revision of the Church Order explained the relationship between general and special discipline as follows:

"This provision embodies the thought that the offense for which an office-bearer might be disciplined with membership [general] discipline must be of such a character that he is also worthy of the special discipline for office-bearers and that this special discipline must be applied before general discipline is applied. The two may run simultaneously, but special discipline must precede general discipline." *(Acts of Synod 1962*, p. 409)

319

IV. THE ADMONITION AND DISCIPLINE OF THE CHURCH
C. THE ADMONITION AND DISCIPLINE OF OFFICE-BEARERS (continued)

ARTICLE 89

GROUNDS AND PROCEDURE FOR SPECIAL DISCIPLINE

a. Special discipline shall be applied to office-bearers if they violate the Form of Subscription, are guilty of neglect or abuse of office, or in any way seriously deviate from sound doctrine and godly conduct.
b. The appropriate assembly shall determine whether, in a given instance, deposition from office shall take place immediately, without previous suspension.

1. Grounds for Special Discipline
   Article 89a lists three reasons for applying special discipline to office-bearers:

   a. Violation of the Form of Subscription
      "Special discipline shall be applied to office-bearers if they violate the Form of Subscription..."
      A copy of the Form of Subscription is found in the back of the *Psalter Hymnal.* (See this manual under Article 5.)

   b. Neglect or Abuse of Office
      "...are guilty of neglect or abuse of office..."

   c. Deviation from Sound Doctrine and Godly Conduct
      "...or in any other way seriously deviate from sound doctrine and godly conduct."

2. Discipline of Officebearers Holding Neo-Pentecostal Views
   The Synods of 1973 and 1974 dealt with problems arising from neo-Pentecostal views held by officebearers.

   a. The Synod of 1973
      1) Declared that "any office-bearer who holds the teaching that baptism in or with the Holy Spirit is a 'second blessing' distinct from and usually received after conversion, should be dealt with according to the stipulations of Art. 88ff. of the Church Order."
      2) Urgently requested "office-bearers who, though disavowing the neo-Pentecostal view of Spirit-baptism, tend to other features of neo-Pentecostalism,

to review their attitudes, practices, and beliefs in order to bring them into harmony with synod's decisions and counsels on neo-Pentecostalism; and instruct[ed] the churches to uphold the biblical qualifications for office as well as the stipulations of the Form of Subscription."

(*Acts of Synod 1973*, p. 77)

b. The Synod of 1974 adopted the following guidelines as its advice to the churches:
   1) "Synod itself has already drawn the conclusion that anyone who holds the second-blessing teaching is thereby disqualified for office in the Christian Reformed Church and must be dealt with according to the Church Order.
   2) "Synod's decisions imply that not everyone who claims to have certain 'charismatic' experiences is by that fact alone to be disqualified for office in the Christian Reformed Church.
   3) "Those who occupy an office in the church, whether that of pastor, elder or deacon, must remember that the church remains judge of what gifts of the Spirit may or should be employed in the exercise of these offices. It is the Spirit-filled church that appoints to office, in the name of Christ, the King of the church.
   4) "Synod's decisions imply that there are degrees to which an office-bearer may display neo-pentecostal tendencies. As long as he has not violated the biblical demands of office and the stipulations of the Form of Subscription, the church must accept him in the performance of his office.
   5) "It is possible that an office-bearer, while disavowing the second-blessing teaching, may still consistently show certain other features of neo-pentecostalism; e.g., it is possible that he uses Scripture in an atomistic and private way, or unduly stresses the extraordinary gifts of the Spirit. In such instances the church needs to determine whether or not he has in fact embraced the second-blessing teaching.
   6) "Evaluations of such office-bearers must be conducted in a balanced way and according to proper procedures." (*Acts of Synod 1974*, p. 31)

3. Procedure for Special Discipline
   Article 89b stipulates that "the appropriate assembly shall determine whether, in a given instance, deposition from office shall take place immediately, without previous suspension."
   Ordinarily the act of deposition by any assembly is preceded by suspension from office in accord with Article 88 of the Church Order.
   Regulations regarding "the appropriate assembly" are found in Church Order Articles 90-92.

4. Discipline of a Consistory by Classis
   a. The deposition of a consistory by a classis was upheld by synod. (*Acts of Synod 1926*, pp. 141-142; cf. report on "Can a Classis Depose a Consistory" in the *Acts of Synod 1926*, pp. 315-332.)
   b. Ordinarily, before a classis proceeds to the deposition of a consistory, or members of a consistory, the classis must proceed by way of suspension in accord

with Article 88a of the Church Order. Before suspension or deposition may take place the assembly must determine which of the office-bearers in the consistory is subject to the discipline imposed. Discipline by its nature must be applied to individuals rather than to groups or assemblies.

c. A classis may not depose a consistory that has appealed to synod (*Acts of Synod 1900*, p. 26).
(See also this manual, Article 91.)

IV. THE ADMONITION AND DISCIPLINE OF THE CHURCH
C. THE ADMONITION AND DISCIPLINE OF OFFICE-BEARERS (continued)

ARTICLE 90
SUSPENSION AND DEPOSITION OF MINISTERS

a. The suspension of a minister of the Gospel shall be imposed by the consistory of his church with the concurring judgment of the consistory of the nearest church in the same classis.

b. If the neighboring consistory fails to concur in the position of the consistory of the minister involved, the latter consistory shall either alter its original judgment or present the case to classis.

c. The deposition of a minister shall not be effected without the approval of classis together with the concurring advice of the synodical deputies.

1. Suspension of Ministers
   a. By the Consistory

   Article 90a requires that "the suspension of a minister of the Gospel shall be imposed by the consistory of his church with the concurring judgment of the consistory of the nearest church in the same classis."

   A consistory may not suspend its own minister without this agreement of a neighboring consistory.

   b. Concurrence of Neighboring Consistory

   Article 90b specifies that "if the neighboring consistory fails to concur in the position of the consistory of the minister involved, the latter consistory [of the minister involved] shall either alter its original judgment or present the case to classis."

   A consistory has two options when the neighboring consistory refuses to agree to the suspension of a minister: Either it must alter its judgment to suspend the minister, or it must bring the matter to classis for decision. In the meantime the minister is not suspended from office.

   c. Meaning of Suspension

   The Synod of 1972, addressing the matter of announcements of suspension, declared that "all consistories should be informed concerning the suspension of a minister in order to prevent the nomination or calling of such a minister during

323

the period of suspension and to prevent a suspended minister from being engaged in the duties of his office" (*Acts of Synod 1972,* p. 26).

This announcement must not be made public by the consistory but must be processed through the classis.

d. Announcement of Suspension

The Synod of 1975 removed the provision for *mandatory* publication of notice of suspension, adopted by Synod 1972 in Article 22, section II, B, 1, "In the case of suspension, the consistory shall notify the stated clerk of its classis. He shall then notify the stated clerks of all other classes concerning the action, and these shall in turn notify each consistory within their classis" (*Acts of Synod 1972*, p. 26).

"Grounds:

"1. The minor assemblies involved in the suspension can judge whether publication of notice of suspension serves the best interest of the minister and of all the churches.

"2. As long as suspension of a minister awaits final disposition, publication of notice of suspension could not only prove unnecessary but also uncharitable and in violation of the ninth commandment. According to Lord's Day 43 of the Heidelberg Catechism we are not 'to join in condemning anyone without a hearing or without a just cause...I should do what I can to guard and advance my neighbor's good name.' " (*Acts of Synod 1975,* p. 19)

2. Deposition of Ministers

a. Procedure

Article 90c provides that "the deposition of a minister shall not be effected without the approval of classis together with the concurring advice of the synodical deputies."

b. Announcement of Deposition

Procedure for notifying the churches about the deposition of a minister is as follows:

"In the case of deposition, the stated clerk of the classis shall notify the stated clerks of all the other classes concerning the action, and these shall in turn notify each consistory within their classis." (*Acts of Synod 1972,* p. 26)

3. Resignation of Ministers

a. Regulations Respecting Resignation

Synod reminded all our churches and classes that "in all cases of resignation a proper resolution of dismissal must be adopted with the concurring advice of the synodical deputies" (*Acts of Synod 1978*, p. 73).

b. Announcement of Resignation

"In the case of resignation, the stated clerk of the classis in which the resignation has taken place shall place an appropriate announcement in the denomination's periodicals." (*Acts of Synod 1972,* p. 26)

324

c. Effective Date of Resignation

Synod ruled "that when a minister of the CRC resigns, his ministerial status in the CRC shall terminate on the date on which his consistory and/or classis determines that his resignation shall become effective" (*Acts of Synod 1977*, p. 66; see also 452-54).

IV. THE ADMONITION AND DISCIPLINE OF THE CHURCH
C. THE ADMONITION AND DISCIPLINE OF OFFICE-BEARERS (continued)

ARTICLE 91

SUSPENSION AND DEPOSITION OF ELDERS AND DEACONS

a. The suspension or deposition of an elder, deacon, or evangelist shall be imposed by the consistory with the concurring judgment of the consistory of the nearest church in the same classis.

b. If the neighboring consistory fails to concur in the position of the consistory of the elder, deacon, or evangelist involved, the latter consistory shall either alter its original judgment or present the case to classis.

(Amended—*Acts of Synod 1979*, p. 67)

1. Comment
   Whereas in the deposition of ministers (Art. 90c) the concurring judgment of both classis and the synodical deputies is required, in the case of other office-bearers only the concurring judgment of the consistory of the nearest church in the same classis is needed. Classis is involved only when these two consistories fail to concur and the consistory does not alter its original judgment.

2. Suspension of a Consistory
   In reply to a question whether a classis may suspend or depose a consistory, synod replied, "In the nature of the case, only a classis to which the unfaithful consistory belongs can exercise the necessary discipline, it being the nearest and broadest assembly" (*Acts of Synod 1926*, pp. 141, 324; see also comments under Article 89 in this manual).

IV. THE ADMONITION AND DISCIPLINE OF THE CHURCH

C. THE ADMONITION AND DISCIPLINE OF OFFICE-BEARERS (continued)

ARTICLE 92

DISCIPLINE OF A MINISTER WHOSE MEMBERSHIP RESIDES WITH A CONGREGATION OTHER THAN HIS CALLING CHURCH

a. A minister of the Word whose membership resides with a congregation other than his calling church is subject to the admonition and discipline of the consistories of both churches. Either consistory may initiate disciplinary action, but neither shall act without conferring with the other.
b. If the consistories disagree, the case shall be submitted to the classis of the calling church for disposition.

1. The Jurisdiction of the Two Consistories

Article 92a affirms that "a minister of the Word whose membership resides with a congregation other than his calling church is subject to the admonition and discipline of the consistories of both churches."

Instances when this situation occurs are rare, but could occur, for example, when a minister is called to serve as chaplain or missionary and transfers his membership to a local church in the area he is serving. In all such cases the minister is subject to the admonition and discipline of both consistories.

a. Emeritus Ministers

The Synod of 1968 made the following declaration with respect to the supervision of emeritus ministers:

"Synod declares that supervision of an emeritus minister (except when he remains as a member in his last congregation, or when the emeritation is expected to be of a temporary nature) may be transferred, at his request, to the church of which he becomes a member after emeritation.

"Grounds:

1) "With a view to supervision over his life and doctrine he should be connected with a local church.

2) "The church in which he is a member is in the right position to exercise that supervision.

3) "This effects a natural relationship between the emeritus minister and church in which he is a member and frees him from the remote involvement of the present situation.

"This transfer is to be made in the following manner: the consistory of the church which the emeritus minister served last formally requests the consistory of the church which the emeritus minister wishes to join, to exercise supervision over him."

(*Acts of Synod 1968*, p. 68-69, 216-22; see also Church Order Art. 18)

The intent of the Synod of 1968 was that every emeritus minister should have his ministerial credentials in the congregation of which he is a member.

b. Ministers Not Serving a Local Congregation

The Synod of 1964 adopted the following regulation concerning the supervision of ministers in specialized ministries:

"He shall be properly ordained (installed) in his office with the use of the form(s) (and adaptations) approved by Synod. His ministerial credentials shall be held by the calling church, and the consistory of the calling church shall exercise supervision over his doctrine and life. His membership shall also reside with the calling church. The latter may be impossible in the case of foreign and home missionaries, and chaplains in the armed forces. However, in all cases where possible, it must be observed."

(*Acts of Synod 1964*, p. 58; see also Church Order Art. 13)

c. Foreign Missionaries

The Mission Order of the Board for Christian Reformed World Missions provides that "the calling or commissioning church [of a missionary] shall have supervision of the missionary's doctrine and life, consonant with Article 12 of the Church Order." (See under Church Order Art. 78 of this manual and Art. VI, section 3 of the Mission Order.)

2. Initiation of Discipline

Article 92a also states that in such cases "either consistory may initiate disciplinary action, but neither shall act without conferring with the other."

3. Disagreement between Consistories

Article 92b provides that "if the consistories disagree, the case shall be submitted to the classis of the calling church for disposition."

Note that the final decision is to be made by the classis of the calling church, not the classis of the church of which the minister is a member.

4. Announcements

See comments on Church Order Article 90 in this manual for the synodical decisions respecting announcement of suspension and deposition.

IV. THE ADMONITION AND DISCIPLINE OF THE CHURCH
C. THE ADMONITION AND DISCIPLINE OF OFFICE-BEARERS (continued)

ARTICLE 93
LIFTING OF SUSPENSION

a. The suspension of an office-bearer shall be lifted only upon sufficient evidence of repentance.
b. The lifting of suspension is the prerogative of the assembly which imposed suspension.

1. Sufficient Evidence of Repentance

Article 93a provides that "the suspension of an office-bearer shall be lifted only upon sufficient evidence of repentance."

Article 93 deals with the restoration of office-bearers who have been *suspended* from office, whereas Article 94 deals with the restoration of those who have been *deposed* from office.

Since an office-bearer may be suspended only for due cause, this suspension may be lifted when the cause has been removed, that is, when the suspended office-bearer demonstrates sufficient evidence of repentance or the charges have not been sustained.

2. The Prerogative for Lifting Suspension

Article 93b stipulates that "the lifting of suspension is the prerogative of the assembly which imposed suspension."

If it was the consistory which imposed suspension, it must be the same consistory which lifts it. Similarly, if it was the classis which imposed suspension, it must be the same classis which lifts it.

IV. THE ADMONITION AND DISCIPLINE OF THE CHURCH

C. THE ADMONITION AND DISCIPLINE OF OFFICE-BEARERS (continued)

ARTICLE 94

REINSTATEMENT OF DEPOSED OFFICE-BEARERS

a. A deposed office-bearer shall not be restored unless he gives sufficient evidence of genuine repentance. It must further be evident that, should he be restored to office, he could then serve without being hindered in his work by the handicap of his past sin and that his restoration would be to the glory of God and for the true welfare of the church.

b. The judgment as to whether a deposed minister shall subsequently be declared eligible for call shall be made by the classis in which he was deposed, together with the concurring advice of the synodical deputies. Upon acceptance of a call, he shall be reordained.

(Amended—*Acts of Synod 1978,* p. 48)

1. Conditions for Reinstatement

Article 94a defines two conditions for the reinstatement of deposed office-bearers:

a. Evidence of Repentance

"A deposed office-bearer shall not be restored unless he gives sufficient evidence of genuine repentance."

b. Prospect of Working Unhindered and without Handicap

"It must further be evident that, should he be restored to office, he could then serve without being hindered in his work by the handicap of his past sin and that his restoration would be to the glory of God and for the true welfare of the church."

2. Reinstatement of Deposed Ministers

Article 94b requires that "the judgment as to whether a deposed minister shall subsequently be declared eligible for call shall be made by the classis in which he was deposed, together with the concurring advice of the synodical deputies."

This article incorporates the decision of the Synod of 1918 that the reinstatement of a deposed minister must be effected by the same classis which deposed him (*Acts of Synod 1918*, pp. 48-49).

In 1978 the synod added the provision that upon acceptance of a call after being declared eligible by the classis in which he was deposed, the deposed minister must be reordained. (Cf. *Acts of Synod 1978*, p. 48.)

A similar regulation was adopted with respect to ministers who are released from their ministerial office without discipline but for weighty reasons according to Article 14 (*Acts of Synod 1978*, p. 47).

3. Reinstatement of Ministers Who Resigned
The same reasons which apply to cases of deposition of a minister (see rule of 1918 above) were judged by synod to apply also to cases of resignation:

"Only that Classis which acquiesces in the resignation of the minister is in possession of all the facts of the case and is thereby qualified to judge of the merits of a subsequent application for readmission." (*Acts of Synod 1959*, pp. 22, 510)

(See also comments under Articles 14 and 17 in this manual for further synodical decisions regarding ministers who have resigned.)

CONCLUSION

ARTICLE 95

EQUALITY OF CHURCHES AND OFFICE-BEARERS

No church shall in any way lord it over another church, and
no office-bearer shall lord it over another office-bearer.

1. Equality of Churches
   Article 95 provides that "no church shall in any way lord it over another church." Illustrations of the implementation of this principle are seen in the practice of delegating two persons to classis, regardless of the size of the congregation (Art. 40), and in delegating four persons to synod, regardless of the size of the classis (Art. 45).

2. Equality of Office-bearers
   In harmony with Article 2 of the Church Order which provides that the offices of the church "differ from each other only in mandate and task, and not in dignity and honor," Article 95 insists that "no office-bearer shall lord it over another office-bearer."
   The article applies in two distinct ways:
   a. Equality of All Offices
      All the offices of the church are on an equal level. No office is to be regarded as higher than another. Ministers, elders, deacons, and evangelists differ only in the task assigned to them and not in the authority or dignity of the office itself. Ministers may not lord it over the elders, or the elders over the deacons, for example. Each office is distinct and responsible in its own function.
   b. Equality within the Offices
      Within the offices, too, there must be equality. One minister does not have official preeminence over another, nor one elder over others, nor one deacon or evangelist over other deacons and evangelists. Each has equal authority according to his mandate and assigned task.

3. Equality of Office and Special Mandates
   From the beginning Reformed synods have maintained that certain tasks require that office-bearers be given the requisite authority to carry out their mandates. It was judged, therefore, that a person serving as chairman of an ecclesiastical assembly who exercises certain prerogatives and authority in the assembly is not violating the spirit of the Church Order when he officiates in that capacity. Likewise, executive secretaries of denominational agencies, the president of the seminary, stated clerks

332

or interim committees all find it necessary at times to exercise within their mandates some form of authority. Recognizing this, the church even seeks out persons with administrative gifts when making appointments to such positions, and does not regard their use of these gifts within the discharge of their mandate as in any way "lording it over" other office-bearers.

Prior to the adoption of this present Church Order, the Committee for the Revision of the Church Order explained its formulation of this article as follows:

> The article "continue[s] to give expression to the treasured and typically Reformed principle of the essential equality of all local congregations, and of all office-bearers in Christ's church." *(Acts of Synod 1962*, p. 411)

CONCLUSION
(continued)

ARTICLE 96

REVISION OF THE CHURCH ORDER

This Church Order, having been adopted by common consent, shall be faithfully observed, and any revision thereof shall be made only by synod.

1. Faithful Observance of the Church Order
   Article 96 requires that "this Church Order, having been adopted by common consent, shall be faithfully observed."
   Prior to 1965 the Church Order specifically prohibited any "particular congregation or classis from altering, augmenting, or diminishing the Church Order," and insisted that "they shall show all diligence in observing them, until it be otherwise ordained by synod."

2. Amending the Church Order
   Article 96 also requires that "any revision thereof shall be made only by synod."
   Article 47 of the Church Order provides that "no substantial alterations shall be effected in these matters unless the churches have had prior opportunity to consider the advisability of the proposed changes." (Cf. also under Art. 47; *Acts of Synod 1972*, pp. 27-28.)
   In 1963 the Committee for the Revision of the Church Order acknowledged "that a Church Order cannot possibly be formulated in such a way, that everyone will be completely satisfied with every detail of the document. The present Church Order and also the Revised Church Order reckon with the fact that there is always room for improvements or alterations which may be for the welfare of the churches" (*Acts of Synod 1963*, p. 110).

3. Historical Notes
   a. Prior to 1965 the Church Order provided the following:
   "These Articles, relating to the lawful order of the church, have been so drafted and adopted by common consent, that they (if the profit of the church demand otherwise) may and ought to be altered, augmented, or diminished. However, no particular congregation or classis shall be at liberty to do so, but they shall show all diligence in observing them, until it be otherwise ordained by synod."

334

b. The Committee for the Revision of the Church Order reported concerning its abbreviation of this article: The article continues "the provisions now expressed in the final article of our [former] Church Order, Article 86. We have abbreviated the statement, but essentially it is expressive of the same principles and provisions" (*Acts of Synod 1962*, p. 411).

See Article 8

Letter Of Call

to: ....

....

....

Dear Brother:

The Consistory of the ....Christian Reformed Church at
.... has the honor and pleasure to inform you that you have been chosen
by majority vote at a local congregational meeting held on the ....day of ...., 19........,
to be their minister of the Word.

On behalf of our congregation we therefore extend to you this letter of call, and urge you to come and help us.

The work which we expect of you—should it please the Lord to send you to us—consists of: preaching twice on the Lord's day, attending to catechetical instruction, family visiting and calling on the sick, and all things that pertain to the work of a faithful and diligent servant of the Lord, all these in accord with the Word of God as interpreted by the doctrinal standards and the Church Order of the Christian Reformed Church.

Knowing that the laborer is worthy of his hire, to encourage you in the discharge of your duties, and to free you from material need while you are ministering God's Word to us, the Consistory of the ....
Christian Reformed Church promises to pay you the sum of $.................... annually in .... payments while you are the minister of this church. We also agree to grant 1) the use of the parsonage (or a housing allowance of $.... .... annually), 2) parsonage telephone, 3) $ ....parsonage utilities, 4) ..... weeks of vacation, and 5)

the following fringe benefits		the business expenses of your work	
a. Social Security Off-Set	$	a. Automobile Expense	$ ....
b. Hospital & Medical Insurance	....	b. Other Travel	$ ....
c. Group Life Insurance	....	c. Continuing Education	....
d.	....	d. Hospitality	....
e.	....		

We also promise and oblige ourselves to review with you annually in the light of the synodical Ministers' Compensation Guidelines the adequacy of this compensation prior to the adoption of the church budget.

We promise to underwrite all expenses incurred in the transportation and moving of yourself, your family, and your belongings, in accord with synodical regulations of the Christian Reformed Church.

May the King of the church impress this call upon your heart and give you light, that you may arrive at a decision that is pleasing to him, and, if possible, gratifying to us.

Yours in Christ,

The Consistory of the ....

Christian Reformed Church at ....

....

Done in Consistory this ....day of ...., 19........

Signature of Classis Counselor ....

See Article 10

1982 UPDATE:
Manual of
Christian Reformed
Church Government

The following collation is presented with the purpose of updating the *Manual of Christian Reformed Church Government* (1980 edition) and includes decisions of the Synod of the Christian Reformed Church for the years 1980-82. In addition attention is called to other important synodical decisions which clarify and expand the contents of this *Manual.* Page references refer to the *Manual* (1980 edition).

Reference will also be made to the 1982 edition of the "Rules for Synodical Procedure," copies of which have been sent to all CRC consistories. Others interested in receiving a copy may obtain this from the Board of Publications, 2850 Kalamazoo Ave. SE, Grand Rapids, MI 49560.

I. Corrections

A. *Article 5*

3. The Form of Subscription (p. 45)

Several lines were dropped from the Form of Subscription when it was printed. The Form should read as follows on the top of page 45, line 3:

"...synod, but that we *are disposed to refute and contradict these and to exert ourselves in keeping the church free from such errors. And if hereafter any difficulties or different sentiments respecting the aforesaid doctrines should arise in our minds, we promise that we* will neither publicly nor privately..."

(Italicized words were omitted.)

B. *Article 10*

3. The Effectiveness of the Ministerial Testimonial (p. 73)

The last line should read: "brief description in its testimonial *with the knowledge of the minister involved.*"

C. *Article 15*

3. The Fund for Needy Churches (p. 91)

The children's allowance of section d was modified by the 1980 Synod to include:

"every child up to twenty-two (22) years of age, excluding those who have reached the age of nineteen (19) and who are no longer enrolled in an educational institution." *(Acts of Synod 1980,* p. 84)

D. *Article 83*

b. Exclusion of Unfaithful Baptized Members (p. 309)
Since Article 83, as adopted in 1965, has revised the rules of discipline, this first paragragh should read:

1) "Members by baptism who willfully neglect to make public profession of faith, or are delinquent in doctrine or life, being unfaithful covenant members, become the objects of ecclesiastical discipline, and when they persist in their sin, should be excluded from the church."
(Acts of Synod 1965, p. 91)

II. Church Order Changes Proposed and Awaiting Ratification by Synod of 1983

A. Modifications of the Church Order and the Form of Subscription for use by the churches of Classis Red Mesa. See the "Rules of Synodical Procedure" under the specific articles and the *Acts of Synod 1981,* p. 15 ff.

B. Church Order Articles 3, 14, 17. See the *Rules for Synodical Procedure* under the specific article; also, *Acts of Synod 1982,* pp. 71-72, 76.

III. Miscellaneous Decisions

A. *Article 8*

Add the following section on page 65:

7. Stated Supply
Synod clarified the regulations governing the employment of unordained persons as stated supply in vacant churches as follows:

"a. It is highly inadvisable to have a man without a proper theological training serve as stated supply.

"b. The employment of a stated supply should not delay the calling of an ordained man.

Grounds:

"a. The underlying assumption throughout the Church Order is that the churches are to be served by ordained pastors unless special circumstances make this impossible.

"b. The reservation of 'official acts of the ministry' to ordained men, cf. Church Order Art. 11 (now Art. 12) and 53b, means that full ministerial service cannot be rendered to a congregation by an unordained man."

(Acts of Synod 1971, p. 65.)

B. *Article 10*

Add the following paragraph to the end of section f on page 72:

"A candidate whose case has been appealed to synod may not be called by another church nor examined by another classis" *(Acts of Synod 1912, p. 53).*

C. *Article 18*

Replace section 5 on page 100 with the following:

5. Readmission of Ministers Retired for Reasons Other Than Age.
Synod declared that "a retired minister, who wishes to reenter active service, cannot be called again unless the consistory and the classis which recommended him for retirement judge that the reasons for his retirement no longer exist."

(Acts of Synod 1928, p. 138)

D. *Article 27*

Replace section 4 on page 122 with the following:

4. The Authority of Assemblies
Each consistory is called by Christ to build his body for his work. Ministering to and with the members of the church constitutes the basic or original mandate of Christ to the church.

The major assemblies are duly constituted assemblies of the churches, and consist of delegates authorized to "take part in all deliberations and transactions of the assembly and transacted in agreement with the Word of God and according to the conception of it embodied in the doctrinal standards of the Christian Reformed Church, as well as in harmony with our Church Order." (Adapted from the "Credentials for Synod." See p. 341 for a copy of these credentials.) The limitations of the work of major assemblies are prescribed in Article 28.

Add the following reference to the last line on page 122:

Acts of Synod 1970, pp. 92-93.

E. *Article 42*

Add the following section on page 189:

7. The Relation of Consistory and Church Visitors

The chairmanship of consistory during church visiting, the nature of church visiting, and the authority of the church visitors were defined by synod as follows:

"At the meeting one of the visitors shall function as president and the other as clerk" shall be interpreted to mean that the respective visitors are to function as president and clerk *of the visiting committee*, and that the president of the consistory functions as chairman of the meeting.

Grounds:

1. Article 44 of the Church Order, dealing with the task of church visitors, defines this task to be a task of 'visiting,' 'taking heed,' 'admonishing,' and 'helping direct.' This article does not speak of any task of governing.

2. The meeting convened for church visitation is a meeting of the consistory receiving the church visitors. It is not a meeting of church visitors having invited a consistory. In a consistory meeting the chair is to be occupied by the chairman of the consistory.

3. Every appearance of hierarchy must be avoided.

(*Acts of Synod 1958*, pp. 93, 94).

F. *Article 49*

2. Churches in Ecclesiastical Fellowship (p. 209)

An updated list of Churches in Ecclesiastical Fellowship can be found in the *Acts of Synod 1982*, pp. 289-290.

G. *Article 53*

Add the following to section 2 on page 224:

"With the exception of licensed students, no one has the right to 'speak' in public worship unless he has received such right from his classis, after it has examined him relative to his orthodoxy, his godly walk, and his ability to address a congregation. Whether a person who has been examined and admitted by one of our classes shall have the privilege of 'speaking' also in other classes, is to be determined by the respective classes, each for its own territory."

(*Acts of Synod 1924,* p. 93)

H. *Article 56*

Administration of Infant Baptism

Add the following to section 3 on page 231:

Note that Synod of 1982 declared that Church Order Article 56 applies also to adopted children. (See *Acts of Synod 1982,* p. 86)

I. *Article 62*

Add the following to section 2a on page 246:

An explanation of this system of giving was offered the churches by synod:

1. With respect to all the work in God's kingdom, for which we as a Christian Reformed Church are jointly responsible, we use the term 'quota' to indicate the amount per family recommended by Synod to the congregations.

2. Synod reminds the consistories of the urgent necessity to keep before their congregations not only the privilege but also the sacred duty to contribute liberally toward the work of the Lord, which we have taken upon ourselves as the Christian Reformed Church.

3. The classes shall (may) consult with delinquent congregations through the consistories and, if necessary, admonish them to become more abundant in manifesting their love for the Lord's cause. However, if the classis is satisfied—with or without investigation—that a congregation has done what it could, the matter shall rest there; nor shall any unpaid portion of any quota be thereafter held against such a congregation as a debt."

(*Agenda I, 1939,* pp. 19-26; *Acts of Synod 1939,* p. 72; *1981,* p. 82.)

J. *Article 66*

Add the following to section 4 on page 261:

C. Membership Transfers RCA/CRC

Synod decided with respect to membership transfers between the Christian Reformed Church and the Reformed Church of America:

"Recognizing that churches in our sister denomination (RCA) often receive members of (our) denomination under discipline or with spiritual problems without becoming informed of these facts, and at the same time recognizing the need for mutual freedom and openness on the part of the churches, the practice of discipline and pastoral concern presently outlined in the church orders of the two denominations be respected in the following manner:

"1. That the pertinent information about the member(s) in question be shared by the pastors and/or elders of both the sending and receiving churches. Such exchange should be promptly expedited upon request to avoid undue delay for the member(s) concerned.

"2. That such members not be received officially until the elders of the receiving church consider their circumstance and status of discipline based on the information supplied by the sending church.

"3. That no member be publicly received until the consistory of the former congregation has been informed of the request for transfer of membership." (*Acts of Synod 1981,* p. 99)

K. *Article 69*

Add the following note to section 1, page 274:

[For comments on this general principle, see the report to the Synod of 1980, Para. II, "Biblical Teaching Regarding Divorce and Remarriage" (*Acts of Synod 1980,* pp. 473-480) as well as this manual, Article 69, 4a & b.]

L. *Article 76*

A revised statement of the four stages of organizational development (p. 291) was adopted. See the *Acts of Synod 1981,* pp. 30, 195.

M.*Article 81*

Add the following section on page 307:

m. Bankruptcy

Synod decided not to make a general rule in this matter, and added that "each instance of this character is to be judged individually."

(Acts of Synod 1892, p. 16).

N. *Article 90*

Add the following to section 1 on page 324:

e. Classis Right to Suspend

In response to a specific case and appeal synod declared: "Article 90 of the Church Order concerns itself with normal situations. The language of the Form of Subscription as interpreted by the decisions of the Synods of 1926 and 1936 give to the classis, in abnormal situations, the right to begin suspension proceedings" (*Acts of Synod 1970,* p. 92; see also *1926,* pp. 141-142; *1936,* pp. 146-147; *1980,* pp. 28-29; *1982,* p. 55).

f. Emergency Prerogatives of Major Assemblies

The Synod of 1982 declared "that it is indeed proper according to Reformed church polity for either classis or synod to intervene in the affairs of a local congregation if the welfare of the congregation is at stake" (*Acts of Synod 1982,* p. 55).

The synod of 1980 in a specific case decided that a classis was not guilty as charged of abusing its "God-given authority by lording it over a local consistory and exercising ecclesiastical authority in a hierarchical manner not in keeping with the domain and character of the authority entrusted to it by delegation."

Grounds:

"1. Christ gave authority to the church as a whole and entrusted authority to the occasions of its exercise in classis and synod as gatherings of the churches to maintain the unity of the congregations in both doctrine and discipline.

"2. The gathering of churches and their representatives in Jerusalem set a pattern of authoritative decisions which pattern is followed in principle in the deliberations and decisions of the major assemblies.

"3. To contend that (a classis) had no proper jurisdiction over the...consistory proceeds on a misconception of the relation of the minor assembly to the major assembly. The same authority, constituting the same standards and same goals, is applied by the several assemblies. Classis...adhered to the correct use of the authority delegated to them by Christ.

"4. The manner in which classis handled the protests and appeals, and other procedural matters did not impair the rights of nor prove to be harmful to the position of the complainants. Substantial justice has been effected, contradicting the claim that the classis lorded it over the consistory.

"5. It is in order that a classis act where a consistory fails to do so (Art. 27, C.O.). Classis' action was within the range of delegated authority.

"6. The classis found that an intolerable situation existed. . . . The synodical deputies concurred in the action. The fact-finding committee and the church visitors made the same appraisal. This breadth of responsible action negates the allegation of lording it over and of exercising ecclesiastical authority in a hierarchical manner."

(*Acts of Synod 1980*, pp. 28-29)

O. *Article 96*

Add the following section on page 335:

c. An interesting observation was made by an advisory committee to the Synod of 1979 to the effect that "the Church Order ought not to be subject to frequent change because nonessential, nonprincipial, detailed items have been included in it. The Church Order should remain as brief as possible to guarantee to the churches the necessary freedom to work out its provisions within these statements of general principles" (*Acts of Synod 1979*, p. 65).

IV. Decisions of the Synod of 1982

A. *Article 14*

Add the following to page 87:

8. The status of ministers not serving as pastors of congregations must be reviewed annually by classis (*Acts of Synod 1982*, p. 72).

B. *Article 52*

3. Synodically Approved Liturgical Forms (p. 219)

See *Acts of Synod 1982*, pp. 84-85, 122, 370-379 for additional liturgical forms adopted by Synod.

C. Article 84

Add the following to page 311:

These decisions of 1908, 1930, and 1961 were superceded by the Synod of 1982 when it declared that "this manner of reconciliation by members who have offended in doctrine or in life be determined by the consistory in all instances; and urged all consistories to be diligent in seeking to effect such reconciliation," adding that "there is no evidence in Scripture that sin against the seventh commandment be singled out" (*Acts of Synod 1982*, p. 40).

See Article 10

CHRISTIAN REFORMED CHURCH
Minister's Consistorial Credential

The Consistory of the Christian Reformed Church of ....

declares by these presents that the Rev. ...., in this

church from ...., 19........ to ...., 19........,
has ministered in the office of minister of the divine Word faithfully and diligently, adhering in doctrine and life to the Word of God, as interpreted by our Forms of Unity and the Church Order.

And considering that sufficient reasons have been adduced for the Consistory to acquiesce in his acceptance of the call of the church of ....,

we unhesitatingly recommend him to the Classis of ....

and to the church of ...., with the prayer that the great King of the Church, who says to this one of his servants "go" and he goeth, and to that one "come" and he cometh, may make him there also a rich blessing.

Resolved to grant him this testimonial of dismission at our meeting of ....
..................................., 19........

The Consistory of the above named church,

....President

....Clerk

Classis .... in which the congregation of ....

.... belongs, approves the above credential and transfers our beloved

brother in the ministry to the Classis of .... in whose midst our

brother expects to serve the church of .... as pastor and minister.

On behalf of said Classis,

....

....

....

Done this .... day of ...., 19........

The Classical Committee of the Classis of ...., having
examined the above credentials, approves them and herewith authorizes the counselor of

the church of .... to proceed to the installation.

The above named Classical Committee,

....

....

....

See Article 34

CLASSICAL CREDENTIALS

To the Classis of _____of the Christian Reformed Church, to convene

_____, 19_____, at_____

The Consistory of _____Christian Reformed Church at _____

has appointed _____ and _____

as delegates to represent said Church at the meeting of the Classis above referred to. The alternate delegates are:

_____ and _____

We hereby instruct and authorize them to take part in all deliberations and transactions of Classis regarding all matters legally coming before the meeting and transacted in agreement with the Word of God according to the conception of it embodied in the doctrinal standards of the Christian Reformed Church, as well as in harmony with our Church Order.

By order of the Consistory,

_____, President

_____, Clerk

Done in Consistory _____

QUESTIONS UNDER ARTICLE 41, CHURCH ORDER

(Consistories will please answer the following questions in writing)

1. Are the consistory meetings held regularly in your church; and are they held according to the needs of the congregation? _____

2. Is church discipline faithfully exercised? _____

3. Are the poor adequately cared for? _____

4. Does the consistory diligently promote the cause of Christian education from elementary school through institutions of higher learning? _____

5. a) Have you submitted to the Secretary of our Home Mission Board the names and addresses of all baptized and communicant members who have, since the last meeting of Classis, moved to a place where no Christian Reformed churches are found? _____

   b) Have you informed other consistories or pastors about members who reside, even temporarily, in the vicinity of their church?_____

   c) Have you, having been informed of such members in your own area, done all in your power to serve them with the ministry of your church? _____

6. Does the consistory diligently engage in and promote the work of evangelism in its community?_____

7. Is there any matter in which you need the advice or the help of Classis?

_____

Done in Consistory,

_____, President

Date _____   _____, Clerk

(See other side for Instructions and Overtures)

340

See Article 34

Credentials for Synod

To the Synod of the Christian Reformed Church

to convene.., 19..............

at...

Classis...has chosen the ministers

....and..

and the elders

....and..

as delegates to represent said Classis at the meeting of the Synod above referred to. The alternate minister delegates are

....and..

and the alternate elder delegates are

....and..

We hereby instruct and authorize them to take part in all deliberations and transactions of Synod regarding all matters legally coming before Synod and transacted in agreement with the Word of God according to the conception of it embodied in the doctrinal standards of the Christian Reformed Church, as well as in harmony with our Church Order.

By order of Classis...

...., President

.... , Stated Clerk

Done in meeting of Classis...

Date...

(over)

341

See Article 66

STATEMENT OF MEMBERSHIP

The Consistory of the _____ Christian Reformed Church of

_____ , at the request of our member(s) listed below, presents this statement of

membership to you, the _____ Church of _____

We commend them to your Christian fellowship and request your consistory to receive them with Christian love and

provide them with appropriate pastoral care and counsel.

MEMBERSHIP RECORD

Last Name _____ Phone No. _____

Address _____

Given Name	Date of Birth	Date of Baptism	Date of Profession*	Prior Membership
Single				
Husband				
Wife				
Children				

*To be filled in only for professing members.

ADDITIONAL INFORMATION:
(Involvement in church functions, special gifts or abilities, special needs, etc.)

_____ , President

Done in Consistory _____   _____ , Clerk
　　　　　　　　　　(date)

MEMBERSHIP RECEIPT
please return as soon as possible

This is to certify that the membership of _____

from the _____ Christian Reformed Church

of _____ has been received and accepted.

_____
Receiving Church

_____   _____
Date   Clerk

See Article 66

Front side

STATEMENT OF DISMISSION

This is to certify that ....
(has, have) until this date been a member(s) in full communion (by
baptism) of the .... Christian Reformed Church
of ...., and at .... request .... hereby
dismissed to unite with the church ....

By order of the Consistory of the Christian Reformed

Church of ....

.... *Pres.*

.... *Clerk*

Done in consistory on

the .... day of ...., 19......   **(over)**

Back side

MEMBERSHIP RECORD

	Date of Birth	Date of Baptism	Date of Confession of Faith
Adult Single Person	....	....	....
Husband	....	....	....
Wife	....	....	....
Baptized Children	....	....	....
	....	....	....
	....	....	....
	....	....	....
	....	....	....

General Index

A

Acts of Synod (minutes of assemblies), **32:3c,** p. 145; **46:3c,** p. 199
Admonition and Discipline *(see* Discipline)
Adopted Children and Baptism, 56:2d p. 231
Adult Baptism *(see* Baptism; Neo-Pentecostalism)
Adultery, 84:2, p. 311
Advisory Committees *(see* Committees of assemblies)
Affiliated Churches *(see* Interchurch relations)
Agenda
    of assemblies, **32:3b,** p. 145
    of consistory meetings, **35:3c,** p. 166
    of deacons' meetings, **25:5,** pp. 118-19
    of elders' meetings, **35:3c,** p. 166
    of synod, **28:5h,** pp. 127-28
Aid to Churches *(see* Fund for Needy Churches)
Amusements (worldly), **81:2i,** p. 306
Annual Day of Prayer, 51:2c, p. 217
Appeals
    definition of, **28:3,** p. 125
    distinguished from revision of an assembly decision, **31:1a,** p. 140
    elements of, **30:1b,** pp. 132-33
    Judicial Code, **30:2,** pp. 133-39
    legally before synod, **28:5c,** pp. 126-27
    of rejected overtures, **28:5d,** p. p. 127
    proper procedure, **30:1c,** p. 133
    right of appeal, **30:1a,** p. 132
    status of matters under appeal, **p. 30:1e,** p. 133
    time limit for, **30:1d,** p. 133
Approbation
    by congregation necessary for call to office, **2:2b(5),** p. 35
Archives, 32:3d, p. 145
Articles of Incorporation *(see* Incorporation)
Ascension Day, 51:2a, p. 216
Assemblies
    agenda of, **32:3b,** p. 145
    appeals *(see* Appeals)
    authority of
    —disciplinary, **27:6,** p. 122
    —nature of, **27:1,2,5,** pp. 121-22
    —original and delegated, **27:3,** p. 122
    —relative character of, **27:4,** p. 122
    character of decisions, **29,** pp. 129-31
    classis *(see also* Classis), **39-44,** pp. 176-93
    committees *(see also* Committees of assemblies), **33,** pp. 153-62
    composition of major assemblies, **34:1,** p. 163
    consistory *(see also* Consistory), **35-38,** pp. 165-75
    credentials *(see* Credentials)
    defined, **26:1,** p. 120
    delegation to, **34,** pp. 163-64

files and archives, **32:3d,** *p. 145*

financial transactions, **32:3e,**
pp. 145-46

general provisions, **26-34,** *pp.*
120-64

incorporation
—congregational, **32:4a,** *pp.*
146-47
—denominational, **32:4b,** *pp.*
147-48
—synodically approved form for
congregational incorporation,
32:4a, *pp. 146-47*

Judicial Code, **30:2,** *pp. 133-39*

limitation of voting by delegates, **34:4,** *p. 164*

matters of concern for major
assemblies, **28:2,** *pp. 124-25*

officers and their responsibilities, **32:2,** *pp. 143-44*

provisions for conducting business, **32:3,** *pp. 144-46*

responsibilities of assemblies,
26:2, *p. 120*

responsibility and freedom of
delegates, **34:3,** *pp. 163-64*

rules of procedure for assemblies, **28:4,** *pp. 125-26*

synod (*see also* Synod), **45-50,**
pp. 194-213

Authority in the Church
disciplinary authority of assemblies, **27:6,** *p. 122*

exercise and nature of, **24:6,** *pp.*
115-16

of ecclesiastical assemblies,
27:6, *p. 122*

original and delegated, **27:1, 2,**
5, *pp. 121-22*

relative character of assembly
authority, **27:4,** *p. 122*

B

Baptism *(see also* Forms: Liturgical;
Sacraments), **55-58,** *pp. 28-37*

administered outside the worship service, **56:5,** *p. 232*

adopted children, **56:2d,** *p. 231*

adult baptism, **57,** *pp. 233-34*
—form must be used, **57:3,** *p.*
234
—profession of faith required,
57:1, *p. 233*
—rebaptism, **57:2,** *pp. 233-34*

baptism with the Holy Spirit,
58:3, *pp. 235-37*

infant baptism, **56,** *pp. 230-32*
—administration to sick children, **56:5,** *p. 232*
—adopted children, **56:2d,** *p.*
231
—children whose parents have
not professed their faith,
56:2a, *p. 230*
—doctrinal basis, **56:1,** *p. 230*
—failure to present children for
baptism, **56:2b,** *p. 231,* **81:2a,**
pp. 304-05
—form must be used, **56:3,** *p.*
231
—infant baptism and church
membership, **56:1,** *p. 230*
—must be requested, **56:3,** *p.*
231
—parents under formal discipline, **56:2c,** *p. 231*
—recording of baptism, **56:4,** *p.*
232
—valid baptisms, criteria for,
58, *pp. 235-37*

Baptized Members *(see* Church membership; Discipline)

Basis of the Church Order: biblical and
confessional, **1,** *pp. 28-31*

Belgic Confession
Article 7, **1:2b,** *pp. 29-30*
Article 28, **66:7,** *p. 262*
Article 29, **1:2a,** *p. 29*
Article 30, **1:1c,** *p. 29*
Article 34, **56:1,** *p. 230*
Article 35, **55:2,** *p. 228*

Benediction, 53:1, *p. 224*

Bible
contemporary versions, **52:2b,**
p. 219

recommended versions, **52:2a,** *p. 218*

synod to designate versions, **47:1f,** *pp. 202-03*

Boards *(see* Committees of assemblies)

Board for Christian Reformed World Missions *(see* World Missions)

Board of Publications *(see* Unified church school curriculum)

Board of Trustees—Calvin College and Seminary *(see* Calvin College; Seminary)

Christian Reformed Board of Home Missions *(see* Home Missions)

Christian Reformed World Relief Committee

C

Calling *(see also* Candidacy; Letter of Call)

calling to special offices, **4,** *pp. 42-43*

candidates *(see* Candidates)

ministers *(see also* Ministers of the Word), **8,** *pp. 58-65*

—advertising for available ministers, **8,** *p. 61*

—consistory consent before acceptance, **14:1,** *p. 85*

—from other denominations, **8:5,** *pp. 62-65*

—seeking a call, **8,** *p. 60-61*

missionaries, **77:1d,** *p. 295*

necessity of call by the congregation, **2:2b(5),** *p. 35*

rules for calling by smaller congregations, **38:4,** *p. 175*

Calvin College, 71:3a, *pp. 277-78*

Calvin Seminary *(see* Seminary; Theological training)

Candidacy *(see also* Candidates), **6,** *pp. 48-52*

continuation of candidacy, **6:2,** *pp. 48-51*

eligibility, time of, **6:2b(3),** *p. 51*

Indian mission field: regulations **7:4,** *pp. 55-56*

length of candidacy, **6:2b(3),** *p. 51*

M. Div. degree required, **6:1b(2),** *p. 48*

ministers from other denominations: regulations for admittance to candidacy, **8:5,** *pp. 62-65*

ordination of candidates, **10:1,** *pp. 68-73*

persons not trained at Calvin Seminary, **6:3,** *pp. 51-52*

regulations for candidacy, **6:2,** *pp. 48-51*

required classical and synodical credentials, **10:1c,** *p. 69*

time period for consideration of a call, **6:2b(3),** *p. 51*

without prescribed training, **7,** *pp. 53-57*

Candidates *(see also* Candidacy), **10,** *pp. 68-73*

certificate of ordination, **10:1g,** *p. 72*

classical diploma, **10:1g,** *p. 72*

classical examination, **10:1,** *pp. 68-73*

—credentials required, **10:1c,** *p. 69*

—importance of, **10:1b,** *p. 69*

—ordination and laying on of hands, **10:1h,** *p. 72-73*

—prerequisites, **10:1a,** *p. 68*

—reexamination, **10:1f,** *pp. 71-72*

—schedule for examination, **10:1e,** *pp. 70-71*

—sermon(s), **10:1d,** *pp. 69-70*

moving, **10:1a(2),** *pp. 68-69*

ordination, **10:1,** *pp. 68-73*

provisional nature of call, **10:1a(1),** *p. 68*

setting date for ordination, **10:1a(3),** *p. 69*

Canons of Dort, 1:1a, *p. 29*

Catechetical Instruction *(see also* Unified church school curriculum), **63-64,** *pp. 250-56*
> church's responsibility for, **63:1, 2,** *pp. 250-52*
> content of catechetical instruction, **63:3,** *p. 252*
> definition of catechesis, **63:1a,** *p. 250*
> implementation of, **64,** *pp. 254-56*
> instructional materials, **64:4,** *p. 256*
> integration of catechism and Sunday school, **63:2b, c,** *pp. 251-52*
> neglect of, **81:2d,** *p. 305*
> place of Heidelberg Catechism and Compendium, **64:3,** *pp. 255-56*
> purpose of, **63:4,** *pp. 252-53*
> responsibility of the pastor, **12:2c,** *p. 77;* **64:2,** *p. 255*
> scope of catechesis, **63:1b,** *pp. 250-51*
> Sunday school: purpose of, **64:1b,** *pp. 254*
> supervision by the consistory, **64:1,** *pp. 254-55*

Catechism *(see* Catechetical instruction; Heidelberg Catechism)

Censure *(see also* Discipline)
> mutual censure, **36:3,** *pp. 168-69*
> silent censure, **85:1,** *p. 312*

Certificates *(see also* Forms)
> classical diploma, **10:1g,** *p. 72*
> —copy of, **Appendix,** *p. 338*
> of members from churches in ecclesiastical fellowship, **59:3,** *p. 240*
> of members from other CRC churches, **59:2,** *p. 240*
> of ordination, **10:1g,** *p. 72*
> of transfer *(see* Church membership)

Chaplains: Institutional, industrial, and military, **12:4,** *pp. 79-81*

Charismatic Movement *(see* Neo-Pentecostalism)

Children *(see* Baptism)

Choirs, 52:6, *p. 223*

Christian Education *(see also* Christian schools), **71,** *pp. 276-78*
> Relationship to church education, **64:1c,** *p. 255*
> Support by ecclesiastical office-bearers, **3:4a,** *p. 41*

Christian Reformed Church in North America
> Articles of Association, **32:4b(2),** *pp. 147-52*
> Christian Reformed Church Synod Trustees, **32:4b(1),** *pp. 147-48*
> incorporation, **32:4b,** *pp. 147-52*
> Synodical Interim Committee, **32:4b(1),** *pp. 147-48*

Christian Reformed World Relief Committee
> constitution, **25:4,** *p. 118*
> world hunger, **25:5,** *p. 119*

Christian Schools
> area colleges, **71:3b,** *p. 278*
> duty of parents and congregation, **71:1a,** *pp. 276-77*
> higher education, **71:3,** *pp. 277-78*
> necessity of Christian education, **71:1a,** *pp. 276-77*
> principles of Christian education, **71:2,** *p. 277*
> taxation, **71:2,** *p. 277*

Church Development
> stages of organization, **76:1b(2),** *p. 291*

Church Discipline *(see* Discipline)

Church Education *(see also* Catechetical instruction; Sunday school)
> adult education, **72:1d,** *p. 280*
> congregational societies for Bible study, **72,** *pp. 279-80*

Church Government *(see* Church Order; Polity of Reformed churches)

Church Help Committee, 33:1, *pp. 153-54*

Churches in Ecclesiastical Fellowship *(see* Interchurch relations)

Church Membership
> absentee members, **67:2,** *pp. 263-64*

—admission to communicant membership, **59**, *pp. 238-40*

—communicants from churches in ecclesiastical fellowship, **59:3**, *p. 240*

—communicants from other CRCs, **59:2**, *p. 240*

—persons from other denominations, **59:4**, *p. 240*

certificates of transfer

—copy of, **Appendix**, *p. 342*

—for members by baptism, **66:3**, *p. 261*

—for moving to other CRCs, **66:1**, *p. 260*

—for moving to other denominations, **66:4**, *p. 261*

—issued by consistory, **66:5**, *p. 262*

—required for admission, **59:2,3**, *p. 240*

—signatures required, **66:5**, *p. 262*

—transmitting of certificates, **66:2**, *pp. 260-61*

communicant

—and baptism of infants, **56:2a**, *p. 230*

—meaning in relation to church office, **59:1c**, *p. 240*

—via public profession of faith, **59:1**, *pp. 238-40*

confessional reference, **66:7**, *p. 262*

discipline of members (*see* Discipline)

dismission, **66:4**, *p. 261*

lapsed membership

—of persons who do not move away, **67:2b**, *p. 264*

—of persons who move away, **67:2a**, *pp. 263-64*

membership

—of divorced and remarried persons, **69:4c**, *pp. 268-74*

—of emerging congregations, **2:3e(6)**, *p. 37*

—of foreign missionaries, **67:3**, *p. 265*

—of ministers serving in missions, **12:3d**, *p. 79*

—of released ministers, **17:5**, *p. 96*

—of separated mates, **66:6**, *p. 262*

—resignation of children's membership by parents, **86:4**, *p. 315*

membership papers (*see* Church membership: Certificates of transfer)

membership records, **68:1**, *p. 266*

membership transfers (*see also* Church membership: Certificates of transfer)

—from other CRCs, **59:2**, *p. 240;* **66:1**, *p. 260*

—from other denominations, **59:3, 4**, *p. 240*

—of baptized members, **66:3**, *p. 261*

—of persons under discipline, **66:1**, *p. 260*

resignation under discipline, **86:3**, *pp. 314-15*

retention of membership when moving, **67:1**, *p. 263*

transfers (*see* Church Membership: Certificates of transfer, Membership transfers)

Church Music

choirs, **52:6**, *p. 223*

principles, **52:4**, *pp. 220-22*

Church Order *(see also* Polity of Reformed churches)

adoption of, **47:1b**, *p. 201*

divisions of, **1:3**, *pp. 30-31*

faithful observance required, **96:1**, *p. 335*

historical introduction, **Introduction, B**, *pp. 1-2*

how to use, **Introduction, E**, *pp. 4-5*

need for, *pp. 28-31*

recent trends, **Introduction, D**, *pp. 3-4*

relationship to Scripture and creeds, **1:1, 2**, *pp. 28-30* revision of, **Introduction, C, D, 1**, *pp. 2-3;* **1:2c**, *p. 30;* **2:2b(6)**, *p. 35;* **47:2**, *p. 203;* **96:2**, *p. 334;*

Church Planting, 76:1b(2), *p. 291*

Church Polity *(see* Church Order; Polity of Reformed churches)

Church School *(see* Catechetical instruction; Sunday school; Unified church school curriculum)

Church Visitors, 42, *pp. 184-89*
    appointment of, **42:1**, *pp. 184-85*
    arrangements for, **42:4**, *pp. 186-89*
    availability of, **42:5**, *p. 189*
    benefits of church visits, **42:2, 3**, *pp. 185-86*
    duties of, **42:2**, *p. 185*
    frequency of visits, **42:1c**, *p. 185*
    guide for the examination, **42:4**, *pp. 186-89*
    inquiries re evangelists and ministers in specialized tasks, **42:2**, *p. 185*
    observations regarding, **42:3**, *p. 186*
    qualifications of, **42:1b**, *p. 184*
    questions for church visiting, **42:4**, *pp. 186-89*
    reports to classis, **42:6**, *p. 189*

Classis *(see also* Assemblies), **39-44**, *pp. 176-93*
    approval for organization of a new congregation, **38:2**, *p. 174*
    church visitors *(see also* Church visitors), **42**, *pp. 184-89*
    credentials of delegates, **34:2**, *p. 163*
    —copy of, **Appendix**, *p. 340*
    definition, **39:1**, *p. 176*
    delegates, **40:1**, *p. 177*
    examination of candidates *(see also* Candidates), **10:1**, *pp. 68-72*
    evangelistic task, **75**, *pp. 287-88*
    financial transactions, **40:4b**, *pp. 179-80*
    frequency of meetings, **40:2**, *p. 178*

    home missions committee, **75**, *pp. 287-88*
    interim committee, **33:4**, *p. 155*
    joint action of classes, **44**, *pp. 192-93*
    Judicial Code, **30:2**, *pp. 133-39*
    jurisdiction, **39:2**, *p. 176*
    licensure to exhort, **43**, *pp. 190-91*
    minutes, **32:3c**, *p. 145*
    mutual financial responsibilities, **41:3**, *p. 183*
    officers, **40:3, 4**, *pp. 178-80*
    open to public, **40:1**, *pp. 177-78*
    organizing new classes, **39:3**, *p. 176*
    questions to consistories, **41**, *pp. 181-83*
    redistricting, **39:4**, *p. 176*
    responsibility to unorganized churches, **38**, *pp. 173-75*
    role in discipline, **83:1b, c**, *pp. 309-10;* **85:2**, *p. 312;* **86:1, 2b**, *pp. 313, 314;* **87:1**, *p. 317;* **89:4**, *pp. 321-22;* **90**, *pp. 323-25;* **91**, *p. 326;* **92:3**, *p. 328;* **93:2**, *p. 329;* **94:2, 3**, *pp. 330-31*
    stated clerk, **40:4a**, *pp. 178-79;* **45:3a,b; 4a,b**, *pp. 195, 196*
    synodical deputies, **48**, *pp. 204-06*
    transfer of congregation to another classis, **39:5**, *p. 176*

Colloquium Doctum
    required of ministers from other denominations, **8:5**, *pp. 62-65*

Committees of assemblies
    functions, **33:1**, *pp. 153-54*
    Historical Committee, **32:3d**, *p. 145*
    interim committees, **33:4**, *p. 155*
    mandates and reports, **33:2**, *p. 154*
    membership, **33:3**, *pp. 154-55*
    rules for study and standing committees, **33:3a**, *pp. 154-55*
    synodical advice to churches re committee membership, **33:3b**, *p. 155*

Synodical Interim Committee, **33:5**, *pp. 155-58*

Communicant Membership *(see* Church membership)

Communications to Assemblies
definition, **28:3**, *p. 125*
information to synod, **28:5f**, *p. 127*
legally before synod, **28:5**, *pp. 126-28*

Communion *(see* Lord's Supper)

Compendium of the Heidelberg Cate-chism, 64:3, *pp. 255-56*

Confession of Faith *(see* Profession of faith)

Confessions *(see* Creeds)

Congregational Evangelism, 74, *pp. 284-86*

Congregational Meetings, 4, *pp. 42-43;* **37**, *pp. 170-72*
calling a minister *(see* Calling)
consistory's role, **37:2**, *pp. 171-72*
election of office-bearers, **4:1, 2**, *pp. 42-43;* **37:1a**, *p. 170*
participation in, **37:3**, *p. 172*
purpose, **37:1**, *pp. 170-72*
women's right to vote, **37:3c**, p. 172

Consistory *(see also* Deacons; Elders; Offices of the church), **35-38**, *pp. 165-75*
church visitors, questions for, **42:4**, *pp. 186-89*
discipline of *(see* Discipline)
distinction of functions, **35:3**, *p. 166*
election of, **4:1, 2**, *pp. 42-43*
examination by for profession of faith, **59:1a**, *pp. 238-39*
general and restricted con-sistory, **35:2**, *pp. 165-66*
general nature and function, **35:1**, *p. 165*
officers and duties, **36:2**, *pp. 167-68*
ordination of office-bearers, **4:4**, *p. 43*
organization of new congrega-tion, **38:1, 2, 3**, *pp. 173-75*

regulation of sacraments, **55:1**, *p. 228*
regulation of worship services, **52:1**, *p. 218*
responsibility for evangelism, **74:2**, *pp. 284-85*
responsibility in granting leaves of absence (temporary re-lease), **16:1, 5**, *pp. 93, 94*
supervision, **24:1**, *p. 114*
time and place of meeting, **36:1**, *p. 167*

Counselor, 9, *pp. 66-67*
appointment, **9:1**, *p. 66*
reports, **9:2**, *p. 66*
responsibilities, **9:3**, *pp. 66-67*

Covenant and Baptism, 56:1, *p. 230*

Credentials
authorization of delegates to assemblies, **34:2, 3**, *pp. 163-64*
candidates', **10:1c**, *p. 69*
copy of classical, **Appendix**, *p. 340*
copy of minister's *(see also* Ministers of the Word: Credentials), **Appendix**, *p. 339*
copy of synodical, **Appendix**, *p. 341*
retired minister's, **18:3b**, *p. 99*
submission to synod, **45:3a**, *p. 195*

Creeds *(see also* specific creed)
adoption of, **47:1a**, *p. 201*
received by the Christian Re-formed Church, **1:1a**, *p. 29*
relation to Scripture and Church Order, **1:2**, *pp. 29-30*
relation to synodical pro-nouncements, **29:3**, *pp. 129-30*
subscription to, **1:2b**, *p. 30*

D

Days of Prayer
annual, **51:2c**, *p. 217*
national, **51:3**, *p. 217*

Deacons *(see also* Consistory; Offices of the church)

    agenda for deacons' meetings, **25:5,** *pp. 118-19*

    church visitors, questions for, **42:4,** *pp. 186-89*

    community involvement, **25:5,** *pp. 118-19*

    conferences, **25:4,** *p. 118*

    discipline of *(see* Discipline)

    election of, **4:1, 2, 3,** *pp. 42-43*

    —reelection, **23:3,** *p. 110*

    eligibility for office, **3:1,2,** *pp. 39-40*

    nature of their ministry, **25:1,** *p. 117*

    objects of mercy, **25:2, 3,** *pp. 117-18*

    ordination of, **4:4,** *p. 43*

    provision for institutional care, **25:3,** *p. 118*

    tenure *(see also* Tenure), **23,** *p. 109-12*

    women as deacons, **3:2,** *p. 40*

    work of mercy, **25:1,** *p. 117;* **35:3b,** *p. 166*

    world hunger, **25:5,** *pp. 118-19*

Delegates to Major Assemblies, 34, *pp. 163-64*

    to classis, **40:1,** *pp. 177-78*

    to synod, **45:2,** *p. 194*

Denominational Financial Coordinator

    regulations for position, **33:7,** *pp. 161-62*

    role at synod, **46:4d,** *p. 200*

Deposition *(see* Discipline)

Diakonia

    meaning and application to office, **2:2a(1),** *p. 33*

Diploma

    Copy of classical diploma, **Appendix,** *p. 338*

Discipline

    announcements of

    —exclusion of baptized members, **83:1b,** *pp. 310-11*

    —excommunication, **86:2,** *p. 314*

    —ministerial suspension, deposition, resignation, **90:1, 2, 3,** *pp. 323-25*

—resignation of membership, **86:3b,** *p. 315*

—restoration to church, **87:1c,** *p. 317*

baptism and discipline

—failure to present children, **56:2b,** *p. 231*

—parents under formal discipline, **56:2c,** *p. 231*

censure, silent, **85:1,** *p. 312*

confessional references, **78:1b,** *pp. 299-300*

deposition

—of consistory, **89:4,** *pp. 321-22*

—of elders or deacons, **91,** *p. 326*

—of ministers, **90:2,** *p. 324*

—reinstatement to office, **94,** *pp. 330-31*

—resignation of ministers, **90:3,** *pp. 324-25*

—special and general discipline, **88,** *p. 319*

—without previous suspension, **89:3,** *p. 321*

disciplinary authority of assemblies, **27:6,** *p. 122*

erasure of baptized members, **81:2c,** *p. 305;* **83,** *pp. 309-10*

excommunication, **86,** *pp. 313-16*

initiation of, **81:1,** *p. 304*

Judicial Code, **30:2,** *pp. 133-39;* **82,** *p. 308*

mutual discipline, **78:2,** *p. 300*

nature and responsibility, **78,** *pp. 298-300*

occasions for, **81,** *pp. 304-07*

of ministers *(see* Discipline: Deposition, Suspension from office)

of office-bearers *(see also* Discipline: Deposition, Suspension from office), **88-94,** *pp. 319-31*

—because of neo-Pentecostal views, **89:2,** *pp. 320-21*

—classical discipline of a consistory, **89:4,** *pp. 321-22;* **91:2,** *p. 326*

—grounds, **89:1,** *p. 320*

—procedure, **89:3,** *p. 321*

—reinstatement to office, **94,** *pp. 330-31*

preliminary requirements, **82,** *p. 308*

promises required by forms, **80:2,** *pp. 302-03*

purpose of, **79,** *p. 301*

readmission

—of baptized members, **83:2,** *p. 310*

—of divorced persons, **87:2,** *p. 318*

—of excommunicated members, **87:1,** *p. 317*

reconciliation of disciplined members, **84,** *p. 311*

resignation of children's membership by parents, **86:4,** *p. 315*

resignation under discipline, **86:3,** *pp. 314-15*

sacraments

—restriction from participation, **85,** *p. 312*

seventh commandment violation, **84:2,** *p. 311*

silent censure, **85,** *p. 312*

spiritual character of, **78:1,** *pp. 298-300*

suspension from office, **8:1,** *p. 319*

—lifting of, **93,** *p. 329*

—of a consistory, **89:4,** *pp. 321-22*

—of ministers, **90:1,** *pp. 323-24*

—of office-bearers, **89,** *pp. 320-22*

task of elders, **24:4,** *pp. 114-15* **35:3a,** *p. 166*

transfer of membership to escape discipline, **66:1,** *p. 260*

Divorce *(see* Marriage)

Doctrinal and Ethical Decisions of Synod, 65:5, *pp. 258-59*

Doxology, 52:5, *p. 223*

E

Ecclesiastical Fellowship *(see also* Interchurch relations)

list of churches, **49:2b,** *pp. 209-10*

receiving of members into communicant membership, **59:3,** *p. 240*

Ecclesiastical Matters

definition, **28:1,** *pp. 123-24*

Ecumenical Relations *(see also* Interchurch relations), **49, 50,** *pp. 207-13*

Education

Christian schools, **71,** pp. 276-78

—relation to catechesis, home, Sunday school, **64:1c,** *p. 255*

church education *(see* Catechetical instruction; Sunday school)

duties of pastors, **12:2c, d,** *pp. 77-78*

Elders *(see also* Consistory; Offices of the church)

admonition and discipline *(see also* Discipline), **24:4,** *pp. 114-15*

agenda for elders' meetings, **35:3c,** *p. 166*

church visitors, questions for, **42:4,** *pp. 186-89*

duty to maintain good order, **24:2,** *p. 114*

election of, **4:3,** *p. 43*

eligibility for office, **3:1,4,** *pp. 39-40, 41*

exercise and nature of authority, **24:6,** *pp. 115-16*

ordination of, **4:4,** *p. 43*

pastoral care of the congregation, **24:3,** *p. 114*

reelection of, **23:3,** *p. 110*

relation to evangelism, **24:5,** p. 115

supervision of the congregation, **24:1,** *p. 114*

tenure *(see* Tenure of elders and deacons)

Election
immediate reelection of elders and deacons to special office, **23:3,** *p. 110*
of ministers, elders and deacons, **4,** *pp. 42-43*
Emeritation *(see also* Ministers of the Word: Retirement), **18,** *pp. 98-100*
Equality
of churches, **95:1,** *p. 332*
of office, **95:3,** *pp. 332-33*
of officebearers, **95:2,** *p. 332*
Ethical Decision of Synod, 65:5, *pp. 258, 259*
Evangelism *(see also* Home Missions)
classical, **75,** *pp. 287-88*
congregational, **74,** *pp. 284-86*
denominational, **76,** *pp. 289-93*
office of evangelist, **2:3,** *pp. 35-38*
task of consistory, **74:2,** *pp. 284-85*
task of elders, **24:5,** *p. 115*
task of ministers, **12:2d,** *pp. 77-78*
Evangelist
discipline of, **88,** *p. 319;* **91,** *p. 326*
eligibility for office, **2:3,** *pp. 35-38;* **3:3,** *pp. 40-41*
examination, **2:3f,** *p. 38*
history of, **74:5,** *pp. 285-86*
office of, **2:3,** *pp. 35-38;* **23,** *pp. 109-116*
ordination, **2:3e,** *p. 37;* **23,** *p. 111*
regulations, **2:3a,** *p. 36*
relation to office of elder, **2:3d,** *p. 37;* **23,** *pp. 109-12*
sacraments administered by, **2:3c,** *p. 37;* **55:3,** *228-29*
Examination
candidates *(see also* Candidates), **10,** *pp. 68-73*
persons admitted to ministry without prescribed training, **7,** *pp. 53-55*
evangelists, **2:3f,** *p. 38*
Excommunication *(see* Discipline)

Exhorting *(see* Licensure to conduct worship services; Preaching; Worship)
Expenses of Synodical Delegates, 45:2c, *p. 194*

F

Family
definition re quota system, **62:2d,** *p. 248*
home visitation, **65:3a,** *p. 258*
Files and Archives, 32:3d, *p. 145*
Financial Coordinator *(see* Denominational financial coordinator)
Foreign Missions *(see also* World Missions), **77,** *pp. 294-97*
Form of Subscription *(see also* Gravamina), **5,** *pp. 44-47*
copy of, **5:3,** *pp. 44-45*
guidelines re meaning of subscription, **5:4b,** *pp. 45-46*
occasions for signing, **5:1,** *p. 44*
official copy, **5:2,** *pp. 44-45*
Forms
copies of
—classical diploma, **Appendix,** *p. 338*
—credentials for delegates to classis, **Appendix,** *p. 340*
—credentials for delegates to synod, **Appendix,** *p. 341*
—credentials of ministers, **Appendix,** *p. 338*
—letter of call, **Appendix,** *p. 337*
—statement of dismission, **Appendix,** *p. 343*
—transfer of membership (baptized or professing member), **Appendix,** *p. 342*
liturgical
—adopted by synod, **47:1c,** *p. 201*
—use in worship services, **52:3,** *p. 219*
—use of prescribed forms required, **55:4,** *p. 229*

Fund for Needy Churches
relationship to smaller congregations calling a minister, **3:4,** *p. 175*
rules for administration, **15:3,** *pp. 90-91*
to assist in supporting ministers, **15:2c, 3,** *pp. 89-91*
Funerals, 70, *p. 275*

G

Gifts
for service, **3:1d,** *p. 40*
of those who have not followed prescribed course of study for candidacy, **7,** *pp. 53-57*
Grant-in-Aid Program, 76:1a(4), *p. 290*
Gravamina
confessional difficulty, **5:4c,** *p. 46*
confessional revision, **5:4d,** *pp. 46-47*
definition, **28:3,** *p. 125*

H

Head of the Church, 1:1b, *p. 29*
Heidelberg Catechism
Compendium of, **64:3,** *pp. 255-56*
Lord's Day 12, **2:1b,** *pp. 32-33*
Lord's Day 26-27, **56:1,** *p. 230*
Lord's Day 28-30, **60:2c, 4,** *pp. 242, 243*
Lord's Day 30-31, **78:1b(4, 5, 6),** *pp. 299-300*
Use of
—in catechetical instruction, **64:3,** *pp. 255-56*
—in worship services, **54:2, 3,** *pp. 226-27*
Historical Committee, 32:3d, *p. 145*
Home Missionaries (*see* Evangelist; Missionaries)

Home Missions
Board of Home Missions, **76,** *pp. 289-93*
classical, **75,** *pp. 287-88*
—classical home missions committee, **75:1c, 2,** *pp. 287-88*
—relationship of classical and denominational home missions committees, **75:2,** *p. 288*
—task of classis, **75:1,** *pp. 287-88*
congregational
—consistorial responsibility, **74:2,** *pp. 284-85*
—cooperation with neighboring churches, **74:3,** *pp. 285*
—"Guide for Neighborhood Evangelism," **74:1, 2, 5,** *pp. 284-85, 286*
—minister of evangelism, **74:4,** *p. 285*
—obligation of churches, **74:1,** *p. 284*
—office of evangelist, **74:5,** *pp. 285-86*
denominational, **76,** *pp. 289-93*
—administration of synodical home mission work, **76:2,** *pp. 291-93*
—Board of Home Missions, **76,** *pp. 289-93*
—campus ministries, **76:4a,** *p. 293*
—church planting, **76:1b(2),** *pp. 290-91*
—grant-in-aid program, **76:1a(4),** *p. 290*
—home missionaries, **76:3,** *p. 293*
—home mission fields, **76:1b(2),** *p. 291*
—inner city missions, **76:4b,** *p. 293*
—Jewish missions, **76:4c,** *p. 293*
—minister of evangelism, **76:1a(3),** *p. 290*
—Regional Home Missionaries, **76:2c(6),** *pp. 292-93*

—significant guidelines and
decisions, **76:4,** *p. 293*
—specialized ministries,
76:1b(2b), *p. 291*
—staff personnel, **76:2c,** *p. 292*
—task of synod, **76:1,** *pp. 289-91*
home missionaries, **76:3,** *p. 293*
membership of emerging congregations, **2:3e(f),** *p. 37*
office of evangelist *(see also*
Evangelist*),* **2:3,** *pp. 35-38;*
74:5, *pp. 285-86*
Home Visiting, 65:3a, *p. 258*
Hymnal *(see also* Church music*)*
adoption of, **47:1d,** *p. 202*
principles of church music,
52:4a, *pp. 219-21*
—*Psalter Hymnal* and *Supplement,* **52:4b, c,** *pp. 221-22*

I

Incorporation
assemblies, **32:4,** *pp. 146-52*
Christian Reformed Church in
North America, **32:4b(2),** *pp.
148-52*
Christian Reformed Church
Synod Trustees, **32:4b(1),** *pp.
147-48*
congregations, **32:4a,** *pp. 146-47*
definition of schism, **32:4a(3),**
p. 147
denominational, **32:4b,** *pp.
147-52*
synodically approved form for
the incorporation of con-
gregations, **32:4a(1),** *pp.
146-47*
Infant Baptism *(see* Baptism*)*
Information Concerning Ministers (*see*
Ministerial Information Service*)*
Installation *(see also* Ordination*)*
candidates *(see* Candidates*),*
10:1, *pp. 68-73*
elders and deacons, **4:4,** *p. 43;*
23:4, *pp. 110-11*

evangelists, **2:3e,** *p. 37*
ministers *(see* Ministers of the
Word*),* **10:2,** *p. 73*
Interchurch Relations, 49, 50, *pp. 207-13*
calling ministers from other
denominations, **8:5,** *pp. 62-65*
churches in ecclesiastical fellowship, **49:2,** *pp. 209-10*
—reception of members into
communicant membership,
59:3, *p. 240*
ecumenical organizations, **49:3,**
pp. 210-11
Interchurch Relations Committee, **49:1,** *pp. 207-09*
loaning ministers to other denominations, **13:4,** *pp. 83-84*
Reformed Ecumenical Synods,
50, *pp. 212-213*
transfers of membership between denominations *(see*
Church membership*)*
Interim Committees, 33:4, *p. 155*

J

Jesus Christ
head of the church, **1:1b,** *p. 29;*
27:1b, *pp. 121-22*
Lord of the church, **2:2b(3),** *p. 35*
Judicial Code of Rights and Procedure,
30:2, *pp. 133-39*

L

Labor Union Membership, 3:4b, *p. 41*
Lapsed Membership (*see* Church mem-
bership*)*
Lay Evangelists *(see* Evangelists*)*
Laying on of Hands, 2:2a(10,11), *p. 34*
candidates, **10:1h,** *pp. 72-73*
Leave of Absence, 16, *pp. 93-94*
Letter of Call
copy, **Appendix,** *p. 337*

must be signed by counselor,
9:3, *pp. 66-67*
provisional nature in case of
candidates, **10:1a,** *pp. 68-69*
Liaison with Government, 33:5b, *p. 155*
Licensure to Conduct Worship Services
classical, **43,** *pp. 190-91*
limitation of classical licensure
of students, **43:3,** *p. 191*
regulations re worship, **53:2,** *p.
224*
theological students, **22,** *pp.
106-08*
—foreign students, **22:3,** *p. 107*
—procedures to obtain licensure, **22:4,** *p. 108*
—purpose, **22:1,** *p. 106*
—relationship of synodical and
classical licensure, **22:6,** *p.
108*
students not studying at Calvin
Seminary, **22:5,** *p. 108*
synodical rules, **22:2,** *pp. 106-07*
Limitation of Tenure in Office, 23, *pp.
109-12*
Liturgical Committee, 47:1e, *p. 202*
Liturgical Forms *(see* Forms: Liturgical)
Lodge Membership
an occasion for discipline,
81:2h, *p. 306*
profession of faith and the
lodge, **59:1a,** *p. 239*
Lord's Day *(see also* Worship)
designation for special purposes, **51:1f,** *p. 216*
observance, **51:1e,** *pp. 215-16*
violation an occasion for discipline, **81:2e,** *p. 305*
worship services, **51:1,** *pp.
214-16*
Lord's Supper *(see also* Sacraments)
administration to the sick,
60:2d, *p. 242*
confessional references, **60:4,**
p. 243
consistorial responsibility (supervision), **60:2a,** *p. 241*
frequency of celebration, **60:1,**
p. 241

guests, **60:2c,** *p. 242*
neglect of, **60:2e,** *p. 242*
preparatory and applicatory sermons, **60:3,** *p. 242*
use of the forms, **55:4,** *p. 229;*
60:2b, *p. 241*

M

Major Assemblies *(see* Assemblies;
Classis; Synod)
Marriage
divorce and remarriage, **69:4,**
pp. 268-74
—church membership, **69:4c,** *p.
269*
—readmission of divorced persons, **87:2,** *p. 318*
—remarriage after divorce,
69:4b, *pp. 268-69*
—sanctity of marriage, **69:4a,** *p.
268*
instruction: duty of, **69:1,** *p. 267*
membership of separated
mates, **66:6,** *p. 262*
solemnization, **69:2,** *p. 267*
—ceremony, **69:2b,** *pp. 267-68*
—form, **69:2a,** *p. 267*
—limitation re minister's solemnization, **69:3,** *p. 268*
Membership *(see* Church membership;
Lodge membership)
Mercy *(see also* Deacons)
Christian Reformed World
Relief Committee, **25:4, 5,** *pp.
118-19*
ministry of mercy, **25:1,** *p. 117*
objects of mercy, **25:2,** *pp.
117-18*
—the household of faith, **25:2a,**
pp. 117-18
—the needy in general, **25:2b, 5,**
pp. 118-19
—world hunger, **25:5,** *pp. 118-19*
Ministerial Information Service (regulations), **8:4,** *pp. 60-62*

Ministers of the Word (*see also* Candidacy; Ministry)

administration of the sacraments, **12:2a,** *p. 77;* **55:3,** *pp. 228-29*

a special office, **2,** *pp. 32-38*

—eligibility for call, **8:1,** *p. 58*

—length of pastorate, **8:2b,** *pp. 58-59*

—letter of call (copy), **Appendix,** *p. 337*

—moving expenses when called, **8:2e,** *p. 59*

—period of consideration of a call, **8:2d,** *p. 59*

—repetition of call, **8:2c,** *p. 59*

salary responsibility, **8:2f,** *p. 59*

calling (*see also* Calling), **4,** *pp. 42-43;* **8,** *pp. 58-65*

candidacy (*see* Candidacy; Candidates)

catechizing the youth, **12:2c,** *p. 77*

chaplaincy, **12:4,** *pp. 79-81*

church visiting, guide for, **42:4,** *pp. 186-89*

conduct worship services, **12:2b,** *p. 77;* **53:1,** *p. 224*

credentials, **10:2b, 3,** *p. 73;* **12:3d,** *p. 79*

—of retired ministers, **18:3b,** *p. 99*

discipline of (*see* Discipline)

educational task of, **12:2c,d,** *pp. 77-78*

eligibility for office, **3:1, 4,** *pp. 39-40, 41;* **6,** *pp. 48-52*

emeritation (*see* Ministers of the Word: Retirement)

exchange of pastorates, **8:4,** *pp. 60-62*

from other denominations, **8:5,** *pp. 62-65*

in missionary service

—calling, **12:3,** *pp. 78-79*

—membership, **12:3d,** *p. 79*

installation, **10,** *pp. 68-73*

—necessity, **10:2a,** *p. 73*

—prerequisites, **10:2b,** *p. 73*

leave of absence, **16,** *pp. 93-94*

loaned to other denominations, **13:4,** *pp. 83-84*

marriages: limitation on solemnization, **69:3,** *p. 268*

ministers of evangelism, **74:4,** *p. 285;* **76:2c(3),** *p. 292*

official acts of ministry, **12,** *pp. 76-81;* **53:3,** *p. 225*

officially explain and apply Holy Scripture, **54:1,** *p. 226*

pension, **12:4a(2),** *p. 79;* **18:4,** *pp. 99-100*

release from a congregation

—approval required, **17:2,** *p. 95*

—conditions necessitating release, **17:1,** *p. 95*

—if no call is received, **17:6,** *p. 96*

—membership of released minister, **17:4,** *p. 96*

—status of released minister, **17:4,** *p. 96*

—support for released minister, **17:3,** *pp. 95-96*

—transfer of credentials, **17:5,** *p. 96*

release from ministerial office, **14,** *pp. 85-87*

—conditions for release, **14:2, 3,** *pp. 85-86*

—effective date, **14:5,** *p. 87*

—resignation, **14:4,** *pp. 86-87*

—return to ministerial office, **14:6,** *p. 87*

resignation, **14:4, 5,** *pp. 86-87*

retirement, **18,** *pp. 98-100*

—approval required, **18:2,** *pp. 98-99*

—credentials, transfer of, **18:3b,** *p. 99*

—discipline of retired ministers, **92:1a,** *pp. 327-28*

—eligibility and retirement age, **18:1,** *p. 98*

—readmission to active service, **18:5,** *p. 100*

—status of retired ministers, **18:3,** *p. 99*

—support of retired ministers, **18:4,** *pp. 99-100*

salaries and/or support of ministers, **15,** *pp. 88-92*
—combining congregations, **15:4,** *p. 91*
—Fund for Needy Churches, **15:3,** *pp. 90-91*
—guidelines for salaries and benefits, **15:2,** *pp. 88-90*
—responsibilities of consistories, classes, and church visitors, **15:5,** *pp. 91-92*
—responsibility of calling church, **15:1,** *p. 88*
—support of released ministers, **17:3,** *pp. 95-96*
—support of retired ministers, **18:4,** *pp. 99-100*
specific tasks and calling, **12,** *pp. 76-81*
supervision (*see also* Supervision), **13,** *pp. 82-84*
—and discipline (*see also* Discipline), **92,** *pp. 327-28*
synodical appointees, calling of, **12:3,** *pp. 78-79*
temporary release from service (leave of absence), **16,** *p. 93-94*
transfer from one congregation to another, **14:1,** *p. 85*
transfer of retired minister's credentials, **18:3b,** *p. 99*

Ministry
appointment to particular ministries, **2:2a(9-12),** *pp. 34-35*
comprehensive ministries, **2:2a(1, 2),** *p. 33*
of all believers, **2:1b,** *pp. 32-33*
official acts of ministry, **12,** *pp. 76-81;* **53:3,** *p. 225*
particular ministries, **2:2a(3-6),** *pp. 33-34*
special ministries and the congregation, **24:6d,** *p. 116*

Minutes (*see also* Agenda)
acts of assemblies, **32:3c,** *p. 145*
files and archives of assemblies, **32:3d,** *p. 145*
preparing minutes, **32:3c,** *p. 145*

preservation (Heritage Hall), **32:3d,** *p. 145*
responsibilities of the clerk, **32:2b,** *p. 144*
Missionaries (*see also* Evangelist; Home Missions; World Missions)
calling of, **12:3,** *pp. 78-79*
foreign missionaries
—calling of, **77:1d,** *p. 295*
—membership of, **67:3,** *p. 265*
—support of, **77:1d,** *p. 295*
home missionaries, **76:3,** *p. 293*
—delegate to assemblies, **40:1,** *pp. 177-78*
Regional Home Missionaries, **76:2c(6),** *pp. 292-93*
supervision of, **13:2,** *pp. 82-83*
Missions (*see also* Home Missions; World Missions), **73-77,** *pp. 281-97*
biblical and confessional references, **73:1a,** *p. 281*
church's mandate, **73,** *pp. 281-83*
congregational evangelism, **74,** *pp. 284-86*
foreign missions, **77,** *pp. 294-97*
goal of mission, **73:2,** *p. 282*
Home Missions, **74-76,** *pp. 284-93*
mission principles, **73:1b,** *p. 281*
stimulation of members to missions, **73:3,** *pp. 282-83*
support of home and foreign missions, **73:4,** *p. 283*
Music (*see* Church Music; Hymnal)
Mutual Censure, 36:3, *pp. 168-69*

N

National Day of Prayer, 51:3, *p. 217*
Needy Churches (*see* Fund for Needy Churches)
Neo-Pentecostalism
discipline of office-bearers holding neo-Pentecostal views, **89:2,** *pp. 320-21;* **57:2,** *p. 234*

rebaptism and baptism with the
Holy Spirit, **58:3,** *pp. 235-36*
rebaptism and church discipline, **81:2k,** *pp. 306-07*

New Year's Day, 51:2b, *p. 217*

Nominations

for office, **4:1,** *p. 42*
immediate renomination, **23:3,**
p. 110

O

Offerings (Alms) *(see also* Quotas)

above-quota offerings, **62:2e,**
p. 248
accredited agencies, **62:3,** *pp.
248-49*
distribution of offerings, **62:2,**
pp. 246-48
in worship services, **51:1d,** *p.
215*
quota system, **62:2,** *pp. 246-48*
supplementary contributions by
individuals, **62:4,** *p. 249*
work of deacons, **62:1,** *p. 246*

Office-bearers *(see* Offices of the
Church)

**Office of all Believers, Introduction, D,
2,** *p. 3; * **2:2a(1, 2, 6),** *pp. 33-34*

Officers of Assemblies

duties of the clerk, **32:2b,** *p. 144*
duties of the president, **32:2a,**
pp. 143-44
other officers (treasurer, etc.),
32:2d, *p. 144*
termination of office, **32:2c,** *p.
144*

Offices of the Church *(see also* Consistory; specific offices)

authority of office-bearers *(see
also* Office of all believers),
24:6, *pp. 115-16*
elders and deacons, **23-25,** *pp.
109-19*
eligibility for ecclesiastical
office, **3,** *pp. 39-41*
equality of offices, **95:2,** *p. 332*

evangelists *(see also* Evangelist), **2:3,** *pp. 35-38*
general provisions, **2-5,** *pp.
32-47*
meaning of the word *office,*
2:1a, *p. 32*
ministers of the Word, **6-22,** *pp.
48-108*
nature of office, **Introduction D,
3,** *p. 3*
professors of theology *(see also*
Professors of theology), **20,**
pp. 102-04
Synod 1973: Guidelines, **2:2a,**
pp. 33-35

Old Year's Day, 51:2b, *pp. 216-17*

Order of Worship *(see also* Worship)

adoption of principles and elements, **47:1e,** *p. 202*
elements *(see also* Worship),
51, *pp. 214-17*
local autonomy, **52:5,** *pp. 222-23*

Ordination *(see also* Installation)

candidates *(see also* Candidates), **10:1,** *pp. 68-73*
evangelists, **2:3e,** *p. 37*
meaning, **2:2a(9),** *p. 34*
regulations, **4:4,** *p. 43*
reordination of deposed ministers, **94:2,** *pp. 330-31*
reordination of released ministers, **14:6, 7,** *p. 87*

Organization of a New Congregation

assembly approval required,
38:2, *p. 174*
procedures for organization,
38:3, *p. 174-75*
rules for calling for smaller congregations, **38:4,** *p. 175*

Organization of the Church

necessity for, **Introduction A,** *p.
1; * **2:2b(1, 4),** *p. 35*

Overtures

appeals of rejected overtures,
28:5d, *p. 127*
belated overtures to synod,
28:5e, *p. 127*
definition, **28:3,** *p. 125*

late, **28:5g,** *p. 127*

legally before synod, **28:5b,** *p. 126*

P

Pastoral Care, 65-72, *pp. 257-80*

exercise of pastoral care, **65,** *pp. 257-59*

—over the congregation, **65:1,** *p. 257*

home visiting, **65:3a,** *p. 258*

pastoral tasks defined, **65:3,** *p. 258*

pastoral visiting, **65:3b,** *p. 258*

purpose of pastoral care, **65:4,** *p. 258*

responsibility for, **65:2,** *p. 257*

Pastoral Declarations by Synod, 65:5, *pp. 258-59*

Pension

leave of absence, **16:6,** *p. 94*

ministers

—in specialized services, **12:4a(2),** *p. 79*

—of congregations, **18:1, 2,** *pp. 98-99*

of non-ordained employees, **18:6,** *p. 100*

of retired ministers, **18:4,** *pp. 99-100*

Pentecostalism *(see* Neo-Pentecostalism)

Polity of Reformed Churches *(see also* Church Order)

necessity for organization, **Introduction A,** *p. 1;* **2:2b(1, 4),** *p. 34*

presbyterian pattern, **Introduction A,** *p. 1*

principles of, **1:1,** *pp. 28-29*

Prayer

annual day of, **51:2c,** *p. 217*

at opening of assemblies, **32:1,** *p. 143*

ministry and prayer, **61:1,** *p. 244*

public worship services, **61,** *pp. 244-45*

—elements of, **61:1,** *p. 244*

—liturgical prayers, **61:2,** *pp. 244-45*

Preaching *(see* Licensure to conduct worship services; Worship)

task of ministers, **11:1,** *p. 74;* **12:2,** *pp. 77-78;* **54:1,** *p. 226*

President

consistory, **32:2a,** *pp. 143-44;* **36:2a,** *p. 167*

major assemblies, **32:2a,** *pp. 143-44;* **40:3,** *p. 178;* **46:3a,** *p. 198*

Principles of Church Music, 52:4a, *pp. 220-21*

Principles of Reformed Church Government, 1:1, *pp. 28-29*

Profession of Faith

and eligibility for office, **3:1a,** *p. 38*

and infant baptism, **56:2a,** *p. 230*

announcement of, **59:1b,** *p. 239*

examination by consistory, **59:1a,** *pp. 238-39*

neglect of, **81:2c,** *p. 305*

public, **59:1c,** *pp. 239-40*

request for admission to communicant membership, **59:1,** *pp. 238-40*

Professors of Theology

a special office, **2:1d,** *p. 33*

regulations for nomination and appointment, **20:2, 3,** *pp. 102-04*

requirements for appointment, **20:2,** *pp. 102-04*

role at synod, **46:4A,** *p. 199*

tasks, **20:1,** *p. 102*

to sign Form of Subscription, **5:3,** *p. 44*

Property

safeguarding by incorporation, **32:4,** *pp. 146-53*

Protests *(see also* Appeals; Request for revision of assembly decision)

definition, **28:3,** *p. 125*

rules for submission to synod,
28:5c, *pp. 126-27*
Psalter Hymnal *(see also* Hymnal),
52:4b, c, *pp. 221-22*

Q

Quotas *(see also* Offerings)
above-quota offerings, **62:2e,** *p. 248*
accredited agencies, **62:3,** *pp. 248-49*
effective date for quotas, **62:2b,** *p. 247*
exemption from quotas, **62:2c,** *pp. 247-48*
family unit: definition, **62:2d,** *p. 248*
system, **62:2a,** *pp. 246-47*

R

Racial Prejudice
an occasion for discipline, **81,l,** *p. 307*
Rebaptism *(see* Neo-Pentecostalism)
Recommended Agencies
support of, **62:3,** *pp. 248-49*
Reelection of Office-bearers, 23:3, *p. 110*
Reformed Church Polity *(see* Church Order; Polity of Reformed churches)
Reformed Ecumenical Synods, 50, *pp. 212-13*
Reimbursements of Synodical Delegates, 45:2c, *p. 194*
Relations with Other Churches *(see* Interchurch relations)
Release from a Congregation *(see* Ministers of the Word)
Release from Ministerial Office *(see* Discipline: Deposition of ministers; Leave of absence; Ministers of the Word: Release from ministerial office)

Reports to Assemblies
definition of *reports,* **28:3,** *p. 125*
late reports to synod, **28:5g,** *p. 127*
matters legally before synod, **28:5,** *pp. 126-28*
supplementary reports to synod, **28:5i,** *p. 128*
Request for Revision of Assembly Decision, 31, *pp. 140-42*
definition, **28:3,** *p. 125*
distinguished from an appeal, **31:1a,** *p. 140*
distinguished from revision of a decision during an assembly meeting, **31:1b,** *pp. 140-41*
Resignation
of members, **86:3,** *pp. 314-15*
of ministers, **14:4, 5,** *pp. 86-87*
Retirement *(see* Ministers of the Word: Retirement)
Revision of Assembly Decisions *(see* Request for revision of assembly decision)
Revision of Church Order *(see* Church Order)
Rules of Procedure
assemblies, **28:4,** *pp. 125-26*
classical, **28:4b,** *p. 126*
consistorial, **28:4a,** *p. 125*
synodical, **28:4c,** *p. 126*

S

Sabbath *(see* Lord's Day)
Sacraments *(see also* Baptism; Lord's Supper)
administration, **55,** *pp. 228-29*
administration by missionaries, **55:3,** *pp. 228-29*
baptism, **56-58,** *pp. 230-37*
evangelists authorized to administer, **2:3c,** *p. 37;* **55:3,** *pp. 228-29*
Lord's Supper, **60,** *pp. 241-43*
relationship to public profession of faith, **59:1c,** *p. 240*

restriction from participation, **85,** *p. 312*

Salaries of Ministers *(see also* Ministers of the Word: Salaries and/or support of),* **15,** *pp. 88-92*

Schism, Congregational
definition of schism, **32:4a(3),** *p. 147*

Schools *(see* Calvin College; Christian schools; Seminary; Sunday schools; Theological training)

Scripture *(see also* Word of God)
and the Church Order, **1:2c,** *p. 30*
and the Reformed creeds, **1:2b,** *pp. 29-30*
and the worship service, **54:1,** *p. 226*

Secret Societies *(see* Lodge membership)

Seminary *(see also* Theological training),* **19,** *p. 101*
Seminary, Calvin
—appointment of professors, **19:3,** *p. 93;* **20:3,** *pp. 103-04*
function of the seminary, **19:2,** *p. 101*
government of the seminary, **19:3,** *p. 101*
instructional staff, **20,** *pp. 102-04*
president's role at synod, **46:4B,** *p. 199*
relationship of church and seminary, **19:1,** *p. 101*

Sermons *(see also* Worship)
for reading, **53:4,** *p. 225*
preparatory and applicatory at the Lord's Supper celebration, **60:3,** *p. 242*

Services, Worship *(see* Worship)

Seventh Commandment Violation, 84:2, *p. 311*

Singing *(see* Church Music; Hymnal)

Social Security, 15:2b(5), *p. 89*

Societies, Congregational, 72, *pp. 279-80*
consistorial promotion and supervision, **72:1, 3,** *pp. 279-80*

youth organizations, **72:2,** *p. 280*

Specialized Ministries *(see also* Ministers of the Word),* **12:4,** *pp. 79-81*

Special Worship Services, 51:2, 3, *pp. 216-17*

Standing Committees, 33, *pp. 153-62*

Stated Clerk
denominational, **33:6,** *pp. 158-60;* **46:4C,** *pp. 199-200*
classical, **40:4a,** *pp. 178-79*

Statistics
congregational, **68:1,** *p. 266*
denominational, **68:2,** *p. 266*

Student Fund, 21, *p. 105*

Study Committees, 33, *pp. 153-62*

Subscription to Creeds by Office-bearers *(see also* Form of Subscription),* **1:2b,** *p. 30*

Subsidized Churches *(see* Fund for Needy Churches)

Sunday Observance *(see* Lord's Day)

Sunday Schools *(see also* Catechetical instruction)
integration with catechism, **63:2b, c,** *pp. 251-52;* **64:3c(3),** *p. 252*
supervision, **64:1b,** *p. 254*

Supervision
of all ministers, **13:1,** *p. 82*
of congregational societies, **72:3,** *p. 280*
of ministers in mission service, **13:2,** *pp. 82-83*
of ministers serving non-CRC churches; regulations, **13:3, 4,** *pp. 83-84*
of ministers whose membership does not reside in their calling church, **92,** *pp. 327-28*

Supplements to Church Order *(see* Articles of Church Order, pp. 7-25 of this manual for listing and reference)

Suspension *(see* Discipline)

Synod *(see also* Assemblies), **45-50,** *pp. 194-213*
Acts of Synod, **32:3c,** *p. 145;* **46:3C,** *p. 199*

agenda, **32:3b,** *p. 145;* **28:5h,** *pp. 127-28*

appeals *(see* Appeals)

Christian Reformed Church Synod Trustees, **32:4b,** *pp. 147-52;* **33:5a,** *p. 155*

classification of materials for Synod, **28:3,** *p. 125*

committees *(see also* Committees of assemblies)

—advisory, **45:3c,** *pp. 195-96*

—interchurch relations, **49,** *pp. 207-11*

—program, **45:3c,** *pp. 195-96*

convening

—church, **46:1b,** *p. 197*

—time and place, **46:1a,** *p. 197*

credentials of delegates, **34:2,** *p. 163;* **45:3a,** *pp. 194-95*

delegates to

—election of, **45:2b,** *p. 195*

—information questionnaire, **45:3a,** *pp. 194-95*

—number of, **45:2a,** *p. 194*

—preparation of, **45:3,** *pp. 194-95*

—reimbursement for loss of wages, **45:2c,** *p. 194*

doctrinal and ethical decisions of, **65:5,** *pp. 258-59*

files and archives, **32:3d,** *p. 145*

incorporation, **32:4,** *pp. 146-52*

Interchurch Relations Committee, **49,** *pp. 207-11*

judicial hearings, **30:2,** *pp. 133-39*

location, **46:1a,** *p. 197*

matters legally before synod, **28:2, 5,** *pp. 124-25, 126-28*

meetings, **46,** *pp. 197-200*

minutes, **32:3c,** *p. 145;* **46:3C,** *p. 199*

mission responsibilities

—home, **76,** *pp. 289-93*

—world, **77,** *pp. 294-97*

non-delegate synodical functionaries, **46:4,** *pp. 199-200*

officers, **46:3,** *pp. 198-99*

—clerks, **46:3C,** *p. 199*

—president, **46:3A,** *p. 198*

—treasurer, **46:4E,** *p. 200*

—vice-president, **46:3B,** *p. 198*

overtures, **28:3, 5,** *pp. 125, 126-27*

preparation of delegates, **45:3,** *pp. 194-96*

Reformed Ecumenical Synods, **50,** *pp. 212-13*

reimbursement of delegates to synod, **45:2c,** *p. 194*

reports, **28:3,5a, g, i,** *pp. 125, 126, 127, 128*

representative nature, **45:1,** *p. 194*

request for revision of decision, **31,** *pp. 140-42*

rules of procedure, **28:4,** *pp. 125-26*

special sessions, **46:2,** *pp. 197-98*

synodical agencies' representation, **28:5k,** *p. 128*

synodical deputies, **48,** *pp. 204-06*

—appointment, **48:1,** *p. 204*

—responsibilities, **48:2,3,4,** *pp. 204-06*

Synodical Interim Committee, **32:4b,** *pp. 147-48;* **33:5,** *pp. 155-58*

task of synod, **47,** *pp. 201-03*

time and place, **46:1a,** *p. 197*

Synodical Agencies *(see also* Synod; the name of the specific agency)

speakers for synodical agencies at synod, **28:5k,** *p. 128*

Synodical Deputies

appointment, **48:1,** *p. 204*

responsibilities, **48:2, 3, 4,** *pp. 204-06*

Synodical Interim Committee, 32:4b, *pp. 147-52;* **33:5,** *pp. 155-58*

Synods, Ecumenical, 50, *pp. 212-13*

T

Temporary Release from Office *(see* Ministers of the Word: Leave of absence, Release from ministerial office)

Tenure of Elders and Deacons, 23, *pp. 109-10*
    Length, **23:1,** *pp. 109-10*
    reelection: eligibility for, **23:3,** *p. 110*
    reordination, **23:4,** *p. 110*
    retirement, **23:2,** *p. 110*

Theological Training
    candidates without prescribed training, **7,** *pp. 53-57*
    for persons of more mature years, **7:2,** *pp. 54-55*
    Master of Divinity degree required, **6:1b,** *p. 48*
    persons not trained at Calvin Seminary, **6:3,** *pp. 51-52*
    prescribed for admittance to ministry, **6:1a,** *p. 48*
    seminary (*see also* Seminary), **19,** *p. 101*

Transfer of Membership *(see* Church membership)

Transfer of Ministers *(see also* Ministers of the Word)
    ministerial transfer from one congregation to another, **14:1,** *p. 85*
    transfer of retired ministers, **18:3b,** *p. 99*

Translation of Bible *(see* Bible)

Treasurer
    classical, **40:4b,** *p. 179-80*
    synodical, **46:4E,** *p. 200*

Trustees of the Christian Reformed Church, 32:4b, *pp. 147-48;* **33:5a,** *p. 155*

U

Unified Church School Curriculum, 63:2c, *p. 252;* **64:3c,** *p. 256;* **72:1c,** *p. 280*

Unorganized Churches
    assembly approval required for organization, **38:2,** *p. 174*
    care of, **38:1,** *pp. 173-74*

organizational development, **76:1b(2),** *pp. 290-91*
procedures for organization, **38:3,** *pp. 174-75*
relationship to classis, **39:1,** *p. 176*
rules for calling by smaller churches, **38:4,** *p. 175*

V

Vacant churches
    calling a minister (*see also* Calling), **4,** *pp. 42-43*
    counselor, **9,** *pp. 66-67*
    delegates to classis, **40:1,** *pp. 177-78*
    presiding officer, **36:2a,** *p. 167*
    rules for calling by smaller churches, **38:4,** *p. 175*

Versions of the Bible *(see* Bible)

Visiting
    church (*see also* Church visitors), **42,** *pp. 184-89*
    home, **65:3a,** *p. 258*

Voting *(see also* Congregational meetings)
    freedom of delegates to assemblies, **34:3,** *pp. 163-64*
    limitation of voting rights of delegates to major assemblies, **34:4,** *p. 164*
    nomination and election to special offices, **4:1, 2, 3,** *pp. 42-43*
    right to vote at congregational meetings, **4:3b,** *p. 43;* **37:3,** *p. 172*

W

Weddings *(see* Marriage)

Women
    appointment to committees, **33:3b,** *p. 155*

eligible for office of deacon,
3:2, *p. 40*

right to vote at congregational
meetings, **4:3b,** *p. 43;* **37:3c,**
p. 172

Word of God
complete subjection to: a basic
principle of Reformed church
polity, **1:1a,** *pp. 28-29*

World Hunger *(see also* Mercy)
diaconal responsibility, **25:5,**
pp. 118-19

Worldliness, 81:2i, *p. 306*

World Missions, 77, *pp. 294-97*
administration of, **77:2,** *pp.
295-97*
appointments to board, **77:1b,**
pp. 294-95
calling of missionaries, **77:1d,**
p. 295
Mission Order, **77,** *pp. 294-97*
support of world missions, **77:1,**
pp. 294-95
synodical responsibilities, **77:1,**
pp. 294-95

World Relief Committee *(see* Christian
Reformed World Relief Committee)

Worship *(see also* Licensure to conduct
worship services; Lord's Day)
children's services, **51:1g,** *p. 216*
conducting of worship services,
53, *pp. 224-25*
elements and occasions for
worship services
—benediction, **53:1,** *p. 224*
—doxology, **52:5,** *p. 223*
—elements essential to worship
services, **51:1d,** *pp. 214-15*
—Lord's Day: frequency of worship, **51:1a,** *p. 214*
—music, **52:4, 6,** *pp. 219-23*
—preaching
—essential to worship service, **51:1d,** *pp. 214-15*

—on Heidelberg Catechism,
54:2, *pp. 226-27*
—task of ministers, **11:1,** *p.
74;* **12:2,** *pp. 77-78;* **54:1,** *p.
226*
—second Sunday service,
51:1c, *p. 214*
—special days for worship,
51:2, *pp. 216-17*
—special worship services,
51:3, *p. 217*
—synodical worship service,
46:1, *p. 197*
time and number of services,
51:1b, *p. 214*
order of worship, **52:5,** *pp.
222-23*
pre-synod worship service, **46:1,**
p. 197
regulation of worship services,
52, *pp. 218-23*
sacraments in worship services,
55:2, *p. 228*
sermons for reading, **53:4,** *p.
225*
use of liturgical form, **52:3,** *p.
219*
weddings during worship services, **69:2b,** *pp. 267-68*
who may conduct services,
53:1,2, *p. 224*

Y

**Yearbook of the Christian Reformed
Church**
denominational statistics, **68:2,**
p. 266
responsibility for, **68:2,** *p. 266*

Youth Organizations
consistory's relationship to congregational societies, **72:2,** *p.
280*

Index of Scripture References

Genesis
1:27, **24:6a,** *p. 115*
17:7, **74:1,** *p. 284*

Leviticus
19:15, **30:2b(3),** *p. 134*

Deuteronomy
1:16-17, **30:2b(3),** *p. 134*
16:18-20, **30:2b(3),** *p. 134*

Psalms
147, **24:6a,** *p. 115*

Malachi
3:10, **62:2a,** *p. 246*

Matthew
6:25-30, **24:6a,** *p. 115*
10:29-31, **24:6a,** *p. 115*
16:19, **78:1a,** *p. 298*
18:15-17, **1:1a,** *p. 28*
        78:1a, *p. 298*
        81:1b, *p. 304*
18:18, **65:2,** *p. 257*
28:19-20, **1:1a,** *p. 28*
        12:2a, d *pp. 77-78*
        24:6c, *p. 115*
        27:1b, *p. 121*
        73:1a, *p. 281*

Mark
16:15-18, **73:1a,** *p. 281*

Luke
22:27, **24:6a, e,** *pp. 115, 116*
24:46-49, **73:1a,** *p. 281*

John
3:5ff., **58:3c,** *pp. 236-37*
20:21, **73:1a,** *p. 281*

Acts
1:8, **73:1a,** *p. 281*
2:39, **58:3c,** *pp. 236-37*
6:3, **24:3,** *p. 114*
6:4, **61:1,** *p. 244*
10–16, **74:1,** *p. 284*

Romans
8:1-17, **58:3c,** *pp. 236-37*
15:13, **58:3c,** *pp. 236-37*
12:4-6, **3:1c(1),** *p. 39*

I Corinthians
3:16, **2:1b,** *p. 32*
        58:3c, *p. 236-37*
5:12-13, **78:1a,** *p. 298*

12:3, **58:3c,** *pp. 236-37*
12:4-6, **3:1c(1),** *p. 39*
2:13, **58:3c,** *pp. 236-37*
14:40, **1:1a, c,** *pp. 28, 29*
16:2, **62:2a,** *pp. 246-47*

II Corinthians
5:20, **54:1,** *p. 226*
6:14-16, **78:1a,** *p. 298*

Galatians
6:2, **41:3,** *p. 183*
        62:2c(2), *p. 248*

Ephesians
2:18, **58:3c,** *pp. 236-37*
2:22, **58:3c,** *pp. 236-37*
4:11-13, **11:2b,** *p. 75*
        13:1, *p. 82*
        27:1b, *pp. 121-22*
4:24, **24:6a,** *p. 115*
5:23-27, **1:1b,** *p. 29*

Colossians
3:10, **24:6a,** *p. 115*

I Timothy
2:1-2, **61:1,** *p. 244*
3:1-7, **3:1c(1),** *pp. 39-40*
        24:3, *p. 114*
4:12, **24:3,** *p. 114*
5:19-21, **30:2b(3),** *p. 134*

II Timothy
2:2, **20:1a,** *p. 102*
4:1-2, **54:1,** *p. 226*

Titus
1:5-9, **3:1c(1),** *pp. 39-40*
1:9, **54:1,** *p. 226*
2:7, **24:3,** *p. 114*

Hebrews
13:7, **3:1c(1),** *p. 39*
        24:3, *p. 114*

James
2:1, 8-9, **30:2b(5),** *p. 134*

I Peter
4:10, **3:1d,** *p. 40*

I John
2:20, 27, **2:1b,** *p. 32*

Jude
3, **65:2,** *p. 257*

Revelation
1:5, **24:6c,** *p. 115*